THE

WIZARD

AND THE

WITCH

© Kari Orvik for Photobooth SF

John C. Sulak (San Francisco, California) is a story-teller, actor, filmmaker, and the co-author of the book *Modern Pagans*. He is inspired by journalists like Studs Terkel, Hunter S. Thompson, Tom Wolfe, and Legs McNeil, and it was his idea to tell *The Wizard and the Witch* in the oral-history format and to get involved in the narrative as he was documenting it.

© Julie Epona Photography

Oberon Zell-Ravenheart (Cotati, California) is a co-founder of Church of All Worlds (1962), founded *Green Egg* magazine (1968), is the founder and headmaster of the Grey School of Wizardry (2004), and has written or co-written six books on magickal subjects. Oberon is a regular presenter at Starwood, PantheaCon, and other Pagan festivals. He and his work have appeared in many magazines and books, and on many television and radio programs.

© Oberon Zell

Morning Glory Zell-Ravenheart (Cotati, California) is a Witch, Priestess, and Goddess historian. A published poet, songwriter, and author, she was an acknowledged consultant for Marion Zimmer Bradley's *The Mists of Avalon*.

SEVEN DECADES OF
COUNTERCULTURE, MAGICK & PAGANISM

THE

WIZARD

AND THE

WITCH

AN ORAL HISTORY OF
OBERON ZELL & MORNING GLORY

JOHN C. SULAK

Llewellyn Publications
Woodbury, Minnesota

FIRST EDITION
First Printing, 2014

Cover art: 4741827: iStockphoto.com/stereohype/s. m. Art designs
        1269933: iStockphoto.com/ggodby
        1607906: iStockphoto.com/dra_schwartz
Cover design by Kevin R. Brown
Interior art: iStockphoto.com/4741827/stereohype, 1269933/ggodby,
        1607906/dra_schwartz, 1865745/hanibaram

Llewellyn Publications is a registered trademark of Llewellyn Worldwide Ltd.

Library of Congress Cataloging-in-Publication Data
Sulak, John.
   The wizard and the witch : seven decades of counterculture, magick, and paganism / John C. Sulak. — First edition
      pages   cm
   Includes bibliographical references.
   ISBN 978-0-7387-1482-0
1. Zell-Ravenheart, Oberon, 1942– 2. Zell-Ravenheart, Morning Glory. 3. Neopagans—United States—Biography. 4. Magicians—United States—Biography. 5. Wizards—United States—Biography. I. Title.
   BP605.N46S85 2014
   299'.940922—dc23
   [B]
                        2013037368

Llewellyn Publications
A Division of Llewellyn Worldwide Ltd.
2143 Wooddale Drive
Woodbury, MN 55125-2989
www.llewellyn.com

Printed in the United States of America

This book is dedicated to Alisa Highfill,
my partner in love. Together we make dreams real.
—John C. Sulak

Contents

PART FOUR: The Demise of the CAW

Foreword
by Carl Llewellyn Weschcke

The sixties and seventies of the last century were very exciting times for Pagans and Occultists of all persuasions.

What had been repressed by Church and Society was suddenly being Born Again, and the mood was revolutionary. We were discovering and recovering the Old Ways of Ancient Wisdom, but we were also part of the New Wave of Science and Political Liberation. The Old Ways and the New Wave fed into each other and inspired what we can still, legitimately, call the "New Age."

The New Age shook things up so much that it attracted as many crazy people as it did reformers and people wanting answers to old questions for which old answers were no long accepted. We invented new movements and new institutions, and found alternative ways to see the world. It was as if futuristic science fiction and medieval myths merged and came alive in our time.

Now, in 2013, I can look back over a half-century of publishing for the New Age with astonishment and enjoyment for all we've done and for all the people who played active roles in giving it birth. Today, so much of the New Age is part of the modern world that what was once strange and scary to mainstream America is now common culture in the newly forming global civilization.

Even the pioneers don't appreciate all that has happened. We planted the seeds that burst into New Life; we were the midwives to the birth of a New Earth; we nurtured a New Generation through childhood and adolescence; and now we watch as the Final Drama unfolds, the world-as-we-know-it ends, and a New World Order takes its place.

In the fall of 1973, Llewellyn sponsored an event called "Gnosticon," standing for Gnosis, or Inner Knowledge, in the New Age. Many of these pioneers came together ostensibly to learn from each other but more importantly to "rebirth" one another. The energy of the moment was astonishing and still brings a song to my heart.

At the 1973 Gnosticon, I introduced Morning Glory to Oberon, and sparks flew. Suddenly, where there had been a crowd milling about near the hotel swimming pool, there were only two people. It was a timeless moment when two parts became a Whole Greater than the sum of the parts.

It is said that True Marriages are made in Heaven, but we believe that the Kingdom of Heaven is within—in the Heart of each of us. The Kingdom of Heaven is forever and we can all enter in. A True Marriage is a fertile union that enriches the world around and gives birth to new ideas, new understanding, and renewed devotion to shared ideals.

The life of Oberon and Morning Glory shows all of this to be true, and therefore we can all share in the celebration of that life and the Magick that they have brought into the world and are teaching to another generation.

—*Carl Llewellyn Weschcke*
Planet New Earth, Fall 2013

Introduction
by John C. Sulak

Plenty of books are available with instructions on how to do Magick or be a Pagan, a Witch, or a polyamorous person. But this book is different from those—it's a gonzo document of what it is like to actually *live* a magickal life, to exist as a Pagan or a Witch, and to truly and completely be polyamorous. This is not a book of guidelines—it's a look at what it's like to do those things in the real world. Welcome to the adventures of Morning Glory and Oberon Zell!

When they began their paths to self-discovery, there weren't any instruction manuals available. So, in the tradition of the pioneers, pilgrims, rugged individualists, and inventors who had come before them, they had to create new lifestyles, communities, and worlds. And they've been doing it ever since.

Oberon, then named Tim Zell, was one of the first and hardest-working people to advocate for the use of the word *Pagan* to describe who he was and the kind of folks he was starting to meet. It was in the 1960s, when the astronauts brought back the first pictures of Mother Earth as seen from outer space and people everywhere seemed to be worshipping her. *Pagan* was a word, and concept, that was part of a much larger cultural revolution. He wasn't preaching dogma or trying to set himself up as a guru, which was a trend at the time—he just wanted a religion in which people could think for themselves and make up their own minds about spirituality. The revolution didn't go as hoped for, but his use of the word began to catch on. Today, *Pagan* (with a capital *P*) means many different things to many different people, but it's still being used. It's been more evolution than revolution, and that's part of the story that is documented on the pages that follow.

As Tim Zell continued to follow the Pagan Path, he met the Goddess herself, Gaia, the living Earth, along the way. And then he met his soulmate, Morning Glory, and from that moment on they have walked their beloved Earth together. At the heart of this book is the story of their love, and the people they love and who love them. The Zells were polyamorous before polyamory was cool. Morning Glory *coined* the word *polyamory* to describe what they'd already been doing before they met each other—they were both born that way. The Zells were there for the early discussions of what it meant to live polyamorously, and brought their decades of experience to the conference tables. (Their words of wisdom? "Be excellent to each other!")

Polyamory has, in recent years, been growing rapidly, and the public is becoming more aware of it. There has been a great deal written about poly theory and practice, but no one has practiced it as much and as long as Morning Glory and Oberon. This is the first book to document an open relationship that has been going on for forty years. Anyone wanting to learn about the gritty, messy, yet beautiful truth about the subject can start right here.

Morning Glory was a Witch way, *way* before that kind of thing was cool. Even in the midst of the Neo-Pagan revival that began in the 1960s, Witchcraft was cloaked in secrecy, with mysterious initiations, rituals, and, uh, people wearing cloaks. That didn't stop the teenage Morning Glory, who knew no Pagans or Witches at the time, and had no idea who Gerald Gardner was, from beginning her commitment to being a Witch in the modern world. Just what it means to be a Witch, and what the lineage of Wicca and Witchcraft is, is still the subject of vigorous debate today. Most Witches are "solitary," self-taught and practicing alone. That's how Morning Glory began, but she soon took her practice and her passion public, where her growth as a powerful Witch, a Priestess, and a human being continued.

And there's more, of course, including magic, Magick, Wizardry, and getting legal recognition for Pagan churches. There's the complete saga of how the Zells created the first unicorns in modern times. There are trips to the Underworld, visits to Pagan sacred sites from the old and new world, and Pagan rituals and festivals around the globe. There are not just poly-relationships but child-raising poly-families and poly-breakups, which could offer lessons to present and future readers who are considering some alternative to monogamy. There is social networking in the days before the Internet; there is science fiction and fantasy becoming reality; and there is a sex-positive, *sex-sacred* religion that has some real difficult and scandalous moments as it evolves. There is life, death, and rebirth. And there is, at the very least, some lively entertainment.

All this is told in the words of those who were there. I wanted reading this book to be like the ancient ritual of sitting in a circle with families and friends, paying attention as they each take turns talking. Imagine that! You're being invited to join a circle around a campfire with the village elders!

I was initially inspired to begin working on this project because I personally thought that Morning Glory and Oberon were really awesome and that the world needed to know more about them. Many moons have come and gone since then, and I still feel that way. It has been an enjoyable and educational experience for me. Their story is both a fairy tale and classic Americana: two people who were on the outside of society but believed in each other. Through thick and thin, for better and for worse, Morning Glory and Oberon have stuck together and remain together today. She's in her sixties; he recently turned seventy-one; and they are hanging in there. Their lives have not been easy—they have made countless sacrifices for their spirituality and their tribe. They have worked hard to avoid conformity and compromise. As senior citizens, it is becoming difficult for them to stay healthy and financially stable, but they remain loving and giving.

All of the people who were interviewed for this book were really amazing. Some of them are no longer with us, and we shall not see the likes of them again! You can find more information about each of these participants as they are introduced into the tale by turning to "Appendix II: Cast of Characters" in the back of the book, and there is also a timeline to help put things into context. I feel honored to have had the opportunity to have interviewed each of these people and to share their words with you and future generations of readers. I hope you enjoy what they have to say as much as I did.

"Talking My Walk"
by Oberon

As a young lad growing up in "Pleasantville," I enjoyed reading biographies of people who inspired me in various ways. With such sterling examples, I've tried to live a life that would be interesting enough so that others would like to read about it someday—or even watch the movie version.

Early on I considered that my life was already getting so weird that any biography of me would have to be presented as science fiction! Indeed, much of my life has in fact been inspired and influenced by sci-fi and fantasy novels.

One aspect of my life that others often mention is my propensity for "thinking outside the box." However, I think this is a bit of a misapprehension. For me, it's always been more: "Box? There's a box?" Indeed, through sci-fi, fantasy, and mythology, I have always lived amidst such a diversity of perspectives, opinions, theories, cultures, and customs that any notion of the "One True Right and Only Way," the way things are "supposed to be," has always eluded me. I've just gone along leading my life as I've seen fit to do, blithely oblivious to the opinions of others.

And yet, people would often tell me, "You really should write your autobiography! I want to read it!" A few misguided folks have even said they wanted to grow up to be just like me—and I have had to try and dissuade them, telling them that my life has been shaped by too many mistakes that I wouldn't wish on anyone. And that rather than try to become me (or anyone else), they should devote their efforts towards discovering and becoming who *they* are. Just as I have.

In 1973 I found and married my soulmate, Morning Glory, and my story became inextricably merged with hers. And then there are all our family, friends, lovers, and co-conspirators along the way, who would also need to be included for the story to make any sense. As the years accumulated (over seventy of them now . . .), the prospect of attempting to write my own autobiography began to seem an impossible task!

Then, several years ago, our friend John Sulak approached me with a proposal for writing what he called an "oral history," which would consist entirely of interviews—not only with me and Morning Glory, but also with many of the aforementioned "significant others" in our lives.

Remarkably enough, pretty much everyone—from my parents and siblings to lovers over the decades—was willing to talk to John. And of course, Morning Glory and I also spent countless hours responding to his insightful questions. John has taken these many, many hours of interviews and edited them into sensible commentaries, and then integrated them all into this flowing narrative—as if we are all sitting around the campfire.

People often speak of the importance of "walking your talk," which I certainly agree is a good idea! But I've learned that it may often be best not to try and do so much talking before you've done the actual walking, and so I've tended to just go on ahead and do the thing, and then analyze it afterwards. After all, as the saying goes, "If you want to hear the laughter of the Gods, tell 'em your plans!" So this isn't going to be a book elucidating my philosophies and principles for how to make this a better world. Rather, this is the story of the journey already taken thus far. Where it goes from here, we'll just have to see!

—*Oberon Zell-Ravenheart, Beltane 2013*

"Living Out Loud"
by Morning Glory

This book was in the works for some time, but when I was diagnosed with cancer (multiple myeloma), it put an urgency to telling my life story and personal history that was never quite there before. Also, the birth of my granddaughter added more importance to this effort to leave a written record that will help her make sense out of her wacky grandma's life.

A lot of people have asked me while I was working on this book whether or not I was worried about exposing all these stories in my life, especially the ones that are outrageous or that show so many of the mistakes that I have made in my past. Believe me, it's something I certainly have considered. But I made the decision to tell the story of my life in a straightforward manner and let people make up their own minds about me.

People have always said to me, "Don't you care what people think of you?" Of course I care; I care passionately. But what matters more to me than people's good opinions are their genuine, informed opinions and their understanding, for those are far rarer commodities than just good opinions alone.

I have lived my life pretty much in public. Why have I done this sort of thing? Do I crave attention that badly? Not really. Am I just a media slut? Well, maybe. The reason that so much of my life is an open book about subjects that are controversial or even downright forbidden in some places, is that I genuinely feel that I have something to contribute—especially in the area of changing public opinion in important areas. These areas include freedom of speech, freedom of religion (most especially unpopular religions like Witchcraft and Paganism), and freedom of choice around sexuality—to choose who and how many my lovers will be, and to let them all be known to each other so that there are no shady secrets that can bring a love life crashing down around my ears. Not that that doesn't still happen occasionally anyway, but where sex is concerned, honesty is really the best policy, and in this day and age it can save your life. Besides, it makes you a lot harder to blackmail!

I have had lots of amazing adventures (chasing Mermaids) and done things that no one else has managed to do for a very long time (raising Unicorns); I have even coined a word (*polyamory*) for a lifestyle that lacked a satisfactory name for itself, and seen it adopted—not only by the movement but also by the *Oxford English Dictionary*. I, along with so many of my other brothers and sisters, have left legacies in the form of political and religious activism that will make it harder to persecute my people in the future and will lead to the hope of a living planet for our great-grandchildren to live on. I have also led with my heart, taking risks and making huge and tragic mistakes, which people can point to as lessons about what not to do. After all, how can you grow if you don't admit your mistakes?

At this point I can only point to the words of Sappho, a far greater writer than I will ever be:

"Although they are only breath, words which I command are immortal. Gifts that the golden Muses gave me were no delusion: dead, I will not be forgotten; someone in some future time will think of us . . ."

—*Morning Glory Zell-Ravenheart,*
July 20, 2013

PART ONE

The Early Life of Tim Zell

Chapter 1
A CHANGELING CHILD
(1942–1961)

Come away, O human child!
To the waters and the wild
With a faery, hand in hand,
For the world's more full of weeping
Than you can understand.

—FROM "THE STOLEN CHILD," BY WILLIAM BUTLER YEATS, 1886

NARRATOR: In 1942, pagans were a thing of the past. Gods and Goddesses were what people had believed in centuries earlier; wizards, witches, and unicorns were found in the fiction section of the library; magic was just a stage trick; and fairies lived only in fairy tales.

And in 1942 many Americans were as just as indifferent to the future as they were to ancient history and mythology. Science-fiction authors were writing about space travel, atomic power, computers, and other upcoming wonders, but they weren't being taken seriously. That kind of stuff was considered to be, in the real world, centuries away or impossible.

The United States had just endured the Great Depression and was entering World War II. All that really mattered to most people was the present, and it was bleak. It was in that world that Charles and Vera Zell met and began a family together. Their first son was born on November 30, 1942, and they named him Timothy. He would grow up to be a Pagan and a Wizard, raise Unicorns, marry a Witch, and change his name to Oberon Zell-Ravenheart.

CHARLES ZELL: I was born at home on Labor Day, September 7, 1914. We were poor. I had to put cardboard in my shoes in the winter when there were holes in them. My father was a barber, and when the Depression hit, he was out of work for seven years. I determined when I was quite young that I didn't want to be poor the rest of my life. I wanted to go to college. I graduated from high school with honors. I was very active in Boy Scouts, became an Eagle Scout, and because of that I met a chap who helped me get into Lehigh University. I got a scholarship, and I got a job waiting on tables in a fraternity house for my meals. I played football, basketball, and tennis, all varsity.

I graduated from college in June of 1938 and took a job as a salesman with Rust Craft Greeting Cards. On July 28, my father died in my arms of lung cancer. In December, Rust Craft sent me to St. Louis, where in June of 1940 I met my first wife, Vera. We were married that October 15. When the war broke out, I enlisted in the Marine Corps. That was in September of 1942. My wife was pregnant. Tim was born on November 30. When I got the news of his birth, I was so excited that on the obstacle course that day, for the first time I scaled the wall!

VERA ZELL: My father, also named Charles, was a dentist. And he was a naturalist. He knew the names of birds, insects, and flowers and that sort of thing. He would take yearly ten-day fishing trips that Tim would have enjoyed. He had a flower garden and a fruit-tree orchard in the back, and he grew asparagus and tomatoes. He died in our home of coronary thrombosis on November 17, 1941, a week after Veteran's Day. Tim was born a year later, on November 30, 1942. He was the most beautiful baby in the nursery. Even the nurses said so.

CHARLES ZELL: I was sent to Officers Candidate School in Quantico, Virginia, and became a second lieutenant. Tim's mother and grandmother drove out and stayed with me for six weeks in Dumfries. Then I went to Camp Elliot in San Diego to teach machine guns for six months. Tim and his mother went with me. We were together until he was nine months old, then they went back to the Midwest. I didn't see him again till November 1945.

I went overseas with my battalion. I was sent to Guadalcanal in the South Pacific to join the Third Marine Division regimental weapons company as a machine gun officer. I was in on the invasion of Guam, and survived that. I was in on the invasion of Iwo Jima, where they raised the flag. I survived without being wounded, but most of my buddies were either wounded or killed. I was with my very best buddy when he got hit by a mortar shell and lost his arm. I got him down to the beach and evacuated him.

NARRATOR: While Charles Zell was in the South Pacific fighting in the war, his wife moved back into a big, old Victorian house with her mother and sister in Kirkwood, Missouri—a suburb of St. Louis. At that point in American history, it was not uncommon for extended families to live together. Their living situations were comparable to the way the Addams Family lives in the TV show and movies, with the grandma, uncle, cousins, and assorted oddballs who just happened to drop by all under the same roof. (This was how Tim Zell spent his first few years; and since growing up and leaving his family, that is how he has lived most of his adult life.)

Immigrants often lived in households of this kind. They had come from countries where deep-rooted traditions, customs, and folktales had been handed down from generation to generation. But things like that were being lost, or left behind, as people become assimilated into the new world. Tim Zell's family traditions were passed on even more directly, since he considers himself to be the reincarnation of his mother's father.

OBERON ZELL (OZ): My mother's father had died of a heart attack the year before, and his room in the Victorian house in Kirkwood was made into my nursery. My first memory is of awakening in my familiar room, and there was my family gathered around me. I looked up at them, and they were all looking at me kind of funny. I tried to say something, but I couldn't articulate what I was trying to say. They made funny noises, and I got more and more upset. Finally I raised my hands in front of my face, and they were little, tiny baby hands.

I freaked out and started screaming. I had awakened in the bed that I had died in. I went straight from one life into the next one. It was a direct transmigration. Obviously there was a time gap of a full year, and the birth itself, but I have no memory of any of that. It was like I had gone to sleep the night before, and I awakened the next morning with the same people around me.

As I became more verbal as a child, they would often tell me, "That's just the kind of thing your grandfather would say!" I always felt like, from the time that I was able to talk, that I was somehow older, wiser, and more mature than they were. I never quite could get it that I was the child and they were they adults. It always felt the other way around.

For my first three years, the only people in my universe were my grandmother, my mother, and my aunt Betsy (who never married). So my whole life revolved around the Maiden, the Mother, and the Crone— the Triple Goddess of Celtic lore.

My mother's folks were Presbyterian, but I don't recall ever being taken to church in those early years. But I was baptized. I remember that distinctly because I didn't want it to happen. I screamed and fought it, but they did it anyway. It was very traumatic.

My early years were haunted by recurrent nightmares of dying. I remembered time and time again in my dreams the sensation of dying. It was like falling down a well. The world got smaller and smaller and disappeared. Sometimes I would even get that feeling when I was awake, and I'd have to kind of blink and shake myself.

I was very telepathic. A lot of the time I heard their thoughts as clearly as words. And I just took that for granted as perfectly natural. They didn't have to speak directly in order for me to understand them. I did not distinguish between spoken words and articulated thoughts.

When I was around two or three, there were some women over visiting. I was upstairs in my room, and I remember hearing this commotion of voices. I came down the stairs, and I looked at all these people that I didn't know. There was this noise that hurt my ears. I put my hands over my ears, but it wouldn't go away because I was hearing it inside my head as well. And I yelled out, "Be quiet!"

All these faces turned and looked at me. They stopped talking, but the babble got louder. I looked at them and for the first time understood that their mouths weren't moving, and therefore they weren't speaking, and yet I was hearing them.

I ran back upstairs, hid under the covers, and tried to shut out the commotion that was inside of my head. And that was the last of that. I learned the difference between a thought that was in my head and a thought that was coming into my ear.

My grandmother was very intellectual, so reading was valued highly in my family. I was probably about three when I started being able to read for myself. My mother had been reading me these books, and she would trace her finger along as she was doing it and I would learn it. At first I was just kind of recognizing words, but before long I could read them myself.

NARRATOR: Timothy Zell's religious education after that point came not from his elders, or from other people he knew who were in a position of authority, but from books and direct observation of Nature.

OZ: When I was very small, my mother got me the *Childcraft* books, which were put out for kids by the *World Book Encyclopedia*. There was a whole series of them on different themes. My favorite was the one on world mythology. The very first things I read were Roman versions of the Greek myths, before Dick and Jane or anything else. I'll never forget reading about "Pluto and Proserpine" as a child. These stories introduced me to lots of important concepts, one of them being that there were multiple deities, Gods, and Goddesses of all kinds. So I didn't start off with the assumption that there was only one God; I started off with the assumption that there were many deities worshipped among many people. Later on, when I learned about Christianity, it was not like, "This is the only God." It was just one more story, about one more God.

My father came home from the war in 1945 and became a traveling salesman with Rust Craft Greeting Cards. After four months, he was transferred to Pennsylvania. That's where I really came into my identity. We had this little house and I lived upstairs, where I had my own room and my own desk. My dad and I were very close during that time—he used to tell me wonderful bedtime stories. And there were woods and fields all around us that I used to spend much of my time exploring. I would go hang out with animals and climb trees. I would merge so totally with the place that the animals came to accept me. I would just sit at the base of a tree for hours and hours till the deer would come and graze right next to me without being alarmed. I would climb up into the branches of a tree during the bird-nesting season and just sit and watch them lay their eggs and raise their babies.

VERA ZELL: Tim could spend hours watching a little bug crawling up a wall. Literally. He would go out under the porch and follow the bugs or ants.

OZ: My lifelong interest in Magick and Wizardry was ignited when I first read stories of Magick as a child—such as in fairy tales and the Greek myths. In particular, I was deeply imprinted by the early animated Disney movies featuring magickal characters and happenings. *Fantasia* (which had come out in 1940—two years before I was born) had a huge impact on me. Of course, I loved the whole "Rite of Spring" evolution sequence, with the dinosaurs. But it was the "Pastorale" that really captured my soul. The final scene, when Nyx draws a veil of night like a blanket across the Arcadian sky, and we see a crescent moon which, as we zoom in, resolves into Diana drawing her bow and releasing a meteoric arrow . . . well, that arrow plunged straight into my heart, where it has lodged ever since!

I didn't have any social sense at all as a kid. I got along great with animals, but I never really formed close friendships with other boys. I just didn't understand them—or trust them. And this was reciprocal; I was like a "pink monkey." One time, in second grade, this kid whipped out a pocket knife and slashed the back of my thumb, coming very close to cutting it off. I still have a big scar there, and my thumb has been double-jointed ever since. I couldn't comprehend why anyone would do such a thing. The lesson I got was that there were bizarrely cruel people in the world that I would somehow have to deal with.

I always liked hanging out with girls more than boys. In second or third grade I had two girlfriends, which was the beginning of my lifelong polyamory. They were both named Carol. One of them lived at the bottom of the street; the other lived at the top; and I lived in the middle.

I kept trying to get them to be friends so that we could all three be to-gether and do things.

NARRATOR: Another son, Barry, and a daughter, Shirley, were born into the Zell family. The three Zell siblings all grew up in a time of pros-perity and economic growth. Women who had worked in manufactur-ing jobs during the war were replaced by men and sent home to raise children, and the men made lots of money and spent it on new con-sumer products (televisions, refrigerators, washers and driers, etc.) for their new homes that were being built in the new suburbs. Extended families were being split up, as every couple had to have a house of their own and a garage with two new cars in it. Older relatives had to live alone and take care of themselves.

It was also a time of conservative politics and conformity. The Soviet Union, America's ally in World War II, quickly became America's new enemy, as politicians began talking about the threat of Communism. Any American who had left-wing or liberal political views was perceived as a possible danger to national security, and freedom of speech and thought was actively discouraged. While the Zell children were still in grade school, U.S. senator Joseph McCarthy began what became known as a political "witch hunt" against alleged Communists and sympathizers that would ruin many careers and lives. In 1953 playwright Arthur Miller wrote *The Crucible*, a dramatization of the Salem Witch trials that was actually an allegory for McCarthyism, the House Committee on Un-American Activities, and the resulting blacklisting by the government. Citizens were encouraged to act and think alike, dress alike, and move to identical homes in the suburbs.

OZ: In the spring of 1951, when I was eight, my father got transferred to the Midwest. They had a nice big home built on a large double lot in Crystal Lake, Illinois—a bedroom suburb northwest of Chicago. We moved into the new house in July of 1952, and I lived there from fourth grade through high school. Our house was only a block from the lake, and each of us three kids had our own room. And this place was like the neighborhoods where families that were on TV lived, in shows like *Ozzie and Harriet*, *Leave It to Beaver*, and *Father Knows Best*. I was in high school during the exact same era and setting that all those 1950s high school movies were set in.

My parents joined the Congregational Church, which is a very easy-going, white-bread-Protestant kind of thing. It seemed mostly to consist of social clubs, bake sales, potluck dinners, youth groups, retreats, and things like that. Although my folks were evidently quite active in the church, I don't recall them talking about religion at home. However, I got really into Sunday school. I took confirmation, and I still remember the most important lesson: *Christian* means "Christ-like." So Christians are supposed to be like Christ. The question then becomes, what was Christ like? I took that in rather deeply, and I think I have actually lived in a very "Christ-like" way, even though I eventually came to identify myself as Pagan!

Unlike my parents, who also joined the country club and had many friends and parties, I wasn't much of social person. But I was definitely into the religious thing. I read the Bible as mythology—like the legends of Jason, Heracles, Odysseus, King Arthur, Robin Hood, and all the other stories I had been reading. I got involved in the pageants they would put on for Christmas and Easter, which were the only times I went to actual church services. I usually got the part of narrator, and I loved it. This is where I discovered that I had an aptitude for theater—which I really got into in high school and college.

I read the Bible from beginning to end. There were all these things in there that I thought were really bizarre, but fascinating. But since I'd started out reading Greek myths, it never occurred to me that this was any different, and was supposed to be the one and only true way. And eventually I had this major epiphany: I realized that the entire Bible, from Genesis to Revelation, was the story of a specific people—the Jews. This was all about *them* as the "chosen people" of their tribal God, Jahweh: their origin mythos; their history; their commandments and rules; their kings, prophets, and prophecies; their messiah; their redemption.

But *I* wasn't Jewish! My ancestors were Celts and Teutons. The Bible was not the story of *my* people or history at all—and thus it simply was not relevant to me. Indeed, I realized that *my* people were the ones continuously mentioned throughout the Bible as the "other people" that the presumed Jewish readers were not supposed to emulate. This realization precipitated my liberation from Christianity, after many years of total immersion in it. And eventually, of course, in seeking my own ethnic religious heritage, I came to identify as a Pagan.

At school every classroom had shelves along the window side. And on these shelves they kept the *World Book Encyclopedia*. This was the same encyclopedia that was associated with the *Childcraft* books that I had read before. So I would always come in and take a seat right next to the bookshelf. And so, one volume at a time, I read the entire *World Book Encyclopedia*.

When I got to volume *D*, there were dragons and dinosaurs. I'll never forget my reaction on opening up that two-page spread of Charles Knight's famous mural from the Field Museum of Natural History in Chicago of a triceratops facing off against a tyrannosaurus rex.

And there it was—wow! Suddenly a major-leap epiphany occurred to me: *dragons were real!* Once upon a time, real dragons ruled the Earth! That was really profound, and it's only gotten better over the years as we've discovered that dinosaurs were not reptiles at all, but warm-blooded and intelligent and related to birds. It's made the dragon stories even more fascinating. The existence of dinosaurs validated the stories of dragons in a sense. This was the reality behind the myth. At least that's how I felt as a kid. Now, I think there is actually a lot more to the dragon legends. But nonetheless, this was a significant epiphany.

So, from that point on, I saw all myths through a double lens. One was the story itself, and the other was the reality behind the story. I became like a "myth detective," trying to ferret out the truth behind the mystery. Eventually, this led me to re-create Living Unicorns, dive for Mermaids . . . and write *A Wizard's Bestiary*.

NARRATOR: Tim Zell discovered science fiction at an early age and looked to the genre for inspiration. While at that point it was still mostly considered to be lowbrow entertainment, for Tim the sci-fi library books he was reading weren't merely imaginary tales but visions of possibilities. (He also had a crush on the local librarian-lady, which helped to keep him going back for more.) He read the "juvenile" novels of author Robert Heinlein as they each came out, and Heinlein became a significant childhood mentor, teaching what it means to be human.

Heinlein, and other science-fiction writers, were also helpful to Tim as he tried to understand psychic experiences that he had as he was growing up, and as he began to explore the possibilities of telepathy and the expanded possibilities of the human mind. Tim even tried psychic experiments with his younger brother and sister, and freaked them out in the process. (His photographic memory gave him something of an advantage in the situation.)

OZ: Science fiction took me to the next phase of my magickal training, providing many different scenarios of imaginative possibilities—including those of psychic abilities and the future evolution of humanity. Robert Heinlein wrote a short story called "Lost Legacy" (in *Assignment in Eternity*, 1953) in which he mentioned specific techniques for developing psychic abilities. So I started doing some of those exercises. I read about psychokinesis and started using that as a focus. At that time my family was into playing board games together. I spent hours of practice trying to control dice and coins as they were tossed. I got to be so good at it that my brother and sister complained that I was cheating. I guess I was, technically, although I was using a skill that I worked hard to develop. But it was a skill that went beyond the parameters of the game. I thought it was like somebody being really good at shooting hoops after a lot of practice.

In high school I studied hypnosis and self-hypnosis, and practiced these on myself and other kids. I came to the conclusion that hypnosis could be used to enhance one's psychic and other abilities, because you could tell someone when they were hypnotized that they could do something, and then they could do it. I got to point where I could control pain and didn't need anesthetics.

But there are side effects to these things that you don't necessarily realize at the time. For example, the control over pain that I mastered severely reduced my empathy. I didn't experience other people's pain any more than I did my own. Later I went through a long period of having to re-learn a sense of empathy.

CHARLES ZELL: Tim was very strong. He didn't look strong, but he was. He spent one summer at the Carson Long Military Institute in

Pennsylvania, and they had to engage in sports all the time. I went there to visit one weekend, and he had broken his hand hitting a guy while he was boxing. Sometimes kids would pick fights with Tim because he was different, and, strangely enough, he would always come out on top. So after that they left him alone.

He was very bright. His problem in school was that he was so bright that he often corrected the teachers when they were wrong, particularly in English. His mother had been an English major, so he was very well versed in correct English. The only problem I had with Tim in school was not his grades—those were fabulous. It was his conduct as a student.

One of his tricks he did when he was maybe ten or eleven years old. It was the middle of the winter, and when the teacher opened the desk drawer a mouse jumped out at her. Of course all the kids knew it was Tim. I was called to school, and I said to him, "Where did you find a mouse in the middle of winter?" There was two feet of snow on the ground! He said it was easy. He knew so much about Nature, even at that age.

When Tim was fifteen, I had him tested at the Illinois Institute of Technology. They didn't even want to test him. They usually didn't test anybody that young. But I had some contacts, and I called in my chips. I wanted to see what was happening. They tested people who had high IQs, and I knew he was brilliant. For three days he not only did very, very well at it, but he also knew which test he was taking and why. So I'd meet with him for lunch and say, "How are you doing?" And he'd tell me all about the test. And I'd say, "How do you know so much about the test?"

And he'd say, "Oh, Dad, I read about that years ago!"

When it was all over, the head of the school called me and said, "You have a very interesting son. His tests are just off the chart!"

And I said, "Well, what should I do?"

And he said, "Just stand back and let him go. Don't interfere with him. Just understand that he is one of a kind." And he is.

OZ: From the ages of ten through twelve, I had to go back and forth from Crystal Lake to Kirkwood, Missouri, for months at a time. This was for extensive orthodontic work, as I had really bad buck teeth. I lived with my maternal grandmother, whom I called "Gogi," and my Aunt Betsy, both of whom I loved dearly.

But my memories from those times are quite confused with memories of my former life as my grandfather in that same house and yard—such as that of the giant alligator snapping turtle I recall befriending, who hung out in the asparagus patch. I named him "Rastus," and at the end of the summer, we took him down to the St. Louis Zoo, where I would go to see him every time I went back—even into the 1970s, with Morning Glory. I would identify him because he was the biggest turtle there, in with the alligators.

But a few years ago, when I asked my mother about this, she told me: "That never happened to you. It was your grandfather who brought home a big snapping turtle from one of his fishing trips and kept it for a while in a big tub in the backyard, before giving it to the zoo. He called it 'Rastus.'"

Fairly early on in my childhood, I discovered animal skulls, and I became really fascinated by those. I decided I wanted to collect the whole set, so I started working with road kills to get the skulls. In the process of this, I became interested in the rest of the anatomy as well. I was taking biology classes in school, so I started doing dissections. And as I learned to dissect various critters in biology class, I applied those techniques to road kills. This was a precursor to the idea that I would someday become a surgeon. I had excellent hand-eye coordination and got pretty good at being able to tease out the blood vessels and the nerves from the flesh.

I dissected everything I could get ahold of. Then I preserved the skins, saved the bones, and cleaned the skulls. Each one was like a unique vessel for the soul of the creature. I was more intrigued by the skull structure than I was by the external appearance.

These were what I would now call "Wizardly Studies"—the study of arcane, obscure, little-known, forbidden, and esoteric knowledge. I was fascinated with the stars, and I'd often lie out on the ground (or on the roof) at night studying the constellations, spotting planets, watching meteors, and so on. I read all the books I could find on astronomy and visions of future space travel.

I would shine a flashlight up into the sky to try and signal the flying saucers to come get me and take me home. I felt like an alien in human society—a "stranger in a strange land." The weird thing about this was that I did feel I belonged to the planet. I felt totally at home in Nature and with animals. But I did not feel as comfortable with people, and didn't really feel like I was one of them.

Our house was on the periphery of town. Nearby there were fields, a marsh, a lake, and a forest. There was a big, sprawling golf course a block away that had lots of woods in it. When everybody else went to sleep, I would take off my pajamas and sneak out of my bedroom window late at night, especially if there was a full moon, and go running around naked in the dark. This was a whole world that was mine alone—totally unpopulated by humans. The animals that would come out at night were unafraid. There was something totally magical about that—my "secret life."

This was when I found a lot of critters, because they too were "children of the night." I was always dragging in strange new "pets." I brought home a screech owl that I called "Archimedes"—after Merlin's owl in T. H. White's *The Sword in the Stone.* I had a white rat, lizards, salamanders, toads, frogs, box turtles, water turtles, crayfish, a possum (which I named "Pogo"—the first of many possums I've had in my life), and a little brown bat I called "Boris." And my mother let me keep them all in my bedroom—everything but snakes. She was remarkably indulgent about that, I eventually came to appreciate.

VERA ZELL: One time Tim's father was cleaning out the garage, and he picked up a hatbox and it was absolutely writhing with snakes. Tim was taking care of them and feeding them.

He had a terrarium full of praying mantises, and an ant colony. And he had a whole beehive that he had ordered by mail. He took it to school for show and tell, and they all got loose in the room. You can imagine the chaos that caused!

OZ: One time the housekeeper left my bedroom door open while my mother's bridge club was in the living room . . .

VERA ZELL: All of a sudden the girls started screaming, and here was this bat flying around the room. They were all crawling under the tables. Another time they went to use the powder room that was closest to where we were playing bridge, and there was a screech owl in it. They came screaming out of there fast!

CHARLES ZELL: Whatever he was involved in, we encouraged him to do it. I said to Tim one time, "If you build a better mousetrap, people will beat a path to your door." So he built a very unusual mousetrap and put it in our garage, where it filled up with mice. He took me literally.

OZ: But I was very disappointed that the world didn't beat a path to my door. The concept of marketing wasn't included in the adage! In later years, I came to see my whole life like that—constantly building better metaphorical "mousetraps," and waiting for the world to show up. But first, as I later came to understand, you have to get their attention, and that's the part I've never quite mastered.

NARRATOR: The adolescent Tim Zell was what today would be called a "science geek," though the word *geek* didn't mean the same thing then as it does now. American life was changing rapidly, and the changes included what it meant to be a teenager, and how to describe the way teens behaved and interacted with each other. What was happening with Tim and people his age was a new cultural phenomenon. As the Baby Boomers grew up, they found themselves in the unprecedented position of not having to go directly from childhood to assuming adult responsibilities. They were the first generation of American teenagers to have their own culture—their own music, movies, and a new form of entertainment called television (with lots of new shows for adolescents who had time on their hands).

But Tim Zell was different from other teenagers. He was thirteen when Elvis Presley first appeared on *The Ed Sullivan Show*—the perfect age to be when rock and roll was being invented—but it meant nothing to him. He didn't listen to Buddy Holly or Little Richard; he didn't go see James Dean movies; and he hated *The Catcher in the Rye*. Tim was, instead, the kind of student who joined the debate team, did all of his homework on time, excelled in his lab classes, and created his own science projects. One winter Tim built an igloo in the backyard of his home based on reading he'd done about the Inuit (polar Eskimos), and it was so authentic that teachers would bring their classes for tours.

OZ: Another year I built a sod house in the field in back, like the pioneers used to build out on the Great Plains. I built treehouses and forts. I would totally get into these things. I would read about something, and then I would want to do it. I read about Stone Age technology and learned woodcarving and flint-knapping to make spears, atlatls, arrow points, and stone axes.

My father got me into the Boy Scouts, and I really enjoyed that. I got really good at woodcraft—things like tracking, trapping, fishing, building fires, camp cooking, making shelters, and how to survive in the woods. I learned to identify all the plants and animals. Many years later I did a two-week vision quest in the Oregon woods with only a pocket-knife, and I survived just fine using my Scouting skills.

Insofar as I hung around with other kids at all, I mostly hung around with girls—especially when the girls and boys became more differentiated. I had very few male friends, and none of them really close. I was oblivious to peer pressure, and never got into the guy-culture thing of sports, cars, rock and roll, and stuff like that. Since that wasn't my crowd, I never had the slightest interest in doing any teenage drinking or smoking cigarettes. I just never felt any particular desire to be like other kids, which is unforgivable in teen culture. From being in church pageants I'd learned about drama, so I then began to try out for the plays in high school. And I always got accepted—often for leading roles. I got into all the other aspects of theater in addition to acting—working on sets, props, costumes, and makeup. I loved costumes, and my mother taught me to sew so I could make my own. When I was a junior in high school, I created a costume based on the human-fly character that Vincent Price played in the horror movie *The Fly*. I made a giant fly head with big bulging papier-mâché eyes and movable antennae and mandibles. All this was the best possible preparation for eventually becoming a Priest and ritualist, where I still apply those skills.

That put me in a very different social context. I began seriously dating two girls simultaneously, Judy and Sharon, who got into a considerable rivalry, as often happens. This culminated over who would be the first one to actually have sex with me. That turned out to be Sharon, and it happened right after the end of the semester, at the beginning of summer vacation, in the back seat of the car. I was sixteen, and I thought this was the best thing in the universe! That summer we made love all the time—every place we could find.

I absolutely loved sex, and I determined that this was something I wanted to study and practice as much as possible and get really good at! It totally transformed me in so many ways. Sharon said she'd "made me a man," and I think that was so. Up till that point I'd been obsessively body-modest around other people. And that all just disappeared.

NARRATOR: The fun came to a quick halt in the fall when Charles Zell sent his son to a college prep school for his senior year, where students were closely supervised. Once again the teenage Tim found himself with no friends, and though he had a girlfriend, he was unable to spend time alone with her.

But the future he had grown up dreaming about was rapidly approaching. As a result of the space race against Communist Russia, the United States was emphasizing science education, and Tim would get a scholarship to the college of his choice when he graduated from high school. Other "science geeks" and science-fiction fans like himself would receive similar opportunities, and they would go on to help create the computers, cell phones, and Internet that are in use today. And Tim Zell would go on to create his own church.

Chapter 2
Sharing Water
(1961–1965)

Then two college boys thought it would be a joy
To try and start livin' like Martians in their dorm. (In their dorm!)
So they shared a glass of water and they did what they oughter,
And the Galloping Garrulous Grok-Flock was born!

—FROM "THE GALLOPING GARRULOUS GROK-FLOCK"
BY ADAM WALKS-BETWEEN-WORLDS

NARRATOR: Tim Zell's freshman year began at Westminster College, a small school in Fulton, Missouri, in 1961. Westminster was a men's college, and there was a woman's college across town called William Woods. He chose it because he intended to become a surgeon, and the school was well known for its pre-med program.

John F. Kennedy was sworn in as president in 1961. Unlike his predecessor, Dwight D. Eisenhower, JFK was young, charismatic, and had a beautiful and charming wife. Eisenhower had been an army general in World War II and, during the eight years of his presidency, kept his strict military attitude and maintained the national status quo. At his inauguration, Kennedy declared a "New Frontier" and began working to create positive changes.

This was also a time when the first Baby Boomers began to mature and, inspired by President Kennedy and Dr. Martin Luther King, get involved in politics and social issues like the civil rights and free speech movements. Liberal college students graduated from rock and roll to folk and protest music, and were soon singing along to songs like Bob Dylan's "Blowin' in the Wind" and "The Times They Are a-Changin'." And, following the example of the Beat poets and their interest in Buddhism, they began to explore Eastern religions and other alternative forms of spirituality.

Tim Zell's mystic path would soon take him in a direction much different from even his liberal peers—as usual, he was following his own muse. His life was about to be changed by a friend he would meet and the science-fiction novel they would both read.

OZ: So I started college in the fall of 1961—the dawning year of what would eventually become known as the "Psychedelic Psixties." At Westminster, the first-year students stayed in dormitories, but for your second year you had to live somewhere else, so I decided to join a fraternity. The first weeks I was there, they had the pledge parties. Nobody had explained the concept of the college fraternity thing to me, and, as was so often the case, I didn't quite get it.

NARRATOR: To get an idea of what the frat scene was like back then, check out the movie *Animal House*, which is set in the same period of time that Tim was beginning his undergrad studies and pledging a fraternity.

OZ: I didn't understand that the purpose of the fraternities was to make connections with people who could help you in your future career. Eventually I accepted a membership in the Phi Kappa Psi fraternity, which was, as it turned out, the lowest one on the social scale. Social status was something I've always been pretty oblivious to . . . even to this day.

And at the very beginning of all this I met Lance Christie.

LANCE CHRISTIE: I ran into Tim Zell during the pledge week. We were in the anteroom of one of the fraternities. One or the other of us, I don't remember which, made some sort of wisecrack about the strange customs of the natives. The other one of us responded, "Ah! Somebody else who has the same view of things that I do." Later on he told me that I was the first person he had ever met who seemed to be a member of the same species that he was. We discussed the whichness of what, and we were excited about all the information that we were coming across. We realized that there was a gigantic, wonderful picture puzzle out there that could be put together, that formed a road map to how to build a hopeful and enlightened future. Every time we came across another piece that seemed to fit into the puzzle, or at least told us where to look for the next piece, we would recognize it and be all excited about it. It was very emotional—this stuff was coming from the heart. It wasn't just an abstract intellectual exercise.

From reading science-fiction authors such as Olaf Stapledon and Arthur C. Clarke, we had acquired the concept of the human race evolving. And there being subgroups within the race that were actually different subspecies. We concluded that we were members of a different subspecies than the mass of people. Of course in *Atlas Shrugged*, Ayn Rand described these people as being the innovators, the creative thinkers that the majority of people will then attack because they are different, and they feel threatened by these people operating outside the bounds of safe conventionality. We obviously could identify with that.

OZ: In college I was like a kid in a candy store. I signed up for everything I could—I took the maximum number of hours I was allowed, and continued doing so every year. The first year I took all the pre-med classes, statistics, etc., and I encountered the psychology department. There hadn't been anything like that in high school. I was fascinated by this brand-new field with lots to study.

The head of the psych department, Gale Fuller, was interested in the transpersonal psychology movement of Abraham Maslow, Karen Horney, and Eric Fromm, which was still quite new. The concept of the self-actualizing person, to me, played right into the idea of the next step in human evolution. That was a strong part of the science-fiction vision that I had been exploring. There was a lot of that kind of stuff going on at that time. Gale Fuller was a very impressive mentor. He was brilliant, insightful, funny, and wise, and it was his influence that really inspired me to shift my major from pre-med to psychology, sociology, and anthropology. My folks never quite understood. They had envisioned having a son who was a successful brain surgeon, and they didn't get it that my destiny lay along a different path.

That fall the October selection of the Science Fiction Book Club was a new book by Robert Heinlein called *Stranger in a Strange Land*. Lance was a subscriber, and he got the book. He took it home and read it over Christmas vacation. When he got back, he handed it to me and said, "You have got to read this!" So I did. There was an incredible sense of recognition—here was someone who understood us and was talking to us. And the ideas that he was putting forth were all ones that we resonated with on so many levels.

Having been an avid reader of Heinlein's juveniles all through high school, I was really ready for *Stranger in a Strange Land*. As the protagonists in his previous works had all been about my age progressively, so it was with the newest one: Valentine Michael Smith—as an infant, the sole survivor of the first attempted manned expedition to Mars, which crashed upon landing. The baby is rescued and raised by native Martians, in their ancient and wise culture—with no idea of his human heritage. Twenty-five years later, a second expedition succeeds in reaching Mars intact, and brings Michael back to a home world he's never known . . . with his Martian-trained mental abilities and alien cultural perspective. In the novel, Michael establishes the "Church of All Worlds," built around "nests"—a fusion of congregation, group marriage, and intentional community. A key concept is *grokking* (literally, "drinking")—i.e., the ability to be fully empathic. Thus the sharing of water is the most profound act of communion between two people—or a group.

Heinlein's *Stranger in a Strange Land* introduced us to the ideas of immanent divinity ("thou art God"), pantheism ("all that groks is God"), sacraments (water sharing), Priestesses, social and ritual nakedness, intimate extended families as a basis for community, and, of course, open, loving relationships without jealousy and joyous expression of sexuality as divine union. By defining *love* as "that condition wherein another person's happiness is essential to your own," *Stranger in a Strange Land* changed forever the parameters of our relationships with each other—especially in the sexual arena. And all of this in the context of a legal religious organization—a "church"—that could have all the rights and privileges granted to the mighty Church of Rome! This was heady stuff, and we drank it up.

LANCE CHRISTIE: We talked a lot about the possibilities that were available to human beings to take a different path, in respect to the way society was put together and the premises on which it was founded. That's where *Stranger* had such a powerful effect. Heinlein constellated the idea of trying to work out and install a different set of cultural premises, to develop an alternative human civilization based on more enlightened concepts about human beings—their relationships to each other, their relationships to the natural world, and the purpose and conduct of life, what constitutes right livelihood, what constitutes right action, and so on.

OZ: In *Stranger*, sharing water and saying, "Water shared is life shared," is the fundamental ritual of the book. So on April 7, 1962, Lance and I sat down in a field, shared water, and became water-brothers, dedicating ourselves to creating a life based on the principles that were in this book—and to trying to actualize them and manifest them into reality. That was essentially the founding event of what eventually became the Church of All Worlds—as well as the Association for the Tree of Life.

When our girlfriends (and future wives) returned from spring break, we turned them on to *Stranger* and shared water with them, too. That was on May 25. And so it began . . .

NARRATOR: Using the results of psychology-department personality tests, Tim and Lance were able to find other like-minded students, turn them on to *Stranger in a Strange Land*, and form a "water-brotherhood." They called it *Atl*, which is the Aztec word for "water"—with the esoteric meaning of "original home of our ancestors."

LANCE CHRISTIE: The name *Atl* was chosen because it appears in *Atlantis*, the *Atlas Mountains* of northwestern Africa, and the *Atlantic Ocean*, all of which derived from the Greek mythological Titan Atlas, who carried the heavens on his shoulders.

OZ: Eventually Atl grew to about a hundred people, many of whom had grown up in different religions. We had come from Episcopalian, Baptist, Congregational, Catholic, Jewish, and other backgrounds, but none of us really felt like that was the one for us.

We wanted to create an affiliation that was based on cherishing diversity, and a deeper level of bonds between the people, one that we really felt a natural affinity to. None of us felt like we quite belonged to the families we were born into, but we wanted family! We wanted a tribe. The only way we could get it was to come up with different criteria. The old saying was that "blood is thicker than water." We created a family in which water is thicker (or at least deeper) than blood. And the sharing of water became a stronger bond to us than the blood relationships that formed the basis of all families prior to us. And in our new tribal family, we all took initiatory names—usually from Greek mythology. I was Prometheus, the fire-bringer who defied the authority of almighty Zeus to bring enlightenment to humanity; and Lance was Chiron, the wise centaur and teacher of heroes, such as Heracles and Jason.

And right about then I formulated my lifelong mission statement, which has remained unchanged ever since: "To be a catalyst for the coalescence of consciousness."

LANCE CHRISTIE: Something that was very fundamental to our intuitive take on the world, that we still have, is that instead of the paradigm in which you have a prophet, or authority figure of some sort, or an intellectual leader who reveals or dictates a religious system, we had absorbed the concept that the only way of doing things was individually. What is essential to that process is that the individual actually breaks free of adherence to the normative values of their culture of origin and develops a highly individualized set of tastes, ethics, and understandings based on their particular characteristics of character. Self-actualization involves coming to understand who you are, what your skills are, what your proclivities are, and how to utilize those to both satisfy yourself and benefit the world.

The impulse to benefit the world seems to be a part of the package, because otherwise we would have a bunch of extremely effective raging sociopaths running around. That right there underlines the inherent optimism that you find in Oberon's and my take on the world and its potential. What we both perceive is that when you actually get all the cultural craziness out of the way, and you have people develop and become this integrated human being that is not neurotic, not psychotic, that is not dragged down by all these *shoulds*, *oughts*, and weird cultural control mechanisms, then what you end up with, except for people who have a wiring defect and are sociopathic from the get-go, is a person who is, in fact, beneficent. The enlightened person wishes the world to be a better place.

With the water-sharing ceremony we were recognizing people who seemed to have the ability to look at society from an outsider's point of view, and who were not inferior to the demands of society. Although some mistakes were made there, too. George Bernard Shaw, describing the early Christians in his commentary on "Androcles and the Lion," observed that any progressive social movement attracts not only those who are superior to the demands of the contemporary society, but also those who are inferior to it. And we did acquire a number of people in the water-brotherhood who proved to be outcasts from society not because they were superior to it in the sense of being more intellectually, morally, or creatively developed, but in fact were people who had psychiatric issues that made them unable to function in society. It took some mistakes before we came to understand the difference between an intelligent but damaged individual versus a person who is more advanced ethically and socially.

OZ: We started putting out a newsletter called *The Atlan Torch*, which became the first "underground" paper that the school had ever seen. It was secretly subsidized by some of the more radical teachers, who let us use the school's mimeograph machines and supplied us with paper. We tackled provocative issues like student rights and free speech, and poked fun at the campus socialists.

One of our Atlans was a streetwise New York hipster named Pete. He had been a part of the Greenwich Village Beatnik scene, and he introduced us to pot. It was an elaborate ritual—we pulled down all the shades, stuffed towels in the cracks under the doors, lit candles and incense, sat in a circle on the floor, and ceremonially passed the pipe. That really imprinted me. From that time on, my use of any kind of mind-altering stuff has always had to be done in a ritual setting of some sort—as a sacrament. And thus I never really did that much of it.

But this sort of ritual became a part of our lives. The whole format of sitting around in a circle and passing the sacred sacraments started with that particular event. After that we added wine to our rituals, but I never just opened up and drank a bottle of it on my own or even with a meal. It was always part of a ritual. And so I never got into beer or hard liquor. They just never appealed to me.

NARRATOR: Across the United States, young people were beginning to explore rituals like this. In the newfound freedom of their dorm rooms or apartments and away from home for the first time, they were discovering what opportunities were awaiting them in the brave new world in which they were becoming adults. They had read books like Aldous Huxley's *The Doors of Perception*, and wanted to open those doors for themselves. There were those who had grown tired of their family churches and were trying, on some level, to make a direct connection with what they thought of as "God." They were hoping to do it with drugs, and their numbers were growing.

Tim Zell was not the only one who would go from this kind of ritual to what is now known as Paganism. What the modern Witches were doing in Britain at this same time was not known to Tim or almost anyone else in America then—more on them later. But there was a growing awareness of what shamans were, and of Native American spirituality. Indeed, anyone who had grown up playing cowboys and Indians in their backyard knew what it meant to "pass the peace pipe." For them, this was just a taste of what was to come.

And this was all happening simultaneously with the beginnings of the feminist movement, which Tim and Lance incorporated into their early church philosophy.

LANCE CHRISTIE: We intuitively understood very early on that in order to get the world fixed, we had to reassert the importance of the feminine principle. Through reading history we realized that the Christian church, as an institution, was largely in competition with the Nature religions that preceded it. Those religions, of course, worshiped both the male and the female principle. We also realized that society had made the repression of sexuality a major part of its control mechanisms.

One can tend to rationalize something that one's hormones are driving one to do with what one's philosophies were recommending one do. I'm sure that there were times when we acted in an exploitative fashion. But the thing that would happen with us was that if we were getting out on a limb, most often we would realize it. Because we would start to see the gap between what we knew we believed in and what we were doing.

NARRATOR: During all this, and for years to come, the most important woman in Tim Zell's life was someone he had met right at the beginning of his freshman year at Westminster College.

OZ: The first Friday there was a mixer with the William Woods girls. At that time I was trying to reinvent myself. I didn't want to be a nerdy, nonsocial kid like I had been in high school. I took James Bond and Hugh Hefner as my role models, and I showed up looking very dapper. There was this gorgeous redhead there named Martha.

MARTHA TURLEY: It was love at first sight. We were inseparable after that. We did everything together. We used to call each other Prometheus and Gaea. I thought he was very handsome and intelligent. I was majoring in journalism and drama. In high school I had been the editor of the student paper.

OZ: As our dating got more and more intense, we discovered a great trysting place on the girl's campus. There was a Gothic-style chapel that had a little prayer room up at the top of a small tower that nobody ever went to. I made some adjustments to the lock so that we were able to slip in when no one was watching and make out.

MARTHA TURLEY: I became pregnant with Bryan on December 15, 1962. We had just gone to see some religious epic movie—*King of Kings*. Bryan was born exactly nine months later, on September 15, 1963. We used to have a place in the church that was on the girls' campus. There was a little chapel room upstairs that we used. It was like a tower. Tim had it all rigged up so it looked like it was locked and nobody could come in. Most of the other couples probably had cars they used for doing something like that. But we didn't. This was in the winter when we couldn't go outside.

OZ: Unmarried pregnancy was a very traumatic thing in those days. Of course, we had to talk to our parents about this, which was very difficult. But there was no question in our minds that we wanted to get married. So we arranged to have a wedding that spring in St. Louis. My parents made all the arrangements and paid for it all, and my fraternity choir came and sang. But just a few nights before the wedding they kidnapped me and shaved my whole body, so I was all bristly for our wedding night. This really put me off against the frat scene and their so-called sense of "brotherhood."

Nobody had a clue that Martha was pregnant. We moved into a little duplex for the remainder of the semester, and I quit the fraternity, as it no longer suited my married or social life. Since no one before me had ever quit that fraternity, this didn't set well with some of my fellow frat "brothers," especially the frat president, who declared himself my sworn enemy and tried to make my life miserable clear into the mid-1970s!

I immediately enrolled in a course in developmental psychology, and I read everything I could get my hands on about radical theories and practices of child-rearing and early education. Eventually, these studies led me into a career in teaching and working with children.

In the previous year, one of the books that we'd read in the psychology department was B. F. Skinner's *Walden Two*. It was his vision of a utopian society based on the principles of behavioral psychology. The book had some provocative ideas for communal living that were almost science fiction. And one of these was a crib-type thing that was sort of a habitat environment for infants. So I wrote to Skinner. He had drawn up plans for this thing—which he called an "air crib"—and he sent them to me. It was quite a project—it had to have temperature and humidity controls and a woven nylon frame that the baby slept on with a drip pan underneath to catch pee, a Plexiglas window that could be raised and lowered in front, and shades that could be pulled down. I spent the summer of 1963 building it.

I was with Martha until Bryan was born. That was a very traumatic thing for me because the hospital would not let me attend the birth. And

I had no idea that would happen. I had been reading about innovations in having fathers participate in the birthing experience, and I just naturally figured that was what we'd be doing. But in those days the doctors just went ahead and made all those decisions and never discussed them with the patients at all. So I was utterly unprepared when she was wheeled away into the delivery room and I was forcibly exiled into the waiting room.

There was another man out there with me who was considerably worried. The nurse came out to talk to him. I couldn't help but overhear as she told him that his baby had been born dead. The guy fainted right on the spot. I was completely traumatized by this. I demanded to be let in, but they would not do it.

MARTHA TURLEY: I don't remember the delivery. They knocked me out. I knew that there was no way I was going to have natural childbirth. My tolerance for pain is very low. They say that's typical for redheads. Tim was with me the whole time I was having labor pains. I remember them giving me something in the delivery room, and it put me right to sleep. When I woke up, I was back in my own room.

Back in those days, they didn't allow fathers in most hospital delivery rooms. It was something he maybe should have planned ahead of time and discussed or set it up with the doctor. Knowing Tim, it probably never even occurred to him that you had to do that.

OZ: It had a profound effect on our life. Giving birth is a moment when a woman needs to have her mate with her. And if he is not, the resentment that is created never really goes away. This contributed to the postpartum depression syndrome that she had really badly. After that event Martha completely lost interest in sex and we became alienated from each other. Our relationship was never the same after that.

MARTHA TURLEY: I guess I was scared of getting pregnant again because it was such a traumatizing experience. My mother kept me naïve about everything so I had no idea what was going to happen or what I was going to go through. It was all a big secret.

OZ: Right after Bryan was born, I had to go back to school. Martha stayed with her mom for a while and eventually came back to live with me in our new upstairs apartment. Somehow we got the air crib back there, too.

MARTHA TURLEY: Tim was a good, loving father. Even though he was in school full time, we were equal partners in parenting. As a matter of fact, he was much better at diapering than I was.

OZ: I got totally into being a father. We slept with Bryan cuddled in our bed at night (the air crib was mainly for naps). I kept elaborate logs of his feeding schedules, weight, measurements, and developmental milestones. Other than school, we took him everywhere with us and just doted on him.

Martha and I explored possibilities to heal our sexual relationship. One of the ones that seemed reasonable was opening our marriage. We thought that if this thing was damaged between her and me, perhaps she could heal it at her end by getting involved with other people. It was very trial-and-error and experimental. We didn't have any clear-cut guidelines other than *Stranger in a Strange Land*, which laid out a premise that it was okay as long as everyone was open and honest about it. So at least we had a guilt-free context for this. It took me a while to get into it personally, because I was so busy. But we each managed to have a few other lovers during our college years. That worked out quite well, all things considered. Eventually things came back together between us, but there was always a scar across our marriage.

Martha and I became the first students in the history of Westminster and William Woods to get married while in school, and thus to have independent housing. Every other student either lived with their parents or in a fraternity, sorority, or some kind of school housing. So our place became a hangout for other students like us.

This was in the days of the hootenannies . . . the beginnings of the folk and protest music that came to define the '60s. On weekend evenings there was usually someone with a guitar, and conversation was interlaced with folk singing. We maintained an open house at all times, encouraging people to drop by at their leisure. And because of the influence of

Stranger in a Strange Land, it became the custom to be naked in our home. People would come in, take their clothes off, and hang out. Our apartment became an off-campus, clothing-optional haven for our growing Nest of water-siblings—as well as a trysting place—and we never lacked for baby sitters.

We had a sign posted on the inside of our front door, just like in *Stranger*, that said, "Did You Remember to Dress?" We kept that sign for decades—in fact, its successor is on our front door right now. We even had a bowl of money by the door that people could contribute to or take from. We did everything we could to create a Nest environment like in the book. Our pad acquired the reputation among friends as a place they could be themselves, and among our enemies as a den of iniquity.

We continued to publish *The Atlan Torch*. The articles that I wrote were not just controversial but were considered threatening to some. I attacked the draconian security systems set up by the girls' school to keep them from having sex. (Of course, since we had an off-campus house, anybody who wanted to have a tryst could just come over to our place.) *The Atlan Torch* and our libertine Atlan ways did not set well with the administration of William Woods, and the *Torch* and I were both banned from the WW campus.

NARRATOR: Somewhere in that period, the Zells got a black-and-white television set, and they began watching *The Addams Family* and *The Munsters,* both of which had TV sitcom folks they could really identify with. *Bewitched* was another favorite, and for many years it provided their only example of what a modern Witch might be like. Tim Zell was still interested in increasing his psychic powers, and he thought that if Witches actually existed, they might be able to help him with that. But he didn't personally know any or, indeed, if there even *were* any anywhere.

Another significant part of the Atl mythology came from two Marvel comic books that had just started publishing.

OZ: The first was *The X-Men*, which was based on the idea that some people are just mutants and not part of the same species as everyone else. That was a good metaphor for us, and something we could identify with. The setting also involved a "School for Gifted Youngsters," which became an inspiration that I actualized forty years later with the Grey School of Wizardry. The other comic was *Spider-Man*, with a hero who had personal problems and angst just like the rest of us. His basic principle was that "with great power comes great responsibility."

NARRATOR: The Nest continued to meet in the Zell home during the cold Missouri winters. When the weather was better, the party would sometimes move outdoors.

OZ: Exploring the countryside beyond the school and town, we discovered abandoned clay pits that had been used by the brickworks that had, once upon a time, been a mainstay of the town. There were hills of rejected materials that had been hauled out of the pits. They had been eroding for years and were covered with sparkling calcite crystals. The pits had filled with water, and minerals turned the water different colors—blue, green, and violet. Little marshes, trees, and vegetation had come back in and reclaimed the place. It was this incredibly magical oasis that nobody else seemed to know about. On weekends we would all go out to the clay pits. Lance would make up a big batch of sangria in a wastebasket. We'd go skinny dipping and roll around in the mud; we'd sing folk songs around a campfire; we'd make love under the stars; and on Monday we'd go back to school. Social nakedness and outdoor lovemaking was very liberating.

I continued taking every single course that I possibly could. By the time I graduated, I had the full credits for majors in pre-med, psychology, sociology, and anthropology. I also took every class they had in comparative religion and natural history (including astronomy, paleontology, geology, zoology . . .). The senior colloquium assignment was to design a new religion for a newly emergent intelligent species. My thesis, "Freedom Through Existentialism," drew upon our Atlan perspective in trying to live out our visionary ideas in an experiential experiment, laying the foundations for the actual church we would later come to create.

OZ's BROTHER, BARRY: His college course load was amazing. He had more credits over four years than any other student his college president could remember, in addition to having a very high grade-point average.

NARRATOR: In an isolated town in rural Missouri, Tim Zell had found, and created, many of the elements that would be the foundation for what would become his Pagan church. And the next step in his spiritual and religious growth would come when he graduated from college and began to make contact with other people around the world who shared similar interests.

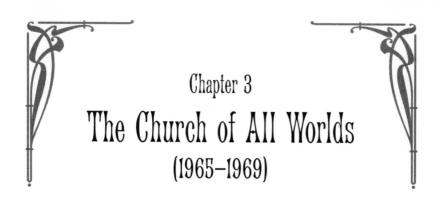

Chapter 3
The Church of All Worlds
(1965–1969)

Long past, in the Days of Legend,
When Star Trek newly had its birth,
Our ancestors met to honor
Sacred Fridays with sweet mirth!
—FROM "WHAT A FRIEND WE HAVE IN CHEEZ-ITS"
BY MAERIAN MORRIS, 1995

NARRATOR: Tim Zell graduated from college in 1965, less than two years after the assassination of President John F. Kennedy. It was the year when there was rioting in the streets of the Watts neighborhood in Los Angeles, and when President Lyndon Baines Johnson began to deploy combat troops to fight in Vietnam. The Selective Service system (a.k.a. "the draft") was used to force young men into the military, and by December nearly 200,000 U.S. soldiers were stationed in South Vietnam. Back home the protests began, and as the war continued to escalate, the protests got bigger and bigger.

In 1965 folk singer Bob Dylan went electric, and the Beatles and the Rolling Stones toured America. Ken Kesey, author of the popular anti-establishment novel *One Flew Over the Cuckoo's Nest*, and Timothy Leary, a former Harvard psychologist, were working overtime to encourage people to try LSD. The drug was still legal, and anarchist chemists like Augustus Owsley Stanley III began manufacturing mass quantities of it that were eagerly consumed by the more adventurous Baby Boomers. The psychedelic experience, as Leary called it, often led to deep reverence for Nature and the realization that everything, including the Earth, is alive and interconnected.

Acid wasn't the only drug being consumed by liberated young adults. They also had access to the new birth control pills, widely available for the first time, which made this generation the first generation anywhere that could have sex whenever they wanted, and as much as they wanted, without having to worry about creating the next generation. And so began the sexual revolution and the era of sex, drugs, and rock and roll.

The British Witch who was the father of modern Wicca, Gerald Gardner, had died the year before, but the news had not made headlines in America. At that point even Tim Zell had not heard of him, and he was not alone. American Hippies and college students were not reading Gardner's obscure occult books—science-fiction and fantasy paperbacks were the hip new campus favorites, and no longer just for kids and geeks. *Stranger in a Strange Land* caught on in a big way as the counterculture book of choice. Tim was joined by, literally, millions of others who began to dig the book's spirituality and its philosophy of sexual freedom. Next to *Stranger* on their bookshelves were *Dune*, Frank Herbert's epic saga of the ecosystem of an entire planet; and J. R. R. Tolkien's novels about Hobbits, Wizards, Elves, and other magical forest dwellers.

And young people were reading the underground newspapers that were filled with information about astrology, Tarot, feminism, reincarnation, pantheism, ecology, Mother Nature, and emerging alternative lifestyles. All these things were part of the fertile ground that American Neo-Paganism was beginning to grow from.

Tim Zell was ready to join the revolution in whatever way he could, and the most obvious way to do that seemed to be by continuing to study psychology.

OZ: I received a full scholarship in clinical psychology from the U.S. Public Health Service, to attend graduate school at Washington University in St. Louis. We rented a house on Park Avenue downtown where we could watch the St. Louis Arch being built way down the street. And in September of 1965, I started graduate school.

While I was in graduate school, Martha pursued her calling to become a Montessori teacher. The nearest place to get her training was in Kansas City, so while I was attending Washington University in St. Louis, she was on the opposite side of the state, over two hundred miles away. I would drive across on weekends to visit with her and Bryan, but being away from my family for so much time was a real hardship on all of us.

As I soon learned, the psych department at Washington University had a very different agenda from Westminster's. Instead of the transpersonal psychology of Maslow and Fromm that had so inspired me, the Wash U. psych professors were all into B. F. Skinner's behavioral psychology. This wasn't about understanding and helping people, but more about doing horrible experiments on animals—such as cutting open cats' heads and sticking electrodes into their brains. And the other grad students didn't seem to give a damn about making a difference in the world and in people's lives; all they seemed to be interested in was making money, and in playing manipulative political games.

In the summer of 1966, my father came for a visit. We sat out in the backyard, and he confided in me that with his kids all off to college and on their own, he was planning to divorce my mother. This decision, he said, had first taken hold in his mind back in 1959, when he had been hospitalized with a nearly fatal attack of kidney stones, and my mother just left him in the hospital and continued on our vacation to the Black Hills of South Dakota, without ever even phoning to see how he was. I hadn't given the matter much thought as a sixteen-year-old kid, as we all just cheerily went along our way. But seven years later, as a family man myself, I found the episode unimaginable, and I totally sympathized with my dad. So later that year, my parents divorced. I didn't see much of my mother for many years, and she never visited me to her dying day. But my dad continued to visit me every few years, in nearly all my different homes.

My father's mother, Mary (Gramma Zell), whom I dearly loved, had disappeared from my life back in high school, when (as I much later found out) my mother had banned her from visiting us. She died on March 28, 1966, but I never got a funeral notice or invitation. I never knew what had become of her until forty years later, when my father finally told me. This still seems incomprehensible to me. What kind of family does that? And how could my father have acquiesced to the banishment of his own mother? I think there are things about my family that I will never understand.

NARRATOR: Instead of returning to graduate school in the fall of 1966, Tim began looking for a full-time job. After trying different things, including teaching grade school, he was hired by the Human Development Corporation as a social psychologist and did that for the rest of his years in St. Louis. His work there encompassed family counseling, job training and placement, arranging educational programs and scholarships, working with abused women and kids, halfway houses, rent control, and emergency food, clothes, and shelter—it was a huge array of programs under President Johnson's "War on Poverty."

Tim's dad gave him the money for a down payment on a house, and Martha got a job teaching at a Montessori school. With a home and a steady job in place, he was then able to continue expanding on the visionary pursuits that he had begun in college. After moving to St. Louis, he had maintained his connections with the other Atlans. In fact, there was almost never a time when one or more members of the Atlan waterbrotherhood weren't staying with Tim, Martha, and Bryan, and living the social experiment 24/7. For the rest of them, he continued to publish separate editions of *The Atlan Torch.*

OZ: I also developed a short column in the *Torch* into its own independent publication, *Atlan Annals.* This consisted entirely of letters written among Atlans, which I would retype and collate into a single newsletter, run off copies on a mimeograph machine, and then mail to everyone.

Lance and I had both moved to different cities, and we continued our conversation regarding our mission of changing the world. We wanted to create a world that would be safe for people like us. One that we could live in comfortably. One where it would be safe to go outside and say (and be) who we were without being lynched.

So, we started talking about how we might best go about that. And two different directions emerged. One of them was to continue to be a secret underground society and work in various revolutionary causes, and inject these ideas into them—just sort of shaping things subtly from behind the scenes. And the other was to go public, with a church that would be right out there. In typical fashion, we decided to do it all. And so we formed two branches. One group we called the Atlan Foundation. Lance headed it up and became its main director. And it was involved in some very interesting stuff. They took lessons from things like *Cat's Cradle*, by Kurt Vonnegut, and especially the final chapter of *The Harrad Experiment* that talks about having this secret group move to some underpopulated state in the western United States and infiltrate the governmental arena. Well, this is what they did. Lance became the director of public health services for New Mexico, and was responsible for some of the earliest reform laws for medical marijuana in that state.

And I was chosen to head up the Church of All Worlds, because I seemed to have that kind of a personality.

LANCE CHRISTIE: Ordinarily when you have people who have been involved in starting something, and they're not working together on it, it's because there has been some sort of a falling out. That's the normal pattern in our culture. But that was never the case with Oberon and me. It was rather that obviously his talent lay in a different form of expression than mine. I viewed us as being collaborators who were walking different paths that were related. Both of us were experimenting. We knew what it was that we wanted to get to, but we didn't know how to get there, because what we were trying to do was not something for which there was a standard cultural template.

I realized that where OZ had a flare for the dramatic and getting out there and blowing minds, I was, and am, a social engineer, in the sense that I have a propensity for solving problems and figuring out how to make things work—in both a technical and a social sense.

Oberon had, and has, a real desire and talent for theater. There is a certain element of the Zen master in it, and a certain element of the little boy showing off. So he was really enjoying creating this Neo-Pagan church, with all the theater and ritual that went with it, and seeing what he could do by way of using that as a vehicle for changing people's consciousness. And also having a helluva good time. Lest all this sound too serious, one of the things that we intuited very early on was, as we put it, "What good is a religion if it doesn't have a good belly laugh now and then?" And of course OZ, very early on, adopted the self-mocking title of "Primate." A lot of the stuff that we put together and did had self-mocking or pun-based connotations. The whole idea was to keep people from getting locked into a rigid seriousness, which gets in the way of examining ideas and learning about yourself, working things out and having a fruitful life.

NARRATOR: Tim and Lance decided to take the Church of All Worlds (CAW) public in 1967. It was the year that the Summer of Love and the Human Be-In took place in San Francisco. On the radio Jim Morrison was living the myth of Dionysus, and the Jefferson Airplane was telling everyone about popping pills, smoking hookahs, and having fun hallucinations. And on Broadway it was declared that it was the dawning of the Age of Aquarius. People were beginning to explore, and exploit, what a few years later would be called the New Age. African Americans, Latin Americans, women, and gay people were learning about liberation. And anyone who had an idea for creating a new social or spiritual movement had the opportunity to bring a like-minded group of people together for just that purpose in parks, communes, collectives, churches, and anywhere else that the spirit moved them. In September of 1967, Tim jumped right in by arranging for a garage sale at a local coffeehouse to raise money to buy a ditto machine to start a CAW newsletter. (A ditto machine is also known as a "spirit duplicator"!)

OZ: After that, people started asking, "Just what is this Church of All Worlds?" So the guy who was running the place asked me if I would come back the next week and talk to people about the CAW.

At that time there was a guy in California known as Omar K. Ravenhurst, whose actual name was Kerry Thornley, and who later became one of the founders of the Discordian Society. He was involved in a San Francisco group called Kerista, a utopian visionary cult that had been founded in New York City clear back in 1956 by John Peltz "Bro Jud" Presmont. Kerista was premised on the creation of intentional "utopian" communities of group marriages. Kerry had written a little article called

"Functional Religion," which came to my attention. In the article, he proposed the use of the word *Pagan* as an identifying term for the kind of religious expression that he felt Kerista embodied.

Before that I had never seen the word *pagan* used in the context of a positive identification, let along a religious one. The "pagans" had always been the people who were not religious and needed to be converted to Christianity. But Kerry applied the term to a particular type of religious thinking and perspective that embraced pantheism, polytheism, classical mythology, ancient cultures, and all that cool stuff. Jud rejected the term, considering himself, as he much later told me, "an authentic Hebrew prophet, not some godless pagan!" But I thought it was perfect for us. Previously, the word had been used to refer to *others* in a derogatory fashion, as "*those* pagans." I seem to have been the first to claim it as a religious self-identification—as "*us* Pagans"—with a capital *P*.

I showed up at the coffeehouse, and I got up there on the little stage with a stool and a microphone where guys wearing goatees and black turtlenecks would usually read poetry or sing folk songs. I introduced myself as "Your friendly neighborhood Pagan," and I proceeded to talk about the Atlan vision in terms of the "First Pagan Church of All Worlds." Afterwards the manager invited me to come back and talk again.

Adoption of the term *Pagan* as an identification of our religious identity precipitated some very profound discussions in the *Atlan Annals*, around the whole aspect of identifying with people who have been misunderstood, feared, marginalized, and intensely persecuted throughout Christian history. In creating a new church, did we really want to take on all that baggage? The other Atlans mostly thought not and chose not to become involved, remaining below the public radar.

But those of us who gravitated to the vision of a public CAW had read Frank Herbert's *Dune* novels, and considered that a certain amount of persecution may be a necessary ingredient to consolidate a group identity. Certainly this had been the case in *Stranger in a Strange Land*. As long, of course, as the persecution isn't powerful enough to destroy the group utterly—as the Catholic Church did with the Cathars! But since America guaranteed freedom of religion, and the Christian churches no longer had the legal right to burn heretics at the stake, we felt we could pull it off with nobody getting killed. Happily, our worst fears of a lethal backlash never materialized; but at that time, who could know?

That fall I came back every Thursday and pretty much talked off the top of my head. I read excerpts from *Stranger in a Strange Land* and Carlton Berenda's *The New Genesis*, and shared the ideas, philosophies, and thinking that we had been doing in the Atlan water-brotherhood for years. And people really responded. They would come back the next week with their professors, and then the professors would come back and bring their whole classes with them. Soon people wanted to join this cool new church; the first one to actually do so was a very fat fellow named John "Tiny" McClimans.

Somewhere in the middle of that scene, a guy by the name of Ravi Kristen, who was the local Boo-Hoo of the Neo-American Church, came up to me and said, "I've got this money in our treasury, but there isn't much interest in doing anything with it. So I'll use it to hire a lawyer to legally incorporate the Church of All Worlds."

Heinlein had pointed out that "religion is a null area of the law"— the first amendment of the U.S. Constitution precludes any governmental regulation of a church. If you set up a church, and get all the paperwork straight, you can pretty much do anything you want to. You can have schools; you can own property and do all kinds of things that other agencies have to have all kinds of elaborate licensing to do. So this looked like a good idea.

We approached Richard Sparrow, the attorney for the local archdiocese of the Roman Catholic Church. I told him that I wanted a Pagan church that was legally structured so that anything the Catholic Church could do, we could do. I especially wanted us to be able to establish subsidiary Orders that would be covered under our group exemption. And any challenge to our legality would impact the legality of the Catholic Church, and therefore we would have to be defended.

He created for us articles of incorporation, and a foundation of by-laws, that were absolutely amazing. Martha, two other Atlans, and I signed the articles of incorporation. On March 4, 1968, we received our legal certificate of incorporation in the state of Missouri. And then began the struggles. The state initially wanted to deny us tax exemption, as they didn't consider us a "real religion." After all, we had no dogma regarding the nature of God, salvation, and the afterlife! That resistance to our legitimization was just what we had been hoping for. We took the matter to the ACLU, and they got involved. We got big write-ups in the paper. And we won! It took several years, but we won. And we got great publicity, which then put us on the map. And we also had to apply to the Feds for a 501(c)(3) religious exemption, which we finally received on June 18, 1970.

NARRATOR: In the decades that would follow, many other Pagan groups would benefit from the legal precedent that was set in St. Louis. The CAW's successful efforts were a major building block for every Pagan group that came afterwards that wanted legal recognition and nonprofit status.

OZ: I also enrolled in a correspondence course in theology with Life Science College in Rolling Meadows, Illinois. They were a small-scale Christian seminary supported by the Life Science Church. I followed the prescription that Heinlein gave in *Stranger in a Strange Land*, where he had Valentine Michael Smith enroll in a small divinity school. I completed the program for a Doctor of Divinity (DD), and become ordained as the first Priest of the Church of All Worlds at Yule of 1967.

Interest in the CAW continued to grow over the winter of 1967–1968. Our activities centered around Gaslight Square, which was kind of the Greenwich Village or the Haight-Ashbury of St. Louis. There was a lot of counterculture stuff going on there.

Some friends of ours opened up a coffeehouse they called "The Agora." Named for the forum in Athens, Greece, where philosophers used to meet and talk, it was sort of a co-op. It was very laid-back and comfy, and I hung out there quite a bit.

As an outgrowth of that scene, I came upon another coffeehouse on Gaslight Square that was called "The Exit" (in reference to Sartre's play *No Exit*). It was run by a collective of Christian churches, and it wasn't accomplishing what they wanted it to (i.e., bringing Hippies to Jesus). Since I had been a guest speaker there, one of the people involved asked me if my church wanted to take over the lease, and we decided to do it.

As of the first of March, 1968, we took over the coffeehouse and renamed it "The Instead." For Spring Equinox we put out the first issue of a little one-page newsletter called *Green Egg*. Run off in green ink on the ditto machine we'd bought with the money from the garage sale, it had a calendar of events and an essay on what we were all about.

The coffeehouse was in the basement of a huge, old, five-story Victorian house, which became our first temple. We called it "Lothlorien Center," after the home of the Elves in J. R. R. Tolkien's *Lord of the Rings*. We painted the interior of the coffeehouse black, with black lights directed at the walls. We put out day-glo-colored chalks, and invited patrons to draw and write on the walls. We got little round tables and covered them with checkered tablecloths. On each table we put a straw-wrapped chianti bottle with a candle in it, all covered with dripping wax.

People would gather around the tables and have great conversations. We had a stage where people could get up and perform. We had poetry readings. People who played regular gigs in the clubs on the strip would come in late at night and jam. One of our most committed regulars was an outrageous folksinger. Another important person was a sweet young runaway named Debbie Dietz, who sort of became our temple "house mother."

DEBORAH DIETZ: I left home when I was fifteen. I was your basic honor student forced to live on the street. I could have stayed at home and been battered, but fortunately there was a Hippie subculture in place to receive me.

I was attracted to the Church of All Worlds because it was outrageous. I lived in the coffeehouse. They tried to do decent things there. There were no drugs to speak of that I can recall. Everyone talked about drugs a tremendous amount of the time, but none ever materialized. There was a tremendous amount of sex. But maybe that's in the eye of the beholder. I hadn't left home so that I could have sexual adventures. I was kind of a bookish person. So when I looked around and saw everyone constantly running to the clap clinic and getting pregnant, I just decided to steer clear of the whole sexual issue.

So I became sort of a mascot for everyone. Me, being such a youngster, there were a lot of people who took care of me. From the best of them I got encouragement to be just as smart as I wanted to be. Women did not get that kind of encouragement back then. And that continues today.

OZ: Once we got the temple on Gaslight Square, then my life split into three aspects that had very little to do with each other. There was my life at home with Martha and Bryan; there was my life at work; and there was my life at the temple with the crowd there. It was a juggling act to keep my three worlds in balance.

I would go to work in the morning. Then I'd come home and have dinner with my family. Then, most evenings, I would go to the Instead. Often I would take Bryan there with me. When he got tired, he would just go to sleep in the corner, and I'd bring him home with me.

NARRATOR: The Instead was like many other gathering places that were opening at that time, most of which weren't considered to be "temples." According to musician and social critic Frank Zappa, all across the nation there were "psychedelic dungeons popping up on every street." They were part of the ongoing cultural changes that were setting the stage for the Pagan revival.

The Instead became a stopping-off point for draft dodgers on their way up to Canada. And there were people who, basically, were living there, and they did things in exchange for having a place to crash. Every Wednesday the CAW would take them out to a Howard Johnson's restaurant for the special $1.19 "all you can eat" clam or fish dinner.

DEBORAH DIETZ: Tim would organize these trips where we would all arrive for "all you can eat" clams. It was a real popular thing for the general public to do. It was like Grand Central Station in there for business, and then we would descend on this place *en masse*, painted and bizarrely dressed. This was the kind of idea that I recall him coming up with. He so enjoyed outraging convention, and providing food for thought for onlookers.

The other people in the restaurant would be pale with loathing. At that period of time there was so much antagonism between conventional people and unconventional people. You'd be walking down the street, and people would just scream stuff at you out the windows of their cars. It was so polarized. It wasn't uncommon for guys I knew who had long hair to have bottles thrown at them out of passing cars.

NARRATOR: The Vietnam War continued to escalate, and the presence of over 500,000 American troops there couldn't stop a brutal defeat in the Tet Offensive. In the spring of 1968, Martin Luther King, Jr. and Senator Robert F. Kennedy were both assassinated. At the end of the summer, protests at the Democratic Convention in Chicago turned into riots as the police tear-gassed and beat the protestors in the streets. And in the fall, Richard Milhous Nixon was elected president of the United States.

Any city that had Hippie hangouts soon had problems with police harassment, homelessness, and crime. The psychedelic drugs that had been so popular were overtaken by hard drugs like heroin and amphetamines. The result was a lot of pushers, junkies, speed-freaks, bikers, and crime. The Gaslight Square neighborhood had the same problems with drugs and violence that places like the Haight-Ashbury in San Francisco and the East Village in New York City did. As a result, in the fall of '68 the Instead was closed. Tim had to start looking for another place for the CAW to meet and, as he often did, got what he wanted as the result of a love affair.

OZ: In October of 1968 I met a woman named Petra. She was a journalist doing a feature story on Hallowe'en for a local newsmagazine, and she approached me for an interview. She took me out to an ancient, abandoned graveyard somewhere in south St. Louis, hidden behind high walls. It was completely overgrown with vines and flowers, and nobody came there. She took me there initially to do photographs for the article. But then that became our private Garden of Eden and trysting place.

Petra was in her early forties, and I was twenty-six. She taught me about courtship, seduction, and exactly how to please a woman. I was determined to be a good student and learn everything I could! The movie *The Graduate* had just come out, and she really identified with the character of Mrs. Robinson. I highly recommend this kind of relationship to younger men!

So then Petra wanted to introduce me to her friends. She took me to the Unitarian Church and I got to be good friends with the minister. I got involved in his church and even taught Sunday school for a year. We went on canoe trips and campouts together, and talked around the fire long into the night. I got some exposure to their liturgy and incorporated elements and style from that, which was very helpful. That gave us something to work with when we were developing things like marriage ceremonies in CAW. Since we were a legal Pagan church, we got a lot of young Hippie couples wanting me to perform their weddings.

Petra was fairly well off, and since the coffeehouse was closed, she invited us over to her house on Friday nights. That was a big deal and a social occasion, and became the foundation of our Nest meetings. She invited her other friends, and we got to meet a different class of people. Then other people began to offer to host the Nest meetings at their houses, so we started to rotate.

NARRATOR: The meetings continued to happen on every Friday. Eventually they were moved over to Tim Zell's house as the full-time location, and the "Did You Remember to Dress?" sign was once again posted on the wall. During this time he visited his old college campus to recruit more Pagans.

TOM WILLIAMS: In September 1968, I was a graduate student at Washington University. I was walking across the campus when I spotted a sign that said, "Have You Discovered Paganism? You may be a Pagan and not know it." The sign announced a meeting of something called the Church of All Worlds the next evening. I went down to the Student Union and sat down in the meeting. It was there I first saw a well-groomed young man with a goatee wearing white slacks, a white turtleneck, and a white sport coat. The young man's name was Tim Zell, and he was talking about a book called *Stranger in a Strange Land*. I listened to his pitch and found it very intriguing. So I went up and talked to him afterwards. He loaned me a copy of the book, which I took home and read.

That book changed my life. What was especially interesting and synergistic about it was that all around me the '60s were happening, and people were proposing, talking about, and actually *living* the very things Heinlein talked about in his book. The hypocrisy of the "normal" society couldn't have been more blatant due to the racism, the war, the lies about drugs, and hollow rewards of material success. Mind you, the '60s were a time of relative prosperity, so while there was certainly poverty, a lot of young folks could exist and even thrive on no work and little money—or so it appeared. So I went to some meetings.

Now, you have to picture the house. On the outside it was a normal-looking suburban bungalow with a lawn and some bushes and a little walk up to the door. But once you went through that door . . .

You found yourself in a large L-shaped room with cushions on the floor and low tables. There were shelves with models of dinosaurs and spaceships (come to think of it, OZ's surroundings aren't much different today). The walls were painted black, and there were day-glo posters on the wall, some plants, a stereo, and over the years a menagerie of strange animals ranging from cats to boa constrictors and pythons to a six-foot iguana, a parakeet that somehow managed not to be devoured, a musclebound tegu lizard, a possum, rats rescued from the psychology lab, caymans in the bathtub, an owl perched on the shower head, geckos roaming about at night, and various species of Hippies and other bizarre life forms.

Now, you've got to remember that the focus of the CAW in the early days was a very secular one. If humans were perfectible or at least improvable, then it could be done by embracing *human* values—that is, values that arise from our intrinsic nature as human beings rather than values imposed by some abstract creed or philosophy. Why, these folks didn't even mention the word *spirituality*.

In the midst of deep philosophical discussions, there would be a break while everyone went into the room where the TV was to watch *Star Trek*, which was then in its final season. It was at this juncture that the CAW came by its tradition of eating Cheez-Its, which were ultimately to become our church "snackrament." *Star Trek* had a special appeal for this crowd. Not only was it the best science-fiction series that had ever—to that date—appeared on television, but it also had a unique message.

Among other things, *Star Trek* celebrated the urge to go out, to explore—not only new worlds but also other ways of being. It was possible to improve society and appreciate and honor diversity among races.

In the midst of the Cold War, here was a Russian ensign in the same crew with a black woman officer and a green-blooded Vulcan—all part of a grand United Federation of Planets. In all the situations that arose, violence was always the last resort and practically never solved anything. *Star Trek* appealed to that desire to improve the human condition by improving humans. And "human" took on a much broader meaning in light of the other races encountered in *Star Trek*—it was more a quality held in common by sentient life forms, a thing that all living intelligent beings shared. It was exhilarating.

NARRATOR: At the end of the '60s, Tim Zell, the changeling child who hadn't fit in, found himself in the center of a very busy circle of friends and activity. The circle would soon be expanded to include a great many people and places far beyond what was happening in his St. Louis living room. And it would include not just living beings all over the Earth, but the living Mother Earth herself.

Chapter 4
"TheaGenesis"
(1968–1970)

And Yes! Yes! to the pulse that flows,
The stream of life's rebirth,
The sacred flame intones your name,
Oh Gaia, soul of the Earth.

—FROM "HYMN TO GAIA" BY TOM WILLIAMS

NARRATOR: Publishing *Green Egg* long before home computers, desktop publishing, or even copy shops was in itself something of a magickal act. In the years that would follow, *Green Egg* grew in size and in circulation, and it went nationwide and global. Tim Zell was able to discover other people, both individuals and groups, who were walking down similar paths, and they were all able to find out about and learn from each other. Tim printed all the letters he got unedited, so there was an ongoing discussion of what was going on and what could happen next. *Green Egg* and its fabulous forum became an important part of the formation and early growth of modern Earth-based spirituality—in all of its many variations.

This was also way before the World Wide Web, search engines, and social networks. But in a way it provided the same services—just at a much slower speed. The basic idea for it came from, once again, science-fiction geeks. For decades sci-fi fans, who typically didn't know too many people with similar interests in their local communities, had been using self-published "fanzines" to communicate with like-minded individuals in other towns. These *zines* frequently featured prominent letter sections—it cost a lot of money to make long-distance phone calls back then. Tim Zell used the same tools and format that they did, and helped create a different kind of "fandom."

One of the first people Tim Zell connected with was an artist and visionary named Fred Adams, who had founded a group he called *Feraferia* ("wild festival") and published a newsletter called *Korythalia* in California.

OZ: What I read in *Korythalia* seemed very much along the lines of what we were looking for. At that time we didn't have much liturgical and theological stuff developed. We had just decided that what we really were was Pagans, but all we had was a rough philosophy. We didn't know how to put it into a coherent form or what to do with it. Feraferian literature was filled with liturgy, ritual, theology, mythology, sacred art, and poetry. It was all about the seasonal cycles of celebration, and that was the first time I came across that idea.

TOM WILLIAMS: In *Green Egg* number 12, dated December 12, 1968, there are the first mentions of Pagan holidays—the periods of Repose and Yule. These came from a little pamphlet called *The Nine Royal Passions of the Year* that Tim got from a group called Feraferia in Southern California. I remember in 1968 when Tim first showed me the pamphlet, which was printed in four colors. I felt a twinge go through me like some half-remembered longing, like some affinity with long-forgotten rituals and connections. It was a brief description of the old Celtic Pagan cycle of the Wheel of the Year, the celebrations and their significance. We started to date our *Green Eggs* according to Robert Graves's tree calendar, which Feraferia followed. These were the first seeds of what was to eventually lead to the transformation of the Church of All Worlds. Or better put—the expansion of our purpose and consciousness to embrace the living planet.

OZ: As soon as we got the information about the Wheel of the Year, we started aligning ourselves with it. There were marvelous revelations around finding out that the annual holidays and celebrations that I grew up with were linked to a greater and more ancient cycle. There was a sense of deepening and of feeling the roots of all these things and weaving them all together. It was very exciting to have a larger context for that stuff. I started researching worldwide holiday customs, and the more I learned, the more I started to appreciate them.

Our central format for rituals, which allowed a lot of this stuff to be woven around it, was that there always a circle where things were passed around. Of course, the first time we did it was with a glass of water. Later it would be food, or stories. We didn't have a "doing" ritual as much as a "sharing" ritual. We would read little passages and poetry that were relevant to the season. It was very simple and unstructured back in those days. Over time these things evolved, and we got better and better at it. We would find out what other folks were doing and take bits and pieces of it and integrate them into our rituals.

These things were foundational to what happened in the '70s. The '60s were all about finding the pieces, bringing them all together, putting them in the same place, and taking a look at them. We started putting out notices and inviting people to join us. People started showing up, and the idea spread.

NARRATOR: As time passed, the CAW purchased bigger and better printing technology, and *Green Egg* continued to grow in page count. Circulation increased; they began to take advertising; and new people were reached not just by word of mouth, subscription, and trade, but also by retail sales in bookstores.

OZ: I did all the typing, layout, and design for each issue. I didn't do much of the actual writing because there was so much stuff coming in from other people. My main job was to be an editor. I would deal with all the letters that came in. I really enjoyed it—I had ink in my blood. I learned how to do every single aspect of publishing.

When the issue was all ready and printed up, we would have collating parties. People really looked forward to this—it was like having a quilting bee. We would lay all the pages out on a long table and sit down around it on pillows on the floor. People would collate the pages, and we'd straighten

them out and staple them. We'd bundle them and put on the mailing labels. Most of it would be done in one day, in one big push.

NARRATOR: The magazine continued to be published, in what was to be
the first phase of its existence, for the entire time Tim was in St. Louis.
During those seminal years, it helped to both create and unify a community and the use of the word *Pagan* to describe it. *Green Egg* had a direct
influence on many, including a young journalist named Margot Adler.

MARGOT ADLER: My book *Drawing Down the Moon* would not exist if
it hadn't been for *Green Egg* and its letters column. When I was coming
into the Pagan movement, there were no festivals; there was no Internet. There were little newsletters. And most of those you found out
about by complete chance, or by knowing someone who knew someone. *Green Egg* devoted some twenty to thirty pages of each issue to
letters, and those letters were from the real theorists and theologians
and thealogians of the Pagan movement. It and *Nemeton* were the first
intellectual Pagan publications. I started doing research for my book in
fall of 1975. I took *Green Egg*, and I looked at every single interesting letter over twenty issues, and I wrote those people letters and said, "Hi! I'm
thinking of doing this book on Paganism. Can I come visit you?" And
that's how I constructed *Drawing Down the Moon*. Once I had a bunch of
people who I went to see, they would introduce me to other people, and
one thing led to another. But *Green Egg* was my best source for guidance.

NARRATOR: Early on in this process, Tim Zell contacted Fred Adams
and discussed the possibility of forming a Pagan ecumenical organization.

OZ: The way my thinking has often gone in my life has been "Let's
throw a party and invite all our friends." Virtually everything I've done
has been a version of that. Fundamentally I'm a host (which would explain the parasites . . .). Fred came up with the name "The Council of
Themis." Themis was the Goddess of harmony in Greek mythology
(Romans called her Harmonia), and is depicted in our modern iconog-
raphy as the blindfolded figure of Justice holding balance scales in one
hand and a sword in the other. The Council rapidly expanded as word

got out. In the process of discussing this grew the term *Neo-Pagan* for the modern groups, to be distinguished from the primordial pagans. Most of the groups that got involved were from California. There were maybe a dozen groups total.

NARRATOR: As editor of *Green Egg*, Tim was probably the best-informed person on the planet about the Pagan population, and at that point he had still not heard anything about the existence of real Witches or a Witchcraft movement. The prevailing mythology then in popular culture was that Witches were different from regular humans, who were referred to as "mortals." One had to be born a Witch—Witchcraft wasn't presented as a religion or something that someone could join or get trained in. And, in fact, this fictional idea of Witches continues today in the *Harry Potter* books, where anyone who doesn't come from a magical family is a "muggle."

Then, in 1968, Sybil Leek published her book *Diary of a Witch*. Her story, which she claimed to be true, was congruent with the mythology. She said she came from a family of Witches in England, that she had magical powers, and that they were hereditary. This was exciting news for Tim—the possibility of psychic abilities had intrigued him since he was a kid. Sybil's book got some attention in America, and she came to St. Louis as part of a promotional tour. Tim figured that if she really was a great and powerful Witch, then he should be able to connect with her telepathically. So, when she visited the campus of Washington University, he sat in the front row and attempted to do just that.

She did not respond as he had hoped. But he was not discouraged. Soon the CAW heard from some American Witches, and they turned out to be human beings just like everyone else. Tim brought them into the growing Pagan movement, and he even met a Witch who was running a metaphysical/occult shop in his own town . . .

TOM WILLIAMS: So Tim and I signed up for a sixteen-week course in Witchcraft taught by a local St. Louis Witch named Deborah Letter (now Bourbon). I still have the course material from that class and was impressed to see that the definitions and orientation of the class do not adhere to any one Wiccan tradition but are general enough to appeal to more general Pagan sensitivities. For example, the definition of a Witch in the first lesson is as follows: "A Witch is a person, either male or female, who has learned to use the powers of the body and mind (as well as those of Nature) to either help or hinder."

That's a definition that could apply to shamans and magicians in general. After we took the class, Tim and I both eventually received initiations in different Wiccan traditions. However, the generalist nature of the background we received in our first encounters with shamanism and Magick (in addition to the "eco-psychic" awareness we had begun to cultivate) made it difficult for us to commit to any single, strictly defined tradition.

NARRATOR: In 1969, Hippie Paganism seemed to take over the world, or at least it seemed like that for one weekend when 400,000 people gathered on a farm in upstate New York for the Woodstock festival. According to Arlo Guthrie, it was "a lotta freaks, man." Author Ayn Rand would later describe Woodstock as being Dionysian. Although she didn't mean it as a compliment, many people agreed and thought it was a great idea.

People were inspired by books like Henry David Thoreau's *Walden*, and there was a lot of talk about getting away from it all and moving to the country. The *Whole Earth Catalog* was published (and regularly updated) to give people access to the tools needed to make the transition. Joni Mitchell told the flower children that it was time to go "back to the garden," and the new comic book hero was a rustic, bearded sage named Mr. Natural (who looked a lot like OZ does now).

OZ: Of course, the most significant event in 1969 was the first moon landing on July 20—which I had been looking forward to all my life. Tom Williams and I watched the whole thing together on TV from start to finish. It was incredibly emotional for us—as I'm sure it was for nearly everyone on Earth. Finally, the world was catching up to science fiction!

So just over a month later, when the World Science Fiction Convention was held in St. Louis, we just had to go! After all, we were a science-fiction-based religion! There we met a seventeen-year-old kid from Winnipeg, Canada, named Bill (his name would later be Orion Stormcrow). He'd hitchhiked down to the con, and we put him up in our room. Over the following years he became very much like a younger brother to me, and along with Tom Williams, we became quite a trio—sometimes like the Three Musketeers, and other times more like the Three Stooges!

NARRATOR: The CAW continued to have weekly Friday-night gatherings and *Green Egg* collating parties at the Zells' house, where the animal menagerie was steadily growing.

OZ: The most special critter in my life during this period was Histah—a lovely boa constrictor I bought as a baby from a pet store. I named her after the ape word for "snake" in the *Tarzan* novels by Edgar Rice Burroughs.

Histah soon became much more than a pet. She was my constant companion and a true familiar. Although I built a really spectacular habitat for her—using a curved truck windshield for a front—most of the time she had free run of the house. At night, I could "dream-fast" with her, and in my dreams I would see through her eyes as she roamed around the house and finally settled on a new place to sleep. Then in the morning I would go straight to her hiding place and take her out, where she spent most of the day wrapped around my shoulders. As she grew, I often took her to children's schools and other places, where she would win everyone over—even confirmed ophidiophobes. Whenever there were people around, she was as social with them as any cat.

I was intensely focused on my work, and I disciplined myself to get by on six hours of sleep a night. My life was a constant training program. I didn't give myself any time to just veg out. From 1970 on, I used to bicycle to work every day, unless it was raining or snowing. It was eleven miles each way. When I was at work I would use my break periods to work on *Green Egg*. I'd take a bag lunch and sit there at my desk eating and typing at the same time. I hung out at the local underground radio station, KDNA, and was a regular guest on Elizabeth Gips's show, talking about the CAW.

I didn't go out and hang out in bars or go to football games. It's amazing what you can do with your life if you make room for it by not doing things that are not productive. Even now I have to make an effort to un-discipline myself, to pry loose and hang out. If I'm left on my own, my default mechanism is this focused behavior. If somebody says, "Hey, let's go for a walk" or "Let's go to a party," then I may break loose and join them. But if I'm left alone, I'll just keep on working by sheer momentum. I was kept going by a utopian vision of creating a new world and new society.

NARRATOR: But Tim's efforts to make the world a better place were causing stress in his family life, and so was their open relationship.

MARTHA TURLEY: I was always the jealous type. Deep down I was probably not happy with our open relationship. Tim was my first sexual experience, so I made up for lost time. I enjoyed being with the other guys, but I was still jealous of Tim. I never really accepted it too much emotionally. That was there from the beginning. I'm a very passive person. I go along with things and don't cause trouble. I think it comes from hearing my parents argue constantly. I said, "When I get married, I am not going to fight." I don't remember Tim and I ever having any arguments. I always did everything Tim ever wanted to do. I'm not saying that he was a domineering, pushy person. I'm kind of a sheep, you could say.

Tim became more Pagan, and I didn't. At our house they used to get together on weekends. If I was there, I stayed by myself in the bedroom. Or else I went out with whichever gentleman I was dating then. I don't even know what they did at those rituals. Bryan was at them, but not me.

DEBORAH DIETZ: There was a period of time when I lived at Tim's house. My function was to take care of his son. I think that Martha was more conventional in many respects. The impression I always had of her was that she was being swept along like in a tidal wave. I remember thinking that she was married to someone who was completely different from her—she was a nice woman in a difficult situation.

NARRATOR: This didn't slow down in 1970, a year of sex, drugs, the first Earth Day, and some major spiritual activity for Tim Zell and his tribe.

OZ: There was a total eclipse of the sun on March 7, 1970. And some of the folks who lived in St. Louis threw an eclipse party that featured a big bowl of electric orange juice (that is, spiked with LSD). At that point I decided that the occasion I had waited years for had arrived. I was waiting for the perfect moment to try LSD, having been given all the big build-up by Tim Leary's writings about having the perfect set and setting.

It was an amazing, totally transformative experience. I had such a great trip—including an incredible sexual encounter in a bathtub full of balloons with two lovely women—that I never actually went out and looked at the eclipse itself! I have regretted this ever since—especially after I finally witnessed such a spectacular celestial event in 1979.

TOM WILLIAMS: In early 1970, some of us decided to get involved with a St. Louis group called The Coalition for the Environment. We attended meetings with some well-intentioned liberal types who were trying to work within the system to address some of the pressing issues of urban and automobile pollution, clean air and water issues, and local environmental concerns. These were the beginnings of what would eventually blossom into the environmental movement.

Also that same spring, for daring to protest a brutal and senseless war that was destroying the soul of America, four students were shot dead by the National Guard at Kent State University in Ohio. Just in case anybody had trouble remembering what his or her ethical priorities were.

Earth Day was a world event, even though we didn't realize it at the time. We did notice that we were the only group at the event that called itself a church. Where were the other churches? It wasn't hard to figure that out. The admonition in the book of Genesis that humans shall "have dominion over the Earth and over every creeping thing" suddenly stood out in sharp relief. Why should Christian churches care about Earth Day when their real goal was Heaven and when their Bible admonished them to exploit the Earth? We began to see ever more clearly why people who called themselves Pagans were basically different.

OZ: We decided that we were going to do the Earth Day thing in a big way, with a booth, presentation, and display. We designed and worked on them for weeks. One of the things we wanted to do was create a big poster based on Robert Graves's thirteen-month calendar of the year. While I was going through *National Geographic*s and selecting pictures to put on the calendar, a young woman came in to help out.

She was just eighteen at the time and one of those beautiful, Witchy, vegetarian kind of girls that you ran into in those days. Her name was Jodie Parker. In the process of working on the calendar, as we got to know each other and talk about what we were doing, we fell in love. Our relationship became quite a romance and a major focus of my life for the next few years. I often refer to her as my second wife, although we were never married.

So on April 22, we toted all of our stuff to Forest Park and set it up. The idea that Earth Day topics could be of a religious concern was unheard-of at the time. So we made our theme all about what would eventually come to be called "Deep Ecology"—or "Green Religion." In addition to our "Eco-Psychic Calendar," we created a pile of trash with a large globe and a human skeleton (from my days in pre-med) tossed akimbo into the heap to convey the idea that trashing the Earth was also destroying humanity, as we were all interconnected. This was the first inkling of the expression, originally stated by Cicero: *Omnia vivunt; omnia inter se conexa* ("Everything is alive; everything is interconnected").

My old Beatnik friend Jim Igoe turned me on to Robert Graves's *The White Goddess*. Until that time CAW didn't have a coherent theology, per se. We vaguely embraced mythology, in general, and used science fiction as a mythic framework. But there was no coherent theological basis of how it all worked. Graves's book moved us in that direction, at least from the point of view of the impact of the Divine Feminine in culture and literature. It gave me something to think about.

My lifetime of interest and pursuit of studies of biology, natural history, evolution, and paleontology all came together over Labor Day weekend of 1970. At that point Jodie was getting ready to go away to college. We decided that we needed to do something really spectacular before she left. Our friend Jim's brother was a prominent attorney with a very nice house; he had gone away for the weekend and kind of left our friend in charge of the house. So he invited us to come over.

Jim had a few doses of what he had been told was organic mescaline, but it was probably acid laced with something else. We went into the backyard in the night where there was a big trampoline. We lay stark naked on it on our backs looking up at the sky. It was easy to imagine just floating off into space. I know the constellations; Jodie, like most city people, didn't. But this was a clear night, and you could see the stars well. I started tracing the constellations to show her what some of the more prominent ones were. Having just learned how to see auras from Deborah, I discovered that if I stuck my finger up into the sky and drew a line with my aura, the line would stay there (in acid-speak these are called "trails"). So it was easy for me to connect the dots.

I made the Vulcan "live long and prosper" sign (from *Star Trek*), and got absorbed in watching the auras of my fingers as they moved back and forth. And in the pattern of the auras, I had a vision of a cell dividing. As the concept of the cell formed in my mind, I linked myself with what I was seeing. I went diving down through the continuity of cellular division, of mitosis. It was like running a film backwards as the cells divided, until I was back to the first cell that I was, fertilized in my mother's womb. I felt how my life began, when I was conceived as a single cell that multiplied and became all of me. And then I went further down, through all the cells that coalesced to form my parents. I kept going through this reverse coalescence all the way back through geological time, experiencing all these cells congealing, all the way back for billions of years, till I reached that first original primal cell that began all life on Earth, and from which we are all descended. And it was like all of us were condensed in that single cell. It was sort of like the Big Bang of biological evolution.

And then I ran the film back the other way—forward. And that cell divided and all the living things came out of it. And the different species emerged, and I saw the whole tree of life open up, down through the different lineages. I traced the protoplasm through all these different divisions, which was like tracing the entire history of the DNA molecule. As that life from the first cell spread out across the planet, my consciousness rose from the surface and looked down on the whole Earth below me.

Just that previous year, the first photographs of the Earth from space had been taken by the Apollo astronauts returning from the moon. So I rose above the Earth, and I saw the life spreading across the planet. And I saw all this connection; I saw all this as one, vast, single organism. Because it was absolutely identical to the way my own body had grown from the first fertilized cell. Evolution was nothing but embryology on a planetary scale.

I looked down, and at that point, the mythology of Gaea overlaid itself upon this entire organism. I suddenly saw the Earth in a whole new light, through this perspective. I saw this living being instead of just a planet full of unrelated creatures. And at that point, it was like She opened her eyes and smiled at me, and said, "Now you know me."

And I did know Her. I was overwhelmed with this incredible sense of love, kinship, and recognition. It was an astonishing epiphany. And my immediate response was, "I shall ever serve you." And I have, from that moment forward.

It wasn't just a vision; it was a Revelation. I felt this in the deepest part of my soul. It is still hard to speak of this without choking up with tears, because it was the most profound experience of my life.

I have no idea how much time passed. When I came down, I went into the house and told Jim about the whole experience. At the end of all that, Jim said, "Well, I knew that if I hung around with you long enough, you would get some great revelation. That's the kind of guy you are. And there you have it." He encouraged me to write it all down, which I did over the next few days.

A week later was our weekly Nest meeting, and I came in with it all written up, and delivered my first actual sermon in the history of the Church of All Worlds. Interestingly enough, I got a considerable amount of argument. There were people who were deeply offended, fearing that this church that they had joined specifically because it didn't have any official dogma was now going to be saddled with such. They thought I was going to establish some orthodox set of doctrines that everybody was going to be required to believe in.

I kept coming back to it over the next few months. Though I contributed the gist of it to a couple of books by Leo Louis Martello (*Black Magic, Satanism & Voodoo* and *Witchcraft: The Old Religion*), I didn't officially publish it in *Green Egg* till the next year. It was so far out there, so radical, that I really wanted to be on solid ground before I tried to bring it out to the world. I sought more information, background, and details on the biology involved. I did research into genetics and DNA and cosmology and nucleotides and the nature of amino acids found in meteorites.

Forty years later, we know a whole lot more. But this was three years before James Lovelock first published his famous "Gaia Hypothesis." He was an atmospheric biochemist on assignment from NASA to help them design sensors for some of the probes they were developing to detect life on other planets. And that led to a lot of additional research, all of which has essentially confirmed the premise that all life on Earth is indeed descended from a single cell. Lovelock got the idea from seeing that same photograph of the Earth. But he saw it from the outside looking in. I saw it from the inside out, equating evolution with embryology.

TOM WILLIAMS: Tim had articulated what came to be known as "TheaGenesis." Basically what that means is that the Earth is a living being; the various biomes and ecosystems, plant and animal communities, and their interaction are analogs to the organs and systems of a living body. In addition, this being has a spirit, a consciousness. That spirit has been instinctively revered and worshipped through the ages by native peoples as a Goddess whose names are as numerous as the cultures and peoples who honor Her. Eventually, we settled on calling her *Gaea*, for the Greek Earth Mother.

The Church of All Worlds transformed that year of 1970 into a new dimension, not abandoning the values on which it had been founded, but adding the ecstatic identity of ourselves and all living things with this grand and nurturing Being, this Divine Mother, and realizing that we were both Her and Her children. The Church of all Worlds had finally become Pagan in the truest sense of the word.

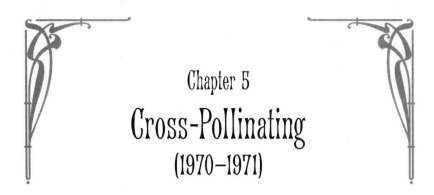

Chapter 5
Cross-Pollinating
(1970–1971)

Of Gaea, Mother of all, strong-founded, I shall sing
Most Ancient, who nourishes all things that are on the Earth,
All that move on the divine Earth and in the sea
And all that fly, all these are nourished by your wealth.
And from thee, revered goddess, are men rich in children and harvests,
Oh venerable one, and you cause the giving or taking of life to mortals;
And blessed is he whom you will wholeheartedly and eagerly honor;
To him all will be abundant.

—"HOMERIC HYMN TO GAEA,"
TRANSLATED FROM GREEK BY ARISTARCHOS PAPADIMITRIOU

NARRATOR: The year 1970 was not just the year of the first Earth Day and Tim Zell's TheaGenesis revelation—it was also the second year of Richard M. Nixon's presidency. With Nixon as commander-in-chief, the war in Vietnam continued and even expanded into the neighboring countries of Cambodia and Laos. In America antiwar activists bombed government buildings and banks, and on the campus of Kent State in Ohio, four students were killed by bullets from the National Guard. *Rolling Stone* did a cover story that declared America to be "a pitiful, helpless giant." In the midst of all this, the CAW decided to try to reach more people by moving from meeting in Tim Zell's house to establishing an actual Church center.

TOM WILLIAMS: We set out to find a suitable center and eventually located a vacant storefront. Interestingly, the place we found was adjacent to another storefront church that was home to a predominantly black congregation called "Mother Martin's Temple of God in Christ." The building, which housed both churches, was long and narrow. Our side had three large rooms arranged in line front-to-back. We decided to allow access according to the "ring system."

The front room (painted green) was open to the public and contained our printed materials and comfy chairs, where we could discuss our philosophy with people who wanted to come by and learn about us. The middle room (painted red) contained desks, records, and files, and had a stairway to the basement, where we kept the newly purchased mimeograph machine that was now used to publish *Green Egg*. The back room—its walls painted black with day-glo posters—was used for rituals and for the inner circle membership. We called it, naturally, "The Inner Sanctum."

I was in charge of making arrangements with the city of St. Louis for occupancy permits, rental agreements with the landlord, and so on. I encountered a lot of bureaucratic resistance from the city, such as impossible requirements for parking spaces, load-bearing specifications for the floor, and such. The fact that there was already a church next door in the same building, Mother Martin's Temple of God in Christ, eventually made it impossible for the city to deny us permits.

OZ: We rented it on the first of March, 1970. We spent much of that month getting it all fixed up and ready to go. There was no real grand opening. We had stuff going on in the temple almost every evening. We had study groups, our human-values reading program, and a comparative religions program. It was a center of activity. We boarded up the windows in the back room—put up a big metal door and completely sealed it off. We made it a place where we could have weekend retreats, which we did eventually.

I paid most of the expenses for the temple myself. Back in those days, it didn't cost much to do something like that. I took a vow of poverty, which meant that my paychecks from the Human Development Corporation were written to the Church, and taxes weren't taken out of them.

I used the money that would have gone to taxes to pay for things like the temple and *Green Egg*, and supported myself and my family with the rest. We put the hat out whenever we did anything.

When we put up the big sign out front saying "Church of All Worlds," Mother Martin and her husband came over to meet us and brought coffee and doughnuts. They invited us to their services. But the services that we held in our inner temple were basically done naked, so we couldn't really reciprocate.

TOM WILLIAMS: We actually formed a good relationship with the church next door. Reverend Martin was a six-foot-four, strapping black preacher with a booming basso profundo voice and a heart of gold. His wife, Mother Martin, was a solid, good-hearted woman who wore a cloth coat, pillbox hat, and purse, and thought it was just wonderful that another church was moving in next door.

OZ: We also used the inner sanctum of our temple for rituals and retreats. It was painted all black—floor, walls, and ceiling—including the windows. There was a heavy, metal, insulated door separating it from the second room (which was painted in red, with little café tables). In addition to a huge altar, psychedelic posters and countless day-glo cutouts of stars and planets adorned the walls and ceiling. When only the black lights were on, the background disappeared entirely, as if you were in outer space. There was a full kitchen and bathroom, and many mattresses and cushions, so the room was entirely self-sufficient for the weekend-long, Esalen-style encounter groups I conducted there. We were totally isolated, with no clocks or contact with the outside world.

NARRATOR: The activities in the temple were unique in St. Louis but not unusual for the times. In other places, feminists were holding consciousness-raising sessions; humanistic psychologists were experimenting with encounter groups; the repressed were working towards liberation; libertines were having orgies; and, oh yes, Pagans, along with countless other seekers of wisdom and truth, were trying to find new spiritualities that were relevant to their lives. And some of this was even happening in rented storefronts.

But the CAW was trying to do all this and more all at once, and in a politically and socially conservative city. If the temple had been in Cambridge, Berkeley, or some other liberal locale, things might have turned out differently. But St. Louis, home of Budweiser beer, is a very conservative city.

TOM WILLIAMS: One night there was a raid by officers looking for drugs and underage girls allegedly staying there. The cops found no drugs but confiscated some switches and wires we had gotten to set up a burglar alarm system. The next day the *St. Louis Post-Dispatch* ran an article on the raid, saying the police had entered the temple where "Charles Manson–like activities were going on," and had seized material used for making bombs.

OZ: The newspapers printed my picture, with my long dark hair and beard, practically side by side with Manson's. Apparently he also was some kind of fan of *Stranger in a Strange Land*, so that also got mentioned. But Mother Martin next door stuck up for us, which helped us turn this around.

TOM WILLIAMS: Fortunately, we had a lawyer who called in the TV people to counter the charges and threatened the paper with a lawsuit. There was a correction printed in the next edition that was followed by an interview with Tim that actually cast the CAW in a positive light. The incident was a net gain for our image in the community. We were also able to go on the local alternative radio station, KDNA, and present our case and our philosophy.

NARRATOR: The temple was closed after six months. After that a lot of the Church activity moved back to the Zells' house, which put additional strain on a marriage that was already having difficulties.

OZ: Martha wasn't opposed to the Church stuff, but she wasn't interested at all in any of it. Both of us during that period were dating other people. I still spent my nights at home—Jodie and I didn't sleep over together, except on the weekends, when the CAW was having seasonal festivals at the quarry along the Mississippi.

During this period of time, my life began to shift in a different direction, away from the urban life and work that I had been doing and towards the rural community life that had always been a dream of mine. We started planning to buy some land. My attention, thoughts, Magick, and correspondences with people all became about that move.

This shifted the dynamic at home. Martha really did not want to do that. She had grown up in the country on a farm, and the last thing in the world she wanted to do was move back to one. At that point we had been together almost ten years. If anything, what she wanted to do with her life was to be more of an urban person. So we started talking about that, and agreed that at some point we would have to go in different directions. In early 1971 Martha started dating a guy named John, who was a lot more like what she had been looking for. She was looking for a father figure, and I just didn't fit that role.

Around spring break, Jodie decided she'd had enough of college. It wasn't working out for her, and she wanted to move in with me. Around that time Martha was spending more time with John and feeling that this was what she was really looking for. So, starting around March 1971, Martha moved out and Jodie moved in—there was a brief overlap period when both of them were there, but we worked it out okay. It was very amicable at that time. Our lives were clearly going in different directions. What we wanted out of life was completely different.

MARTHA TURLEY: As I got older, I became not so much into the Hippie life. I had multiple partners to begin with, and eventually I met my second husband, John, and married him. He was married at the time, too. When that girl Jodie moved in, it became a choice of living with the two of them or moving out. John left his wife, and we got an apartment together. I didn't want to take Bryan out of the school that he was in. So he would stay with Tim and go to school during the week, and I would have him on weekends. Bryan didn't want to eat at their house because Jodie was always making everything out of tofu. He wasn't crazy about that.

BRYAN ZELL: Jodie was a strict vegetarian, and I was a fussy eater. I couldn't stand her food. I called it "hippie goulash." She made her own yogurt, too, but it never had any flavor to it.

NARRATOR: Negotiations began to buy some land in the country. Several people, including two married couples with children, all moved into Tim's house in anticipation of soon leaving the city to form a rural intentional community. Tim and Jodie had to get used to living with each other at the same time that they were sharing a small house with other potential community members. It was not an easy situation for any of them. Then the land deal fell through, and Jodie, Bryan, and Tim were left to build a life together after the other families moved out.

During all this time Tim was a steady worker at the Human Development Corporation and using his salary to fund the Church and *Green Egg*, which were both growing in popularity. There wasn't much time or money left over for his personal life.

Jodie did some nude photo-modeling work to bring in some money to help with their financial situation. One night she brought Tim down to the studio with her to have some professional photographs taken that could be used for PR work.

OZ: I wore my white robes and brought along Histah. We got some really great photos, and then headed home. On the way, we were pulled over by the cops. It seemed they still had a warrant out for me over some case that I had already gone to court over, and had all charges ("suspicion of trespassing") dismissed. But they arrested me anyway and threw me in jail in my robes, which was all I was wearing. So there I was, this white guy in a white robe with a pointy hood, tossed into a cell with a bunch of very tough black guys. Awkward, to say the least. Thinking quickly, I tucked the hood into the back of the robe and came on as a nutty, cartoon-style end-of-the-world street preacher; the beard and long hair reinforced that image. That got me left alone until Jodie could show up the next morning and bail me out.

NARRATOR: A few years later, one of the photos from that shoot turned out to be quite significant. But the money earned wasn't enough to make much of a difference for their household . . .

OZ: I wasn't paying enough attention to my family. Jodie was far too young to be a mother and got into a competitive thing for my attention. My larger vision of the community, and all the activities with CAW and *Green Egg*, took precedence, and I neglected the closer stuff that was really important—especially my wonderful son, Bryan. This is one of the saddest aspects of that period—and one I have deeply regretted ever since. One time we were sitting together at dinner and Bryan asked each of us, "What is the most important thing in the world to you?"

We all gave our answers, and mine, uttered with great pomposity, was, "Why, the whole world itself!"

But Bryan's answer, from his open heart, shamed me: "The most important thing in the world to me," he said, "is my family."

In my fanatic obsession with saving the world, I never could get into just looking out for my own best interest—or that of my family. Most religious people are only interested in personal salvation, not in making the world a better place for present and future generations. But in my whole life I have never given a thought to personal salvation, and I've been disdainful of people who have that obsession. It always seemed narrow-minded, provincial, and selfish to me. Decades later, I finally came to appreciate the importance of family, and I have tried to make up for my early failings as a son, husband, and father.

And then Martha got remarried, and her new husband pushed her to file for custody of Bryan. Essentially, he had always wanted a kid. So it suddenly became an issue. They didn't even have a room for him, but they filed for custody and we went to court. Martha made the case that we were Pagans and that we had nudity in our home and stuff like that. The judge decided that Bryan should go with his mother. There wasn't a whole lot that we could do about it.

BRYAN ZELL: They had snuck into my dad's house and taken a bunch of photographs that they used in court against him. The judge asked me who I wanted to live with. At the time I thought I should stick with my mom. I think that kind of hurt my father's feelings. I sometimes wonder where I would be today if I had stayed in his custody.

NARRATOR: Tim, Jodie, and Bryan were able to take a road trip together at the end of the summer of 1971. This was affordable, even for them, since gas was so cheap, and everywhere they went they stayed at people's houses and apartments. In fact, that was the whole point of the trip. Their goal was to attend Noreascon, the 29th World Science Fiction Convention, which was held in Boston that year. But it was the journey, not the destination, that was most important. And Tim Zell was a man on a Mission from the Goddess.

OZ: In a sense, without being conscious of it at the time, the pilgrimages I was making from one end of the country to the other were seeding events that had never been done before. This was many years before there were festivals where people got to meet each other. So, what you would have would be a small number of groups in a particular area, who may have been vaguely aware of each other, but they didn't have much interaction. There were no big, public gatherings on Beltane or Samhain. But we would show up, and because I was publishing *Green Egg*, and it was the only publication that was interdenominational—it wasn't just one group's own little newsletter—it would be an excuse for people to all come together and meet.

BRYAN ZELL: Dad has always been a great networker. He would do his research in advance. When we went on these road trips, he knew where we were going and who we were going to stay with. Wherever he went, he had a circle of people who were just fascinated by every word that came out of his mouth. As a child I was awestruck by this. I was a little shy.

OZ: That was our first personal contact with the better-known figures in the Pagan community. We had lunch with Robert Rimmer, author of *The Harrad Experiment*. We really hit it off, and he gave me several cases of his book *The Rebellion of Yale Marratt* to circulate among CAW folk. Susan Roberts had just published her book *Witches U.S.A.* In New York City we stayed with her. She took us on a tour to introduce us to many

of the Witches that she had written about, such as Ray Buckland. We
visited several occult stores and spent memorable evenings sitting around
telling stories and singing songs and chants. At that time, the New York
Witchcraft scene was pretty much straight out of the movie *Bell, Book
and Candle.*

NARRATOR: Raymond Buckland was the first British Witch that Tim
Zell met in person. And it was also his first meeting with someone who
had been initiated in the Gardnerian tradition. By then Tim knew who
Gerald Gardner was and had read his books, but he was still surprised by
what he found in New York.

The American Pagan groups that Tim Zell had interacted with up
until that point had typically been started by college students, and their
Paganism had been born from the ecstatic discoveries of the Psychedelic
Psixties. One of the first of these eclectic groups, NROOGD (New Reformed Orthodox Order of the Golden Dawn), had been formed just a
few years previously as a result of a homework assignment to create a
ritual that several students had been given in a class at San Francisco
State College (now San Francisco State University).

But Gerald Gardner claimed to have been initiated by a coven in England in 1939, and he was not a college student or any kind of early Beatnik
or Hippie at that time. He was a retired British civil servant who had just
moved back to England after having spent most of his adult life in southern
and southeastern Asia. When Britain's Witchcraft Act, which had been the
law for centuries, was repealed in 1951, he went public about being a
Witch. He wrote about it, gave interviews about it, and operated the Museum of Magic and Witchcraft. The story Gardner told was that his lineage went all the way back to an ancient, pre-Christian Witch-cult that he
called "The Old Religion," that it had been underground since then, and
that he was trying to keep it alive.

Buckland became friends with Gardner in the early '60s, and was initiated in his presence shortly before Gardner died at the age of seventy-
nine. Buckland brought Gardnerian Wicca to the United States when he
settled down there. Gardner's historical claims were dubious even in 1971,
and in the years since there has been abundant debate and research about
where his tradition really came from. But at that time a good deal of the

details were still being kept secret, and there was intentional mystery surrounding what actually happened in a Gardnerian coven. No Book of Shadows had been published, and there were no public rituals.

Raymond Buckland was the only Gardnerian in New York City who even had a coven, and it wasn't a part of the Council of Themis. The other Gardnerians who lived there all worked as individuals. Today they would be called "solitaries." And, like the characters in *Bell, Book and Candle*, they were urban Witches, and weren't interested in a rural lifestyle. It was a completely different scene from the one Tim Zell was used to.

After that Tim went up to Boston to attend the science-fiction convention, where he hoped to get a glimpse of the future. Little did he know that he had just gotten one in Manhattan.

OZ: On our return trip home, we stopped off in Philadelphia, where we met a couple who had just started up a Pagan Way group, based on liturgy created by Ed Fitch. They wanted to create a Wiccan tradition that would be publicly accessible. It would be sort of like an "outer court" for Witchcraft. But it was an unfortunate choice of name. People who joined the Pagan Way thought of themselves as generic Pagans, but what they really were being considered by the organization was proto-Witches. If they continued on, they would eventually get initiated into Witchcraft. So the idea became embedded in the community that Pagans were simply proto-Witches who hadn't gotten initiated yet. The notion that was promoted was that Witches were the clergy, and the Pagans were the laity. Which was really annoying to Pagan groups, who had their own distinct traditions! We still run into this unfortunate attitude among some Witches.

We were really surprised to learn that these lovely folks didn't include their kids in their religious practice. It wasn't a family thing for them, as it was for us in CAW. They were sending their children to Christian Sunday schools. And when they would have their full-moon Esbat Circles, they would have their kids taken care of by a babysitter, and the kids would never know what they were doing. We thought that was weird. For us, Paganism was a *religion* that included everybody. They were thinking of it more as a lodge or a secret society like the Masons. We hadn't assimilated that that's where a lot of people were coming from until that trip, because we had developed all this stuff on our own over the years, with practically no real connection with Witches.

Today many folks think that Witches founded the Pagan community, but it wasn't that way at all—at least not in the United States. Here the Witches came into a Pagan community that had already existed for at least a decade. What a lot of my work was engaged in at that time was weaving together some of these different threads. I worked hard to do that by the publishing of *Green Egg*, which went out to all these different groups. The Pagan community today has roots in what were at that time very separate communities.

NARRATOR: One more notable event happened while on this trip: Tim wrote his first letter to Robert Heinlein.

OZ: I can't explain why I had never done that before, in all those previous nine years. Probably I was just intimidated. However, I had previously written to B. F. Skinner regarding his idea of the air crib, which I built for my son. So on this particular occasion I decided it was finally time for me to write to Mr. Heinlein. That became the beginning of a correspondence that went on for a number of years. Later on I found out that his letters to me were the only ones during that period where he talked about his philosophy, life, and what he had in mind when he wrote *Stranger*. Apparently many people had written to him and he just sent them back a form letter.

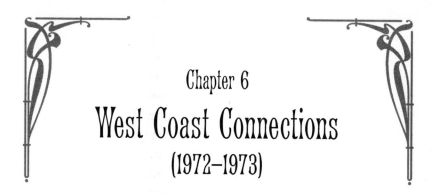

Chapter 6
West Coast Connections
(1972–1973)

Oh we're nifty and keen, our religion is green
And we're proud of our planet up in space! (Up in space!)
And you won't see us grovel 'cause we're from a sci-fi novel,
We're the Galloping Garrulous Grok-Flock in your face!
—FROM "THE GALLOPING GARRULOUS GROK-FLOCK"
BY ADAM WALKS-BETWEEN-WORLDS

NARRATOR: The year 1972 was the tenth anniversary of Tim Zell and Lance Christie sharing water for the first time, and there was a lot to celebrate. *Green Egg*'s circulation was increasing and reaching people around the globe. Tim Zell continued to host the clothing-optional collating parties (eight times a year) and weekly Nest meetings at his house.

And new members continued to join to the Church. Bryan Zell, who may have been the first child to be raised within a modern Pagan family, by then had other Pagan kids to interact with. And some of the new people had homes with big backyards where the CAW began holding seasonal festivals.

DON WILDGRUBE: Our festivals lasted way into the night, and most people stayed all night and crashed in various spots around the house. In the morning, Jodie would fix pancakes for all of us. One Sunday morning, we were sitting on the floor around a very low table, and since the festival the night before, none of us had any clothes on. We were hidden by the low table. There was a knock on the door. Jodie answered it wearing an apron (and nothing else). A few Jehovah's Witnesses came in and started preaching to us. Soon Jodie came in with more pancakes and bent over to serve them. Her bare butt was facing them, and just about that time Tim got up to discuss things more. They looked at Tim's naked body, looked back at Jodie and then the rest of us, and decided that good Christians should not be there and beat a hasty retreat!

NARRATOR: Two of the new, early-'70s members were Michael Hurley and Carolyn Clark. Michael had been a college student at Illinois State University, where he learned about the CAW from a *Green Egg* subscriber who lived in his dorm. Carolyn Clark was a St. Louis nurse. Both of them would go on to become very involved in the Church.

OZ: In the summer of 1972, Michael Hurley was living with us—we always had people staying with us. In late July, Jodie and I went away for a few days, leaving Michael to take care of our animals. At this time Histah was seven feet long, and she lived in the house and wandered around where she wanted to. When we came back home, Histah was missing. Michael had taken her out for a slither in our peach tree, which I used to do with her often, and had forgotten to bring her back in for the evening. I couldn't find her anywhere. I slept in the backyard at night and tried to dream-fast with her, but it didn't work. After several weeks I gave up.

CAROLYN CLARK: I had met Tim at the first Earth Day in April of 1970. It was his snake, Histah, that first got my attention. Tim was in a long white robe, and he had the most magnificent snake I had ever seen. So I walked over and started talking to him. Later there was a little article in the newspaper when the snake was missing. So I called Tim and said I hoped that Histah returned safely. He invited me over to his house to hang out. We talked and then he invited me to their next festival—which in Wicca would have been called a Sabbat. I found out later that that was their way of screening people. They would first talk to them for a couple of hours, and then if that went well, invite them to a festival. And if that went well, they were invited to the weekly Nest meetings.

At the time I joined, the Church had never ordained a Priestess. So I studied, and after a year I became the first—ordained at Beltane of 1973. I took on the duties of Priestess and found a real purpose in life.

NARRATOR: After ten years of spiritual exploration, Tim Zell and his fellow members of the Church of All Worlds had absorbed many influences. The elements of what are commonly used in ritual today were being experimented with (including the Elements!), but there was still much that was free-form and unstructured. They were open to new possibilities: a typical Nest meeting was never very typical, and they continued to follow no leader or set path. The CAW had an extensive recommended reading list that included history, science, science fiction, philosophy, and mythology, but it did not have a guidebook or instructions on how to be an orthodox Pagan.

As the Church grew older, so did its members. There were those who were committed to what was going on, but since no one had ever done anything like the CAW before, it wasn't clear where it was heading and who would stay with it. Many Pagans who had been college students in the '60s were becoming more involved with careers and other responsibilities. The revolution that some had anticipated hadn't happened and didn't seem likely to happen, and Richard Milhous Nixon, the symbol of everything Hippies hated, was re-elected by a landslide.

And in 1972, Tim Zell turned thirty. Jack Weinberg, a leader of the Free Speech Movement at UC Berkeley, had once warned to "never trust anyone over thirty," but when Tim reached that ripe old age, he found himself in the unexpected position of being a tribal elder.

OZ: I have never wanted to join a cult, so I certainly didn't want to create one! I have never understood their appeal to so many people—especially in the '60s. I have always been profoundly suspicious of gurus and cult leaders, finding the entire concept deeply distasteful. It seemed the antithesis of the CAW's "Thou art God/dess" principle of immanent divinity.

NARRATOR: For Tim there was no turning back. He lived in the temple, and when the rituals and parties were over, he didn't go home and return to his normal life because the Church *was* his normal life. He was the one who had to clean up after the party, and then get everything ready for the next one. Tim kept editing and paying for *Green Egg*, where he made more connections and continued to learn what Pagan groups were doing in other cities. And with that information he began planning his next Pagan road trip—this time to the West Coast.

OZ: The 1972 World Science Fiction Convention was to be held in Los Angeles, and we spent months getting ready to go there. Since my previous VW camper had been wrecked the year before, I bought a 1968 Volkswagen van and spent the weeks before the trip building camper components into it. I was in the front yard one day, cutting wood for the project, and I suddenly felt Histah in my mind. I dropped my tools, ran around to the side of the house, pulled away the big sheets of plywood that were leaning against it, and there she was. I picked her up, wrapped her around my shoulders, and I must have been floating a foot above the ground as I carried her into the house.

But as I uncoiled her I saw that she had a serious wound in her side. I took her to the vet, and he cleansed the wound and sewed it up, and gave her antibiotics, but he couldn't do anything more. She wouldn't eat, and she got thinner and thinner. She sustained for some time, but she never got better.

I finished converting the camper, and we hit the road, arriving in Los Angeles on August 29, where we settled in at Lance Christie's house. Harold Moss and Donald Harrison of the Church of the Eternal Source came by, along with Michael Kinghorn of the Delphic Fellowship. We spent a long evening discussing the Council of Themis and the various problems therein. A year or two after the Council had been started, Poke Runyon from the Order of the Temple of Astarte got the notion of appointing himself and Fred Adams as directors. I was not part of that deliberation at all, and I thought I should have some say. But Poke did not feel that the Church of All Worlds was a legitimate Pagan religion because we were based on science fiction instead of something ancient. He dismissed CAW as a "science-fiction grok-flock," a term we delightedly took to heart, henceforth often referring to ourselves as "the Galloping Garrulous Grok-Flock."

I was trying to build an inclusive coalition, but their idea was that only people they approved of should be a part of it. This was one of my first experiences of being cut out of something that I had founded.

NARRATOR: Tim Zell and his van full of Pagans arrived safely at the World Science Fiction Convention in Los Angeles, and I (your narrator, John C. Sulak) was there, too. I was, in fact, at most of the same early sci-fi cons that OZ was at—starting at St. Louiscon in 1969. Unlike the big conventions of that sort today, those gatherings didn't attract a lot of people or get much attention from the media. All the attendees and activities could easily fit into one hotel, and anyone walking by the building would have no idea what was going on inside. So this made it easy for people from different cities and states to have a centrally located place where they could all arrange to safely meet. It was also a fairly cheap vacation—the convention committee would book a block of rooms ahead of time so that anyone attending could reserve one at a discounted rate. They could then split the cost with friends who would crash on floor in the room with them for the weekend. Most of the people didn't spend much time in the room anyway, since there were activities that went on round-the-clock, like rarely screened movies being shown, parties, workshops, lectures, discussion groups, a dealer's room, games, autograph sessions with authors, and of course the hotel swimming pool.

Science-fiction fans in general were not Pagan, but a lot of them were pretty freaky in their own way. They generally didn't fit into mainstream culture or have much of a social life outside of "fandom," so they were tolerant of other outsiders. (Anyone who wasn't a part of their community was called a "Mundane," a term that was picked up by Pagans and is still in common use today. In this context it's synonymous with referring to someone as a "muggle.") And going to a convention was their big yearly chance to cut loose and party, so no one seemed to mind, or even notice, the Pagans.

Science-fiction conventions were also worth a cross-country drive for anyone who enjoyed the art and craft of costuming. Tim Zell had been making his own costumes since he was child. Unfortunately for him, when he reached adulthood, Hallowe'en was still considered to be just for children—unlike now, when it's a very popular time for adults to get dressed up (and spend lots of money doing it). Sci-fi fans, on the other hand, have always created their own reality when they got together, and appreciated creativity and imagination. So going to a con was a chance for Tim to strut his stuff somewhere else besides a Pagan ritual.

OZ: Saturday we finally made it over to LAcon '72—the 30th World Science Fiction Convention. Bryan spent most of the day in the pool and kept asking when he could go skinny-dipping. That evening we went to the masquerade. When Jodie and I stepped onto the stage, painted blue and garbed in the Priestly vestments of an authentic portrayal of Cerridwen and Cernunnos, the Goddess and Horned God of Celtic lore, we were greeted with a thunderous applause. Histah, who was draped around the forked stang I carried, really got off on the good vibes, and scanned the audience. Jodie carried a dry-ice smoking cauldron, out of which she lifted a human skull. At that moment, you could have heard a pin drop. We had several hours of suspenseful waiting for the judging, during which we were photographed constantly, until one by one the names of the winners were announced.

Finally the stage was full; all the best costumes had been awarded prizes, and we had not been mentioned. Just as we were consoling ourselves that our costumes were probably too esoteric, came the final announcement: ". . . and for Best of Show—Tim and Jodie Zell as Cernunnos and Cerridwen!"

One of the judges was Alison Harlow. Afterwards she came up to us and introduced herself and lots of other Pagans. Some of them we had already corresponded with, like neo-Druid Priest Isaac Bonewits, and others we didn't know. It really brought us into connection, in a major way, with many of the movers and shakers in the California Pagan community.

Alison and Isaac invited us to come up north to the Bay Area. When we got there, Alison threw a big party for us at her place. That's where we met Gwydion Pendderwen. Alison and Gwydion were living together in this big house in Oakland, called *Caedderwen*. They were both involved in the Society for Creative Anachronism and the Renaissance Faire crowd that eventually grew out of it.

NARRATOR: Gwydion was the Bard of his Society for Creative Anachronism (SCA) Kingdom. The SCA had been started just six years earlier as a medieval sword-and-shield tournament in the Berkeley backyard of Heathen writer Diana Paxson (then a UC graduate student). It didn't take long to expand from the backyard to the rest of the country. It currently has nineteen kingdoms, where people work together to re-create the Middle Ages "as they should have been, not as they were." Their biggest yearly gathering attracts over 10,000 to a site in western Pennsylvania.

From the beginning the SCA has always been a safe haven for Pagans. One of the original founders in Berkeley was Marion Zimmer Bradley, who would go on to also become friends with the Zells, and to write *Mists of Avalon*, a fantasy novel set in the same time and place that the SCA role-plays in. The premise of *Mists* is that the Earth Goddess is real and Goddess worship still existed in Europe up until the time of King Arthur. Though it's never been official, that kind of medieval Paganism could always be found at SCA gatherings for those who cared to look for it. That's what Gwydion Pendderwen would sing about at night while everyone was drinking mead after a long day of chivalry and combat.

Tim Zell was quick to grok what they doing—it was a group of people who liked to get dressed in costumes and then stay in them for a whole weekend at a time as they acted out their fantasies.

OZ: So that was another community we were weaving into the mix. We became fast friends and lovers with various people in that group. We deeply shared the same vision of Paganism being a community, a tribal kind of a thing, and living on the land. Alison and Gwydion took us up to Greenfield Ranch in Mendocino County, which was just in the process of being acquired at that time.

ALISON HARLOW: In the mid-1970s I was looking for a secluded place in the country to have Pagan gatherings and so forth, where we could be skyclad in the woods and celebrate close to Nature. I wasn't looking for a place to live.

I heard about Greenfield Ranch—5,600 acres of beautiful land in Mendocino County that was once a working cattle ranch. We knew the man who was putting the real estate deal together—he had done something similar before. Basically he would take out an option for some land, and then he would create communities by finding ecologically minded people to buy parcels of it.

At the time I was living in Oakland with Gwydion Pendderwen and his wife. Gwydion and I went up to look at Greenfield Ranch, and we both just fell in love with it. I wound up buying a 220-acre parcel.

NARRATOR: Gwydion was the "craft-son" of an East Bay resident named Victor Anderson, who was the founder of a version of Shamanic Witchcraft. Gwydion named this the Feri tradition, wrote rituals and poetry for it, and generally helped popularize the tradition; Alison Harlow was an initiated Feri Witch. At that time little was publicly know about Feri—there was nothing published about it, and initiations were done privately. Though the teachings differed in style from Gardnerian Wicca, both traditions were kept "underground" in the ways they were transmitted. Victor Anderson and Gerald Gardner were both charismatic, clever older men who enjoyed training and initiating younger women. (Gwydion was a younger man who also really enjoyed the company of women, and there were plenty of women who enjoyed his.) And they all were into the Goddess, sex, and Magick.

By that point Tim had met lots of people who claimed to have some degree of initiation in a tradition, and he respected them all. He had no reason to consider any one form of Paganism as being more important than anything else that was happening at the time—his visions of the future had always included having a lot of different options to choose from. But the Feri Witchcraft that started in California, like Gardnerian Wicca from England, both of which were intentionally mysterious and difficult to get involved with, would become extremely significant and widespread by the end of the decade. Curiously, no psychics, Tarot readers, or other practitioners of divination at the time could see it coming. And when Tim and the gang got in the van and drove home, they had other things on their minds.

OZ: I continued trying to get Histah healed. I tried to stay in constant contact with her. We were psychically bonded—she was the most intense familiar relationship I have ever had. On October 17, at 2:30 p.m.,

I was sitting at work and suddenly I just felt her presence. It was like we were connected, and then suddenly she dropped the other end of it. She dropped her body and was snapped into being in me. I completely felt this. I called home and told Jodie, "Histah just died."

And she said, "No, she's fine. I just saw her in the bathroom." I told her to go take another look. I waited. She came back and she said, "You're right. How did you know?"

And I replied, "Because she's now in me." That was a powerful experience. Ever since then I have felt that inside me is the soul of a serpent. And in the language of J. K. Rowling's *Harry Potter* novels, I became a "parseltongue," able to communicate with snakes ever since.

In February of 1973, Jodie turned twenty-one. She wanted to get some independence because she had moved into my house straight from her parents' home, with only a brief stint at college. So she moved out. That was quite a big thing for me. This was the first time in my entire life that I had lived alone. I felt strongly that Jodie was my soulmate. She was completing her work for ordination and getting right to the edge of becoming a Priestess. But we also had a fairly tumultuous relationship.

I didn't quite know what to do. I wasn't used to not having someone to share my life, bed, meals, conversations, and everything. There were a few people in the community whom I had lover/friend relationships with. That was all very nice, and it helped me get through it. But having someone you can spend the night with isn't the same as having a companion.

One day I went down to the co-op to buy some groceries, and this woman, Kay Brush, came up to me. I'd never met her before. We got into a conversation that somehow revealed that I was alone at the moment, so she invited me over for dinner. I ended up spending the night. At that time I was extremely susceptible and vulnerable. Within a week or so of our meeting, she moved into my house. It wasn't like we planned it exactly. She took the initiative and I didn't say no.

But then it got kind of weird. She borrowed my credit card, which seemed reasonable at the time. I didn't realized until a month later when I got the bill that she was racking up quite a lot of expenses. It got to be pretty intense. After a month or so she moved out again, but we still continued to date.

Jodie then told me that she'd had enough time on her own and would like to move back in. I said I wasn't quite ready for that yet, which was really stupid of me. I don't know if it was my wounded pride or what. I should have said, "Boy, am I glad to have you back! I really missed you." But I didn't. Idiot.

All this led up to Beltane of 1973, when we had probably the most amazingly intense erotic celebration that we had ever had. It was instigated by an astonishingly gorgeous Yemeni belly dancer who did a topless dance for us at the Beltane ritual. Somehow the intensity of the evening precipitated an amazing sexual experience all the way around. It wasn't specifically with her. There were people all over the place feeling aroused and getting it on. This was the evening that went way out there.

DON WILDGRUBE: Two people at the Beltane festival had a contest to see how many people they could screw. The next thing you know, about ten or twelve of us came down with trichomoniasis. At that time, there was a lady named Bobby who was a nurse, and she went to the free clinic, and when the doctor told her what it was, he asked, "How many people were infected?"

CAROLYN CLARK: When she said twenty-three, he said, "That must have been one helluva party."

DON WILDGRUBE: He wrote prescriptions for all of us. So everyone was on Flagyl tablets. It eats up all the yeast. Girls had to take two pills a day, and the guys one pill a day for ten days.

OZ: However, we didn't get the rap about the side effects: an incredible increase in irritability, anxiety, paranoia, and general bad attitudes. Within a fairly short time of everybody taking this stuff, in this very tight, intense community, people started to go nuts. They were going off the wall with accusations, hostilities, jealousies, and weird stuff like that.

In late May we had a Nest meeting that went all awry. It started reasonably enough. Someone suggested that we had to tighten up our boundaries about who we were having sex with and maybe stick with our own Nest mates. Someone said, "I wouldn't want to sleep with anyone who wasn't a water-brother." And then Jodie, who was at this meeting, said, "I wouldn't want to sleep with anyone who was sleeping with Kay Brush."

I was sitting over in the opposite corner across from her, with Kay Brush sitting next to me. In one single movement I rose up from the couch, swept across the room, and backhanded Jodie across the face. Even thinking about it now, it seems utterly unconceivable that I would have ever done such a thing. But I did. It was devastating. We rushed Jodie to the hospital, where it was determined that I had broken her nose.

DON WILDGRUBE: Well, weeks later I happened to be doing some floor work in a hospital, and at lunchtime I was behind the nurse's station, and I got out the *Physician's Desk Reference*, a big, thick book that gives you the breakdown of various medications. And I looked up Flagyl. And there is a long list of side effects. And that's when I realized what had happened to Tim. He's a pacifist. When we were all taking Flagyl we were always at each other's throats, always arguing, always fighting.

CAROLYN CLARK: That was why he hit her. He was angry with her, and under ordinary circumstances it would have stopped with raised voices. Immediately afterwards he was horrified, ashamed, and broken up that he had actually become violent towards anyone, especially Jodie.

OZ: So, there I was. It was the summer of 1973, and I'd lost the woman I'd expected to be with forever. I'd blown any chance of getting her back, and I had no one to blame but myself. I'd heard about the Rainbow Family gathering, which that year was being held in Wyoming on the Fourth of July. And I decided that what I needed to do was go walkabout and find myself.

I realized that up until that point in my life, I had taken everyone around me for granted and focused on my own mission and desires. I really got a chance to see that a bit more objectively, and I felt like an ass. If I had just paid a little more attention to what it was that other people needed or wanted, things could have been very different. The fact that they went along with it was all I needed. I just automatically made all the decisions and presumed that it was all up to me. I got perspective on this and felt terrible.

I realized that one of the things that Jodie had hated the whole time she had been living with me was that the living room had been painted black and that I had day-glo stars and planets all over the walls. So the first thing I did when I got back from the trip was repaint the whole place white. I threw away all of my black clothes, which is mostly what I'd been wearing since the Beatnik days. I started wearing more white and light colors. I looked at the images I surrounded myself with, the music I listened to—I spent the rest of the summer going through my life and tried to turn around everything that I could.

I had to accept that there was no way that anything I did was going to get Jodie to come back to me. But I still fantasized and hoped that it might happen—it was too little, too late, but it did change me. There had been something built into me from the time I was a kid and had to deal with bullies. I didn't want that to be there at all. I had to abandon the whole concept of being a powerful, alpha-male, dominant figure.

During the last couple of years, my writings on TheaGenesis had been spreading throughout the community. It became a unifying mythology. As Joseph Campbell said, "The only myth that is going to be worth talking about in the immediate future is one that is talking about the planet." My articles from *Green Egg*, which I had expanded forth from the initial idea, had been reprinted in other places. Llewellyn Publications reprinted one in their publication *Gnostica News*. And they also invited me to come and do presentations as a keynote speaker at the Gnostic Aquarian Festival in Minneapolis that was to occur on the Fall Equinox weekend of 1973. This was a big deal for me—my first major public-speaking gig. A bunch of people wanted to come along, so we made plans to have a CAW table there.

Just before we left, we had our Mabon celebration. Carolyn Clark, being our high Priestess, conducted the ritual. She asked everybody to write down on a piece of paper what they would like to harvest for the year. We each had to think about what seeds we had sown, and what we would like to receive as our reward.

CAROLYN CLARK: During the time that I was active, I wrote and conducted many rituals—it was like being the conductor of an orchestra. I wrote them so that other people would be pulled into the action and not be spectators. That Mabon ritual was the first one I had done that involved that kind of requesting the Goddess through writing down our petitions and burning them.

OZ: I got my paper and pen, and I started to write down, "Let me be reunited with Jodie . . ." But something stayed my hand, and instead I wrote, "Let me be united with my true soulmate." I was shifting my thinking from my directing how I wanted things to be, to trusting the Goddess to know what was best for me.

That went into the cauldron, and I didn't really think about it much more because then we were on our way. We packed up a van full of people and headed up to Minneapolis. When we got there, we looked around and realized that it was not a gathering of our kind of people at all. They were into astrology, Tarot, crystals, reincarnation, and other New-Agey kind of stuff, but they weren't really Pagans in the religious or cultural sense.

Well, the other occasion for this was that Llewellyn's owner, Carl Weschcke, decided that they would also be having a gathering of Witches. So a lot of big-name people in the Witchy world had been invited. They had just gotten Isaac Bonewits on the staff of *Gnostica News* as their editor, so he was there. And they had brought in people like Ray Buckland and Margot Adler. The ulterior agenda for all this was to introduce a woman named "Lady Sheba." She had put together a grimoire, which, it later turned out, was essentially the Gardnerian *Book of Shadows* slightly altered. She was going to be presented to us as the new Witch Queen of America. Needless to say, that didn't go over very well among a bunch of radical anarcho-Pagans who had no use for British-style royalty!

NARRATOR: Although she was never recognized as royalty, Lady Sheba's book went on to become quite influential. She didn't claim to have written the book herself, and that was indeed true. The source of it was eventually traced to an Alexandrian Book of Shadows, and a lot of people got really angry because those kinds of things were supposed to be kept secret.

But, as they say, the cat was out of the bag. After that, it wasn't a secret anymore! Even though there were errors in it, Lady Sheba's book was still a source for all kinds of information about Witchcraft and rituals that was available to anyone who wanted to become a Witch or to do Witchcraft and Magick that worked. And that's just what a lot of folks began to do.

OZ: While we were getting our table set up in the lobby, I looked around, and coming in through the door I saw a gorgeous Hippie woman dressed in a flowing, beautiful San Francisco Gold Rush dress, all purples and lavenders, with creamy lace and long, frilly sleeves. She had long, dark hair and huge deer eyes and incredible breasts. That was more along the lines of what we had been hoping to find!

Unfortunately, I didn't have a chance to talk to her, because right at that time I was being hauled away to do interviews, and then I had workshops and a lunch engagement with a reporter from *Playboy* lined up. When I came back, Orion was telling me, "Oh, man, you have got to meet this woman! You and she have so many things in common." But by then she was gone. This kind of thing kept happening. She would come by the table when I was gone, and people would tell her about me. And then I'd come back, and people would tell me about her.

This went back and forth until finally I came back to the table and she was there, and we talked for a few minutes. We didn't have a chance to do much because I was just there to pick up some copies of *Green Egg* and head down to do the first of my TheaGenesis presentations. I told her I had to leave and she said, "Can I walk with you?"

I said, "Okay, but I've got to go do this workshop."

And she said, "Where is it?"

And I said, "It's downstairs."

She said, "I'm going downstairs to a workshop, too, so I'll just go with you."

So we walked and continued talking. When we got down to the room, I walked up to the front and set the box of magazines down on the table. She sat down in the front row, and that was the first time she realized that I was actually the speaker at the workshop she was going to.

There was a whole room full of people, including Robert Anton Wilson. I presented my "TheaGenesis" paper. And at the end of the presentation, they all came rushing up to talk to me. And this girl was at the head of the line. She said, "We have to talk."

And I said, "Right." I grabbed her hand and just walked out of that room, leaving everyone else standing there watching us go.

I took her upstairs to a secluded bench behind some potted plants, and we sat down next together. As we turned to look at each other face to face, suddenly, for both of us, the whole rest of the world just disappeared. For me, there was nothing else except her eyes, and I fell into them like diving into a deep pool. I felt we were completely and telepathically bonded, as if our souls had merged. It was love at first sight, but beyond anything that you read about. I heard the voice of the Goddess in the back of my head saying, "This is the one you asked for."

Her name was Morning Glory.

PART TWO

Enter
Morning Glory

Chapter 7
Good Morning Glory
(1948–1973)

I saw your face once in my dream
A thousand miles and years away.
Then Fate began Her cosmic scheme
To bring me to your side that day.

I'd travel far, to where you are
Favorite Lover, my Best Friend!
I'd do it all the same again;
I'd do it all the same again.

—FROM "LOVE OF MY LIFE" BY MORNING GLORY ZELL, 1993

NARRATOR: When Tim and Morning Glory met, it was like something out of one of the many myths or stories that they both knew so well, but it was real. And as they got to know each other, they found out that though their family histories were very different, they had many things in common with each other. And so we will now go back in time and look at what Morning Glory's life had been like before her fateful meeting with Tim Zell.

Morning Glory was born in 1948 in Long Beach, California. She was the only child of Polly Browning and James Moore, who had moved to Southern California from Mississippi during World War II.

MG: My parents were a traditional couple, with the father who worked and the mother who stayed home with the child, at least for the first eight years of my life. I was an only child; my mother wanted to have thirteen children, but instead she had six miscarriages and almost died in fifty-four hours of labor with me. I was born by cesarean section. So I was her sun and moon and stars; she decided that all my friends (and later my lovers) would be the adopted other children she never could have.

We had a pretty good life, and we should have been relatively comfortable, but when I turned eight my father developed emphysema. He worked in the oil fields in an increasingly smog-ridden city and smoked Kool cigarettes at a time when they advertised that Kool cigarettes were "doctor recommended." Once he got sick, he could no longer work enough to make a living wage even though he tried. But he spent more and more time in the hospital until the doctors and hospitals ended up owning all his hard-earned money and property, and we were forced to move into an eighteen-foot travel trailer and become Gypsies. He suffered from the stress of losing everything, the constant struggle to breathe, and all the steroids and other weirder drugs he was given while the doctors used him as a guinea pig. After a couple of years of this, he went pretty crazy—from being a terrific dad to being perpetually ill, irritable, and violently abusive.

Every summer we would drive back to Mississippi to stay with our relatives there. A couple of times when my dad got too weak to work and too debilitated by the smog to live in Southern California, we would go back and stay for longer periods. When I was ten we stayed for a whole year and a half in Mississippi and I went to school there; I shunted around from one group of relatives to another in the summertime. I learned to milk cows, take care of 66,000 chickens, and harness a horse and plow a field. I learned to love the rural lifestyle, but I never fit in with the people; I was picked on a lot and was always in trouble.

NARRATOR: She began learning about, and loving, dinosaurs at an early age, just as Tim Zell had.

MG: When I was in the first grade, I discovered a Little Golden Book called *From Then to Now*. It was a child-sized bite of the evolutionary history of Earth, which was pretty wonderful in and of itself; but the real thrill for me was that it introduced me to dinosaurs! They were my first great passion. I read Darwin because I was a dino-brat, and I pretty much grew up with the notion of evolution as a given. I discovered that most of my relatives, including my mom, believed that evolution contradicted the Bible.

Surprisingly, my grandfather, who was a Methodist minister, did not believe that at all, because he did not believe in a literal translation of the Bible. He once told me, "The Bible, like all the other great, sacred works of mankind, is a metaphor, and anyone who believes in the literal truth of every single word of it is an ignorant idiot." He didn't see any problem with evolution as a process of Creation at all.

At that point in my life I still considered myself to be a Christian, but it was Granddaddy Moore who made the first real dent in my belief in the rightness of those teachings. It was around a discussion that I was having with him about my horse, who was twenty-three years old and didn't have many more years left. I said to Granddaddy, "I guess I will see him in Heaven someday."

He then informed me, complete with cited scriptures, that my horse would not be in Heaven because he did not have a soul; only humans had souls and went to Heaven. So I told him that if my horse wasn't going to Heaven, then I didn't want to go either. He asked me if I was planning on going to Hell instead, but I said, "No, I'm not. I'm going wherever the horses and other animals go." Oddly enough he didn't get mad at me this time; he just burst out laughing and called me "his little heathen." Talk about prophetic words . . .

I frequently had dreams that would come to be true, and sadly I learned not to talk about them to other people. I dreamed that my dad's boat was going to capsize and sneaked out to put in extra life preservers. That night he came home from an ocean fishing trip drenched and shivering but still alive. That was the first time people called me a Witch. I could feel spirits speaking in the wind, and every time I would smell burning leaves in autumn or fresh cut grass in spring I would get a frisson of delight, and the hairs on my neck would stand up and shiver. I would spend hours looking at the face of the moon, seeing the large, round, and slightly sad eyes of the Lady (it never looked like the "Man in the Moon" to me).

Going from California to Mississippi, back and forth like a ping-pong ball, had a strange effect on my upbringing. For one thing I was always "the new kid" wherever we went, and the culture shock was enough to give anyone psychic whiplash. I just got used to never fitting in anywhere and developed coping mechanisms. I was always outgoing and I made friends pretty quickly—but I made enemies pretty quickly, too. So I learned to tell stories to entertain other folks and keep them from picking on me.

I was a voracious reader, and no matter what town we traveled to, if we stayed more than two days I would beg to go to the library. It was my haven and my sanctuary. I would weave the stories I read into the tales I told, and that is how I learned to teach people—by telling stories and anecdotes. The downside of all this was that I learned early on that in order to keep from being picked on or whipped by my dad, or getting into trouble about stuff, I had to lie. So when I told stories I often embroidered them significantly; there were fantasy tales that I would tell as if they happened to me. My mom and grandma used to use the term *story-telling* as a euphemism for lying. So it all sort of got blurred together in my mind. I learned to tell stories to get attention and to distract people from being angry with me. I learned to tell them in odd ways because I never knew what it was that I was going to get in trouble for, since every place I went to the cultural norms were different. This behavior, in both positive and negative ways, would play a very large role in my life.

I mostly grew up in my mom's church, the Pentecostal Assemblies of God. They practiced an ecstatic form of Christianity, with baptism of the Holy Spirit, speaking in tongues, and dancing in the Spirit. I was fully involved in it and deeply immersed in the emotional gestalt of the experience. When the Holy Spirit was with me, I always felt a strong, uplifting feminine presence, but I never really talked about that part of it to anyone.

But all the aspects of that brand of religion are male: God the Father, the Son, and the Holy Spirit; even the angels are portrayed as masculine. It is a religion that is all about men and run entirely by men, but its congregations are much more female than male. But it was what I knew, and I got along without asking too many awkward questions, until one day I went to the pastor and said, "Look, I'm concerned because my father beats my mom and me. Where is God's will in this? What recourse do we have?"

Back then, there weren't any battered women's shelters, and at one point I went to a psychiatrist to try to get family-counseling help, but he told my parents that I was crazy and needed electroshock therapy. So when I went to our pastor, he told me that it was the woman's duty to surrender to the will of her husband, and that if my dad killed my mom or me, we would get crowns in Heaven someday! He said that my duty was to be obedient and not rock the boat, and that really tore the mask off for me. After that, all the bits and pieces that never quite fit started coming faster into a rushing torrent of questions and doubt. All this was coincidentally right about the time of my puberty.

POLLY LOVE MOORE: Jesus says to love your companion—this is to the husband: "You have to love your companion like you love me." And if you really have that nature of Jesus, and that husband offers that wife that sweet nature, the fruits of the spirit as the Bible says—love, peace, joy, and all that—then that wife is just going to be thrilled to death to fall in that shadow. Because then you're going to get all that love that anybody is looking for.

MG: I loved my mom so much, but I couldn't stand it that she was like a doormat. Whatever my dad did was okay with her—I guess it had to be, because periodically he would beat her and threaten to kill us both. That kind of behavior shaped me, but I never gave in; it never broke me. She was always terrified, but I just got angry and would argue right back at him and try to show him proof when I was right about something and he was wrong. I guess I was a smart-aleck kid who acted like I was his equal and he hated that—so we would get into these huge fights. Also, I would jump between him and my mom when he was hitting or kicking her. I can remember a time when he was threatening to kill me and I tried to bite his hand. He looked down into my eyes blazing back at him, and I guess he must have seen a piece of his own fighting spirit reflected there and he couldn't bring himself to snuff that out.

Paradoxically, I never stopped loving my father; I know I must have loved him as much as I hated him. My father was my window and door into the natural world—he was sort of a deistic naturalist who loved Nature and introduced me to Her wonders. In spite of his craziness, he imparted that gift to me. My mother gave me deep love and appreciation for the spiritual world. She was an incredibly nurturing, loving parent. She taught me by example about unconditional love and a reverence for life. Hers grew out of devout Christianity, and though I took it in a different direction, we still shared in common a belief in the transformational power of unconditional love, a reverence for life, and a commitment to spiritual practice.

What I did not get from my mother was her fear. She led a fear-driven life from the time she was a child—even her faith was rooted in a fear of God and Hell—but I rejected that whole fear component. Perhaps her love gave me the strength to do that, but I think that it probably saved my life, because if I had reacted to my dad's threats with fear instead of the anger he recognized in himself, he might have killed me. I took away a lesson in survival: to not back down, to stick up for what you believe in, and to be strong and not let yourself be intimidated by someone who is trying to bully you.

Not long after all this, when I was about thirteen, I had an opportunity to visit my aunt and my cousins in New Orleans and attend Mardi Gras. I glimpsed another entire universe. It was so exciting that I was overwhelmed, and I felt my spirit leaping up and exclaiming, "Wow— that's what I want! Somehow that is my religion!"

That's where I met Bacchus. He tapped me on the shoulder and said, "Girl, follow me!" And I did. After that revelation I knew that I was not suited to be a Christian.

POLLY LOVE MOORE: When she got old enough to know what she wanted, it never did bother me anymore. She's just as sweet as ever and I love her just as much as I ever did. I still had to accept the fact that she had her right, her prerogatives, to choose whatever she wanted. Of course, I still always pray for her and for every one of her friends that they will be safe.

MG: Right about that same time, I discovered the works of Ayn Rand and became an outspoken and somewhat obnoxious Objectivist/atheist. But I had always been psychic, and there was no place in her universe for mysticism. So I began a conscious deliberate religious search. I studied a little bit about Zen Buddhism, Islamic Sufism, and Yoga philosophy, which eventually led me to a Hindu temple where I first heard about Goddesses in the world today. And I was amazed and awed: "Wow, what an idea! You mean there are living Goddesses in the universe still?" I had read lots of Greek mythology as a kid—I was originally named for the Moon Goddess Diana—and that was fascinating. Learning about Lakshmi and Kali Ma and the power of Shakti was such an awakening. But when I started studying the actual practices, I found myself dealing with the same old bugaboos of celibacy, sexism, and obedience to male dominion. So I came to the sad conclusion that that just wasn't quite it either.

Next I moved into more magickal realms. I read *Lord of the Rings*, and for a while I wanted to be an Elf more than anything else in the world. I guess on some level I always will . . . But I read other fantasy stories, classical fairy tales, Romance literature like William Morris's *The Wood Beyond the World*, and Celtic lore like *The Mabinogion* and the *Táin Bó Cúailnge*. I read *The White Goddess* by Robert Graves and later the series of *Teachings of Don Juan* by Carlos Castaneda.

Somewhere along the line, I got hold of a book called *Diary of a Witch* by Sybil Leek. I was about nineteen or twenty, and it all just clicked into place. The book told how the "Old Religion" had been suppressed by Christianity; it described a Horned God like Pan or Cernunnos, and His consort, the Goddess of many names. It all woke this deep feeling of recognition inside me. Like all the other bits and pieces I had been striving for were clues to this divine puzzle, and when it fit together it all made perfect sense: a true revelation! I realized that I was a Witch in this life and had been a Witch in other lives before. Unfortunately, Leek's book also said if you're not born a hereditary English Witch, you don't get to be one at all. But I was not going to let what one person said about how one became a Witch stand in my way. This was before the books by Gerald Gardner were readily available in the United States.

Based on my eclectic reading, I decided that what I needed was an initiation. So in the summer before my senior year, I conceived this whole story in my imagination about an English Witch that I had met in Venice (California, not Italy) who was teaching me about Witchcraft. I gave her a name: Vashti Esterath, and invented a lineage for her. I can still see her face in my mind's eye. Maybe I knew her from some past life, but in this one she was someone I dreamed about.

That summer I took off for Big Sur for a month. First I lived off the land for a week, then I fasted and took a major LSD trip. At Lime Kiln Creek, I dedicated my life to the Goddess, and then I climbed up the side of a big rock by a waterfall and dove into the pool of water. The person who dove off that waterfall was a girl named Diane, but the person who climbed out of that pool was a woman named Morning Glory. That was my initiation.

The next morning I awoke, and three other Hippie-type folks were sitting around my sleeping bag and they had covered it with little field morning glory flowers while I slept. They all said, "Good morning, glory!" and that is how I got my name. Oh, lots of people laugh because I am certainly not a morning person, far from it, but it was not the time of day that convinced me to take that name. Morning glory seeds contain trace amounts of lysergic acid, and they are part of the ancient shamanic pharmacopeia; their bell-shaped flowers, like Datura, resemble the skirts of the Cretan Goddess. They are common and unassuming but hide a potent secret in their hearts. All of these are the reasons why I chose that name.

Why would I change from a perfect Witchy name like Diane? The answer is that I love the Goddess and I respect Her, but I did not presume to take Her name, especially after I came into my sexuality and began to follow the ways of Aphrodite. As a young girl Diana protected me, but in order to stay with Her as an adult I felt that I would need to give up my love of men. She can be very possessive, that Goddess, and I did not want to end up like Callisto or so many of Her maidens that strayed from Her side to follow the love of a man or a God. So whether it seems to fit or not, Morning Glory I became and Morning Glory I remain. Even if I mostly see the dawn these days about the time I am heading to bed. Hmmm . . . maybe I should have called myself Nightshade. Oh well, too late now!

After this experience I embroidered it and wove it into my story about Vashti the English Witch and how my initiation had been under her tutelage, so that I could convince others that my initiation had been legitimate. Oh, what a tangled web we weave . . . But regardless of what stories I spun about it, I always felt in my heart of hearts that it was a legitimate initiation.

NARRATOR: Though the details of her story would come back to haunt her years later, Morning Glory was actually way ahead of her time: self-initiation rituals would become very popular in the decades that followed. And there were probably other Witches around then who had done the same thing, but back then everything was shrouded in secrecy, a lot of tall tales were told, and no one was recording any statistics. Indeed, even Gerald Gardner claimed to have been initiated by an old Witch that no one had ever met, and to this day there is still speculation about who she was and what really happened.

Morning Glory remained independent in all things, and even while she was still in high school and living at home, she was working so that she could have a horse and her own car.

MG: In high school I took three years of Latin, biology, world history, and literature. But in the drama club I found a social circle I could relate to; I was also involved in the speech club and the debate society. I learned a lot of the best elements of creating a good ritual and about the Bacchic religious roots of the theater from our drama teacher.

I was working part-time at a local hospital in the laboratory and also did some emergency services work like EKG monitoring and collecting specimens and phlebotomy. I did other assistant lab work as well as grungy jobs like washing test tubes and specimen jars. I spent time up to my elbows in the midst of life and death there, attending to people in crisis and also sometimes when they died. These experiences really made me want to understand the passages between the worlds.

I remember a watershed moment for me was when a woman came in to the ER with chest pains; she and I had the same doctor. He came into the room and was laughing with us as I took her EKG. It was supposed to be more of a precautionary test, and then suddenly her back arched upward and her eyes rolled back. I thought my machine had broken because the needles went haywire, but she had just suffered a massive myocardial infarction. We tried to save her—the doctor, the nurses, all the tools of the crash cart; they hit her five times with the defibrillator, but it was just not going to make any difference.

Finally, there comes this nervous moment when everyone looks around sort of sheepishly at each other and shrugs. And then everyone looks at the doctor, and he sighs and shakes his head and we all start packing up our gear while he has to go and tell this woman's husband the life-shattering news. The room emptied out and I was left alone with the woman, sort of lying like a broken doll on the gurney. One moment she and I had been laughing about some TV show and the next she was just lying there like a carved wax figure, her eyes still open, staring into infinity. When I bent over her to disconnect the leads, I stared into her eyes and sent out my thoughts to her as hard as I could: "Where are you now, and what is it like?"

I held very still and listened inward, and I heard her voice say to me with this silvery little laugh, "Don't be in too much of a hurry; you'll find out everything soon enough." I thanked her and gently closed her eyes, then left with my machines and my question.

I was still living off and on with my parents, but I also shared an apartment with a girlfriend from drama club who had graduated the year before me. I turned eighteen on May 27, 1966, but I graduated in June. I moved out completely the day I turned eighteen, bought myself a seven-foot boa constrictor that I named Baby Doll, and for a year or so I pursued a career as a laboratory histologist for a private lab.

So, I worked and partied and went to junior college for a while, enjoying being a free bird entirely on my own, until my awareness of the political scene with the war in Vietnam and the repression of the antiwar and civil rights movements here began to overwhelm my consciousness. More and more of my time was spent working at the Peace Center or going to antiwar demonstrations or to love-ins, and it cut into my work and my school life. The Psychedelic Psixties had arrived in full tilt! I had actually gotten an awesome education in high school, and we were too poor for me to go to a four-year college, so I ended up at a second-rate junior college. But I got so frustrated with the poor level of education that was being handed out at the junior college that I followed Tim Leary's suggestion: I turned on, tuned in, and dropped out.

I felt that I needed to start a new life in a new place. A friend of mine from the Peace Center wanted to come along as far as San Francisco, so we headed north in the warm summer sunshine. There was an on-ramp near the gas station where I filled up, and my friend pointed out some hitchhikers on the ramp, so I pulled over and gave this guy a ride. I recognized him from the Peace Center and also from driving around and smoking pot in the back of his tricked-out old psychedelic panel truck. His name was Gary, and he said he was also headed for San Francisco and that he had just got kicked out of the military for being too weird.

Our first stop was Big Sur, and I was planning on staying there for at least a month before I went any further north. I knew that I needed to touch the Earth and clear my head of all the bad vibes I had picked up traveling in the South and in the cities. Big Sur was always my magickal touchstone; it was like wandering through Middle Earth. When we got to Big Sur I offered to share my sleeping bag with Gary, because he had only brought a bedroll. But the deal was: if he wanted to do that, he had to help me keep my boa constrictor warm!

GARY FERNS: We met originally down in Orange County for a few months before we left for Oregon. I had just gotten thrown out of the Air Force and was sort of kicking around—a freewheelin' Hippie. I met Morning Glory at one of the local head shops in Santa Ana. She was the "snake chick," the one with the boa constrictor under the black light. We used to hang out with the same people and go to the beach or concerts. She decided to move to Oregon. I was kind of bored when I heard about it and it sounded like it might be fun, so I decided to go along for the ride. We stopped at Big Sur and made this intense psychedelic connection, and we decided we were married from that point on. We stayed at Big Sur for a couple of weeks and then ambled on up the coast. Eventually, we arrived in Eugene and connected with this other family from Orange County that we knew from the Peace Center who had migrated there earlier.

NARRATOR: MG and Gary co-created a commune with their friends. Eventually they merged with another, larger group that had a communal-style farm and they all moved out to the country. Then MG and Gary decided to have a child together.

MG: My daughter was born on November 11, 1969. I had a home birth in town, in the back room of a friend's house. In those days, fathers were not allowed in the hospital delivery rooms, and Gary and I both felt that was really unfair. We had started this together, and we wanted to make it through together; so many women cut off from their partners become estranged by undergoing the pain and magick of the birthing process without them. I had a sixty-year-old midwife who was an osteopath who had delivered lots of babies, including the husband of the nurse who assisted us. We were just down the street from the hospital in case anything went wrong, but I was convinced from all the books on natural childbirth I had read that my birth would be a snap. When I went into labor, I thought there must be something really wrong because it hurt so badly. But once I got over the shock, I was able to use the meditation and breathing techniques I had learned, and it was all totally worth every minute of it. There were no complications at all, and Gary was able to help and to be there as my supporter all the time. And finally there was the baby. She was this beautiful copper color like an Indian child; we named her Rainbow Galadriel.

NARRATOR: The social experiment of communal farm living didn't work out the way they had hoped, so MG and Gary moved with their newborn baby back into Eugene. They eventually settled down in a loft-like space where they formed a new community that included their downstairs neighbors.

CATHERINE CROWELL (C9): A friend of mine told me that there was a Witch living upstairs from her. It was the spring of 1972. So I went up there to meet Morning Glory. She and I started talking, and I didn't come back downstairs for forty-eight hours. We stayed up night and day talking. She was fascinating and truly living a self-made life. That was a very valuable thing in 1972—my entire generation was really about redefining life and not simply accepting the mantle of suburbia.

She lived in an amazing little apartment with Gary, Rainbow, and an eight-foot boa constrictor named Ophelia that they kept in a hollowed-out TV set. The place was painted the colors of peacock feathers. It was a sort of converted attic. Gary had a love for antiques, so they had Victorian-style furniture, which one could pick up at the time, and it was always filled with candles.

MG: I started writing a column called "Magick Words" for *The Augur*, a local underground newspaper, and I was reading Tarot cards, teaching classes, and giving little seminars. I had lots of wonderful friends, and Gary was a great guy, but more of a retiring Buddhist-type spiritual person. He wasn't cut out to be a Priest to be the partner to my Priestess self; I just didn't have any magickal peers. I wanted to share my spiritual visions with the world, but there were no other Pagans or Witches there. I kept looking for other people to connect with; we even drove down to San Francisco looking for Witches, but we couldn't stay long enough to make any real connections. Everyone was really underground and secretive in those days.

However, I did pick up a copy of Llewellyn's *Gnostica News* at a psychic bookstore. I subscribed to *Gnostica* and finally heard about the Gnostic Aquarian Festival, or Gnosticon, to be held in Minneapolis over the Autumn Equinox weekend of 1973. So I decided that I was going to hitchhike to Minneapolis, go to the con, and finally meet some people like myself.

CATHERINE CROWELL (C9): She functioned alone as a Pagan in Eugene. She would always get interviewed by the newspaper at Hallowe'en, but there really wasn't much of a community of that sort there at the time. Still she seemed fine and happy—she wasn't always yearning and grumpy. Around the time of Elvis Presley's concert from Hawaii, Morning Glory heard that there was a big festival that was going to be in Minneapolis. She was desperate to go there. They didn't have any money, so I went to my father and I lied. I said I needed the money, I borrowed it from him, and I funded her trip. We sent her off with great love and encouragement, because she meant so much to all of us. She was an inspiration and a constant joy. And we knew that her religion was the foundation of that for her. So Gary and I did what we could. We sent her off. And she did not come back.

MG: When I got to the convention, I took a deep breath and looked around. It didn't seem like there was anyone there that looked at all like me. They were mostly older, straight-looking folks. I finally saw a bunch of folks with brightly colored clothes, Renaissance-style tunics, and cloaks at the Church of All Worlds booth. I asked this one long-haired fellow how to get to my first workshop, and we exchanged some mutual excitement about the event and he gave me directions. After my workshop was done, I returned to the CAW booth and hung out with the folks there; everyone kept telling me that I had to meet this guy who was with them because we were so much alike. He even had a snake.

And eventually, when we did meet, it became a magickal meltdown. I hadn't really read his articles in *Gnostica News* before I came, but I realized that I had signed up for all of his lectures based on the titles he had created from popular rock songs; they were all about Nature and the Goddess. He gave this amazing lecture on the TheaGenesis principle (later called the Gaea Thesis), which was the whole idea of the Goddess as an evolutionary force in Nature, and how we were all part of that one planetary consciousness. It was all the missing pieces of my own home-grown theology and answered all the biological and historical questions that had been plaguing me—wrapped it all up and tied it up with a neat bow and ribbon. I was completely blown away and so were most of the other people in the room.

I may seem like a pushy broad, but in many ways I am kind of shy; I'm especially nervous around people who I think are "famous" or more educated than I am. But I couldn't stop myself from going right up to the front of the room at the end of the lecture and telling this man, "I really need to talk to you!"

I had meant it in a sort of "We should find time to have a conversation about this stuff" sort of way, but to my amazement he just took my hand and said, "You're right!" and walked me right out the door, leaving all those other people behind with their mouths hanging open in astonishment. We went off to a little alcove behind some potted plants in the lobby and sat down and took a deep breath, turned to each other with a million things to say, and found ourselves . . . speechless, timelessly falling into each other's eyes, into each other's memories, into each other's lives. It was like the dreamfasting experience for the Gelflings in the movie *The Dark Crystal* (which hadn't been made yet).

It was the most profoundly important magickal act that had every happened to either of us. We were so in love that we could hardly speak.

But I have always had the ability to step back from my feelings (it's a Gemini thing), so I paused and took a deep breath and said, "This is amazing and wonderful, and I love you so much I can't even think straight. But I must be honest with you. I need you to understand that as much as I love you, I can never be in a monogamous relationship; for one thing I already have a family. Monogamy is just not in my nature and I don't want to deceive you. I want to be free to have other lovers, and you're free to do that as well. I'll give you my whole heart and soul, but I cannot give you monogamy. There are other people in my life, and there always will be other people. Yet what we have together is special and unique beyond any measure; nothing will ever take away from that."

And he looked back into my eyes and smiled like he had just found the Holy Grail.

OZ: I'd never had anybody present it to me as what they wanted. It had always been me saying that. Everything that we touched on was like that. We started coming up with every possible thing we could think of, and every time we did we found a complete match. From that moment on, we were totally inseparable. The whole rest of the weekend was like a dream. Everybody who had come up there with me was packed into one hotel room. (This was a custom I had picked up from going to science-fiction conventions. We had all brought our sleeping bags with us.) The closet was just big enough for Morning Glory and I to lie down in, so that became our private space. Though I think we probably kept everyone else awake all night with the sounds we were making!

MG: I have always been a "True Dreamer"—that is, from childhood I would have dreams that would come to be real. About two years before Gnosticon I had dreamed that I was going to meet a man who was going to be a teacher for me. The Goddess spoke to me and told me that I was to follow him, and he would lead me into a completely new life. When I woke up, the dream was so vivid that I told Gary about it. So I went about my life, sort of looking for this person and wondering when I was going to meet him. I had memorized his features exactly in the dream by sort of freezing the action and had never forgotten them. When I met Tim I kept thinking, "This must be the guy in the dream, but there is something different about him; he doesn't look quite the same." I just couldn't put my finger on it.

And then I finally got a copy of the Gnosticon program book; I was flipping through it and I saw his picture. And it was literally like it was cut with scissors out of the dream. And I told him, "Wow, this picture doesn't really look that much like you."

And he said, "Yeah, it's an old picture. It was taken two years ago." *Wham!* There it was. It was truly Destiny, in my face staring back at me. And there was no way I could deny it, explain it away with logic, or escape from the inevitable reality of it. It was like the Gods said to me: "You have always asked for proof of real Magick; you asked for a miracle; now here it is. Deal with it!"

Many people go through their whole lives begging for just one scrap of true Magick and then rarely recognize it when it finally does arrive. But I was so blessed that I was not going to make that mistake; I was not going to lose this perfect, shining, Goddess-given gift. At that point I decided, "Okay, I have to accept that this is genuinely my karmic fate; so now what am I going to do?"

OZ: We became the darlings of the entire con. At the big banquet, they set up a special table just for speakers. Of course, I insisted that an extra place had to be set for Morning Glory! Right across from us was Isaac Bonewits, and he had two questions for us: "When are you going to get married? And can I perform the ceremony?" This was like twenty-four hours after we had met.

Well, we turned to each other and said, "Next year at the spring gathering." Because they were going to be having an Aquarian Festival and Witchmeet on the 1974 Spring Equinox. "And yes, you can perform the ceremony." And that was that; we just acted totally on impulse, even though we knew there was a lot that had to be resolved before it could happen. I mean, she had a loving husband and daughter and a whole community of friends out in Oregon.

MG: Gary and I had always had an open marriage, but it's quite another thing to have two primary relationships over two thousand miles apart. The whole drive back to St. Louis I was pretty much a basket case. I sat in the back seat weeping inconsolably. It was definitely a case of "be careful what you wish for"—it will come about, but at what cost? The price was my relationship with my husband and daughter and my wonderful community of friends in Eugene. I came to understand why the ancient Greeks feared the power of Aphrodite, the Goddess of Love; it was because Her gift was irresistible and caused lives to be torn apart and communities to be thrown into chaos.

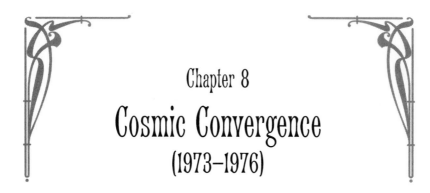

Chapter 8
Cosmic Convergence
(1973–1976)

We took our vows to never part
We pledged for Life and then for more.
You kissed my lips and stole my heart
In front of people by the score.

In velvet green, our wedding scene
Was filled with portent now and then.
I'd do it all the same again;
I'd do it all the same again.

—FROM "LOVE OF MY LIFE" BY MORNING GLORY ZELL, 1993

NARRATOR: Morning Glory and Tim did not have a lot of time to prepare for their wedding. MG was traveling back and forth between Eugene and St. Louis, where Tim was still a very busy man. The Church of All Worlds had invested in a real printing press, and *Green Egg* had gone "semipro": there was a wrap-around cover and articles by people like Robert Anton Wilson, and they were publishing a lot of advertising. So Tim Zell, as editor, publisher, and typist, had to do what basically became his second full-time job. Though *Green Egg* was doing a fantastic job of connecting Pagans with each other and nurturing the growth of earth-based spirituality, it was not a financial success. Tim and everyone else who worked on it were doing it voluntarily.

The relationship between Morning Glory and Tim was tumultuous from the start, and not helped by the environment Morning Glory suddenly found herself in. It was difficult for her to trade the lifestyle and mild climate she was used to for harsh winters and a rough, inner-city neighborhood.

MG: I was totally unprepared for living in a hard, cold, big city. I had been living in Hippie communes and a liberal college town. Here I was in a situation where I was with the person I was supposed to be with and this church that I loved. But his whole universe was wrapped around this organization that was embedded in this really awful big-city environment. Some people thought the city was great, but for me it was a nightmare. It wasn't safe to go out on the streets after dark. Two of the women in our community had been raped and brutally beaten. I grew to love most of the people in the church, but they were all part of this toxic environment and some of them were not at all supportive of Tim and me. They saw me as a self-righteous interloper; and to be perfectly frank, they were pretty spot-on about the self-righteous part. I just didn't get how people could deal with the noise, the pollution, and the violence; I was so homesick for Eugene that I was miserable and made other people around me resent me.

NARRATOR: And from the moment that they had first met, OZ and MG had had almost no privacy. Tim's house in St. Louis was a center of activity, and there were always people coming and going. That was the way he had lived his entire adult life. Finally, right before they were to be married in the spring of 1974, the couple had an opportunity to be alone together.

OZ: Some friends of ours who had a summer cabin in the Ozarks offered this to us for a weekend to go have a retreat and get ourselves together before the ceremony. We went down there, and it was beautiful—spring was springing forth all over the place. Flowers were all in bloom. We made a little fire in the fireplace, and we tripped on acid. In the process of this, we bonded in an amazing way.

Strongly in our minds at that time was the whole vision of the Awakening of Gaea, and the coalescence of planetary consciousness. We still hold that as a central myth in our lives and in our work. And one of the concerns that was going around among ourselves and our friends, who were also caught up in the Gaean mythos that we were developing at that time, was, "What happens when Gaea really does achieve consciousness? Do we all just get lost like drops of water in the ocean?"

Because we were so focused on this stuff (and the Magick, and our impending marriage), we became One. We were able to look out through each other's eyes, and completely be within each other. We had this epiphany that in the emergence of planetary consciousness we would not be lost as individuals, but rather our individual consciousnesses would expand into the larger awareness. So that rather than just seeing out of only one pair of eyes, we would see out of everyone's eyes. And everyone else would have that same experience.

We found that, in our combined essence, our general magickal capabilities were vastly expanded as well. We were sitting in a clearing in the middle of the woods. At one point we reached out to the sky and called out, and a hawk started circling around above us. We reached up and looked out of the eyes of the hawk, and we were able to look down and see ourselves and the forest all around us. We reached out and called butterflies, and swarms of butterflies came flying in from all over the place and landed on us. We called the wind, and the wind started picking up and whistling through the trees. We kept on doing that till the intensity got to be almost like a tornado, so we had to stop and slow it down. The wind slowly receded back to normal.

We picked violets to make violet jam, and it was the only time in our life when we were in a place where there were enough wild violets to do that. At the end of this retreat, when it was time to return home, we felt, "Okay, we know who we are." It was one of the great romantic high points of our life. We were totally bonded—forever.

NARRATOR: The Gnosticon in Minneapolis, where the wedding was scheduled to take place, was also being promoted as a "Witchmeet" where the newly formed (and short-lived) Council of American Witches was to create and adopt what is now known as "The Principles of Wiccan Belief," which were later incorporated into the U.S. Army's chaplains' handbook, in 1978.

But the real center of attention for the weekend was on April 14, 1974, when Morning Glory and Tim were handfasted and legally married in a huge Pagan ceremony.

MG: It was the very first public Pagan wedding ever; we wrote and created the entire ritual ourselves, and it was really stressful. Partly because I was trying to handle things at a convention that was hundreds of miles away from St. Louis, which is where I was living, plus I was still going back and forth to Eugene. I had brought Rainbow to live with us for a while, and she was only four years old and was very confused about the changes in our lives. Then at the con we had to set up a CAW booth, plus we were both keynote speakers. I wrote an article and did a speech about my own understanding of what being a Witch was, which was that it was a form of European shamanism. This was a very controversial idea at the time.

And it turned out that the date that we had picked, unbeknownst to us, was Easter Sunday. Just try and find flowers or a wedding cake on Easter Sunday! Plus I had friends flying in from all over the country. (Unfortunately, I couldn't afford to fly in my parents.) The wedding went off without too many hitches, pretty much. Tim and I both had tears streaming down our faces, but our voices were still strong enough that you could hear the words of our vows. We got all the way through it, and it was wonderful.

OZ: The story and photos appeared on the front page of the local paper, and they upstaged the Pope's Easter message to the world. Bryan was the ring bearer, and even my father attended it. Rainbow wore this little pink faerie gown and was the flower girl. She was given a basket of petals to scatter on the pathway for us to walk on. Not having any experience, or been given any instruction, she plucked the petals out of the basket one at a time and very carefully placed them on the carpet. Margot Adler sang Gwydion's "The Witches Coven Dance" song. Isaac and Carolyn performed the ceremony. Both of them had long hair down to their waist, and in the process of leaning over the altar, both of them set their hair on fire from the candles. That was very impressive and every-body applauded. Fortunately, neither of them were hurt.

At the dinner after the wedding, my dad sat with Morning Glory, the kids, and me. At one point I went off to the restroom, and one of the other people at the table asked my father how he felt coming to this thing and seeing that his son was such a prominent figure in the com-munity. He said, "I feel like I've given birth to the anti-Christ." But he said to me that he thought it was a very nice ceremony.

And then Morning Glory ended up getting quite ill.

MG: At the time I had a condition called abdominal epilepsy. And it was a seizure disorder that affected my stomach, bowels, and uterus—all my plumbing. So I would lose urinary control and bowel control and start vomiting. I had that disorder from the time I was a teenager. I had always had problems that were sort of like that from childhood, but it got worse when I hit puberty. I was on Dilantin, but I did not like to take it. That really screws up your red cells, and it has a lot of negative mental side effects also. I had heard about new research about alpha and theta waves, and that you could reprogram your brain out into a healthier pattern of rhythms and prevent seizure patterns from recurring. When I told my neurologist about this research, he didn't want to have to deal with it. He told me to take my medicine and not argue.

It just so happened that when Oberon and I got together, he had the right kind of biofeedback headset. So I was in the middle of the process of learning this new technique of seizure control, and I had also chosen, foolishly, this time to get the meds out of my system. So I was loaded down with all the stress of the wedding weekend, and on top of it Oberon and I had done some deep inner work and he had this whole vi-sion that when we got together something really significant was going to happen. But we didn't know exactly what it was going to be.

After the ceremony and dinner were over, we went back to the hotel suite. It was time for the consummation of the wedding, and *Wham!* I felt the beginning precursor wave of a seizure. And I thought, "Omigod, what am I going to do?" So at that point I took some of the women who were part of our intimate circle and already in our room aside, and I said,

"I need you take over for me, and be my proxy. Are any of you willing to help me with this?"

There were three women who happily volunteered and were in bed with Oberon, and so I lay down there next to them. I used the energy that was generated by them all to block the seizure and stop it from happening. So towards the end I was able to be a part of it. And that was my wedding night!

OZ: Morning Glory and I had spent months creating the ritual. We published it in *Green Egg* and it became the template for Pagan handfasting and wedding ceremonies throughout the community. Decades later we would encounter Pagan groups who pulled out their ancient, passed-down-through-the-ancestral-lines Book of Shadows—and we would discover that it was our ceremony they were using!

After the wedding Rainbow came back to St. Louis to live with us for a while. Morning Glory and I gave each other snakes as wedding presents. I gave her a baby male Burmese python, which she named Ananta, and she gave me a baby female boa constrictor I named Tanith. They grew up together.

Over the following months Morning Glory continued her studies towards ordination as a Priestess in CAW. We counted all the previous stuff she had done before, so she moved ahead pretty quickly and ended up being approved for ordination in about nine months.

At Lughnasadh, on the first of August, MG was scheduled to be ordained. Several of the folks in our community knew people with rural land, so we found ourselves with access to new sites. One place had a cave, a pond, and a marsh. In preparation for the festival, Michael Hurley's wife, who had a kid Rainbow's age, said she was going to be going back to that farm where we had held previous events and spend some time out there, and she invited Rainbow to come along. We said okay— we knew her, we knew her kids. Rainbow really wanted to go, and we thought that would be a lot of fun for her.

MG: The following weekend we went out to the place where we were having the ordination ceremony. Gary, who had come all the way from Oregon to be at my ceremony, went with us to the site of the gathering, and Orion drove to the farm to pick up Rainbow. When he got there with her, it was a shock. Her hair, which had never been cut in her life and had been down her back, had been cut short. She and all the other kids there had been dosed with LSD. This phony guru had shown up on the scene, and unbeknownst to any of us, the women we knew had become his followers. He was calling for people to bring their kids so that he could begin a new order and purify the kids with drugs. The guy's name was Gridley Wright. He believed that all children belonged to him, and that they should all be dosed with acid, and that the fathers should all bow out and acknowledge him as the alpha male, and of course the women should all be subservient to him. He had all the women shave their heads. I had no idea of any of this. The woman with whom I had trusted my daughter had been a strong feminist. But she had joined that cult. She had shaved her head and given my daughter as well as her son over to the cult.

GAIL SALVADOR [formerly Rainbow]: At first I was happy to be there. It was fun. There were other kids, and it was a communal, collective feel, but very rugged as well. The house was stripped down to a bare floor and cots. We were there for a few days, and then it changed. I went for a walk one day, and all of the foliage started dying. I kept walking, and I ended up down at the river. I was really afraid. There was another little girl who was laughing and having a good time. Then I started hallucinating even heavier. Giant anchors started falling out of the sky and into the water. Later I was on a blanket with a woman who was supposed to be my caregiver, and Gridley was on a blanket next to us. I think he was giving us the acid in Kool-Aid. He said, "Do you want to come with me?"

And I said, "No, I don't like you. You're a bad person." Then the whole earth cracked open on both sides of us. I said, "I want my mom, I'm scared." And he told me that my parents were dead and that I belonged to God.

MG: When Orion brought Rainbow to me and told the story, Gary and I went off with her alone in the woods, and we just held her and told her she was safe now and we weren't going to let those people ever come near her again. I was in a quandary, because on one hand I just wanted to take my child and leave but on the other, I did want to complete the ordination ritual that I had worked so hard for. So I asked Rainbow if she wanted to leave right now or stay for the ceremony, and by that time she was starting to have a good time with us and some of the other kids so she said that she wanted to stay. And that was my final ordeal before I went through my ordination ceremony; the symbolic ordeals that were part of the ritual were just that: symbolic. The real ordeal had torn my soul into pieces, and I was furious at myself and at the universe but most of all at this Gridley-monster and the women I had trusted. I took deep breaths and got myself centered and then made myself get through the ceremony, but then we packed up and left. We went back to the farm and confronted the guy.

OZ: I was absolutely livid. He had two biker guys who were his guards. I went into complete overdrive, in full warrior mode. At that time I had the ability to morph into incredibly fast, reflexive moves. I could snatch bats, butterflies, and hummingbirds out of the air, and catch striking snakes behind their heads. So as I charged in, I took two guns away from two different guys—a rifle, which I broke over my knee and threw into the swamp, and a pistol, which I tossed to MG. Once these guys had been disarmed, Gary was able to hold them at bay. I landed on Gridley, slammed him to the ground, and sat on his chest.

MG: I was haunted for years because Oberon took the guns away from two of the bikers, and I had the pistol and held it at this guy's head, and I could have pulled the trigger. I stopped and I didn't do it, because I knew that if I did that I would go to prison, and my daughter wouldn't have a mother. At that point I backed away and instead I called a curse down on his head—I asked the Mother Goddess to take him down for what he had done in his arrogance and madness.

You have to understand that our attitude about psychedelics was that these were sacred medicines; they were magical allies. No one should ever be forced or tricked into taking them; they were not tools for brain-washing, and to do this to a child was the ultimate betrayal of trust and profanation of the sacraments.

OZ: We tried to file charges against Gridley and got nowhere with that. You would think that the child protection agency or the police would want to do something. But they just figured that we were a bunch of Hippies, and we had left our kids with him, so we had no case. We were quite astonished by that. One cop actually said that they could prosecute us for trespassing and assault.

GAIL SALVADOR: After that I was really depressed. A lot of my parents' friends told me that I was never the same after that, that I wasn't the same happy-go-lucky kid. My innocence was gone. My dad took me back to Oregon. We hitchhiked back together. I hated hitchhiking. It used to terrify me. I felt insecure about the whole process.

MG: Years later we heard that Gridley Wright had fled the country and gone to India with his followers. He declared that none of them would be allowed to have any vaccinations or Western medicine; they were in a primitive commune. The children all got serious illnesses and died. A father who had been tracking him down got there a week after they buried his children. When he found out what happened, he pulled out a big knife, carved Gridley up (twenty-two stab wounds, the report said . . .), and left him. And because of the orders Gridley had given, his followers let him die slowly and painfully of septic poisoning. So it was Kali who took him in India, but it was at the hands of Shiva, the avenging father.

In retrospect, bringing my daughter to live with us in St. Louis was the biggest mistake I ever made in my life. There were a series of tragedies that happened when she was staying with us, such as the whole Gridley Wright thing. Partly that was because I was a new parent and my natural approach to child rearing was to shower my child with everything I ever wanted when I was a child, which was lots of freedom and adventures. I didn't understand until years later that you have to give a child what they want to have, not what you want to give them. In Rainbow's case, what she wanted was security, and that has never been important to me so it wasn't even on my radar.

I do need to say that my experiences in St. Louis were not all negative. It is important to remember and celebrate the good times, too. It was wonderful meeting all the people, making new friends, and learning about the hodgepodge of bio-theology, science-fiction mythos, complex ritual creation, family celebrations, Cheez-Its eating, magazine printing, and bad-pun-telling traditions that formed the Church of All Worlds in those days. Nest meetings were homey and down-to-earth, and since they changed with whoever was in charge of it that week, you got a large variety of experiences, a real communal spiritual smorgasbord. A Nest meeting could be anything from an all-out formal Wiccan-style Circle to a Tantric group meditation, or a trip to the zoo. It was and is a marvelously flexible way of worshipping, and when it is really practiced, it becomes the backbone of a strong spiritual community.

OZ: Don Wildgrube and Tom Williams started taking turns holding Nest meetings at their places. A gradual mitosis happened, and we ended up with two Nests. Don's Overland Nest was largely an entry-level group, with classes and teachings. The group that met at Tom's was the Dog Star Nest—the joke was that we were the Sirius group. That was mainly for the inner-circle people who had been around for a long time. We tried to schedule things in a way that they didn't conflict with each other, so some people could go to both. But there still arose a certain inevitable tension.

DON WILDGRUBE: I took over the central Nest. We would have an open house every Tuesday. Then on Friday or Saturday we would get together for our Nest meetings. The open house was for anybody who wanted to show up—that way we could weed out the people that we wouldn't invite back for the weekend meeting. For example, one guy was there and we were talking about nudity, because at our Nest meetings most people were nude. And this guy said, "If I have a problem with nudity, I'll just make loincloths for everybody."

NARRATOR: There was nothing else happening anywhere else in the world that was quite like the scene in St. Louis (and there still isn't today). Writer Margot Adler was doing research for what would become her book *Drawing Down the Moon* and visited the Nest to check the facts in person. The cutting-edge style of journalism at that moment was called "gonzo," which meant that the reporter became a part of the action that they were writing about. When Hunter S. Thompson was working on his groundbreaking book about the Hell's Angels, he got on a motorcycle and rode with them. So when Margot checked out the CAW, she didn't just watch and take notes.

MARGOT ADLER: CAW and the Zells were very into sexual experimentation. When I went to interview them in the fall of 1975, I spent a week living and sharing their life with them. I remember going to a CAW Hallowe'en party in St. Louis. I remember being very aware that there was a lot of sex going on, people pairing up and going into corners and stuff like that. I will confess that I was fairly prudish, and I found myself very uncomfortable. I was single, and at that point my response was to take the one person there that I really liked and disappear with him into a bedroom so I didn't have to deal with the all the other stuff that was going on.

At the same time, truth be told, I thought Tim and Morning Glory were beautiful, loving people: loving towards each other and towards me. I thought, "This is definitely not what I normally do, and I am not really comfortable, but I'm just going to throw myself into this and see what a threesome is like." I'm not a very sexual person. Now, in the present day, I've been living in a monogamous relationship for the past thirty-three years. So this was definitely not typical for me. But I remember they had a mirror on the ceiling of their bedroom. I would look up and feel that we were all in some Renaissance painting.

When I returned home I was very freaked out. I felt that I would have gone completely crazy if I'd lived their life for more than a week. It wasn't only the sex; there was a level of intensity that was hard to deal with. So, I went to a psychologist and said, "I don't know what I'm feeling about this. Should I have felt more comfortable? Is there something wrong with me?"

And she said, "You know, there are some people who are champion skiers. And there are some people who are champion tennis players. And these two people were champions at sex. And that doesn't have to be who you are." And I laughed with relief. So I ended up thinking: they were really good at sex, and incredibly open, warm, loving, and inviting. It was easy to get swept into their lives. But for me what was most important was realizing that their life was not my life. I had to make my peace with who I was.

MG: At the time I just thought everybody was like that. It's not that I thought everybody was like me, but I thought that most Pagans took this kind of Hippie/poly/sexuality thing as a matter of course. After all it was straight out of *Stranger in a Strange Land* and *Island* by Aldous Huxley. I guess because I was a Hippie Witch and Priestess of Aphrodite, I didn't see why we shouldn't be living the way the people were in the books. That was where I was coming from. I didn't think about other people having—I hesitate to use the word *hang-ups*, so we'll just say inhibitions about it. Because I just didn't have any inhibitions. A lot of the sexual adventures that I had around that time were kind of all joy and enthusiasm, and "Welcome to my bed," and "Welcome to my life," and "We're all gonna be lovers and friends, and it's gonna be a wonderful world." And I didn't realize that some people weren't comfortable with that. It never would have occurred to me in a million years.

NARRATOR: The Church continued to evolve. The individual members were also evolving, but not all at the same pace and in the same direction. MG tried her hardest to go with the flow, but, in spite of her best efforts, it didn't work out.

MG: One night I went to a laundromat and I took my snake with me—a six-foot Burmese python named Ananta. It was cold out, so he was tucked inside my clothes. While I was in the parking lot, two carloads of inner-city teenage boys pulled up, jumped out of the cars, and started heading my way and talking trash to me. After what had happened to the other women in our community, I could see my death looking at me, and every single pore in my body just squirted adrenaline. When that happened, Ananta smelled my fear, came out of my clothes like he was shot from a gun, and started making these loud hissing sounds like letting air out of a truck tire. The kids yelled, "Holy shit, man, that chick's got a snake!" and jumped back into their cars and rolled out of there. I got back in the car, locked the doors, held Ananta, and said, "Thank you, thank you, thank you! You saved my life!" I couldn't have been better defended if I had been packing a gun.

At that point I told Oberon, "I love you, but I can't live in this environment. I'm going. I've given you two years of my life, but I can't do this anymore. You can come and join me, but I know you have a whole life here. You have to choose. If you choose to stay here, I can't live here." It was the hardest decision I ever made.

OZ: At that point I would have agreed to anything to stay with her. I started telling people what was going to happen. This produced a reaction against her. When she had first arrived in St. Louis, Morning Glory had been welcomed and embraced. And she had made an effort to connect with people in the Church. She understood the value of the bonds that form between lovers and the levels of trust that occur. There is a certain loyalty and commitment you have to people you have slept with that you don't have with other people. But when it became clear that she was going to take me away from them, it created a backlash.

MG: It was hard on OZ. He was working full-time at a regular job, publishing the magazine, and running the Church. Even at that time I was quite amazed by the lack of respect he was routinely given by other members of the organization. Maybe I just didn't understand their personal style or their interpersonal history, but it seemed as though he was constantly fighting an uphill battle with these people who claimed to love him so much.

NARRATOR: At least one person that I interviewed said that there was talk about Morning Glory's relationship with the Church being comparable to the one that Yoko Ono had with the Beatles: Yoko got the blame for the band breaking up after she married John Lennon. (In this scenario, Tim Zell and Tom Williams were considered to be the CAW equivalent of Lennon and McCartney.) But listening to the later Beatles recordings, now it's clear that they were already in the process of going their separate ways before Yoko entered the picture—in fact, it's amazing that they stayed together as long as they did.

The same might be said for what happened with Tim Zell and the Church of All Worlds. After all, this was a group of people that had partly modeled themselves after a spaceship crew that was on a five-year mission. More than five years had passed since the Nest had gathered in front of a TV to watch *Star Trek* every week. It was, for Tim, time to prepare for his next mission: to explore strange new worlds, to seek out new life and new civilizations. To boldly go where no one had gone before!

OZ: November 30, 1975, was my thirty-third birthday. Thirty-three is a significant year in many men's lives. Both Jesus and Alexander the Great died at that age! On my birthday, I resigned from my job as director of social services at the Chouteau Russell Center of the Human Development Corporation. They threw a great big going-away party for me. After nine years on and off, I had been there longer than anybody.

But at that point I'd had enough of that kind of work. I was working more and more with abused women through the family-counseling program. I would try to help them get out of the bad situation, and I had a huge emotional investment in that. Being a man, I felt a personal responsibility to redress the suffering they had experienced at the hands of other men. But invariably, after we had put all this energy and resources into getting these women away from the abusive bastards, they would go back to them. They'd be back in my office a month later covered with bruises again. And then one of them was murdered by her ex-husband whom she'd taken back. I didn't have any real training in how to deal with this. I just didn't understand why they did it. It cost me a lot emotionally, and when it was time to leave, I didn't ever want to go back.

Now there are recovery programs and whole institutions set up to deal with these situations, but there wasn't any of that stuff at that time. In my entire background and years of study in college and special training seminars, I never got any information about abuse, childhood sexual molestation, alcoholism, drug addiction, or recovery programs. Today most of the field of social psychology is about addiction therapy and abusive relationships, but at that time these situations were treated as individual anomalies, not as a widespread phenomenon or syndrome.

As part of our plan for leaving, we started liquidating things. Most of my vast library I donated to the Church. I started training Tom Williams to be my successor as editor of *Green Egg*, and by the time we left, it was completely in his hands. In December of 1975 we rented out my house, leaving the furnishings, and moved out of it. For a while we crashed with Tom and had our stuff in storage. Bryan continued to stay with Martha and go to school. He entirely cut himself off from us, refusing even to talk to us on the phone. This really hurt a lot, but it was his choice, and I had to accept it.

BRYAN ZELL: I purposely avoided my dad and stepmother during the time of transition when they were getting ready to move out to the West Coast in the school bus. Morning Glory would call and ask for me, and I would refuse to talk to her because I was afraid they were going to kidnap me.

OZ: We bought a used school bus (a 1954 Chevy), about twenty-five feet long. It had a five-foot-nine-inch ceiling, and I'm 5' 10", so that made it difficult to walk around inside. We started fixing it up to put it on the road. I designed, cut, and constructed an elaborate RV-type interior. I made seats that converted into benches and beds, tables that would fold up and down, a ten-foot-long kitchen, a toilet, a closet, and a whole side for bookcases and animal cages. Since it was already painted red, we named it the "Scarlet Succubus." It's one of those magickal things—you give a name to virtually everything that has any investment of energy. We refer to it as "animating inanimate objects." The bus had previously belonged to a fundamentalist church, and we left the name of the church painted on the side. It was a great disguise. Later, as we traveled, we were able to stay overnight in church parking lots, and nobody bothered us.

In June 1976, we left for good. I settled up with Martha. We got together and figured out what she would want for her equity in the house, which I then gave to her. Then I put the house into the name of the Church. The idea would be that after we left they would sell it, and then the money would be transferred into the branch of the Church we were going to set up in Oregon. We would then have a foundation for whatever we were going to do. It seemed like a perfectly good plan to me. Money itself has never really been particularly important to me. Maybe it should have been more so.

MG: A number of people who loved him dearly tried to talk him out of this. They said, "This is your life savings. Suppose the board of directors changes, and they're not your friends? You could lose everything."

And Oberon was like, "No, no, that could never possibly happen. We're all in this together."

NARRATOR: From the beginnings of modern Paganism, and continuing on up to the present, there seems to have been an unwritten rule within the community that the "clergy," in whatever way the people involved care to define that term, are not to be paid. People in positions of service to their Pagan groups are more often than not expected to somehow take care of themselves and their own finances—even if what they're doing is full-time work, and they have duties that would be properly compensated for in some other religion. There are those who have been performing services at births, weddings, funerals, and other rites of passage for decades who now have no retirement funds, insurance, or any place to live out their old age that is connected to the spirituality they've dedicated their lives to.

Which is not to say that they are not loved or in or other ways rewarded. People do these things voluntarily. But their lives can be tough. Tim Zell was not paid for his years of service in St. Louis, and as we have seen, he in fact personally helped finance the Church and its publications. He made a lot of sacrifices, not thinking about what might happen to his own security. The decision to donate his house to the Church was just one more sacrifice, and not one that would work out as he hoped it would after he left St. Louis.

OZ: After paying off Martha, most of the money I'd saved went into the bus itself. It was a matter of completely cutting loose and casting myself into the unknown. I had no idea of what I would do to make a living once we got to the West Coast.

On our last night in St. Louis, we stopped by our old house, parked the bus in the driveway, and went to sleep. We were going to get up the next morning and leave. But it turned out there was still a warrant out for my arrest.

The first week when Morning Glory moved to St. Louis, one night the police showed up at the doorstep and hauled me off to jail. That was not a good way to start things off. Orion, who was crashing with us at the time, had been working on his car and had a bunch of parts spread out in the driveway. He went into the house to make himself some lunch. When he came back he put the car back together, and we thought that was the end of it.

But I was under continual harassment by an ex-fraternity "brother" who had become a city prosecutor. He really hated me because I had rebelled against the fraternity system. When he found out I was living in his town, he kept having me arrested on one trumped-up charge after another. One time, when my iguana, Gryf, got loose, I was charged with "harboring a dangerous animal"! I'd go to court and the charges were always dismissed. I didn't even have to hire a lawyer. In this particular case I was charged with littering—in my own driveway! This one was also dismissed, but somehow some lingering echo of it remained.

So there we were, sleeping in the bus, and there was a knock on the door.

MG: The police were beating on the door and trying to get in. They had another warrant for his arrest. The door was locked. We didn't have any curtains on the windows, so they could look in. So we just pulled the covers over our heads and lay *verrry* still—because the monsters can't get you when you're under the covers! They finally gave up and went away. At that point we jumped up, put our clothes on, and hit the road for Oregon.

Chapter 9
The Magick Land
(1976–1979)

We wandered West and made a Home
With Unicorns and baby deer;
When round the country I would roam,
I knew I'd always find you near.

Adventures bold and Dreams we told;
We never knew just where or when.
I'd do that part the same again;
I'd do that part the same again.

—FROM "LOVE OF MY LIFE" BY MORNING GLORY ZELL, 1993

NARRATOR: By 1976, when the Zells headed west in the Scarlet Succubus, a new age had dawned. Or, to be more precise, *the* New Age, which was a label used to describe all the spiritual/metaphysical/occult kind of activity that had sprouted up in the wake of the '60s. Hippies weren't a "counterculture" anymore—their haircuts and clothes had generally either gone away or been absorbed by mainstream society. The Dionysian ecstasy that had started at the Woodstock festival had become a part of the corporate music machine in the '70s, and drugs and sexual freedom were there for anyone who wanted them, not just the young and rebellious. (And there was an even larger menu of drugs and sex to choose from.)

The draft and the war in Vietnam had both ended a few years earlier, not too long before Nixon had left the White House in shame. A Democrat (and peanut farmer) named Jimmy Carter was elected president. Everything just seemed kind of mellow.

The 1970s were nicknamed "The Me Decade" by journalist Tom Wolfe, and he was referring to the social change from political activism to personal growth. After working to do what they could for the world, people were starting to look at what they could do for themselves, and New Age activity was a part of that. Lots of different things were considered to be New Age, including stuff like pyramid power, crystals, astrology, and Tarot readings. The New Age was open to the public and becoming very commercial and popular. Pagans were still mostly underground, but as a result of the New Age phenomenon they had access to more resources, and eventually each other. The center of all this kind of activity was California, of course, and that was where the Zells stopped off on their way to Oregon.

MG: It was great to do a Circle with Ed Fitch in Southern California and then later on go up to Northern California to do a Circle with Gwydion. It was so exciting to see Witches and Pagans everywhere I went, in places where you would never think to find them—even in Orange County, where I went to high school. One evening my dad came to pick us up from a full-moon ritual; he was asked what he thought about having a daughter who was a Priestess and he said, "My old man was a preacher, and as far as I can tell, she's just some other kind of preacher. Doesn't matter what kind; they're all the same to me." But my mom was really happy to meet Oberon, since he was all I'd ever talked about from the day I met him. She always was happy to love the people I loved.

NARRATOR: Before they got to Oregon, the Zells went to a Solstice party at Greenfield Ranch. Tim fell in love with the land and decided he wanted to live there some day. And both Tim and MG met many new friends along the way.

CERRIDWEN FALLINGSTAR: I first met the Zells in 1976. Alison Harlow held a big Summer Solstice festival at Coeden Brith ("Speckled Forest," her parcel on Greenfield Ranch). I saw Morning Glory dancing and was very attracted. After the festival there was an afterparty at Alison's in Palo Alto that some of us attended. I saw them there and went up to Alison, suggested that I was interested in them, and she said, "Well, if you play your Tarot cards right, you could probably end up with them tonight."

So I approached Tim rather than Morning Glory, because I was a woman who had never been turned down by a guy. I felt confident, even though in some ways it was Morning Glory that I really had eyes for. But they were a package deal, and so were my husband and I at that time (he was not with me at that party). The three of us did end up getting together and making love that night. When I went back to L.A., I told my husband about these fine people I had encountered. He met them later on, also liked them, and we embarked on about a five-year affair with them.

I became Rainbow's honorary aunt and Goddess-mother. Even after I wasn't romantically involved with her mother and stepfather, I continued to see her. They would send her down to spend time with us.

MG: The day we finally arrived back in Eugene, I was ecstatic! We pulled our bus into a parking place at my friend Lucy's house, where Catherine was visiting. The other folks staying there were the Flying Karamazov Brothers—a traveling troupe of jugglers and stage performers that were regulars at the Oregon Country Fair. Everyone piled out of the house to welcome us and supervise while we parked the Succubus. Howard and Paul were using batons to guide us into place like an aircraft ground crew, and then more people arrived with musical instruments from a marching band. Talk about a real "Welcome Home"! I was so relieved to be back in my own town with my own people.

OZ: Later, we met Anna Korn, who lived in an all-women communal house with a long driveway next to it.

ANNA KORN: I was in graduate school in biology in Eugene. Right after the Zells moved there, they had put a notice up in a women's bookstore. I guess most of the people in Eugene weren't aware of *Green Egg* at that point, but I knew what it was. So I contacted them and invited them to my house for dinner. We all hit it off, and I invited them to join our collective household.

The next day, they parked the Scarlet Succubus alongside our house in the driveway, and ran an extension cord through our bathroom window. They would use the phone and kick in for the electric bill. And so we just shared things. If they got a phone call, we would go to the bathroom, lean out the window, and knock on the side of the bus. My roommates, even though they weren't all Pagans, felt that it was peculiar and interesting to have them around.

One of the first things they did, as I recall, is they got a teaching position in the extension courses of the local Lane Community College, where they taught a course called "Witchcraft, Shamanism, and Pagan Religion" for three trimesters. It was really quite a good survey course. The students in the course would come to Circles that we had, and formed the core of a little group of Pagans in Eugene. We formed a coven called *Ithil Duath*, which is Elvish for "Moon Shadow."

MG: I really was hoping that Gary, Oberon, and my daughter could all become one family, but too much water had gone under the bridge at that point. Gary was living in an apartment and didn't want to give that up. I tried, but I couldn't make my two universes come together.

GAIL SALVADOR: In Eugene I stayed with them sometimes in the bus, but I went back and forth. It was a bus! That's not where you raise a kid. With my dad I had my own room. In the bus I had a bunk.

I would always have them drop me off blocks from school. I didn't want them to come to school. But one time, though, my mom did come to my school on Hallowe'en. She was all dressed up as a Witch. And she told a ghost story to the entire school. And everybody thought I was the coolest thing ever after that. Sometimes they would bring the snakes to school for show and tell, and then it came in handy to have the freaky, weird parents. This was in the third grade.

For a little while as a pre-teen I did embrace the Witch spirituality. I guess I decided that a lot of people involved in that world are drama geeks, and I am not a drama geek. I don't have a theatrical side to my personality.

I'm a very pragmatic, practical person. I like my reality. My therapist says that your personality is completely formed by the time you are three. So basically I was scrambling for stability as a child, because I didn't have it at all.

Oberon was a fun guy, like a kid himself. I used to love the way he cooked, because he fried everything. When you're a kid it doesn't get any better than that. But he went through this really weird George Orwell–esque phase where he thought the world was going to end in 1982. We'd be staying up late listening to talk radio or something, and he'd be like, "Oh yeah, it's all gonna end in 1982." He had me convinced for a little while there that that was it, that I only had a few years left. This still pisses me off now, because I would never do that to my daughter.

OZ: I got very caught up on a 1974 book called *The Jupiter Effect* by astronomer John Gribbin. He proposed that on March 10, 1982, a rare planetary alignment of Mercury, Venus, Earth, Mars, Jupiter, Saturn, and Pluto on the same side of the sun could trigger a series of geological events that might spawn devastating earthquakes and massive tidal waves. It was much like the later mythos around the year 2012, and I felt I needed to spread the word so that people would be prepared. But I deeply regret conveying these concerns to our kids, as it cast a Damoclean shadow over their lives for many years—much like the shadow of a seemingly inevitable nuclear apocalypse that had haunted my own youth. I learned a profound lesson from this: never promote a mythos that has no future, especially to the next generation,

NARRATOR: Along the way, Tim and Morning Glory had come up with their idea to raise Unicorns, which they eventually did, and we'll learn more about that in the next chapter. So whatever plans they were making and wherever they were traveling, this was on their minds as their eventual goal.

MG: The hitch in all this was where we were going to do this thing with Unicorns. I desperately wanted to stay in Eugene with my family and my community, but we couldn't seem to manage to find a real place to stay. My idea was to connect with some folks who had land that were looking for people to rent space or to work on a nearby farm where we could raise the animals, where there were barns and so forth. There were a fair number of properties of that nature still around the area.

Then we had a phone conversation with our friend Alison Harlow, who owned the 220-acre parcel called Coeden Brith on Greenfield Ranch in California. Gwydion and Alison had had a falling out, and he had moved off the land that he and Alison had originally talked about becoming partners on. She was offering to let us live there for free in exchange for being caretakers! We were friends with both Alison and Gwydion, and we thought, "Well, maybe if we move down there we could kill two birds with one stone. We could raise Unicorns, and maybe we can manage to patch up the rift between Gwydion and Alison." We were very naïve in those days about these kinds of things!

MG: The idea was that Rainbow would come and live with us, and go back and forth. By that time she was seven, and I let her decide where she wanted to live. And she opted to stay with her father because he had electricity, running water, and television.

I wasn't eager to leave behind my daughter again. But I felt that since Oberon had moved away from St. Louis to be with me, I had to move with him this time. I went ahead and caved in because I could not bear to be parted from Oberon. But I was pretty bitter, angry, and unhappy about it. I felt that he was making me chose between my child and him. I couldn't verbalize my anger, or entirely even bring it up into consciousness. But it was there. A million times a day, all of our stresses of living in a school bus kept bringing these things up and out. We were both headstrong people, and we were always butting heads and constantly bickering. I can see that it wasn't a very appealing thing for a child to want to live in a school bus on raw unimproved land with no running water or electricity with two bickering adults. But at least Rainbow decided to come and visit us in the summer when school was out.

OZ: So on July 4, 1977, we arrived at Greenfield Ranch, posting our old "Did You Remember to Dress?" sign at the gate. We told Alison what we were going to do with the Unicorns and got her involved in the project. To this end, the three of us formed the Holy Order of Mother Earth

(HOME) as a monastic order of stewardship and ritual, and chartered it as a subsidiary of the Church of All Worlds.

ALISON HARLOW: The Zells and I were close friends. I loved them both very, very much. They were living on my land for free, but it was a benefit for me to have them there because they were taking care of things. Oberon had gotten his Unicorn idea some years prior. It seemed like an interesting thing to try to do. Nobody else was doing it. I had to advance them the money to pay for the livestock, but they did ultimately pay me back.

OZ: We pulled up to the parking spot on Coeden Brith and immediately shed all of our clothes. It was hotter than blazes. Ace, the Ranch caretaker, showed up in a pickup truck and said, "Let's go up to the pond and take a dip." We got as far as the Ranch House and the fire alarm was going off. There we were, stark naked in the back of a pickup truck, and the entire Ranch was mobilizing to go fight a forest fire!

We dashed into the Ranch House and managed to find something to put on in the free box of discarded clothes. We then spent the entire day and night fighting the fire. In the night, roots underground were catching fire and glowing. You'd walk around the landscape and it was like Dante's *Inferno*. Many people became seriously sick from breathing the smoke of burning poison oak. That was our first day in our new home!

After the fire we got to meet more of the people who were living there. We were told by several of them that we should connect with Anodea Judith, as she was another Pagan, so we resolved to look her up. Several folks who owned a parcel together had a dairy, and they called it the "Udder Truth." MG and I hiked on up there, and there was a cow with human feet sticking out from under it. We looked over the top of the cow, and there was a long-haired, blond Hippie girl down there milking it.

ANODEA JUDITH: One morning I was milking a cow, up in the shed, and Oberon and Morning Glory came up to visit and were standing on either side of me, and they said, "Anodea, we have come for you." They took me up to their bus, and I think I came out three days later.

We became fast and furious friends. We really related on a meta-physical level. I was already doing rituals and things on my own before I met them, so things kind of linked right up. We started working to-gether producing events, Circles, and magickal trainings. Before I met them I had mostly been doing rituals with women, because I hadn't known any men that were into it.

OZ: We hadn't been up on the Ranch for too long before Orion also moved there from St. Louis, followed soon by Michael (later Brendan) Hurley. Some of our closest Pagan friends on the Ranch in the early years were Bran and Moria Starbuck. Moria was (and is) a truly gifted graphic artist and sculptor, who turned me on to Sculpey (a kind of modeling material that could be baked hard in a regular oven) and thus helped launch my own eventual career in sculpting. They had moved up from Los Angeles shortly before we arrived, and settled on the parcel that had orig-inally been "reserved" for Morning Glory and me. It was in part to accom-modate them that Alison agreed to let us move onto her land instead.

Across the valley from us were Marylyn Motherbear and her family. Troll was her second husband and the father of four of her six kids. They became some of our closest friends. They were fundamental homesteaders, and had once worked with Stewart Brand on the legend-ary *Whole Earth Catalog*. They built a huge, sprawling farm and a vast house that was always being worked on. They had a bunch of kids, and that's why she took the name "Motherbear." Morning Glory and I be-came aunt and uncle to their kids (including LaSara Firefox). We often spent Thanksgivings and other holidays with them. It was quite a hike across the valley, through the creek, and up the ridge to get there from where we were. Getting around the Ranch was not always easy.

One of the things Greenfield Ranch was famous for was rattlesnakes. Gwydion wanted to rename the place "Rattlesnake Acres," because he felt that Greenfield sounded too attractive. One of his favorite songs that he used to sing at parties was "The Last Resort" by the Eagles. There was a line in it about how if you call a place paradise, you can kiss it goodbye. The idea being that if you make it sound really attractive, everyone wants to move there, and before long it is overcrowded and polluted. So Gwydion was always agitating to emphasize the less desirable aspects of country life.

MG: Gwydion had a gift for what we sometimes call "toxic nomenclature." He named a meadow on Coeden Brith "the Battlefield" after a dream he had about a Native American testing ground, and he and Alison fought over it for years. He named his truck the Red Dragon and it blew up and burned a piece of his land. And of course he named his land Annwfn, the Celtic Underworld, and now he's buried there. But we were all into naming everything and everywhere—it's a very animistic thing. Oberon and I most often drew our nomenclature from Tolkien and Greek mythology.

MG: Rainbow spent summers with us, and in the winter she would go live with Gary and go to school in Eugene. We developed this rhythm of the seasons, sort of like the story of Demeter and Persephone. I would go spend Christmas, birthdays, and spring break with her in Eugene. After a year or two of that, she did stay with us for one year and went to the Ranch school.

She had a bunk bed inside the vehicle, but she couldn't take the crowdedness, so we built her a treehouse fort outside to go to when she wanted to get away; we fixed it up with cushions, blankets, and dishes so she could even spend the night there if she wanted to, but she was not too keen on sleeping alone in the woods. I never understood the idea of being scared in the woods because I loved it so much even when I was a little kid. I was always wandering off and getting lost because I didn't worry about that sort of thing. The forest always seemed like a safe haven to me, but I came to realize that's not how many folks think of it.

GAIL SALVADOR: When I went to visit them, I had to take the Greyhound bus by myself. I hated that stupid bus. I never had any bad experiences, but it just stunk. People could smoke cigarettes on the bus back then. And for some reason, the bus always left at three in the morning, so we had to get down there in the middle of the night. I tried to go to school on the Ranch, but it was a Hippie school and it was not working for me. I had dyslexia, and I needed more than what was being provided.

MG: Actually, in spite of both the public schools and the private school that Gary sent her to, when Rainbow was ten years old she still could not read, so I finally put my foot down because I did not want to have an illiterate child who would suffer for it her whole life. So I told her that she was going to spend the next winter with us, and we would make sure she learned to read. She didn't like it, but it worked. There was no TV or mall or other distractions through the long winter months of rain, and the only other kids lived miles away on twisted muddy roads.

But what we were rich in was books, lots of books—and especially lots of comic books. OZ is a comics collector, and he turned her on to *ElfQuest* comics by Wendy and Richard Pini, which was a turning point in her life in many ways. The pictures told the story, but it made her want to learn to read the words and find out more. Then we would work with her sounding out the words until she got it and something clicked in her head and the words finally made sense. After that she never looked back, and she started reading for pleasure: first comics, then kids' books, and finally full-length novels. She once told me years later that was the point at which she became a time-binding being; she learned to judge duration by the six-week intervals she had to wait for the next installment of *ElfQuest*.

GAIL SALVADOR: Oberon and Morning Glory had a really intense relationship. They fought very intensely for years. The whole time they were on Greenfield, they fought like cats and dogs. They had screaming matches that would go on for days. They moved to the woods because they thought it was going to be all groovy and harmonious, and all they did was try to kill each other.

CERRIDWEN FALLINGSTAR: Oberon and Morning Glory fought constantly. It was distressing to my husband and me to see them fighting, and they kept trying to pull us in. So we would talk to them and try to give them a different perspective, and then they would get back together and do it all over again. There was no commitment on their part to learn to be responsible with their emotions, to treat each other and their kid responsibly.

They never fought with us. We didn't have those kinds of conflicts with them. But it became more difficult to be around them. I think that part of it was that life on Greenfield was hard. They were living in a very small bus on a remote piece of land. I'm sure they got on each other's nerves, and that their circumstances were very challenging.

MG: OZ and I were both strong, independent personalities, and we both had a stubborn streak about always having to be right in any argument. Part of it was that we were so much alike in so many ways that when we came upon a real difference, we just couldn't abide it. Also both of us tried to always have the last word in any conflict. Talk about "cabin fever"! Cooped up in a school bus all winter long for many years was more propinquity than we were prepared to deal with. But at the same time we had a personal mythos that we were an ideal couple of soulmates. Gwydion joked around that he would not be surprised to visit us someday and find me cooking Tim for dinner.

OZ: We loved each other desperately and had worked so hard to carve out a life where we could be together 24/7, but once we had that ideal life it didn't seem so ideal, especially to Morning Glory. She really missed her family and friends in Eugene and resented me for leaving there to come to Greenfield. I kept trying to do things to make her happy, but you can't "make" another person be happy. They have to do that for themselves, and at the time I just didn't get it.

MG: There were lots of wonderful things about living on the Ranch so close to Nature that I loved, but it was a very hard and uncompromising existence. It might have been a lot easier if we had enough money to buy some basic amenities like a hot water heater or a refrigerator. But we arrived with just the bus and its contents. We didn't even have a second car, so that anytime we wanted to go grocery shopping, we either had to catch a ride with someone else or we had to drive the twenty-five-foot school bus down the mountainside to town.

NARRATOR: The Zells didn't have any money and had a hard time surviving on Greenfield Ranch, just as they'd had in Eugene. They kept expecting that they'd get some cash from the sale of the house that used to belong to Tim in St. Louis, but there had been some major changes in the

Church after they had left town. Tom Williams had taken over as editor of *Green Egg,* but within a year he quit and moved out to California, too. There was one more issue after he left, and then the magazine folded. Tim's house was sold, but after paying off the remaining debt on the loan for it and other fees, there was only about $2,000 left, and that was then controlled by a newly elected CAW board of directors, only two of whom were personal friends of the Zells. Half of that money was used to pay off bills that had been accumulated by publishing *Green Egg,* and the rest was eventually sent to California. All the remaining back issues of *GE* got taken to the dump. The whole CAW in the Midwest ended up crumbling in the next year or two. A couple of outlying Nests survived because they were family-based and continued to meet. But the foundational infrastructure of the central Church itself collapsed.

OZ: Bryan was still in St. Louis. We weren't really in touch with him. That is one of the things I regret. During the final months in St. Louis and while we were putting the bus together, we tried to phone him many times. But every time we were told that he didn't want to talk to us. So eventually we just gave up. I wasn't in contact with him for a number of years. After we moved to the Ranch, we didn't even have a phone. I could have written, but I didn't. I kind of dropped off the map. Just disappearing was somehow part of the whole thing of going to live in the woods. And since *Green Egg* was no longer being published, I didn't have any way to keep in touch with all the people I used to know.

MARTHA TURLEY: I think the worst thing Tim did in regard to Bryan was having nothing to do with him once he left St. Louis. I don't know why he did that. He always loved Bryan so much when he was younger. It was like he just gave up that whole world when he moved out there. Bryan was upset. Tim never wrote to him or sent him any cards.

BRYAN ZELL: I didn't hear from my dad for years. I had no idea where he was or what he was doing. I believed that Dad didn't want to pay child support. My stepfather wanted to have the law pursue him for that, but my mom refused. She didn't want that to happen.

But I don't think my dad should feel guilty about not being there. There were times I didn't want him to be there. I was afraid of change, and I needed some stability in my life. After knowing what he went through after leaving St. Louis, I feel I made the right decision. So I forgive him for that. But I often wonder where I'd be now if I'd gone with him; that's something in the back of my mind all the time.

NARRATOR: With help from some Pagan friends in California (including Gwydion, who had previously worked for the IRS), Tim was able to get the CAW incorporated in California on September 14, 1978, but they had no money to do anything with it. It would not be until 1985 that the church would truly come back to life again.

But OZ has never been the kind of person who would let finances stop him from pursuing a dream. While the CAW was inactive, and before he got totally absorbed in raising Unicorns, he and MG hooked up with some people in the Bay Area who were forming a group called the Covenant of the Goddess. It was going to be an umbrella organization that would provide a legal structure for little groups that were not legally incorporating to join underneath it for legal protection. The Zells would take trips away from the Ranch to work on that, which led them into an unexpected adventure.

OZ: Throughout my life I've been involved in every effort I could possibly get involved in to form associations and alliances to try to create a game that everybody could play in. I've always felt that there needed to be someplace that all the different Pagan groups could come together. Most of these—like the Council of Themis—were short-lived. But the Covenant of the Goddess was destined to become a significant one.

This involved a lot of trips to different places. One of the first ones was down in L.A. Allison and Gwydion went with us on our bus. One of the people down there was Poke Runyon. At one point, Poke came up to me and said he wanted to make an apology for having been such an ass many years before when we were both involved with the Council of Themis. I accepted, and we smoked a peace pipe together. It was quite nice. We've gotten along ever since.

A few months later, in February 1978, we were doing the same thing up in Seattle, continuing to recruit people for the Covenant of the Goddess. While we were up there, Morning Glory got a call from her mom. Her dad had had a serious heart attack and was in the hospital and wasn't expected to live. She left and flew to L.A. That left me all by myself on the Scarlet Succubus.

Driving back home through the Pacific Northwest, I was looking at postcards of things in the area, and one of them showed Stonehenge. It was restored—not the ruins that you normally see. I turned the card over and read that it was quite nearby, in Maryhill, Washington.

So I went to check it out. It was amazing—a full-scale concrete replica of Stonehenge as it had originally looked before it fell into ruins. It was out in the middle of nowhere. I was able to find out that it had been built by railroad executive Samuel Hill as a memorial for the people who had died in World War I. He had this notion, which was popular among people in those days, that Stonehenge had been built by the Druids as a temple where human sacrifices were conducted. Of course that is not a true account of what happened at the original Stonehenge, but it gave him a justification to do it. He picked the location because it was the only place in North America where two paths of solar eclipses would ever cross. They would form an "X marks the spot." The first crossing had been in 1921. And the next one was due in 1979, on February 26! The altar stone in the center of the ring of the Stonehenge had been laid into place for the eclipse in 1921. Subsequently everything else—trilithons, heelstone, menhirs, portal stones, and the great outer ring of lintel-capped stones—was built around it. It was all prepared for this coming eclipse—just a year away!

I was blown away by the whole idea. It occurred to me then that we ought to do something about it. Shortly afterwards, two events occurred. One was the Oregon Country Fair, which was the weekend before the Fourth of July, followed by the Rainbow Family Gathering, which was happening in Oregon that year. I went back to Greenfield Ranch, and Morning Glory returned from Los Angeles. MG was sick with the flu and didn't feel like going to Oregon, so Rainbow and I hitchhiked up to Oregon together.

We went to the Oregon Country Fair and were hanging out with the Flying Karamazov Brothers and their friends, many of whom were performers. I decided it would be a great time to trip. There was a huge tree with a multilevel treehouse built in its branches, like the flets of Lothlorien. I was up there for quite a while, and I had an amazing vision. I saw a black sun over a trilithon, and heard the following words: "The prophecies will come when shadow mates with sun. Be there. You know where." This burned itself into my brain. I came down from this and started drawing pictures with the date and verse on it and putting them around places. Shortly after that, Rainbow and I went to the Rainbow Gathering, and I handed out cards with the image and date on it.

After the Rainbow Gathering, I continued to print up flyers and send them out to people. Of course this was in the days before email. But it still got around a lot. We started making plans for going up to the Maryhill Stonehenge and doing a ceremony for the eclipse.

At that same time, MG and I were on the land, planning on raising Unicorns. We were building pens and barns and looking for suitable livestock and setting everything into place. During that time we were mostly engaged in that process. But we were also preparing for the eclipse ceremony. We contacted other Pagan leaders we knew—mostly people from the newly formed Covenant of the Goddess. The Stonehenge was on the property of the Maryhill museum—we contacted them and got their permission. They were enthusiastic and cooperative in every way.

The following February, up at Maryhill, the museum curators talked to the local media about the upcoming eclipse and the plans for a huge Pagan ritual there, and set up a press conference for a few days before the event. When we all got there, we explained to the media what we were going to do. They said that we were crazy. It was the middle of winter, and in that part of the country you can rarely see the sky at that time of year because it's so rainy and cloudy all the time. So Isaac popped up and said, "We've got a bunch of weather workers with us. We'll just clear the clouds out of the way." We realized that we had to actually deliver on that!

On the day of the ritual, people started showing up. The museum had put out port-a-potties. The police were there to direct traffic. More than three thousand people drove up and started setting up camp.

The night before the eclipse some folks built a fire in the middle of the Stonehenge circle. They began to play drums and dance. As people danced around the fire, they cast shadows on the stones. The size of the shadows exactly matched the size of the stones. It was as if the stones had been built specifically to be screen backdrops for shadows of dancers. We recalled that one of the obscure and odd names of Stonehenge was "The Giants' Dance." And that was what we were seeing—the stones themselves appeared to be dancing. The energy was incredible. At one point the energy was so intense that we all lifted our hands up to the sky and screamed. There was a clear sky up above us, and nothing but stars. Not a cloud. We looked at each other and said, "Okay, we've done our work here."

We got up at dawn, put on our ritual robes, and processed through the morning mist. The crowd parted as we approached the altar stone.

As the sun rose and the edge of it started being eaten away by the moon, we began chanting the most effective, universal weather chant: "Rain, rain, go away, come again some other day." And the clouds parted. The sky went completely clear. It was an utterly blue, clear sky. We looked off towards the distant horizon and we saw, heading towards us, the shadow of the moon rippling across the landscape. And then we were engulfed in shadow. The sky went completely black, and stars came leaping out. All the birds that were flying squawked and dove for cover because they thought night had suddenly fallen. You could hear cows mooing and lowing as they went to lie down to sleep. There up in the sky above us was this great eye. Because when the surface of the sun was completely covered by the moon, what leaped out from behind it was the corona. It looks like the iris of an eye, with the pupil at the center of it. And we suddenly understood the image of the eye of God that you see on the back of a one dollar bill and in all kinds of Masonic and ancient art. It's the image of a solar eclipse.

ANODEA JUDITH: We did a Nature ritual inside the Stonehenge. It was early in the morning, and I played the Element of Air. What an eclipse is, is that the moon goes in front of the sun; that is what is literally happening. So for our ritual we had a woman carry a big Venus of Willendorf statue. She was playing the moon, and we had somebody playing the sun.

So it was the Goddess coming in front of the sun, and the feminine kind of eclipsing the masculine and getting some notice. And I think at that time the feminine was really starting to come back alive. People were starting to rediscover the Goddess, and we were bringing notice in the world to the feminine. Not that the feminine is better than the masculine, but it had been so repressed and hadn't been seen. So for a short time it got to stand out in front of the masculine.

OZ: It was at that same time that the planet Pluto moved into the solar system, inside the orbit of Neptune. Normally it lies outside of it—it has this long elliptical orbit. For a twenty-year period it would be inside the orbit of Neptune and therefore inside the solar system. That twenty-year period would end in 1999, and on August 11 of that year, the last total eclipse of the sun in the millennium was due to fall over southern England, where there are numerous ancient stone circles. Stonehenge would be just outside of the range, but there were others inside it. So that was pretty exciting. We set the first piece of a twenty-year working into place as the beginning of an Awakening. What we wanted to do was infuse the shadows that moved across the face of the Earth with an energy field that would carry with it a sense of awakening among the people, which would eventually lead to a planetary Awakening of Gaea.

MG: After it was all over, we gathered up our stuff, and people broke camp and headed off in their different directions. That evening we went back to our hotel and turned on the news to see if it had anything to say about us. We saw satellite photos of the shadow moving across the face of the Pacific Northwest. And there was nothing but solid clouds until it got to right where we were. And the clouds opened up like the iris of a camera for the length of the eclipse. And when the shadow moved on, it closed again, then a little further down it opened up again at the Warm Springs Indian Reservation in Oregon. In the Pacific Northwest, those were the only two places that the eclipse could be seen at all.

OZ: Commenting on this phenomenon on the *CBS Evening News with Walter Cronkite*, Terry Drinkwater reported, "Nearby, at a replica of Stonehenge, Druids, Neo-Pagans invoked their Gods, Mother Nature, and

Father Time, to ensure cloudless skies. And, generally, the heavens were clear for eclipse viewing. [. . .] As the totality of the eclipse approached, the Druids at Stonehenge seemed almost spellbound. And finally, at the moment the moon passes between the sun and this spot on Earth—total darkness." The next days we were in all the newspapers. They wrote about how the Druids cleared the sky so that the people could see it. And all the good photos came from the Maryhill Stonehenge.

MG: Right after the eclipse we had to go down to Berkeley to spend a few days with Isaac Bonewits. It was the beginning of March 1979, and the weather was bitterly cold. We had our snakes, Ananta and Tanith, who needed to be taken care of, but Ananta weighed nearly one hundred pounds at this point, and so this time we decided to leave them behind because we were hitchhiking down to the Bay Area. Oberon had made a box for them that they could be kept in. It had a shielded light bulb in it to keep them warm. But it had to be plugged in somewhere, so we took them and the box down to the auto shop where Orion was working, in the small, nearby town of Calpella. All he was supposed to do was keep them warm for a couple of days.

We were in Berkeley with Isaac and Anodea, when Orion showed up on their doorstep. He said, "I hate to be the bearer of bad news, but your snakes are dead." Apparently just after we left, there had been a heat wave. Nobody had thought about the snakes—out of sight, out of mind. Because of the temperature change, they had baked to death in their box. We were totally stricken by this.

We returned to the Ranch and buried them next to where we were building the barn for the Living Unicorns. That was quite a blow. We were wondering what it all meant. We had just been through this incredible eclipse ritual, and then we had the backlash of losing the snakes that we had been so bonded with. And now we were about to embark on our venture with the Unicorn.

OZ: So we walked down to the stream that ran through the land. Called Eldritch Creek, it was one of those Northern California creeks that in the summertime is just kind of a loosely connected sequence of stagnant puddles, but in the winter it becomes this raging torrent because of all the rain. We wanted to check on how the erosion-control work we'd done during the summer was holding up. And, most importantly, we needed to talk about our lives and our plans for the future.

One of the things that I wanted to discuss with MG was my name. Many people who moved to Greenfield Ranch just took another name, a mystical or magickal name.

Now, I am fundamentally an aquatic creature. I had grown up by a lake, and in my youth I spent much of my summers swimming—mostly underwater. When I come up for air I roll around. I swim like an otter, and Morning Glory had taken to referring to me as an "Otter in the water." It had sort of become a nickname, but only in the context of swimming, and not a name that I had taken seriously. She suggested that I take that name, and I said it wasn't really dignified enough. If all went according to our plans, I said, in a year we were going to be out in the world with our Unicorns, and media people would be talking to us, and I would need to have a really cool name to go by. I needed something mystical and arcane—appropriate for a Wizard.

We were having this conversation on the high bank overlooking Eldritch Creek. Below us the stream was roaring by in full flood. Morning Glory said, "Why don't you ask the Goddess for a sign?"

So I did this little invocation: "Oh Goddess, Mother of all living, give me a sign for a name in which I may continue to do your work and be known in the world." No sooner had the words left my lips than a wild otter popped out of the foaming water. It was the first one I had ever seen. It climbed up onto a rock, looked right at us, spun around in a little pirouette, and disappeared back into the froth.

Morning Glory and I turned and looked at each other. I shrugged my shoulders and said, "I hear and I obey." So after that whenever people asked about my name, "Otter," I would say that it was the name my mother gave me.

Chapter 10
The Return of the Unicorn
(1975–1991)

Now not so long ago a Wizard looked round;
He said, "All the people of the Earth seem down.
It's too beautiful a world to look so forlorn—
I think I'll bring back those Unicorns!"

Well he sat down to thinking and it gave him a pain,
Readin' and researchin' in the sun and rain,
Until he learned the secret of the ancient Unicorns:
That the lovely creatures were made, not born.

—FROM "THE UNICORN—PART 2" BY ORION STORMCROW, 1986
(for Oberon on his forty-fourth birthday—November 30, 1986)

NARRATOR: The story of the Zells and their Unicorns takes place over many years and overlaps with many of their other adventures. It started off when Morning Glory and OZ, who was then still Tim Zell, were living together in St. Louis.

OZ: In 1975 or thereabouts, we were sitting around our living room with a bunch of folks and talking about myths, legends, and different mythical beasts and creatures. Somebody asked, "What's the difference between a basilisk and a cockatrice?"

We pulled out a volume of the *Encyclopedia Britannica* and found a fascinating discussion relating the basilisk, cockatrice, and Medusa to the Egyptian spitting cobra, which is a real live animal that can spit its venom in your eyes and blind you and then kill you. But as people got further and further away from the source, it became a creature whose gaze would paralyze you or turn you into stone. (The venom would cause paralysis, which is close to being turned into stone. And snakes have no eyelids—they have an unblinking gaze that can seem very intense and hypnotic.) So stories about a real, actual creature can build up into an entire mythos.

MG: We then thought that we could write a book about what was the grain of truth behind the fantasies and fairy stories. For unicorns, dragons, phoenixes, and all different kinds of creatures—what is the story behind the story?

OZ: For years I'd been collecting news clippings; some of my folders were several inches thick. There were files in my cabinets going back to the '50s that I'd kept for future research. With this whole new vision of a project in mind, we started gathering more stuff together. We went to libraries and looked for accounts, records, reports, drawings, bas-reliefs, sculptures—anything we could find.

NARRATOR: When they relocated to Eugene, Oregon, they began teaching an extension course in "Witchcraft, Shamanism, and Pagan Religion" at the local community college. This gave them access to the school library, where they were able to continue working on their project.

OZ: Morning Glory and I did research in the college library. And there I came across an obscure reference to some experiments that had been performed in the 1930s by a veterinary physician named Dr. Franklin Dove. At that time everybody thought that animals' horns just grew straight out of the skull. But he discovered that horns were precipitated and stimulated into growth by a node in the skin, not in the bone. They were pulled out of the skull, rather than pushed out, stimulated by a node known as the horn bud that releases enzymes that cause a horn to be produced.

Dove discovered that you could move these buds, and wherever they were they would cause the horn to grow from that spot. You had to do all this, though, within a very few hours after the birth of the animal. But it seemed to work on all horned animals, including deer, cattle, goats, sheep, and antelope. Dove decided to see if he could create a unicorn by causing the buds to be brought together and fused. He used a calf, which is part of why his discovery was pretty much unregarded—it didn't strike anybody's fancy.

MG: Franklin Dove's unicorn was the very first unicorn of modern times. It was a beautiful white and brown unicorn bull with a horn in the middle of its forehead. Dove described the animal as being unusually assertive; it used its horn as a tool and seemed more adept at problem-solving. It also appeared gentler and more intelligent than the other cows and bulls on the farm.

OZ: Shortly after that, World War II happened and people didn't pay much attention to what Dr. Dove had done. I Xeroxed this article and brought it back to Morning Glory. We pulled out our "Unicorns" file and started looking at all the articles and images we'd collected. The earliest images date from about 4,000 years ago, and depict the unicorns as bulls. In old Persian bas-reliefs they appear identical to Franklin Dove's animal, and they're depicted fighting with lions. In fact "the Unicorn vs. the Lion" became a motif all the way through history; it's still on the contemporary British royal coat of arms.

The popular images in the Cloisters tapestries from medieval and Renaissance Europe were clearly based on goats—they are cloven-hoofed and have the giveaway little beard. We speculated that unicorns were a deliberately created phenomenon, like a bonsai tree, a mule, or a beefalo. It seemed possible that the unicorn had always been a product of deliberate human manipulation.

The unicorn was not a natural animal, for he can only come into being by deliberate intent. Therefore unicorns are magickal! Because the essence of Magick as we understand it is coincidence control and probability enhancement—intentionally redirecting natural forces and energies to the purpose of a creative will. Planting a garden, irrigation and erosion control, and cross-breeding for diversity are all magickal acts, and it was in this context that we understood the creation of the Living Unicorn.

MG: So we asked ourselves, "What is involved in this?" Dove's procedure was apparently very simple. Both OZ and I had a fair amount of basic veterinary and barnyard medical skills. We realized that with a little topical anesthesia, we could probably do what he did ourselves.

OZ: We looked at each other and said, "Wow! We might be able to produce a real live Unicorn—we could bring Unicorns back into the world! What an incredible magickal act that would be!"

And I said, "This is what we've been looking for—this is clearly our next assignment from the Goddess."

NARRATOR: The synchronicity of getting an assignment from the Goddess is something that OZ likes to explain in terms from 1960s popular culture: at the beginning of every episode in the TV show *Mission: Impossible*, which ran from 1966 to 1973 and was quite different from the Tom Cruise movies of the same name, the leader of a team of secret agents would go to a different surprise location where a tape recorder would be waiting for him. He would start playing the tape and hear a message that always began with "Your mission, should you decide to accept it, is . . ." (At the end of the message the tape recorder would self-destruct!) And OZ has pointed out to me on numerous occasions that if the character in the show *didn't* accept the mission, then the series would have been cancelled, because then there would have been no stories to tell. So whenever OZ received what he perceived to be his next mission, then he too had to accept it for similar reasons.

And then, as they were trying to figure out just how to do this, they got the offer from Alison Harlow to be caretakers on Coeden Brith. After moving there they were able to raise some money for the project. It came from investors, who expected what they were doing to be a profitable as well as magical—for them the Unicorn project was comparable

to a venture capital start-up. (For many years this money from the investors was the only source of income for OZ and MG, and eventually the
money all had to be paid back.)

The Zells began building a barn before they even built a place for
themselves. (They continued to live in their bus until they were able to
build and move into a yurt.)

MG: We did some research and decided to use Angora goats as our Unicorn breeding stock. They have beautiful, white, fleecy hair that can be
groomed and trimmed into an artistic mane, with tail and fetlocks resem-
bling the classical unicorns in the tapestries. There's a bronze medallion by
Pisanello to Cecilia Gonzaga, from the fifteenth century, of a unicorn that
is clearly an Angora goat with its head in the lap of a young virgin.

We ended up driving to Calaveras County, buying four pregnant
does, and bringing them back. This was just before Hallowe'en 1979.
Now, our research had indicated that it's almost impossible to make a
Unicorn out of a female goat, and our first goat baby, born on Ground-
hog Day, 1980, was female.

OZ: We named her Milkmaid. This was our first birth, so we were quite
green at parenting. We took turns sleeping in the stall all night with Milkmaid's mother, Amalthea. A month later our first male was born. When
I discovered him in the stall with his mother, I scooped him up in my
arms (he was no bigger than a housecat) and carried him to the bus to
show Morning Glory. Tears were streaming down my face as I said,
"Unto us a child is born; unto us a son is given."

We named our first Unicorn Galahad as an indication of our high
hopes (we had already decided that we would name our Unicorns after
the Knights of the Round Table).

It was then time to perform the operation. I had plenty of skills and
experience to prepare me for doing it. When you live on a farm and take
care of animals, you have to routinely do things like de-horning, de-
clawing, dis-budding, castrating, and tail docking—it's a completely different way of life that people who live in the city and just have animals
as pets don't understand. I'd had experience on farms as a kid, and when
I was an Eagle Scout I learned how to hunt, trap, and fish. In biology

class I became really good at dissection of specimens and continued my education on my own with roadkills for years. Then in college I was a pre-med student and was so good at anatomy and dissection that I became the teaching assistant and instructed other people in how to do it in lab class.

So I had the necessary background. All I needed was a final bit of information that hadn't been in the article by Franklin Dove, and I had figured that out by dreaming it. I used the same technique that Crick and Watson used to find the model of the DNA molecule. They basically put all the information and all the electron-scanning things out there and got obsessed with "What pattern could explain this stuff?" Watson then dreamed of two snakes intertwining, and correctly intuited the structure of the double-helix spiral.

Well, I put out everything I could find about this and I asked the question, "How can this be done, exactly?" I knew that I had to perform a manipulatory operation that would take two separate horn buds, on opposite sides of the skull, and somehow fuse them together in the center without interrupting the blood flow or the continuity of the skin. It meant a rearrangement of tissue in a complex way that minimized any potential damage.

When I woke up in the morning, I had it. This complex little design, like a sigil, had appeared in my dream. A sigil is a magical sign or symbol—usually a unique, special design. I realized that if I cut that sigil pattern I could then rearrange the components. And that was the answer.

ALISON HARLOW: The newborn goat is completely anesthetized and doesn't feel a thing. It isn't traumatic. There is no way Oberon would ever hurt an animal. Working with any animal creature is one of his big strengths. I remember one time he found a turtle that somebody had run over. The shell was completely cracked. After months of nursing that turtle back to health, it was totally fine again. That's one of his great gifts.

MG: We were advised to neuter him. Experienced goat raisers told us "no one wants a male goat that is intact!" So we neutered the animal almost immediately after it was born, then we did the Unicorning procedure at the same time. But to our utmost chagrin, the little guy never grew much of a horn. You have to have that testosterone on board, or else the horn doesn't grow! After that didn't work, we went, "Hmmm."

We realized that in order to get maximum horn growth, it has to be an intact male. Of course there is some phallic symbolism there. The whole point of the Unicorn experience for us was how much all the things we found out utterly fell into place and dovetailed with the legend.

So often, legend is truer than the modern world would have us believe. Mainstream science is very frustrating to deal with because they ignore things the size of elephants sitting right in their living room. The Unicorn was actually an exercise to point this out to the world. One of the things was to say, "Look! Ta-da! Everybody said this can't be. There is no such thing as unicorns. But here is one. So what else is there that you're saying can't be existing that might be there, too?"

OZ: In March 1980, Morning Glory went to San Francisco for a big Spring Equinox parade. I was up the hill working in the orchard when I heard the now-familiar cry of a doe in labor. I dropped everything and ran down the hill, arriving just in time to discover a wet and wobbly newborn male goat. I snatched him up right away and carried him to the bus, where I performed the operation. For the next two weeks I slept with him in my arms every night and kept him with me in the orchard and garden all day. Morning Glory returned to find a cute, adorable little baby Unicorn. The following weekend, on the full moon, another one was born.

MG: He performed the surgery on the baby boy, whom we named Lancelot. Then another one was born two weeks afterwards and we named him Bedivere. Orion helped with the third surgery, but unfortunately he had a bad cold. Even though he was wearing a mask, Bedivere got a terrible infection. I spent many days and nights caring for him: treating the infection with antibiotics, hot packs, and frequent changes of the dressing. Both animals' horns sprouted up just like Dove's bull, but on Bedivere one side partially died in spite of all my care, so at first his horn was much thinner. Lancelot grew a great, prominent central horn, and eventually so did Bedivere.

ALISON HARLOW: They never mistreated the Unicorns. They were never lazy about feeding the Unicorn babies. They took them away from their mothers and nursed them, and that's very important. Here, again, is something that Otter was really smart about. When you do the Unicorning process to a goat, it actually stimulates their pineal gland, so you get a creature that is a lot stronger and a lot smarter than the average of the species. He was convinced, and I think that he was absolutely right, that if they just let them grow up as goats, by the time they were adults they'd be much too dangerous to have around. A billy goat that can impale you with a sword, and is smarter than a dog, is a dangerous creature.

So what they did was, from the time they were born and they'd done the Unicorning process on them, they took them away from the mothers, and when they were really tiny they lived in the house with the Zells. They milked the moms and fed the babies with their own mother's milk from a bottle, holding them themselves so that they bonded with people. The Unicorns were then completely oriented towards people, and that is why they were so trainable. Because then you could use all of those smarts to get them to do what you wanted.

NARRATOR: Alison talked the Zells into getting an attorney. His name was Matthew Eberhard, and he and his wife Bernice were both fantasy and science fans. They became friends and supporters of OZ and MG, who ended up staying in the Eberhards' Los Gatos house for several months and using it as a base of operations. Together they created a corporation, The Living Unicorn Project, to own the Unicorns and provide funding, and began the process of putting together a patent application for the Unicorning process.

The Eberhards set up a "coming out" party for the Unicorn at their house on Mother's Day 1980 and invited the media. After that the Zells began doing interviews, and there was a lot of publicity, but they didn't reveal the secret of the Unicorning process—they wanted to write that story themselves and sell it to a science magazine. A professional animal trainer was hired, and Lancelot learned how to perform in front of an audience.

OZ: Matthew arranged for Lancelot to be exhibited at Marine World/ Africa USA, an amusement park with animal shows in the Bay Area, where a whole special pen was built so that people could come see him. They built a castle house for him, and a photograph of him standing in front of it ended up in the *Encyclopedia Britannica,* identifying him as a genuine Unicorn. Marine World had a huge billboard up next to the highway with a picture of Lance on it. The billboard said "Come to Marine World and See the Living Unicorn!"

NARRATOR: When OZ called up his dad and told him about the Unicorns, Charlie, who was in the gift and card business, asked him to make some Unicorn figurines and jewelry designs that he could put on the market. This was the first time Charlie had ever asked his son to create something for his company, and it was also the beginning of OZ's career as a sculpture artist.

In the fall, OZ got a new opportunity to promote the Unicorn when Matthew and Bernice Eberhard booked a gig at the Renaissance Faire in Novato, California.

MG: We told the management at the Ren Faire, "Wow! We've got this Unicorn!"

And they were like, "Yeah, yeah. You're just another act." To them it was all just theater. But at least they reluctantly decided to bend their rules a bit to allow us to have a photo booth.

They just didn't get that it was a real Unicorn. And we couldn't imagine that they couldn't get it.

OZ: At that point we had to come up with an appropriate way to present ourselves. You don't do the Renaissance Faire in street clothes—you have to dress up in costume.

So we came up with the idea of the Enchantress and the Wizard and made the appropriate costumes and adopted the personae. But when we were out in the rest of the world doing interviews, we had adopted the personae of "naturalists." Unlike a scientist, you don't have to be accredited to be a naturalist. So in the mundane world we were naturalists, and in the magickal world we were an Enchantress and a Wizard. It was a perfect segue. After all, Wizards ("wise ones") were also called Philosophers ("lovers of wisdom"), and early scientists were initially referred to as "Natural Philosophers." So it all worked perfectly.

That was when I fully adopted the identity of Wizard; before that, MG and I had been a Priestess and a Priest. At that time my concept of a Wizard was based entirely on stories and myths. In these, the Wizard is a lore master. I grew into a deeper appreciation as it unfolded, much like the Unicorn thing itself. Ever since then, I've been exploring that role and now that is pretty much the best way of explaining who I am.

So we did the Novato Renaissance Faire. We set up a corral for Lancelot and a photo booth where people could have pictures taken with the Unicorn in front of a big tapestry background.

ALISON HARLOW: The first year they were doing the Ren Faire with Lancelot, I went for one weekend. The kids just loved the Unicorn. But I don't think people really got it. They didn't understand.

And Oberon would explain and explain to people, and they still wouldn't understand. That was one of the areas in which he has always been really naïve: the feeling that if you explain something carefully to somebody, then they'll understand. But people don't, necessarily. They think what they want to think, no matter how carefully you explain it.

Oberon really believed that when the world saw that there really were Unicorns, that there would be a general mystical turning back to magical ways. He had, and has, a very strong mystical streak. I did not believe that it would automatically transform the world, but I thought it was a pretty cool idea.

Actually, much to Oberon's disappointment, the world did not change itself instantly on the reappearance of Unicorns. Realism has never been his strong suit, let me put it that way.

NARRATOR: During that time, the Zells were generally not in touch with the growing Pagan community. When they left their Nest, and *Green Egg* folded, they lost contact with most of their old friends. The international Pagan scene was changing rapidly, and they had very little awareness of the many newcomers, new publications, and new developments.

OZ and MG were following their own path: attempting to do ritual and Magick not just for themselves or a Circle, but for the whole world.

So they then traveled all over, presenting the animals wherever they could, and their experiences were not unlike those of a rock band on the road. They were featured in parades and they were the guests of honor at the Luckenbach "World's Fair," where the Unicorn was named the official animal of the state of Texas. They hooked up with the Flying Karamazov Brothers juggling troupe and became part of the "The New Old Time Chautauqua" traveling entertainment and medicine show caravan.

But OZ, by any name, has always been good at getting attention, and not so good at making money. And such was the case with the Unicorns. Even with all the publicity they got, there wasn't much income generated. Raising Unicorns was an expensive and ongoing activity that was unable to pay for itself, and there were additional expenses like legal fees for getting a patent on the Unicorning process. They weren't able to sell the Unicorns or the story. (They eventually did get the patent, but it took years and by then didn't do much good.)

I heard lots of talk about what could have been done differently and why things didn't go as hoped for. The consensus seems to be that everyone did the best they could, but, well, since no one else had raised unicorns in modern times, they just weren't sure what to do with them. And who would have known? Matthew and Bernice Eberhard decided they had spent enough money and gave up.

And then, in 1981, someone new entered the picture.

JEFFREY SIEGEL: I was the art director of the Minnesota Renaissance Festival. A little context for you: Renaissance Faires initially burst onto the scene in California. The Minnesota Renaissance Festival was the first serious expansion of the concept outside of California, and it actually became the hub for most of the expansion of the concept nationwide. The Minnesota Renaissance Festival had a unicorn in the Festival's logo, and it had a life-size unicorn puppet as part of the daily performances. I was a voracious reader of newspapers and publications, and I found this obscure reference to these "naturalists" in California who claimed that they had solved the riddle of the unicorn, and had a unicorn. So I contacted them and made an arrangement for them to come to Minnesota to do a personal appearance. And we had a very successful experience with that.

The Zells then asked me if I would consider representing them. At that point in my career, I had already been reasonably experienced and successful in several aspects of the entertainment business. But I also had an extreme interest in circus, carnival, sideshow, vaudeville, and all those related crafts. I had turned down artist management my entire career. I wasn't interested in managing anybody else's career but my own. However, as a circus enthusiast, it occurred to me that I would probably have no other opportunity in my life to have, literally and figuratively, a P. T. Barnum experience in modern history. So I agreed to represent them. I took it on because I felt it was going to be a total carnival experience.

I spent a good amount of time shuttling back and forth between Minnesota and Greenfield Ranch to meet with them, and to meet with people in California who purportedly thought they had some rights to the animals, or various images or whatever. I had to extricate them from a variety of situations, and then once we consolidated that, my next task was to put together branding, marketing, and packaging.

Then I started knocking on doors everywhere I could go, in Hollywood, on Madison Avenue, and elsewhere, to convince people that there was some great potential idea there to take this Unicorn and achieve a great deal of attention for a product, a concept, a movie, or whatever. I put together a nice, organized little roadshow, with our merchandise program, presentation, and displays.

I would typically call a very high-powered agency, or product marketing manager, or Hollywood studio or office, and start with a telephone answering person, typically a female receptionist. Almost invariably, the receptionist would find it incredibly interesting, want to see this for herself, and would convince her employer to make the appointment. Once I got a foot into the door, everybody was interested. But at the end of the day, nobody could exactly put their finger on what to do with it.

We flew them to several Renaissance Faires, sometimes two shows at once. Trotting the Unicorns around the United States for a couple of years was a really great experience.

OZ: With Jeffrey as our booking agent, we basically lived for two entire summers (1982 and 1983) at Renaissance Faires, sleeping in the stalls with the Unicorns in tiny dome tents. In 1982, we did twelve Faires, with three different Unicorns! Rainbow went with Morning Glory, and Bryan accompanied me.

From that point on, at every Faire we did, we became a major promotional attraction. Often we would stay for the entire time of the Faire, which would be several weeks. On weekdays we would do promotion. We would do local TV shows and newspaper interviews to promote the Faire. We would remain in costume and in the personae constantly. Then on the weekends we would be doing the Faire.

So for at least four months out of each year in 1982 and '83, Morning Glory and I didn't even see each other. It was the first time we'd been separated from each other since we'd gotten married. Suddenly we were on the road at different Faires with different Unicorns. From 1975 until 1982, Morning Glory and I had been almost always in total physical proximity. Towards the later part of that time, there came points where we had really intense conflicts. It was almost because we were so alike, and so much almost clones of each other in so many ways, that whenever there was some minor disagreement about something, tiny things would seem to be monumental because they stood out above this totally smooth surface. We had these insane arguments, and since we were out in the middle of nowhere, we could yell and scream.

Some of the people who were close to us at the time were frequently urging us to break up. But these people never really understood that we were utterly bonded. It didn't matter what kind of conflicts we were in— we could not separate because we were so connected. So we had to work it out. Whatever we have done, it has been with such intensity and passion that nothing else can stand in the way of it.

Then we went off to separate parts of the country with different Unicorns. For four months we were apart. It was really quite intense. During that time each of us met other lovers who became important parts of our lives. This was not because we were estranged; we just do that anyway. But the other lovers we met had to put up with hearing us spilling out our hearts about the grief we were experiencing with our soulmates! So the kind of people with whom we connected were never intended to be replacements or anything like that. They almost ended up being counselors and sympathizers to unburden ourselves to, and that became the basis of some of the relationships.

MG: It was a rough time for us. We started out being really together around the Unicorn issues, and then he and I had a really major falling out about the issues around secrecy and credibility and all of that. We were just getting pulled along by other people's advice when they were only in it for the money and we were just "going with the flow," but we were losing our credibility and our focus and were in danger of selling out our values. I'm afraid that, in the long run, I was probably right about this particular thing. Unicorns are a function of innocence and a magickal belief system, and that is fundamentally incompatible with the hardheaded business world, which is all about corporate secrets and one-upmanship. There were a whole lot of real mistakes that I kind of saw coming and tried to talk him out of. It became a real bone of contention in our relationship, and we ended up almost breaking up.

By the end of that summer, I actually had no intention of getting together with Oberon again. I also didn't have a clue as to how we were going to make it without each other, but I'd just had it with the whole scene. Perhaps I had become hyper-acute to anything that felt like a lie by omission, and not telling the whole story—that Unicorns are created by a surgical process—just felt false to me. Yet all the lawyers and agents insisted that we must keep this part of the mystery until we could write a book or publish the truth in a reputable scientific journal. They felt, perhaps correctly, that once the secret was out, the mystery would be gone and nobody would be interested anymore.

OZ: After the summer of 1982 was finally over, she finished with her tour somewhat before I did. She drove to the airport in our pickup truck to pick up Lancelot and me. On the way back home, in Richmond, a city in the East Bay, our truck broke down. It was nighttime, and we managed to get it into an empty parking lot.

MG: So there we were, with all of the camping gear from a summer tour, boxes full of brochures, and a Unicorn in a pickup truck, in the worst possible part of town. It was 3:30 in the morning in a neighbor-hood that the Mafia wouldn't go to for a short-order pizza. We were right next to this junkyard.

I was furious, because I knew that my pickup truck, Helva, was on its last legs. I was angry that I'd had to come pick him up, because I was afraid that the truck was going to break down. I had tried to explain to him, "Look, I don't think that Helva is going to make it. Can't you find somebody else to come get you?"

So I was really angry. "Oh, well, here we go!" I was thinking to my-self. "I'm back involved with Otter again, and the first thing that hap-pens is this!"

OZ: And so now here we were, broken down in the middle of the night. What could we do? We had no way to protect ourselves from anybody who wanted to mug us or rob us. That was the first time we had been back together in four months. We still didn't know what our first meet-ing was going to be like. Were we going to get back together only to file divorce papers, or what? We'd had no contact at all for four months.

MG: Oberon was like, "Well, now what are we going to do?"

"We're going to have to wait here until dawn," I told him. "There's nothing else we can do."

It started off with us being in this incredibly adversarial headspace. We both vented for a while. Lancelot was hanging out in back, and I'm sure he was glad that he didn't have to listen to us fight.

Then we talked, and it was more like, "Well, how was your summer?"

"Okay. How was your summer?" So we explained about each other's summers. He was telling me about all these things that he had seen, and I was telling him about all these things that I had seen.

And both of us kept saying, "I wish you could have seen this thing I saw," or "I wish you could have heard this thing."

Suddenly, I had this epiphany. In spite of the good times and the good people, I had just spent the most miserable summer of my life. I was being mad and pissed off at Oberon for things that certainly were not all his fault, and that were really rather minor in the scope of things. I had spent the whole summer missing him and seeing all of these wonderful things, and all I could think of was that I wanted to be able to share it with him. That summer I hadn't had a person in my life that could share those things with me.

I had my daughter and that was wonderful, but she was still a child, and Oberon was my soulmate, who just shared so many things in common with me! When I came to that conclusion, we both broke down and cried. We embraced and hugged each other and forgave each other and reconnected.

OZ: We held each other, and it was a deep and moving experience. Because both of us knew that we would rather be together, sleeping in a junkyard on the side of a road in a broken-down pickup truck, than to be apart from each other and be the king and queen of the Renaissance Faires. Our whole life and relationship turned around from that moment, and our partnership got into a new kind of synergy. And that was the last time we ever really had that kind of estrangement.

NARRATOR: The Zells went back to the Ranch for the winter, and in 1983 once again split up to go to separate Ren Faires with different Unicorns. Jeffrey Siegel continued to try to get a deal for the Unicorns. Jeffrey had a circus background, and early on he had approached the Ringling Brothers and Barnum & Bailey Circus, asked for a lot of money, and hadn't gotten it. In 1984 he decided to lower the price and try again, and the second time he was finally able to work something out. The negotiations took place at the circus winter home in Florida. OZ flew there with Jeffrey but was not present for the actual meeting. When the deal was sealed, Oberon was waiting outside and for the first time met Irvin Feld, the owner of the circus, and his son Kenneth.

OZ: I had dinner with them and we got along famously with Irvin. We had a great time. He told me all these stories about his life, and I told him stories about mine, and we really hit it off. We signed a contract for a four-year exhibition lease for four Unicorns, which was the number that we had available at that time.

We made the transition in the summer of 1984, right around the Fourth of July. We flew down to Texas, where the circus was currently showing, with four Unicorns. We got the sealed contract and we made the deal with Irvin Feld. The circus was scheduled to shut down in October and go back to Florida for the winter season. Irvin assured us that then they would have us come down and talk to their people about the lore and the legend of the Unicorns. He also wanted us to show them the training stuff and go over the grooming procedures and teach them Lancelot's performance signals.

Our contract said that we could not do anything independently. Anything we did we had to do with their permission. We had to work with them and promote it through them. We were supposed to go there in November of 1984. But in September we got the word that Irvin had died.

The promotion came out and it totally ignored us. The circus spokesmen would go around and tell people, "The unicorn just appeared on our back lot." They wouldn't acknowledge our existence or that we had anything to do with it. Kenneth just cut us out and wouldn't mention us to journalists. So what happened was that journalists started thinking that it was a fraud, because it was clear that they weren't being honest about it.

But they wouldn't talk to us. All this stuff that we had set up never went anywhere. The whole thing was tied up with them because we had this contract, and we couldn't talk to anybody. We couldn't talk to the media, and the circus wouldn't use any of the validating materials we provided for them. This went on for four years, and it was enormously frustrating to us.

JEFFREY SIEGEL: Otter thought and assumed that when the Unicorn landed with Ringling, that he too would land with Ringling, and that he would spend time with them and the Unicorn and that he would be a big part of the attention. But in reality, they wanted the Unicorn; they didn't want the Zells. Keep in mind, we're talking about an organization filled with exotic animals. So they have trainers, groomers, and veterinarians. They didn't want the story to be about the Zells; they wanted the story to be about "Come see the magic! We have found a real live Unicorn!" We were selling exclusivity. That was the product.

I'm not saying that I supported that idea. If they had wanted Otter, I would have been just as happy. Did they lead him on? Not exactly. Everybody was back-slapping them, and "Who loves ya, baby?" and "This is gonna be great!" and then they bought the Unicorn; they didn't buy the Zells.

Otter is correct, though. His assumption was that he was going to be a part of it. But I don't think it was ever Kenneth's intention, and quite frankly Kenneth was really running the show at that point. His dad was pretty much retired.

If the father hadn't died, he would have seen his son have the biggest publicity coup in modern circus history. Kenneth Feld was quoted in *Time* magazine talking about the Unicorn, and the increase in business that it generated in Madison Square Garden. New York City is, I think, their longest run of the year—it's one of their biggest markets. And in that one city alone, the Unicorn generated so much press and attention that it increased their sales from 20 to 30 percent, which translates into millions of dollars. I think it's safe to say that it was probably the biggest circus publicity coup since the passing of P. T. Barnum, when he presented Jumbo the Elephant, Jenny Lind, and on and on. I think it's the first time in modern circus history they had anything quite close to that P. T. Barnum–type of experience. The press went worldwide. The story was covered on the front page of the New York newspapers multiple times. Johnny Carson talked about it. *Saturday Night Live* did skits about it twice.

When protests arose in New York City about animal welfare and abuse, somebody was called in to investigate. And that individual said, essentially, the animal was not abused, and that it was in fact a unicorn, because it is a single-horned animal. He didn't say how or why it became single-horned. That was the golden ticket for Ringling, because they had all this controversy and were getting all this attention.

They didn't want the discussion of Franklin Dove. They wanted to purchase this exotic animal; they wanted to exhibit this exotic animal; they wanted to draw attention and sell tickets; and then they wanted to move on the next idea. They used it for two years as an attraction, and retired the idea when it had played out its performance value to the circus.

OZ: They paid us in bits and pieces, spread out over four years. Stretched out over that amount of time it wasn't such a lot, but it was sufficient to take care of our needs at the time. Having the money coming in from these things allowed us to survive and make the next few moves in our lives. Mid-America Festivals took most of the money that we got from the initial payment. They claimed all these expenses and stuff for promotion and setup that they were to be paid back.

JEFFREY SIEGEL: Did they get ripped off? Not in my opinion. Did they get as much as they wanted? No. Did I get as much for them as I wanted? No. I literally went in there and was asking companies for millions, because everybody thought it was worth millions. And that's one of the reasons it didn't go very far. It wasn't quite worth as much money as they hoped. But I do think they were treated fairly.

I equate this to a check you would have gotten back in the eighties if you had a hot new rock band that was getting some buzz, and somebody wanted to take a chance on you. They'd give you a certain amount of money, some studio time; they'd give you some touring money, and they'd give you a record deal. If your record made money, they'd take back a reimbursement for the studio time, and they'd take back money for the touring expenses.

NARRATOR: To make matters worse, in 1985 Leonard Lake, a former resident of Greenfield Ranch, was arrested. He committed suicide while in police custody, and it was soon discovered that he had been a serial killer. At the time of his arrest and suicide it had been several years since he had lived on the Ranch, and he hadn't started killing people until after he left there. He had moved to Calaveras County, where the remains of more than twenty victims were found buried near the survivalist bunker that he had built.

Leonard had helped the Zells in the early days of breeding Unicorns. After it became known that he was a murderer, a picture of Lake (and the woman he eventually married) with a Unicorn that had been taken at the Renaissance Faire was published in national newspapers.

OZ: After that, Leonard became known as the "Unicorn Man." And people began to confuse him with me. The name I was going by then was Otter, which obviously was not a birth name. So they figured my real name must be Leonard.

That was devastating. And it happened in the summer of 1985, just when the circus was doing big shows with the Unicorns. And there was a picture in a lot of papers around the country of Leonard with the Unicorn! Our contract with the circus prohibited us from talking about this without their permission. And they weren't about to give in. It was quite a blow. We didn't suffer physically; he didn't kill any of us. But our whole vision, plan, life, and everything involving the return of the Unicorn was completely blindsided by this event. There was even a set of "mass murderer" trading cards that was put out. Leonard Lake was featured on one of them, and identified as the creator of the Unicorns!

MG: The whole Unicorn visionary thing came to a wild careening halt with the Leonard Lake fiasco. It was bad enough that the circus had blown off the scientific credibility of the animals, but now their images were being dragged through the mud and blood of a mass murderer. I felt like I was living in a waking nightmare, that all trust and everything good and innocent had been ravaged and wrecked beyond all salvation.

NARRATOR: While Morning Glory and Oberon had sold two of their Unicorns to the circus, who were never returned, Bedivere was never sold or leased, and his brother Lancelot was leased and then returned to the Zells by the circus at the end of their contract. The situation only proved to add anguish to their already troubled hearts.

MG: Lancelot we refused to sell, yet when we got him back, he was never the same. Lancelot's horn had collapsed, hanging down practically onto his nose; it was hard for him even to eat that way. The circus folk wouldn't listen to us when we tried to tell them about all the special attention that it took to keep a Unicorn's horn in proper condition. I guess they felt that he was just a "property" to them that they didn't even own. He seemed pretty sad and tired. He left us all happy and excited to be performing for people, and when he came back he was a broken-spirited creature. I felt like we had sold one of our children for thirty pieces of silver. I cried for a week.

NARRATOR: Lancelot stayed with the Zells until he died in 1991. At that point they had long since left Coeden Brith and were living in a house by the Russian River in Mendocino County.

MG: I would go out to the barn that we had built for Lance; we called it Fort Unicorn. It was huge and totally overbuilt because we thought Lance would be coming back strong and full of piss and vinegar. Instead, of course, he wandered around the huge corral like a wraith in a castle.

We would bring him in to watch television sometimes like he used to do when he was a little kid, but even that didn't seem to bring him out of his funk. We did persist for a while in trying to re-socialize him, but every time OZ would look at him, he would get so upset that he would just leave.

The circus, however, for all its harm, did further one aspect of our agenda: millions of children saw the Unicorns, and even though many adults told them, "No, it's not a real unicorn," they saw it with their own eyes and it became part of their personal reality. We have tried to bridge these universes our whole life long and in all our workings, and we've seen that there are lots of magickal things that the world does not want to believe are so. People wanted the Unicorns to be all sweetness and light; they wanted ethereal, white horses with sparkly horns. They didn't want to have to see that a live Unicorn was an animal who eats and craps, that it is a sexual creature, that it is a real thing with its own needs and desires. Most people really don't want their fantasies to become real, because there might be some work or disillusionment in it.

It's a lot like the difference between fantasy magic and real Magick. With fantasy magic you just wiggle your nose or wave your wand, and the television or movie special effects make it happen. The real Magick is stuff that involves the living world, and it's often a grubby, messy, sticky, organic kind of a thing with lots of prickly wild plants and animals and cold, rainy weather. It involves a lot of effort. You don't just become a magickal person by—well, you *do* become a magickal person by believing you are one. But from that point on if you want to actually practice a discipline, you have to become disciplined, and most people resist that. They would rather wiggle their nose and have their wishes come true . . . as if. When they find out that real Magick isn't like that, then they usually lose interest or become disillusioned and are quick to proclaim, "See! That proves magic isn't real." The truth is that real Magick isn't about illusions as much as it is about a deeper reality; we discovered that with the Unicorns and we found the same phenomenon in all the years we've worked on bringing Paganism, Witchcraft, Wizardry, and magickal worldviews into the world at large: we've tried to get the world to acknowledge that Witches are real just as Unicorns are real. But that reality is very different from the one in fairy tales.

Our observations about the Unicorns showed us that even kids seem to break down into two categories, and, barring some miracle or catastrophe, they pretty much grow up to be adults who are in those same categories. I hate breaking people into categories, but just bear with me a moment. The first category are kids who want to debunk everything, and thereby prove that they are cooler, because they're not going to be fooled by anything. You've got to be the coolest thing around, and anything else that's cooler than you detracts from your coolness. Therefore, you can only be cool if you don't think anything else is cool. So you have to debunk it; you have to cut it down to your size and disprove it. Unfortunately, too many of those kinds of kids use this tactic to gain the alpha status and grow up to be scientists, politicians, and parents, with that particular egotistic attitude in mind: "If there is anything around bigger than my ego, I want it hunted down and killed!" I guess it's a way of thumbing your nose at the universe somehow. Perhaps it's because they are really insecure inside themselves. Perhaps they think that in order to survive, they have to make themselves bigger and better than everything else, and they do it by tearing down rather than building up. It's a sad but common story.

But the second category are the kind of kids who saw the Unicorn and would recognize it for what it was—not a fantasy creature made of moonbeams, just a small white animal with its own kind of beauty and heart and horn. A creature somewhat like themselves, with its own charm and uniqueness but something real to touch and hold. You could watch it happening in their eyes. Those kids would make the connection and see that Magick was possible and then go on to create their own contribution to that unique world-view. Those kind of kids grow up to be people who really are empowered, who really know that they can make their life be whatever they want it to be. They realize that they don't have to just believe what they see on television or read in the papers; they don't have to blindly believe what the government or churches tell them. They have seen that when it comes to the amazing and miraculous versus the dominant paradigm—grown-ups can be wrong.

So I guess the Unicorn was somewhat subversive, and millions of kids saw it. What we hope for is that all those kids who saw the Unicorn and knew it was real will grow up to be different kinds of scientists and politicians and teachers—as well as parents who will believe their kids when they say that they saw a Unicorn in the garden.

Though Oberon and I were often upset by the vagaries of the mundane world, Lancelot and Bedivere themselves never took it to heart whether the mass media believed they were real Unicorns or not. They knew what they were, and they only cared that they had lots of love and attention and good things to eat. Both Lance and Bedivere outlived all the male goats that were born in their generation by a long shot, and they had amazing adventures and very rich and exciting lives. Yet ultimately not even Unicorns are immortal; sooner or later we all grow old, and life can be pretty harsh at times. The question is: "Would we do it all over again?" The answer is blowing in the wind . . .

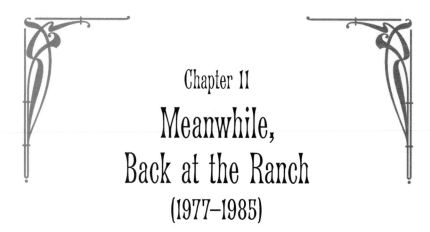

Chapter 11
Meanwhile,
Back at the Ranch
(1977–1985)

Some fields grow in clover, some fields grow in wheat.
Greenfield's growin' all over with love beneath my feet.
Now I have been a travelin' across the whole wide world,
But the country is my oyster, and Greenfield is my pearl!
—FROM "GREENFIELD" BY GWYDION PENDDERWEN, 1981

NARRATOR: For many people who had known the Zells in the Midwest, when they split the St. Louis scene, it was as if they've dropped off the face of the Earth. Prior to that, I used to run into Tim Zell at least once a year at a science-fiction convention somewhere. I'd expected to see him at the 1976 Worldcon because Robert Heinlein was the guest of honor, but he wasn't there or at any other con I went to after that. I had no idea what happened to him.

Eventually I learned some news about the activities of the Zells when I got ahold of Margot Adler's book *Drawing Down the Moon*. It was released in 1979, but I didn't pick it up until a few years later, when I bought it at an East Village store called Enchantments. Margot devoted one chapter to the Church of All Worlds, but by the time the book was in print, the Church had long since split up and *Green Egg* had ceased publication. The CAW was already a part of Pagan history, and its eclectic mix of spiritual exploration was in the past. In the rest of the book Margot emphasized Witches and Witchcraft, and, indeed, by the early 1980s Witchcraft had become the predominant Pagan ritual practice.

The rise of Witchcraft had happened slowly but steadily at first. When Lady Sheba's book was released, there was already a small but enthusiastic community of Witches. Then her *Book of Shadows* made becoming a Witch a real possibility for countless more. Before long, there were many more books with details about the art and practice of Witchcraft, and even more volumes about history and theory. They were publicized mostly by word of mouth, and sold in a growing network of New Age shops and occult bookstores. (These were places where books were allowed to stay on the shelves for years, waiting to be discovered, and employees got to know their customers and made recommendations.)

The Spiral Dance, published on October 31, 1979 (the same date as the publication of *Drawing Down the Moon*), broke all the previous records. It was written by a San Francisco Witch who went by the name of Starhawk. She was a political activist and feminist who had a background in creative writing and psychology, and she had been trained and initiated in the Feri tradition by Victor Anderson. *Spiral* went on to become the Big Kahuna of Witch books in the eighties, and during that time Starhawk was the best-known Pagan on the planet.

And all of this happened, more or less, without Morning Glory or Otter being involved or even being very aware of what was happening. When the Zells were on the road with the Unicorns, they spent their time at whatever Faire they were at. They didn't visit local Pagans, and lost track of that kind of activity for many years. When they were in California, their lives mostly centered around Greenfield Ranch—that was their home and that was where the Unicorns were kept off-season.

Not much in Starhawk's book, or anyone else's, was news to the Zells. They were already living on Feri land, and their next-door neighbor was the *Fäerie* Shaman himself (for such was the title of his second album), Gwydion Pendderwen. In this chapter we'll look at what their life on the Ranch was like, and how their spirituality grew the old-fashioned way.

OZ: For five years we lived in the Scarlet Succubus. After that, for the next five years, we lived in a yurt that was smaller than the living room in our current home. The first year we worked on the yurt, we got the frame put up, but the winter came before we could get a roof and sides on, so we had to cover it with clear plastic. That actually worked quite well. It didn't take much to keep the place warm, as we didn't have really severe winters. A little tin woodstove could get the job done. It was like being inside a giant faceted crystal. That was our first year. But then we put up siding and a roof. I made skylights so we could still look up at the sky. It was a twenty-foot-diameter space—there were no partitions or divisions. It was just one round, open space.

It was a remarkable life. We totally threw ourselves into it. We thought that we were going to live, grow old, die, and be buried on Greenfield Ranch. All those years on the land imbued us with a deep grounding in what Morning Glory and I felt was true Paganism: community, tribal life, and the Village. It was there that the changing of the seasons and the waxing and waning of the moon really mattered. You go through all the stuff together—life, death, and birth. Babies are born and raised. People die and are buried and mourned. The trees and gardens grow, and you harvest the food you planted. This sense of connection and continuity is a precious thing that has been lost to modern civilization. For eight years we were immersed in it. It totally informs and suffuses every aspect of our lives to this very day, and it will forever. Everything that has happened in our lives since then is rooted in that experience.

AYISHA HOMOLKA: One of the things that I learned, not just from Otter and Morning Glory, but from that whole group of people on Greenfield, is an appreciation and understanding of the importance of community. Even though my daughter has become an agnostic and didn't get involved in the whole Pagan scene, one of the things that she treasures and values is community and extended family. I know that Otter and Morning Glory were like an uncle and aunt to her, as were many of the other people up on Greenfield. The people on the Ranch looked out for each other. When you were part of that community, it was probably like it was in the old days, when people all lived in the same village. The adults would take an interest in the children, no matter whose children they were. There was something really special about that. In this world we live in now, everybody is so separate. Even in regular families people don't always live near each other, much less in extended families. It's a richness of living and learning that is priceless. And I think Otter and Morning Glory epitomized that.

MG: Lest people get the impression that our life was one great big party, I do want to talk about the work that we did on the land, which was such a major part of our lives there. Every day there were animals to feed and care for, goats to milk and milk to process into the cheese, which was our major source of protein. In the summer there was digging out the spring box, setting up water tanks, and repairing water lines down to the gardens to irrigate the fruit trees and veggie garden. There was roadwork and erosion control, as well as building sheds and barns and working on the yurt.

In the fall there were weeks of nothing but harvesting downed wood and cutting it up for firewood for the winter, and repairing the roof and other essentials. Also, there was the harvest season and making all kinds of good things to preserve or to eat from the garden or from the wild blackberries that grew by the creek, or were gleaned from farmers' surpluses down in the valley. In the winter there were days and days of rain when the roads would wash out and the only way to get to town was to dig your way out of the mudslides. I remember once when we were shoveling tons of mud that just kept flowing right back on top of us, Otter, Gwydion, and I all looked at each other and said, "What would Heracles do?" So we diverted one of the rivulets that was trying to wash away the road and instead used it to wash away the mudslide, just like Heracles diverted a river to clean out the Augean stables.

In winter we spent a lot of time indoors out of the incessant rain, reading, writing and talking, and having bouts of cabin fever. But the rain in California is a life-bringer, so you were always grateful for its presence; you knew that the water table was being recharged and that the amount of water in your well next August would depend on how much rain you got in November through April. Winter was tree-planting time, and Gwydion started having tree-planting parties in January.

ANODEA JUDITH: Gwydion and I were lovers. He was a very magical fellow. We did tree-planting ceremonies to do something for the Earth. People really got into it. We started having work parties on the land. We did that on New Year's weekends. We would get forty or fifty people to meet at the Ranch house, and we would feed them and teach them. We planted trees on the land in places that had been deforested. And of course this was thirty years ago, so if you go there now, you can see some really big trees that we planted.

MG: The hardest thing about winter was not having hot showers. Going out and working in the mud, cleaning out plugged-up water lines or ditching the roads or clearing out culverts, would leave you cold and wet and muddy, and the only way that you could get clean enough to climb into bed was by heating up water on the stove and mixing it in a bucket and having someone pour it on your naked, shivering body while you washed off the grime. It was definitely not the fun part of living in the country; neither was the lack of indoor toilets. We had a simple privy system that used a low-tech form of composting using plastic pickle barrels and a compost pit. We never used the human waste on the garden, but it did get buried to go back to the Earth in an environmentally friendly fashion.

We were not really very good at the *Mother Earth News* style of "homesteading." We didn't build elaborate wind generators or fancy compost toilets or that sort of thing. Partly because we simply had no money to buy these things, and partly because Alison always kept us hanging as far as giving us permission to build anything was concerned. But mostly I guess it was because we were spending all our time and energy on the Unicorn project. We became very proficient at minimalist survival tactics; for instance, it was two years before I even bought an axe to cut wood, so we got really good at breaking up branches on a sharp boulder half buried in the ground—manzanita and madrone were the best woods to break and to burn. We never cut live wood; we only gathered deadfall. But there were 220 acres of it, so it was never a problem; it just took a lot of time and effort.

Springtime brought more rain and what we called "trash movers," or gully washers, when all the fallen leaves and branches would sweep down the rivulets and streams and plug up the ditches and culverts so that the roads or gardens or dwellings would be in danger of washing away; so you had to don your rain gear and go clear the ditches and culverts fast before the water did irreparable damage to the fragile works of man. You really had to respect the power of Mother Nature and the inexorable way that She moved things around; at times we felt that we were just chips on Her vast tides, just a little anomalous blip on Her cosmic curve.

OZ: We talked our friend Eldri into moving to Greenfield. She brought a big green step-van with her and parked it on the hill during the time we were building our yurt. While she fundamentally lived in the van, she spent a lot of time with us, as we had the only kitchen. It's amazing that we managed to live in that tiny space and share it with people. And we didn't kill and eat each other, which is truly remarkable!

ELDRI LITTLEWOLF: It was cool. They made Unicorns and I watched. I was the home crew—the person who milked the goats and fed the other animals while they were gone. If Morning Glory was at home, I had the morning milking and she had the evening milking. I made sure the fruit trees got watered. The community kitchen was down in the main yurt. We never did have a refrigerator there, just a couple of coolers and buckets of spring water. But we always had fresh goat's milk.

On a typical day we'd hang out, maybe gather some firewood. We'd tell stories. We'd wander off in the woods, visit neighbors, and come back. I spent a lot of time lying on my tummy looking at newts.

In the evening we would play Elven chess, or tell stories, or read aloud to each other. If someone is doing the dishes, it's nice to have somebody in the background reading stories. The *Dr. Demento* radio show was a big deal. Otter would make popcorn, and we'd all listen to that show together.

Otter and Morning Glory are like my long-lost siblings. We were science brats and dinosaur kids, and we wanted to grow up and live in a museum. We liked to talk about natural history. They brought me back a coyote head once from the Anderson Valley for my birthday. They knew that I would like it, and I did. But nobody else is going to hand you a maggoty coyote head as a birthday present!

OZ: Around Beltane of 1980, shortly after the Unicorns were born, I came upon a baby deer in the woods. I knew that I could take the fawn home with me and raise it up—we just had to change the imprint. We named her Marena, after a doe in the book *Bambi* who believes that one day man will come to the forest not to kill but to be friends with the animals. We adopted her to be a sister to Lancelot and Bedivere, bottle-feeding all three of them on goat's milk. She was still a wild deer—she lived with the other deer and wandered out in the fields where they grazed. But we could go out into the field and call out her name, and out of this herd of wild deer one of them would perk up its ears and come trotting over to us.

MG: We ended up raising several orphaned fawns. Though they were all precious, one of the deer that we raised was the most special to me; I called her my Deer Daughter. She was born in the spring of 1982, and Oberon brought her home and put her in my arms. I named her Kira after the Gelfling girl in the *Dark Crystal* movie.

I used to go walking in the cool spring afternoons along the Glory Trail. I would don my purple jogging suit and sneakers and start walking down the road, and often Kira and Octobriana (our kitty) would go along with me.

One day on one of these walks, as we came around the bend we encountered another fawn just about Kira's age standing alongside the road. The other fawn saw us coming and startled, running up the hillside to her mother. Kira saw the fawn and was so excited to see someone like her that she took off after the fawn and ran up the hill to where the fawn was hiding behind her mother. Kira practically slid to a halt when the big doe snorted and stamped a hoof in warning at her. She looked long and carefully at the mother doe and at the fawn peering at her around her mother's flank. Then she looked down the hill at me in my purple jogging suit, then back at the doe and fawn. You could hear the wheels turning in her head: "That baby looks like her mother, but I don't look like my mother. Could it be that I'm adopted?" But then she spun around on her heels, sproinked down the hillside, and ran to hide behind me, peeking out smugly at the other fawn. I could almost hear her blow a raspberry: "Well, I've got a mommy who loves me too, even if she does look funny!"

OZ: One day Morning Glory and I were walking across a field, and we surprised a big wild sow with a batch of piglets. I said, "I bet I could catch one of those and we could raise it up."

MG said, "No way could you catch one!" So I took off running as the whole litter scattered, and I caught one of the babies. She imprinted on us immediately, and soon followed us everywhere, even sleeping inside my sleeping bag with me when we camped out (she would crawl out when she need to pee or poop, and then crawl back in). We named her "Ankh-Ankh," telling people that she knew the secret of eternal life in ancient Egyptian.

That Summer Solstice, we had a mini-parade up to the pond led by Sharon Devlin and her partner, Sean, in yellow Bardic robes playing the bagpipes. MG and I followed, and behind us in a line came Lancelot, Bedivere, Marena, Ankh-Ankh, and finally our wonderful kitty Octobriana. One of our neighbors, John Amon, drove by in his truck and commented laconically, "Must be Summer Solstice!"

The Summer Solstice parties were an amazing annual activity for everyone who lived on the Ranch. They were held down by the pond, which was in a canyon that had been dammed. It went up very steeply on either side, but with a wide bank on one side where people could spread blankets and hang out. On the opposite side was a huge spire of rock like a castle tower. You could climb up there and look down on the whole area. A steel cable was strung across the pond to the rock pinnacle, with a rope swing attached to the center, and a high wooden platform on the near side to jump from. You had to climb up a tall post and stand upon the very tip-top to actually grab the rope! There was a big knot at the end of the rope, and you had to seize hold above it and then jump onto the knot as you fell. With your weight on it, the cable would stretch like a bowstring, and you would plunge nearly to the water before being catapulted back up by the recoil, like a released arrow. The trick was to let go right at the top of that arc, and then, in free-fall, you could get real acrobatic.

ZACK DARLING: There was this big rope swing—there was a cable that went across the pond, and a rope that was tied to it, and this deck that people would swing off of. This was back before the days of people being afraid of lawsuits. It was a pretty dramatic rope swing. Oberon was the only one crazy enough to do a back flip off of the rope swing. He used to be a pretty fit dude.

OZ: And of course lots of people were naked and skinny-dipping. We held watermelon races and a water ballet that we rehearsed beforehand. In the water ballet of 1980, I was the last in the line, and our feral piglet Ankh-Ankh followed me. When I dove in, she was right behind me, and she swam half the circle in perfect formation, to the delight of everybody. But when we got to the opposite bank, she climbed out disgusted, to hang out with MG for the rest of the day.

One of the things that became a part of the Solstice every year was a big ritual, which MG and I co-created and led. We would take a long procession of people and we would walk up to the "Tor"—an ancient volcanic protrusion forming a rough, natural stone circle that was maybe a hundred feet in diameter. We would form a circle of people around it, and create a bubble of protection over the whole Ranch. We would expand our circle to become a huge umbrella, and then extend it outwards to become a bubble that we envisioned as being mirrored on the outside to make the whole place invisible.

MG and I became two of the main ritualists for all kinds of stuff there—whenever there was something to be done that required a ritual or ceremony. So we honed our skills over the years to be able to pull together really good rituals for any size group under any circumstances.

NARRATOR: Gwydion Pendderwen lived on fifty-five acres of land next to the Zells. He had originally planned to be partners with Alison Harlow on the land that she bought, but when that didn't work out he bought the parcel next door and named it *Annwfn*.

OZ: He often helped us and we helped him. Helping your neighbors work on projects was part of the practical work ethic that built our rural way of life. During the years that Gwydion was our neighbor, we would often walk the mile or so over to his place and visit him, and he would do the same for us. He was always writing songs. Music was his great gift.

NARRATOR: OZ had known Gwydion since 1972, when he met him during his trip west to go to the World Science Fiction Convention in Los Angeles. In 1975 Gwydion recorded his first record album and named it *Songs for the Old Religion*. The music and lyrics on it, which were published in a book called *The Wheel of the Year* in 1979, gave Pagans everywhere something in common. Whatever their tradition was, they could all join together and sing Gwydion's songs when they gathered for ritual or social purposes. It helped unify the community, and made him well known.

ANNE HILL: Gwydion really planted the flag, so to speak, and said, "This is Pagan music." He recorded himself, and then started up the Nemeton label, so he was kind of a visionary in that way. Gwydion kept his own publicity going in a way that's fairly modern. He had a lot of correspondence with people. He taught himself Welsh and went to the Royal National Eisteddfod of Wales—it's an annual poetry competition that goes back to medieval times in Wales, when all the national poets would get together. It was kind of like a medieval poetry slam. So not only did he put out his albums, but he was an active participant/creator in the whole Pagan scene and Pagan music scene. I think the styles that he chose to pursue—blending in the whole Celtic themes with the Earth tradition themes—became thick strands in the rope of Pagan identity in the United States.

NARRATOR: Gwydion traveled to Pagan events, where he sang and sometimes did his Faerie Shaman rituals. Those have become legendary, especially among a group of people who can trace their lineage back to someone who was originally initiated by Gwydion himself.

OZ: Gwydion was quite a ritualist. He had a common theme that was running through his mythos and his rituals. He was very tied to the Celtic mythos of the two brothers who were opposing twins, and there was always tension and a constant struggle between them. They could be called the Red Man and the Green Man, or the Holly King and the Oak King, or the Stag King and the Bull King. He would create dramatic rituals for the different seasons that enacted this conflict and struggle, where the two brothers have to fight and determine who was going to be the king for the next half of the year, for the next season.

But there is something fundamentally flawed with that kind of myth. It is a myth that says you can't get along; that you have to struggle and fight. It is not a myth of cooperation. One of the things that we learned when we worked with Gwydion was that you have to be very careful about the myths that you enact, that you call into being in your life—the ones you identify with. These will shape your life. It's not a simple little thing that you just do. It does you too. What you call into being magickally, becomes real.

Gwydion and Alison were part of the Feri tradition that was taught by Victor Anderson. That included having a tree that is your soul tree, and is identified with you. And the fate of that tree is bound to your fate. It comes from an old Celtic tradition—when children were born in the village, the afterbirth would be put in the ground and a small apple tree would be planted with it. And as the tree grew, it would be bound to the person. It would be given their name, and the fruit of the tree was their fruit. Eventually when they died, they would be buried under that tree.

In December of 1981, Gwydion's special tree, which was by the creek on Coeden Brith, came down in a flood. He was quite stricken. In his mind, his fate was bound to the tree.

MG: Samhain of 1982 arrived cold and clear, and Oberon and I donned our handmade woolen cloaks for the ritual. We walked up the hill and met up with Orion, and we three headed to the Shaggy Mushroom, which was the name of Gwydion's yurt. We knocked on the door and he answered, "Enter freely and of your own will," which of course was Dracula's line to visitors at his castle, so we chuckled and pushed our way past the creaky, old green door with the brass fox's head knocker. He was sitting in his beautiful, old, massively carved chair with the lions' paws for arms and legs and a medieval-style lion tapestry for upholstery. He was wearing his cloak with the hood over his head hiding his face somewhat, and he held out a chalice that looked like it was carved of gray marble. "Would you care to drink from the Cup of the Dead?" he asked us.

I eagerly reached out and took the cup because, after all, it was Samhain night and thus an exceedingly appropriate time to drink with the dead. But when my lips touched the cup and I tossed it back, I discovered it was empty, not just out of wine but empty as never having held any. I paused a moment and reflected in the silence—yes, indeed, this would be how the dead would drink; they would drink of emptiness. So I looked into Gwydion's eyes in the candlelight, tipped the cup back, and took a deep draught of the emptiness, thinking of the ones who had passed beyond the veil that year. I didn't let on to the others what I learned; I didn't want to spoil the secret; I wanted them to share this magickal moment of emptiness, too. Gwydion was always a master of secrets, and the Cup of the Dead is still one of our favorite Samhain traditions.

OZ: After sharing the Cup of the Dead with us, Gwydion got up and suggested that we go out into the moonlight. He came out in his cloak, which he had turned inside out to reveal its silvery, pale satin lining. It was a full moon, and he stood out like a ghost in the moonlight. He was luminescent. Now, there is a rule that if you find yourself in Faerie and want to return to the mundane world, you take off your coat, turn it inside out, and put it back on again. So to start out by putting it on inside out, in traditional Faerie lore, is to invite going into the Underworld.

So this was all very strange. We felt there was something eerie about it. But we went ahead and had our ritual. Part of that was to pass around a bowl of beans, pick one out, say the name of someone who had died in the past year, and toss it into the fire. Beans are associated in many myths with being repositories of spirit. Because, of course, if you eat beans it makes you fart. So the idea would be that is the spirit escaping, and thus throwing beans into a fire was a way of calling the spirits.

As was our tradition, we called all the names of people we had known who had died that year. And there weren't very many of them whom we had known personally. But there is always a point in a ritual like that where you look around the Circle and wonder, "Is there anyone here whose name will be called next year?"

After that, we closed the Circle and went our separate ways. Gwydion left the Ranch later on some mysterious errand, and on the way back home he had a fatal car accident. We were eventually able to reconstruct what happened. It seemed he swerved to avoid a deer crossing the road and lost control of his car. It rolled over, and he was thrown out because he wasn't wearing a seat belt. The car flipped over again and came down on top of him. He was killed instantly. The car kept rolling and then stopped right-side up. It was pretty much undamaged except for a broken window. Gwydion was found the next morning.

FARIDA FOX: I had seen Gwydion the night before he died. We both sang in the Ukiah Chorus, a choral group that did concerts and sang major liturgical music by composers like Beethoven and Mozart. It was an opportunity to sing complex, polyphonic music. I sang in choirs for many, many years and I really enjoyed it. Gwydion was an accomplished musician and could read music. Most of the people on the Ranch didn't have much of a background in classical music, but he did. He had sung in choruses and different kinds of things before that.

We had been at a rehearsal. I asked him if he wanted to go out for coffee or something afterwards, and he said, "No, no, I've got to get up really early tomorrow morning." Well, he didn't go home that night. He went to Lake County. It was on his way back from that that he evidently hit a deer on Highway 20. And that was it.

NARRATOR: Every person I interviewed that had known Gwydion had stories about what he was doing and talking about right before he died. He had even gone back to the Bay Area to, what looks like in retrospection, say goodbye to his family and friends. There was also lots of speculation about what happened to him after he left Farida Fox on the last night of his life, and why he didn't go directly home.

This much is certain: he lives on as a kind of Jimi Hendrix, Kurt Cobain, or Jim Morrison of the Pagan scene, someone who was around for a short amount of time and burst like a supernova with creativity. OZ likes to talk about how Jim Morrison was living the myth of Dionysus and that's why he died so young. Gwydion was living the myth of the Green Man, and he felt that his death was near, and so he stopped taking care of himself, didn't buckle up his seat belt, and his myth, too, became a reality.

ANODEA JUDITH: When he died, he left the land to five women, all of whom had been his lovers at one time or another. And we were called the Stewards of Annwfn, because the land was actually in the name of the CAW, and the Church still owned it (and does to this day). But he left it to us to run it. At that point I moved there. I lived there for a couple of years. I was a single mother at the time.

OZ: We held a big memorial up at the Ranch. John Solo, one of the original Ranchers, made a very memorable observation. He said, "Those of us who live the longest will have the task of burying our dearest friends." That was our first wake. Gwydion was the first person whom we were close to in our community to die. We had to learn how to do a wake. We told stories and shared Gwydion anecdotes. Some who knew how to, sang his songs. It was very sobering, and yet deeply moving.

Our 1982 Yule festival was the first Yule that Gwydion wasn't a part of. His singing and Bardic craft had always been an essential part of it. And he had always been *the* Bard. Because he was so good at it, and his songs were so brilliant, nobody else even bothered to participate or try to create music or poetry. We were all just his audience. Moreover, Gwydion was rather contemptuous of people who didn't have a great Gift. He thought they shouldn't bother, and thus he discouraged them from trying.

So there we were, sitting around Sequoia's woodstove. There were all these songs that Gwydion had written, and there was no Gwydion to sing them. So Mari picked up her dulcimer and played a tune. Then other people just started playing music and singing songs—some by Gwydion, and some by themselves and others. Out of that moment was born a true

Bardic tradition in which everybody could participate. Up until then it had just been Gwydion. So, in a sense, the spirit that he had brought became embedded in the larger community. And that, in many ways, was probably the best memorial that there could have been for him. His Bardic gift was bequeathed to the community. After that our Circles were just cranking out songs and poetry. We developed a huge liturgy of stuff for every possible occasion, eventually including much of it in a book, *Creating Circles and Ceremonies*, published in 2006.

FARIDA FOX: After he was killed in the car crash, all of us who were still around started really developing festivals eight times a year at Annwfn, and there was a kind of coming together of the Church of All Worlds as an entity.

NARRATOR: In addition to the stress of losing Gwydion and keeping the Unicorning process a secret, Morning Glory had the additional stress of some things from her past that she was still keeping hush-hush.

Around this same time, some radical psychotherapists were experimenting with giving the drug Ecstasy, which was then still legal, to their patients. There were reports of people getting major insight by doing that. Morning Glory, in her true shamanistic style, began experimenting on her own.

MG: We had a friend who was doing guided visualizations and mediations using Ecstasy. I never, ever did an acid or Ecstasy trip that wasn't very intensely and carefully planned and where we had set and setting and structure, and a goal and a magickal purpose. I had never been the kind of person who would say, "Yippee! Let's drop acid and go to a Dead show."

I had done four of these Ecstasy trips in a row over a series of two or three months. It was right after Gwydion had died. Then, all of sudden, not stoned and all by myself, it was like the biochemical change that had happened in my brain as a result of doing the Ecstasy just dissolved the barrier that was between one part of my informational system and my memory. I discovered that I had created false memories, and suddenly the X enabled me to look at a remembered experience and to perceive that some of those memories were false, to see that I had created them.

This breakthrough was precipitated by the X experiences, but it was not itself a drug experience. It was a psychological breakthrough that happened, a moment of satori. And that made a profound difference in my life from that moment on.

Part of the problem was this really schizophrenic part of me. I'm a Gemini, and I had some really serious kinds of problems based on the way my brain had evolved living in an eighteen-foot trailer with a father who would go into these rages and beat the crap out of my mother and me. And that whole situation kind of forged who I was, and there were some real problems with that in terms of my ability to embroider what was and turn it into what I really wanted it to be, as opposed to what it really was. And sooner or later, that was going to come apart. And that was what happened. It was the Ecstasy that allowed me to break through the psychic illusion that I had about who I was.

Suddenly I was faced with the knowledge that all the stuff that I had said just wasn't so. Starkly, all at once as part of my internal dialogue, I saw that I was living a lie on a lot of levels. And I was mortified. My first instinct was, "I can't live with this." My entire magickal world, the foundation of my magickal training, was founded on a lie. And to have to face that, it was like my mind just snapped. The first thing I did was to pick up a knife, and I was going to kill myself. I said, "I'm gonna end this. I can't possibly live with the contradiction of who I am."

Right at that moment this little voice came into my head; it was like the Ecstasy Faery, and she said, "Awww, don't kill the poor little girl. She didn't mean any harm. She was just trying to tell stories, and just trying to get out of trouble. She's not really bad. She just needs to get straightened out."

The next thing I heard was the powerful voice of the Goddess. And she said, "You wanted a second-degree initiation"—and that was another thing. I told everyone that my first initiation was a life-or-death ordeal, and in a sense it was. But I had said that that was what I wanted for a second-degree initiation, and I was looking for some system or somebody on a shamanic level that could give me that. And it had never materialized, because nobody wanted to take that on—nothing was good about it. And it was because I had this fantasy that wasn't real.

And when I confronted that, at that point the Goddess spoke and She said, "Did you think that the Gods were all made up? That you made us up? That we weren't real? Did you think that if you dangled yourself as bait, in a lie, that we wouldn't snap you up and take your life if you offered your life to us? Did you think that if you offered your life as a lie that we would let you go on living like that?"

I was sitting alone in my little trailer, not on drugs, having this amazing psychological breakthrough, and I was shocked into stillness, but I managed to croak, "No, I don't know what I was thinking. I don't think I was thinking."

And She said, "Well, if you want a real life-changing second-degree initiation, here is what you must do. You have now had your life-or-death experience! You have now had the challenge. You have put down the knife. You have survived. Now here is the challenge. You have to go to everyone that you have ever lied to, and tell them the truth, and ask their forgiveness. And promise that you will never lie to them again. And that is your second-degree initiation. That is gonna be what will change your life. That is going to burn out the impurity and corruption and festering selfish pride that you have built your magickal life on."

And that's what I did. I started with Oberon and I went through, one by one. It took me five years. Some of my lies were written in books, and they had to be corrected for the second editions. I went through and told everybody that I had ever lied to about anything that was significant, and that I could remember; I would tell them the truth, and I would apologize, and I would ask their forgiveness. Then I would promise that I would never lie to them again.

And that has been my yoga. Changing my life and making things right, and trying to create restitution and wholeness. And gradually that humbled me and healed me. And once I was a whole person, I had to go through my own personal rebuilding of "Who the hell am I?"

Chapter 12
The Hunting of the Ri
(1983–1985)

Now the Wizard and his wife's tale's not told.
For what did they do, you ask, with their gold?
Did they bank it or invest it or buy Bills of T?
No, they spent it chasing Mermaids in the Coral Sea!
—FROM "THE UNICORN—PART 2" BY ORION STORMCROW, 1986

NARRATOR: After the Unicorns had joined the circus, then MG and OZ had to figure out who the hell they were, as individuals and as a team. "What to do next?" became the big question. So much of their time and energy had gone into the Unicorns, and they had expected to continue in that direction, and couldn't. But they had always had other things going in their lives. One of them was OZ's artistic pursuits. In the fall of 1983, after the Faire season was over for that year, OZ signed up for art classes at the local community college in Ukiah. While he was there, he met someone who became in important part of both his life and Morning Glory's. Her name was Diane, and she would join them on their next adventure, and many of the ones that would follow. She had a son named Zack, and he would grow up with all of them as parents and become Pagan in a way that the Zells' own children hadn't.

OZ: I enrolled in some pottery classes, and they were great. That was where I made my first sculptures of Goddesses. I was doing that for a couple of weeks, and then it was time for a field trip. This was an annual event that the whole art department went on. They took students down to visit art studios in the Bay Area. We went to glass-blowing, leather-working, tapestry, and wallpaper studios.

The bus left at like 6:00 a.m. This lovely red-headed woman sat down next to me, and we started chatting it up. We hadn't met each other before, and we really hit it off. We were the only Hippies!

DIANE DARLING: I was recovering from a broken heart, and I went on the field trip because anything was better than hanging around in my own head. I just walked down the aisle of the bus until I found the most interesting-looking person. I sat down next to Otter and introduced myself. We kind of hung out the whole field trip.

OZ: Throughout the day the other people were observing this budding romance grow into something quite amorous, so we became the darlings of the field trip. It was sweet, sort of like when Morning Glory and I had met at Gnosticon. People create a support system around something like that. On the ride home late at night we got to be really close, canoodling in the back of the bus. By the time we got back from the trip, we were madly in love with each other.

DIANE DARLING: He was very solicitous and courtly. He was telling me stories about his wife and his Unicorn, and I was taking it all in. At that time he smelled liked a goat. I didn't mind because I'm an animal person. I was in a period of celibacy because I was so screwed up by my previous relationship. He courted me for a period of six months, which I thought was really sweet. He would come down from the mountain and into town to hang out with me.

After about six months we decided to go ahead and have a love affair. I went with him in his beat-up old pickup truck to Greenfield. The Ranch road back then was very bad, and this was at night, in the winter-time, in the rain. So it was a harrowing drive. I used to say it wasn't in the middle of nowhere, but you could see it from there. We got out there and Morning Glory, who had said she was sick and would not be joining us, joined us. So we had a threesome, and that was kind of how we went on from there.

OZ: She also had a young son, Zachariah, so both of them started spending time with us out at the Ranch. After a short amount of time, they both moved there. We had just acquired a large, quite nice, prefabricated, canvas-covered yurt from a community that no longer needed it. We set it up on Coeden Brith, and in the spring of 1984, Diane and Zack moved into it. For the next few years, they were with us on the Ranch.

ZACK DARLING: I was seven years old when I met the Zells. I was born in Minneapolis, Minnesota. My mother was into Zen Buddhism. The reason we moved to California was to live in this Zen Buddhist commune called Spring Mountain in Potter Valley, which is near Redwood Valley. So my mother was a pretty devout Buddhist for most of the early part of my life. Then, through Otter and Morning Glory, she discovered the Goddess.

We became very close with them as the years went on. I remember Otter's long hair and bushy beard when I was a little kid. I don't really know my father. There were three major men in my mom's life who were great for me in the sense that they were willing to step up and take me under their wings and be real strong male role models. Otter was definitely one of those. Otter and I would play "Primate." We would find some trees that we liked, that we could climb on, and we would jump around like monkeys, pick imaginary fleas out of each other's hair, swing from the branches, and make a lot of noise. He was really great with kids.

OZ: While she was still in Ukiah, Diane was making a little money by selling freshly pressed carrot juice to restaurant and health food stores. So when I stayed with her, we'd get up in the morning and press the juice from the carrots that we'd gotten the day before and go with her on her rounds to deliver the stuff in the morning. Well, MG and I were well known in the Ukiah area, so that kind of made a ripple in the community. Then in the afternoons Diane and Morning Glory would come into town to do things together. But when all three of us started showing up together, people just gave up and accepted that we were some kind of a set.

NARRATOR: In 1985 Otter got his next assignment from the Goddess: to go to the South Pacific and look for Mermaids.

OZ: Right around the time that we were making the arrangements with the circus, there were a number of intriguing articles appearing in various magazines, newspapers, and other places. I had just joined the International Society of Cryptozoology (ISC), founded by the legendary Bernard Heuvelmans (who coined the term), and was getting their annual journal, *Cryptozoology*, including back issues. In Volume 1 (Winter 1982) was an article about an interesting new unknown critter, said to be analogous to the Mermaids of legend and lore. These were being seen off of a little island north of New Guinea called New Ireland. Of course, native people's reports of strange things in the jungle are always coming in. That sort of forms the background of the whole cryptozoological field (*cryptozoology* meaning "study of hidden animals"). But rarely do any of these quite get a solid confirmation.

But in this particular case, the report had come from Roy Wagner, a linguist and cultural anthropologist who was the head of the department of anthropology at the University of Virginia in Charlottesville. He had been studying the people of New Ireland to try and document their languages before these unique and varied tongues completely died out and were replaced by the traders' language Tok Pisin. Part of the process is recording and translating the vocabulary. One of the things that they came up with in a coastal village called Nokon Bay was a sea critter. In other areas it was called a *Ri*, but there it was called an *Ilkai*. The natives described this as a real living animal, not some fantasy or mythological creature. Wagner asked them what it was. So they took him down to the beach and pointed to the ocean. And there was an unidentifiable creature bobbing up and down out in the waves! At that distance, Wagner couldn't see a whole lot, but there was obviously something out there, and it looked like it had a head and shoulders. He could see that there was more than one and that it might have been a family with a child.

Wagner asked them more about what it was, and they pointed to the picture on the label of a can of Chicken of the Sea tuna. They told him, "You catch 'em and eat 'em, just like some other fellas do here." They thought that whatever was pictured on the label was in the can—just like there was a picture of a tomato on the label of a can of tomatoes! But Chicken of the Sea tuna didn't have a picture of a tuna on it; instead, there was a picture of a Mermaid. So naturally they figured it was canned Mermaid. And the word for that in pidgin, which is what they were speaking, is *pishmeri,* which means "fishwoman." And that is pretty much the same thing as *Mermaid,* which literally means "seawoman."

Wagner was pretty amazed. His follow-up report in Volume 2 of *Cryptozoology* (Winter 1983) included the traditional, fuzzy, out-of focus photos that he had taken of something bobbing around out in the sea. At one point Wagner convinced one of the villagers to take him out in a little boat that they had. They went out in that, and Wagner definitely saw something there. It swam around, and when it dove, it would raise its tail up above water. It was this beautiful fluked tail—it looked just like a whale tail, only smaller. It wasn't like a dolphin tail or that of any other animal Wagner could identify.

In describing it, the natives insisted that in the upper parts it is just like a human woman—that it had a woman's breasts and genitals, but that the lower parts of it were fish. The natives absolutely insisted that this was, in fact, a Mermaid as we understand it. Articles about this critter ended up not just in mainstream journals but also in the *National Enquirer,* an airline in-flight magazine, and many other places. So we decided to mount our own expedition with the money that we got from the circus for the Unicorns, and go see for ourselves. And we would take along a professional video crew to document the trip. We hoped to be able to recoup the costs of the trip by selling the documentary to some TV adventure or nature show.

We assembled an expedition of thirteen people, sponsored by our own Ecosophical Research Association (ERA), which Morning Glory had founded and chartered under the CAW. We corresponded with Bernard Heuvelmans, president of the ISC, and received his encouragement. Roy Mackal, ISC vice president, and Richard Greenwell, secretary-treasurer, were also very supportive. Dr. Wagner and Greenwell considered joining us but were unable to do so. We started taking scuba lessons and got our diving gear. And we hired a film crew that had done the underwater footage on the movie *The Deep*.

We spent the summer and fall of 1984 getting prepared—taking diving classes in the cold waters and kelp forests off the Northern California coast to get scuba-certified for the expedition. My son Bryan got out of the Army in September and went to diving school in Florida. We rented a dive boat in Australia that would take us on the trip. Orion was one of the major coordinators of all this. He was perpetually doing this—I would come up with some big thing that involved logistical coordination, and he would be right there doing the roadie work. He was quite good at that. In March of 1985 we left for the expedition. Besides Morning Glory and myself, our members included Tom Williams; Orion Stormcrow; Bryan; Diane Darling and her lover at the time; our old friend from the early days of *Green Egg* Daniel Blair Stewart and his wife, Meadow; the film crew; and a couple of other friends.

BRYAN ZELL: We flew into Sydney, Australia. And waiting at the airport was this group that Dad had been corresponding with for a while. They were Gardnerians. They were all in robes at the airport. I attended one of their rituals.

OZ: This whole bunch of wonderful Aussie Pagans, Witches, and Magicians took us home with them and put us all up and had a marvelous time showing us around. In fact, our visit evidently became part of a precipitating series of factors in what became the emergence of a significant Australian Pagan community. At the time that we arrived, the only Neo-Pagan influences in Australia—I'm not talking about the native Aboriginal religion—were Alexandrian Witchcraft and a little bit of Gardnerian Wicca. These were two competing branches of very similar forms of Witchcraft. So you had these various covens that didn't talk to each other or have anything to do with each other. There were also some Ceremonial Magickal Lodges, but they mostly kept to themselves also. So when we came in, everybody wanted to meet us because they had read *Green Egg* and they knew who we were. Now for the first time a bunch of people from different traditions came together and had a big party so that they could meet us. There were too many of us for any one group to take on, so they set aside their conflicts and cooperated in order to make it happen.

We spent days talking to people, promoting the idea that they could have a movement that was bigger than any single group, and that could embrace all different traditions. It was a novel concept that a number of folks thought was great. A lot of people joined CAW at that point, and that eventually mushroomed into something pretty big. Later there were major festivals, publications, and an entire Australian Pagan movement that were all galvanized by this event. So we felt pretty good about how it all went down. It was a wonderful event. Eventually, in 1992, CAW became the first non-Christian church to become legally incorporated in Australia!

We left Sydney and flew on up to Port Moresby, New Guinea. We stopped in the Trobriand Islands that Margaret Mead had made famous, and hiked through the woods to the ruins of an ancient temple. The people told us that the missionaries had told them that it was a bad place and they shouldn't come there. We asked one man if there were any stories the old people told about the place before white people came, but he just shook his head and shrugged his shoulders: "Maybe everyone has forgot now." We told him to keep asking the old folks if anyone knew any stories because it was not good to forget what your ancestors made.

MG: The thing that I most liked to do when we dropped anchor and rowed into shore was to greet the children who gathered on the beach to meet us. I decided that I wanted to put a little magickal energy into everyone I could, so I bought a dozen or so boxes of those little gummed-paper foil stars that teachers give out to grade-school kids on their papers. I bought gold and silver, red, blue, and green, and every time I would land on the beach I'd stick a silver star on my forehead and show them the box and ask if they wanted one too. They always did, and so I had fun sticking colored stars on the foreheads of hundreds of kids of all ages. They would run off and gather up more brothers and sisters to bring them back; there was no need to fight over anything because there were plenty of stars for everyone.

Even the moms would come around and ask for stars and we would laugh together, sharing the excitement of the children. Once, one of the women asked me in pidgin what the stars were for. Maybe she was concerned that her kids were joining some weird religious cult or that they were being marked for kidnapping or something. After all, we were certainly not at all like any of the other white folks they had ever encountered before, so I guess a little caution was justified. I told her that in our schools when a child was good, the teacher would give them a star like that; then I asked her, "Aren't all these good children?"

Of course she laughed, and I saw the relief bloom in her eyes: "Oh yes, yes, all these children are very good!" Then shyly, she asked me if she could have a star too.

When we got to New Ireland, we stopped at a town called Namatanai, and I decided to go ashore in search of ice cream. I had been craving it the whole time we'd been in the tropics because it was too difficult to keep on board the ship. I went into this small convenience store run by a Chinese couple and asked if they had ice cream; they just shook their heads. Undeterred, I kept looking around the store because it looked exactly like the kind of store that should have ice cream bars. Finally, I went back to the Chinese proprietors and asked them again if they had ice cream; this time I asked them in pidgin, in French, and in Spanish, but they still shook their heads.

Then a very tall, Papuan native man walked up to me. His hair was fanned out into an Afro-type style with many small, elaborate braids in the front. He had intricate swirling facial tattoos and a kina shell piercing his nasal septum; he also was wearing a suit and tie. He spoke to me in flawless English with a slight British accent: "Madam, if you want to find someone who speaks English, you will have to ask one of the tribal folk; these people don't speak any language but their own." I blinked and stood there speechless for a minute and then thanked him profusely. Next he directed me to the tiny freezer with ice cream. I laughed at myself all the way back to the boat. My bubble of Western provincial assumptions had been thoroughly popped.

Everywhere we went, we asked about the *Pishmeri*. Most of the places we visited with Melanesian populations said, yes, they knew about such creatures and would tell us a story. One tale was that the Pishmeri followed people in boats, and if you threw trash into the ocean she would reach out and grab you and drag you in. But everyone said that nobody had seen any of them for a long, long time. Only the Polynesian people in the Trobriands said that they didn't know of anything that looked like that; they identified dolphins, whales, sharks, and dugongs—but no Pishmeri. They were significant seafarers, fishing for their living as well as annually sailing their ceremonially decorated Kula canoes all over their island chain to renew the cultural bonds between them.

We sat in a dozen or more quiet bays overnight up and down the coasts of New Guinea, New Britain, and New Ireland, and we scanned the waters with binoculars when the sun came up because that was the time that the creatures most often appeared to feed.

We felt that we needed to get grounded because our luck just wasn't working. But we were in the middle of the ocean, so we decided to hold a Circle in the water. Everyone donned their gear and swam out away from the boat and held hands while we called upon Mama Yemaya to help us and I sang an Irish song that Ruth Barrett had taught me to call the Silkies. We saw dolphins and turtles and, most wonderful of all, a whale shark, but we never saw anything that fit the description we were looking for—until we got to Nokon Bay in New Ireland.

I was up on deck on watch with the divemaster, and suddenly I saw tail flukes rise up out of the water. I called him over to check it out, and as we both watched we saw these rolling dark backs and then, after a three-to-five minute pause, would come this graceful long tail waving up and out of the water as the creature used it for leverage to dive down deep. We had found the Pishmeri exactly where it was supposed to be!

OZ: Eventually we got to Nokon Bay, along the north side of New Ireland. We pulled into the harbor and dropped anchor in the evening. And there out in the water were the critters we'd come to find. It was clearly a family—two adults and one child. From the vantage of the boat we couldn't get a good look, but we were pretty excited about it. In the morning the same family showed up again.

The next day we got up and we saw the Ilkai coming in. We were going to send some divers down to try and get pictures, but the captain said that it was likely that the bubbles from regulators would scare the critter away. So he volunteered to swim out with just a snorkel and shoot some pictures. It was a long swim but he was really good, and he came back saying he got a look at the animals even though the water was a little murky and thought he might have gotten a good picture. But these weren't digital cameras—the film had to be sent to Australia and developed before we knew what we had captured on the film. All we could tell at the time was that these animals were real. We spent the day diving in the reefs and around, gathering seaweed, shellfish, and other things that might be food for the creatures, but we didn't see them again.

In the evening on the second day, the local people invited us to come on shore for a sing-sing, which is sort of like a beach party. They had a fire and cooked up a bunch of fish and shellfish, coconuts and papayas, and we brought some hot dogs and marshmallows from the boat. We all shared the food around, and we sang songs around the campfire.

Just before we left the boat for the sing-sing, we saw a little tugboat pulling into the harbor and dropping anchor. But they didn't make any contact with us. It had a Japanese flag and the lettering on the bow identified it as *The Cuddles*. We asked the natives about it. Lined up along the shore on one side of the dock was a huge raft of logs. What we were told was that some Japanese representative had come to the village and asked if they could cut down some trees. These were big, old teak trees. They offered to give them a jeep in exchange for the trees. The natives didn't really think it would be much of a problem, because the forest was huge, and the wood of the trees was so hard that it was almost impossible to cut—especially with just axes.

So they made a Devil's bargain, and then the Japanese showed up with these tree-cutting machines the size of houses that came onto the island like a lawnmower and denuded half of the entire forest. They would take the logs down to the water's edge, float them, and bind them together. And then every few months a big ship would come, anchor out at sea, and the tugboat would come to shore, lash onto the raft of logs, and haul it out to sea where it would be taken aboard the ship. All the arrangements had been properly made, but the natives were embarrassed about it. They had made themselves a deal with the Devil, with no idea what they were getting into. It was horrible, and a total environmental travesty. The villagers told us this was one of those tugboats.

We started singing. Some of our folks knew how to play guitar. We sang some of our favorite Grateful Dead songs. Then they sang us their songs; even though the songs were in their own language, the tunes sounded familiar. When we asked what the songs were about, they apologized, telling us, "Our traditional songs are lost to us. When the missionaries came, they forbade us to sing our own traditional songs. But they taught us Christian songs in our own language." So they sang "Away in a Manger" and "Jesus Loves Me" in Sursurunga, which is the language of that village. It's spoken by maybe a hundred people.

There were no artifacts in the village because traders had come and taken them all. We're talking a culture that goes back 40,000 years, clear back to the Ice Age. And it was all gone. The people had no heritage to pass on to their kids. And now their forest was being taken away, and the kids were learning English in Australian schools and losing their language.

We went back to the boat and went to bed for the night. We had people set to get up at dawn and watch for the Ilkai. But the next morning the person on watch hollered and woke us up. He said there was some commotion going on down at the beach that we needed to see. We could see that on the beach the natives were clustered around what appeared to be a large, dead creature floating in the water. We realized it was a dead Ilkai. And the Japanese tugboat was gone, without taking the flotilla of logs.

At that point I dove overboard and swam to shore. I didn't wait for the dinghy to row ashore. We got there and found that the female of the family had been shot. There was what looked like a bullet hole in her side, right behind her armpit. She was dead. We arranged for local guys to drag the body up on shore.

Now we could see clearly what it was: an Indo-Pacific dugong, which is a relative of the manatee. It is a sleeker, more slender, silvery creature with a beautiful whale-like tail. It has arm-like flippers. It has a head that looked somewhat like a manatee's head but not exactly. The peculiar arrangement of the jaw and facial parts did, from a distance, look much like a human face, only with the wrong components. So there was a vaguely human look to it even if it was pretty homely by anyone's standards. And it clearly had a distinct head and shoulder arrangement.

So we recognized the species. But the behavior that had we had observed didn't correspond to what had been officially known about dugongs. It became clear to us at that point that this creature was the foundation of the legends of the Mermaids. Their skeleton, which we were later on able to study at the Australian Museum in Sydney on our return trip, has arms that are nearly identical to human arms, but with longer fingers that form a flipper when they're covered with skin.

I did a bit of an autopsy to determine what had caused its death. One of the natives thought that it had been jabbed with a hot spear, but that seemed awfully unlikely. I pretty much determined that it was a bullet hole, but I was not able to dig deep enough to find the bullet, which would have confirmed it. So we decapitated it and took the head to be able to preserve the skull. We tied ropes on the body and towed it out to sea behind the ship and set it adrift. Morning Glory was pretty upset about it all and sang some dirges when we cut it loose. I spent the next few days cleaning the skull. There was no reason to stay there anymore, so we sailed on up to Madang, a port city on the north side of New Guinea.

MG: I guess that among all my regrets about this adventure, the one that comes to haunt me the most is the disrespectful way we dealt with that animal in front of the people of the village. I couldn't help but cry over the body of this poor mother dugong, one of the last of her endangered kind, which I'm sure must have seemed strange to the local people, but I still can't help but feel that it was a very bad decision to do a necropsy in such a public way. At the very least we should have towed the intact body to a more private location.

It was bad enough that the Nokon people had lost their Ilkai, their good-luck bringer. The men and all their wild stories had been disproved and shorn of all their glamour, and I think the women seemed a little smug about that, but the village as a whole lost something precious and unique: they lost their Mystery. Like their missing songs, their missing artifacts, and their missing forest, now strangers had come and taken away one more irreplaceable treasure. I know we were definitely not the ones to kill the creature, but I don't know if the people believed that in the end, especially after we cut it apart and took its head away.

It was the breeding female of a small family group of critically endangered animals. All the other dugongs in villages all up and down the coast had been killed and eaten because those people did not have a taboo about eating it. The very word *Ilkai* in Sursurunga means "not to eat," and so this little family had managed to survive in this one small pocket of safety thanks to this one tradition that the Nokon people had hung on to, even in the face of all the overwhelming changes the modern world was bringing them. We traveled halfway around the world to solve a Mystery, and instead we arrived to witness the death of one.

DIANE DARLING: We were just devastated. Because it's likely no one would have shot her if we hadn't been there to draw attention to the animals, or at least that's what I think. When it turned out to be a dugong, people started behaving badly. There were fights, people yelling at each other. It was pretty miserable to be on that boat after the disappointment.

DANIEL BLAIR STEWART: Everybody had their sights aimed a little bit too high. We wanted to discover a new species. We thought it was going to be some kind of semi-aquatic descendent of some local primate—some primate that branched off from some ape lineage, say, during the Eocene period about thirty-five or forty million years ago, and just took to the water. But when we got there, it was no such creature. It was the Indo-Pacific dugong. And I, quite frankly, felt that it was a successful expedition because we did put the lid on the mystery. We found out it was what they all turned out to be: dugongs or manatees—depending on which ocean you're in.

I'd been doing a bit of dabbling in personally investigating unexplained phenomena, and I always found the best you really can do is close it up and say, "Hey, now we know what it really is." Because when you come up against something unexplained, all too often the phenomenon itself doesn't show, or when it does, it gets away, or half the people see it and half don't. You try to solve as much as you can, because what is left is the real unexplained factor that you have to deal with.

TOM WILLIAMS: The results of the expedition, while not what we had fantasized, nonetheless constituted a contribution—modest though it may be—to the body of science. Our activities had also attracted the attention of the provincial government of New Ireland. We had promised to deliver a report to the governor, and, during our stop in the provincial capital of Madang, I was able to arrange a meeting with the governor and presented a written report. I also wrote a detailed account of the expedition that was published in *Cryptozoology*, the publication of the International Society of Cryptozoology (ISC). In addition, Oberon and I attended the annual meeting of the ISC in San Diego, where I gave a presentation with slides from the trip.

OZ: A couple of years later when I was traveling in Europe, I discovered a little anthropological museum in Florence, Italy. And one little room there was stacked floor to ceiling with artifacts from Nokon Bay. I saw, there, all the stuff that they had taken from that village. It wasn't on display. It was just stacked in boxes with a sign on the door that said, "Nokon Village, New Ireland." I opened the door, and that's where it was. That sort of wrapped up the mystery of what happened to all their stuff. I wish I could have bought the stuff and taken it back to Nokon to give to the people there.

That tiny anthropology museum had a remarkably large collection of tribal artifacts from aboriginal peoples worldwide. I couldn't help but be struck by the observation that all this stuff is in this museum, and in countless other museums the world over, and thus no longer accessible to the very people whose heritage it is. The tribal villages and council houses are empty of their treasures and artifacts—stolen to reside permanently in glass cases, drawers, or storerooms in stone buildings in faraway cities, no longer to be passed on as the cultural heritage to a new generation. Considering how small most tribal communities are, and how many of these sacred artifacts are now in public and private collections, it's no wonder that tribal people are perceived as "primitive" and "culturally impoverished." We Westerners would be pretty impoverished too if everything we owned, and all the trappings of our history and civilization, were removed to some remote and inaccessible location . . . say, on another planet.

PART THREE

Back in the Real World

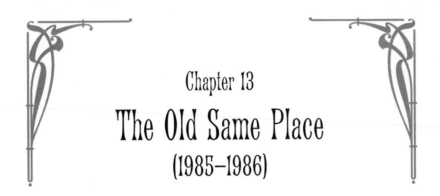

Chapter 13
The Old Same Place
(1985–1986)

Through bitter strife, as man and wife,
We started life anew as friends.
I'd do things better over again;
I'd do things better over again.
—FROM "LOVE OF MY LIFE" BY MORNING GLORY ZELL, 1993

MG: As exciting as it was, I had been deeply worried that we might end up footing the bill for an expensive expedition that would siphon off the nest egg that we had managed to build out of the Unicorn project. I wanted to use that money to buy land, to pay Alison for half of Coeden Brith so that we would finally be landowners and not just tenants. But we never could manage to set up a meeting with her to discuss this. Partly it was the eternal problem of no telephone, but we also got the impression that she might have been dodging this issue with us.

More and more it seemed that Otter was more interested in listening to Orion's grand plans for spending our money to fund the expedition and then trying to recoup the money by selling a documentary. I remember a huge argument where Orion accused me of selling out the future if I didn't go along with this plan. Why was I so opposed? Well, for one thing, we'd had some hard recent experience in trying to interest either Hollywood or the scientific community in real live Unicorns to no avail, even when the animals were standing there and crapping on their floors, so I seriously doubted that there would be a great overwhelming rush to buy a video of real live Mermaids from us, whatever they turned out to be. Otter originally proposed that we would create a complete budget for the entire expedition and then all the members of the expedition would contribute equal shares for making this thing go forward. But it quickly became apparent that most of the friends who wanted to go along could barely afford the airfare and maybe to pay something for their berths on the dive boat; but no way could this bunch of fellow Hippie explorers pull together enough dough to invest in renting a whole boat to sail a very long distance, as well as all the equipment, and to pay professional photographers to shoot a film. We were able to get a few outside friends to invest some money in buying shares of the profits (if any) of such an endeavor; but at the most, when the deadline came for putting the down payment on the dive boat, we only had raised about $12,000 additional funds for all our efforts.

Oberon told me at that point that he had talked to his father and that after the financial success with the Unicorn, his dad was considering funding this trip. He went off to talk with his father, and when he returned he told me that everything was taken care of and that we had a green light to go forward. As it turned out, that was not in fact the case, but I will be generous and say that there was perhaps a miscommunication between them.

OZ: The Mermaid expedition had cost about $30,000, and we paid over half of that out of the $50,000 we got up-front from the circus—the rest being paid by investors. After also paying off our bills and credit cards, and putting in a pond on the land, there wasn't a whole lot left. We held our big Beltane Festival on the land, and we asked people to contribute $25 to help pay for the feast and the new campsites we had put in. It was a small charge to pay for meals and a four-day festival, but people just had a fit, because up until then we had never charged for anything. The idea that we would charge even a small amount that would just pay for the food was an outrage to people. But over two hundred people did come anyway—although many of them refused to pay, because Alison told them that they were her guests and did not have to pay for anything. So we went even further into the hole with that.

A few weeks after Beltane, Alison finally showed up. And we thought we were going to finally have our meeting that we had been waiting for. She had some Ecstasy, and offered it to us. Apparently she had gotten involved with this new fellow who had turned her on to that drug. They had bonded pretty tightly. What seemed to be going on, which we didn't understand at the time, was that he wanted to move up to the land. He was basically talking her into getting rid of us and putting himself there in our place, which eventually happened.

Somewhere in the course of the experience of tripping and being opened up, she said, "Okay, I've decided that I want you guys to leave." We thought that she had finally come to talk to us about selling us a piece of the parcel; we expected that we were going to be there forever. We were stunned. At that moment we were pretty broke, but the deal with the circus would give us nice monthly payments over the next four years. But instead she gave us an ultimatum to go and a few months to do it. She said, "Just be gone by the fall."

OZ: Marylyn Motherbear, in a true act of generosity, invited us to come up and live at her family's place, called Castle Yonder. But we had decided that we really ought to move off the land altogether and make a clean break. We started looking for a place to live in the Ukiah area.

While we were looking elsewhere, one thing came down that was devastatingly painful to us. We were told by the folks then living at Annwfn, which had been deeded to the CAW by Gwydion, that under no circumstances should we consider moving up there. Even on a temporary basis. To be told that by our own people, who were our Nestmates and waterbrothers in our own Church, really hurt; and they would never tell us why. What we eventually found out (fifteen years later) was that it was a campaign that was waged by Orion himself. He had been up there as a caretaker, and had cheerfully helped us spend the money for the Mermaid expedition. But we could never understand Orion's antipathy towards us; I always thought that he was my good buddy. This cast a shadow over our relationships with other people in the Church as well at the time. It felt like a deep betrayal. It was a closing of the doors by people we trusted and considered our closest friends.

MG: Right after Alison evicted us, I had just had a hysterectomy and I couldn't walk very well. And that's when we were told we had thirty days to leave. It got down to the wire, and there were rumors that Alison was going to call the sheriff. We were packing up our belongings and trying to find a place to live. Right about that time my grandmother died, and she left me a small bequest. It was just enough to put the first and last month's rent down on a place to live. We had been searching for housing for months, and there was just nothing available that time of year. It was looking like we were going to have to move into a one-room shack behind a Mexican bar. But I had a dream one night that we would find a place where we could live with our family and our animals; in the dream it seemed as if this refuge would be "between two things"—we had a Unicorn, a whole menagerie of other critters, and at that point my teenaged daughter, Rainbow, was living with us too. She could have gone home to Gary, but she said she didn't want to abandon us in our hour of need.

NARRATOR: By that time Morning Glory's father had died, and her mother had moved up to Northern California to be near her. Polly then came to the rescue.

MG: Literally at the eleventh hour, I went down to my mom's, and she had just found a place in the paper and called them up for us. I drove right over there as fast as I could. There, between the highway and the river, was this little place between the worlds. We went in. There were a bunch of people who wanted to rent the place, and I thought that I had to do something to make us more desirable than any of the other people that they could rent to. So I said, "Is it okay if we have pets here?"

And they said, "What kind of pets?" I told them we had a Unicorn, and I pulled out a picture of Lance and showed it to them. That pretty much sealed the deal. When I went back to see the landlady she had a whole collection of china unicorns, so the unicorn magick came through for us when we needed it the most.

OZ: We had expected to live out our lives in the woods when we moved to Greenfield Ranch. We thought we would die and be buried there. But we'd been there on a Mission, and now our assignment was over. That completed our whole Greenfield Ranch phase of our lives. But we retained the lessons that we learned, and the wisdom and the experience. The new Mission became to take it all back out into the world in a new way. When you're an explorer you really don't complete the Quest until you return to the place from whence you came with the gifts that you have gained from the adventure. Whether it's maps of new territory or magical treasures that you have found, whatever it is you have to bring it back.

NARRATOR: Morning Glory and Otter Zell returned to live full time, once again, in the outside world. It was a different place from what they had left behind eight years earlier. The plague known as AIDS had appeared and there was no cure, or even hope, in sight. In his first four years in office, Ronald Reagan had not mentioned AIDS once while talking to the public, and had done nothing to impede its spread. When the Zells left the Ranch, Reagan was in the second term of his presidency and spending huge amounts of money to build up America's military power.

But there were reasons to be optimistic. In 1982 *The Mists of Avalon*, the novel written by Marion Zimmer Bradley, had come out in hardcover. Bradley was friends with the Zells. They had been to literary salons at her house in Berkeley while she was writing it, and listened to her read early drafts of some of the chapters. She acknowledged them in the credits of the book, which became a national bestseller and helped to increase public awareness of Goddess spirituality. Witchcraft had grown in popularity while they were away from the Pagan community, as well.

It was time for them to pay attention to their families and friends, to get jobs, to find a new community, and reconnect with the rest of the world.

FARIDA FOX: I think that moving off the land was the best thing that ever happened to them. Then they had to start dealing with a different reality, the one that the rest of us were all living in. They had to start seeing how they could blend their concept of things into the larger world.

And there were a lot of hair-raising things that happened and many things that were difficult. But there was more development that took place as far as really discovering what their true talents and abilities to do things were. I think they're doing much more of the things that they were meant to be doing, and the things that they do best.

NARRATOR: When I was interviewing Oberon about their move from Greenfield Ranch, he referred to their new home as "the Old Same Place." It was on the Russian River (which, in a reference to Tolkien's Middle-earth, they called the "Rushing River") at the corner of Highway 20 and the road up to Potter Valley. Once upon a time it had been a kind of a roadhouse, so there were a couple of farmhouses, a number of small cabins, a social area that had been the bar and restaurant, and a big lodge their landlord built for his family.

I didn't have to ask OZ what "the Old Same Place" meant; that name is from a comedy recording, released by the Firesign Theatre in 1969, called "The Further Adventures of Nick Danger, Third Eye." It was on side two of their LP *How Can You Be in Two Places at Once When You're Not Anywhere at All*. Getting together to listen to the Firesign Theatre was a ritual not just in CAW Nests but in dorm rooms and Hippie pads across the country. The records were intentionally multi-layered, so there were always new things to be discovered by listening to them over and over, and doing that with friends was a real bonding experience. Something like "the Old Same Place," which doesn't make much sense when taken out of context, can be simultaneously symbolic and hilarious to a Firesign fan.

There are a couple of reasons why I am mentioning these things. First, the experience of getting together with family or friends to listen to a story is not something that is a regular part of life for most adults today. But it is an activity with a long history, and it is very much a part of the Zells' spiritual world. Telling a story to a group of people sitting in a circle is what they are all about.

And secondly, I think it's important to point out that Morning Glory and Oberon have been through some tough times, and as we begin this chapter they are in one of the toughest. But something that has kept them going, and kept them together, is their shared sense of humor. No matter how difficult their lives have been, they have always been able to step back for a moment and find something amusing in what was happening. And that is a part of their magick.

And so I return you now to our story, which is already in progress . . .

OZ: During that same period of time we started reviving the Church. It hadn't been very active in the years since we'd left St. Louis. We held festivals on Coeden Brith and Annwfn, but we didn't deal with any kind of national organization or do anything on a larger scale. We rarely even had board of directors meetings or elections, just the legal minimum. Our biggest events during those years were the tree plantings that Gwydion held over New Year's, where we planted thousands of trees. We didn't do anything on a larger scale than what we did on the land. The day after Alison told us we had to leave, we held a CAW board of directors meeting on Annwfn to begin the process of getting the Church back on its feet. It was a matter of re-creating the whole Church from the ground up—not for the first time, nor the last. Indeed, we evoked the legend of the Phoenix as a metaphor for CAW's second resurrection (the first having been in St. Louis).

We held our first Clergy Retreat at the Shaggy Mushroom temple (Gwydion's old yurt) on Annwfn for the purpose of envisioning the new CAW as we wanted it to be. It was a very beautiful experience, as each of us in sequential order told of how we first came to the CAW—starting with me. I was profoundly moved as each of my beloved Waterkin recounted our first meeting (for, in every case, I was their first connection). We all shared water and had a big snuggle-pile that soon developed into sweet lovemaking. This was the most profound bonding experience we'd ever had all with each other, and with that foundation, we knew we could build a powerful Church.

Out of that experience and that wondrous weekend, we formulated our new CAW mission statement: ". . . to evolve a network of information, mythology, and experience to awaken the divine within and to provide a context and stimulus for reawakening Gaea and reuniting Her children through tribal community dedicated to responsible stewardship and the evolution of consciousness."

We moved into the Old Same Place in the beginning of October. That was a big thing for us. We had been living on the Ranch for eight years! We got one of the three-bedroom farmhouses with a fenced-in backyard where we could put Bedivere (Lancelot was still at the circus at that time). There was an almost identical house right next to it, but it wasn't immediately available. So Diane and Zack stayed with some friends on a farm.

The Old Same Place had a beach that was totally private, and our landlord Johnny was pretty tolerant, so we could have skinny-dipping parties there as long as none of the other residents wanted to use the beach and objected to nudity. We had our Beltane Festival up at Annwfn and started having our summer Sabbat festivals on our beach: Litha (Summer Solstice—June 21) and Lughnasadh (August 1). We took over having those because it was not really a good idea to have campfires up on the Ranch in the summertime for events at Annwfn. The risk of California wildfires are a very real and present danger, and besides, the roads were all dusty and dry and not good for cars. So we started holding the Church's annual membership meetings on the beach as well.

MG: We loved living on the river and doing rituals there; it lent itself to so many wonderful possibilities. We would have ceremonial baths and ritual baptizings; we had brightly colored clay pits dug into the soft beach sand to do body painting and mud baths; we could send inner tubes down part of the river to the beach, where the rafters would be greeted with ceremony.

NARRATOR: Another major change in the world had happened while the Zells had been in the woods: Apple Computer had released the first Macintosh in 1984. Imagine what it would be like to live in a world without home computers, to go away for years, and then return to find Macs waiting for you. That's what happened to OZ. He jumped right in and got a job in Ukiah at the Green Mac, which was one of the first desktop publishing businesses. He quickly learned how to use a Macintosh 512 computer, which is extremely primitive by today's standards but for those days was phenomenally advanced.

OZ: I started learning the desktop publishing programs—especially PageMaker. That was a big thing. There had never been anything like that before. I enjoyed doing that work, and I was very much in demand because I could create original art as well as do the layout and designs for the projects. Some of these were quite complex, such as intricate, pop-up 3-D card models of ferryboats, cruise ships, cable cars, and the Golden Gate Bridge for souvenir packets—I loved designing these, as paper models were something I'd been into since I was a kid. I also illustrated and formatted restaurant menus, New Age workshop brochures, book and record album covers, billboards, and even entire books.

After about a year or so, a vacancy came up in the house right next to ours, and Diane and Zack moved in there and became our next-door neighbors. And so we were able to completely unify our family at that point, and we did everything together. We ate dinners together. We watched TV shows together. We went to movies together. We traveled together down to San Francisco for rituals, sci-fi cons, and other events. We had three kids at that time—Morning Glory's daughter Rainbow was living with us, plus Zack and my son Bryan, who'd come back after completing his stint with the Army.

This way our kids got to have siblings—being an only kid is kind of tough. It is ecologically appropriate for people to be satisfied with having one offspring, but it doesn't entirely work for kids who are growing up. So the perfect solution is to have one kid from each of several relationships, and have the kids all grow up together; that way they get to have the brother and sister thing.

DIANE DARLING: I eventually moved up to the place that they had found, in another house on the little compound. We lived up there happily for quite a long time.

My house was Honeydew Cabin. My son was growing up. Morning Glory's daughter was around some of the time, and Otter's son was also around some of the time. Morning Glory's mother, Polly, lived in Redwood Valley, and she was a big part of our family. She was a fundamentalist Christian, but she was a true Christian that Jesus would have recognized. She called herself Pollywog. So we had a lovely family. Otter was part of Zack's upbringing.

At Thanksgiving we invited our Pagan friends who were like orphans to come over. We'd cook a turkey, and Morning Glory would always make her pumpkin soup. Of course we celebrated all the Pagan holidays, too. We basically wanted to celebrate anybody's holiday, especially if it had food! Polly was a major Christian, so we would do stuff like get together to go sing Christmas carols around her trailer park. She was proud of us because we knew them all.

ZACK DARLING: Otter used to have Archimedes, the great horned owl. He had this perch behind Otter's easy chair, and he would just sit there and chill throughout the day. He had a broken wing because he had been hit by a car. We got him through Critter Care, which was this group that we were part of that took care of animals that had been hurt. Archimedes was our watch owl—we used to say that if anybody came and robbed the house, he'd watch 'em. The Jehovah's Witnesses came over one day, and they were sitting there yakking with Otter, and Archimedes turned his head and looked at them. The woman was totally shocked, and said, "Your owl is not stuffed!"

And Otter said, "What kind of a man do you think I am? I wouldn't have a dead owl in my house! That's disgusting!"

OZ: Archimedes was a wonderful member of our little family. We got him very shortly after we moved to the Old Same Place. During the daytime, he stayed in the house, mostly sitting quietly on a perch I made for him behind my big comfy chair (with a litter box on the floor below). In the evening, I would take him out into the big aviary I built over Bedivere's corral. I would have to kill a rat for him every night, and place it on the platform in front of his owl-house. So I also had to raise a colony of rats—for both Archimedes and Fluffy, Diane's enormous Burmese python.

Owls are marvelous birds to have as house pets, as I discovered when I was a kid and brought home little screech owls to live in my bedroom. Archimedes was calm and mellow, and would never dream of biting or hurting anyone. I took him around to schools just to introduce kids to him. We did the same with Fluffy.

Archimedes and Octobriana—our awesomely intelligent tortoise-point Siamese cat we'd acquired when we first moved to Greenfield—were quite competitive, and were constantly playing "Gotcha!" with each other. I think it was because they were different versions of the same archetype—night hunters of small mammals, with huge eyes and round heads, as well as moveable ears. I think Octobriana, however, regarded Archimedes as some sort of an insult—a parody of a cat, as it were.

Often Archimedes would sit on the inside sill of our big picture window, looking out in reverie at the world he couldn't return to. Octobriana would be outside, and spot him there. She would sneak quietly up to right underneath him, and then she would suddenly leap up onto the outside sill right in front of him with a flourish. Archimedes would nearly topple backwards in startlement.

But one day he got his revenge. Octobriana was curled up asleep on Morning Glory's comfy rocking chair, at the other end of the sofa from my chair and Archimedes's perch. I saw him watching her thoughtfully, rocking back and forth on his feet. Then he quietly hopped over to the back of the sofa and edged along it until he was on the arm. And with a sudden flourish of wings and clacking of beak, he leaped onto the arm of the rocker, going "Boo!" Octobriana levitated a foot into the air and took off with all legs spinning. Whereupon Archimedes, very well pleased with himself, sauntered calmly back to his perch and preened. For the rest of the day, I could hear him periodically chuckling to himself: "Gotcha! Hee hee hee."

Morning Glory, Diane, and I got to be very well known in the local community. In addition to my participation in the chamber of commerce, I even joined the Odd Fellows. People would come to us for readings, spells, advice, mediations, magickal training, initiations, rituals, and so on. We did presentations in the local schools for such occasions as Hallowe'en. With a supportive team of other members of the Church and the Ranch, we created major public rituals, celebrations, and events—such as the Human Be-In; the Summer of Love twentieth anniversary; a Hallowe'en haunted house; a Beltane Maypole dance and festival; weddings and funerals; installations of political offices; and presentations to local groups, such as during National Women's Week.

As a family, we were a bonded team. When Zack got into trouble at school, all three of us "parents" would show up to talk to his teachers. We'd go to his soccer games and concerts. It was pretty clear to everybody that we were a family. And it was not that unusual, in that there were a lot of kids whose parents had been divorced and remarried, but were still friends, so it wasn't at all uncommon for kids to have three or four parents. We even home-schooled Zack for a while. He was having some academic problems at school, so we took him out and did the whole independent study program.

ZACK DARLING: Otter was my science and history teacher. The lessons that he gave me were so much better than any schoolwork I had ever experienced in a classroom. It wasn't exactly home-schooling—it was called independent study. I was officially enrolled in the school, and I was getting school credits for it.

Being a Pagan kid was really challenging, because there were a lot of Christian kids in my school and I found myself under scrutiny. The Christian kids would always want to debate me, or they would just call me "Satan worshipper." That put me in a position in which I needed to learn a little bit more about it than the other kids because I felt a need to articulate it. So at a young age I had to come up with a lot of information about Pagans, Witchcraft, and Magick, and the history behind it and how to help people understand it. I told the Christian fundamentalists that it wasn't really possible for me to believe in Satan, because he wasn't part of my religion.

GAIL SALVADOR: I went to Ukiah High for a year. It made me appreciate my nice, liberal schools in Eugene. My mother and I did not get along very much. We fought a lot. We had kind of a love/hate relationship. She was kind of a Stormin' Norman, because her father was that way. So that's what she knew.

I never identified with the names that they gave me. "Rainbow Galadriel" is not me. I chose the name Gail really quickly the morning I was registering for Ukiah High. I had this epiphany that I was going to a very small, redneck high school in a redneck town, and I was going to be the new kid, and my name was Rainbow. And I thought, "Oh God, I can't face it. I can't do it." I thought that I could seize the opportunity for a fresh start. Right then and there I wrote "Gail" down on the registration forms. It was basically a shortened version of Galadriel, because I was not a seven-foot-tall blond Elf queen. I still have Rainbow as my legal middle name. When I was about sixteen, I had my name legally changed to Gail.

Tim's parents, Charles and
Vera Zell, October 1940

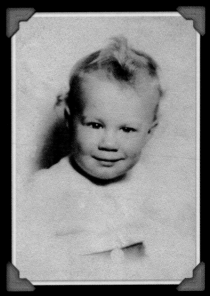

Timmy Zell at sixteen months

Barry, Tim, and Shirley in
Crystal Lake, Christmas 1960

Barry, Shirley, and Tim
in Crystal Lake, 1953

Tim working at the Prudential
Building, 1960

Tim Zell at his high school
graduation, 1961

Tim in his dorm at
Westminster College, 1961

Bryan in Skinner Air Crib, 1963

Bryan Zell, 1968

First Church of All Worlds altar,
St. Louis, 1967

Little Diane, a.k.a.
Morning Glory, in 1952

Diane and her daddy, 1959

Diane and her mama, 1959

Morning Glory, High School
Drama Queen, 1966

Diane on Prince, Forest, Mississippi, 1959

Morning Glory with baby Rainbow
on Crow Farm commune, 1970

Tim Zell's famous
publicity photo, 1971

Morning Glory, Gary, and Rainbow
on an Oregon beach, 1971

Tim and Histah, 1971

Tim and Morning Glory with
Tanith and Ananta, February 1974

Tim and Morning Glory,
February 1974

Carolyn Clark and Tim Zell,
Beltane 1973

The incomparable
Morning Glory, 1974

Green Egg collating party, 1974

OZ-MG handfasting, April 14, 1974

MG at Rex Rotary press printing
Green Egg, 1974

Handfasting of Morning Glory and Oberon,
presided over by Archdruid Isaac Bonewits
and High Priestess Carolyn Clark, at the
Spring Witchmeet, April 14, 1974
(photo from Llewellyn archives)

Tim and his mom in Scarlet
Succubus, Summer 1976

The Scarlet Succubus, 1976

OZ and MG as Peter Stag and
Virginia, Discon, September
1974; "Most Primal"

Tim and Morning Glory with
Tanith and Ananta in Eugene,
Oregon, Mabon 1976

Morning Glory Godiva
at Coeden Brith

Tim the Mountain Man,
Greenfield, 1977

Snow Mom on Coeden Brith

OZ in his deerskin shaman's robe
(note emanations near waist)
Coeden Brith, Litha 1976

Solar Eclipse at Maryhill
Stonehenge, Washington,
February 1979

Rainbow, the Unicorn Maiden,
1981 (photo by Ron Kimball)

OZ and MG with baby Lancelot,
1980 (photo by Ron Kimball)

MG and Kira Deer on Coeden Brith,
Summer 1983

MG, Bedivere, and OZ at
Washington Stonehenge, 1981

Queen of the Unicorns (MG with
Lancelot and Avalon)

MG and Bedivere at Washington
Stonehenge, 1981

Beltane at Annwfn, 1984

Gwydion Pendderwen,
the Faerie Shaman

Gwydion's Shaggy Mushroom
home and temple

OZ and Lancelot at Canada's
Wonderland, 1982

The Wizard and the Accountant:
OZ and his brother Barry, in Derry,
New Hampshire, September 1982

Coffee klatch—Oberon the Unicorn
and Oberon the Wizard, March 1990
(photo by Malcolm J. Brenner)

MG and OZ's yurt on
Coeden Brith, 1985

MG and Bedivere as the Empress
Tarot card

OZ at Mycenae, Greece, March 1987

MG with early Goddess collection

Wizard and son (OZ and Bryan), Old
Same Place

MG, Histology Assistant, Ukiah General Hospital, April 1989

Gary and Diane's wedding, June 25, 1989

he Triskelion Family: Zack, Gary, ne, OZ, MG, 1990 (T-shirts by OZ)

OZ and MG with Tim Leary, Starwood 1993

IG, Miriam Robbins Dexter, and de Cles conducting Panathenaia

MG doing Goddess presentation at Gathering of the Tribes, Tennessee,

MG and Talyn

MG and Wolf, October 1993

...nd MG perform handfasting for Joy
...and Tom Williams, April 16, 1994

MG and OZ pyrates—Aarrrh!

OZ working on Eros sculpture, 1996

Jumping the Broom—OZ, MG, and Wolf handfasting, September 1997

Protégé Priestess: Wynter and MG at V-M Ranch, 1998

MG at the entrance to the Halls of Hades. Eleusis, Greece, September 1997

L-R: OZ, father Charles, sister Shirley, brother Barry, at Shirley's fiftieth birthday, March 27, 1998

OZ's Millennial Gaia statue

On the Bus—OZ presents Millennial Gaia to Ken Kesey, August 12, 1999 (photo by Ariel)

Ariel and OZ at the Roman baths of Bath, England, August 1999

Christmas dinner at Shady Grove, 2001. L-R: Polly, Zack, MG, OZ, Gary, Diane, Gail, Malcolm (the cat).

Wolf and Wynter's handfasting, August 5, 2000 (photo by Richard Ely)

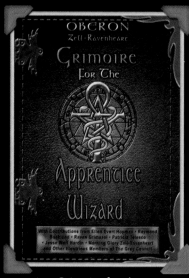

OBERON
Zell-Ravenheart

GRIMOIRE
FOR The

APPRENTICE
WIZARD

With Contributions from Ellen Evert Hopman • Raymond Buckland • Raven Grimassi • Patricia Telesco • Jesse Wolf Hardin • Morning Glory Zell-Ravenheart and Other Illustrious Members of The Grey Council

Grimoire for the Apprentice Wizard, 2004

PanGaia cover with OZ,
Autumn 2007

MG and OZ celebrate their thirtieth
anniversary at Big Sur, April 2004

MG and Liza at Eleusinian Mysteries,
Pinnacles National Monument,
September 2004

Polly at Gail and Joe's wedding,
October 1, 2004

Wolf and MG at Mythic Images booth,
INATS, Denver, June 2005

OZ and Lance Christie, Arches National
Park, Utah, June 2005

MG and OZ cuddling koalas in
Australia, January 2006

Alessandra's first Hallowe'en:
the little Witchlet, 2007

MG and OZ at Yellowstone, June 2008
(photo by Julie Epona O'Ryan)

OZ as Phoenix, Occidental Fools Day
Parade, April 2009

OZ with his first teacher, Deborah
Bourbon, St. Louis, June 2009

Witchy Women: Morning Glory and
Julie Epona, February 2009
(photo by John Sulak)

I felt like I pretty much blew off my entire sophomore year at Ukiah. I had this learning disability that I never got help with until I got to college. I struggled and worked really hard to finish high school. It was not easy for me. But I was determined not to be a dropout like a lot of my friends. I had been hanging out with all this riffraff, the rockers and stoners in Eugene, and then I went to Ukiah.

In Ukiah I started liking the preppy aesthetics. So when I moved back to Eugene I decided I wanted to hang out with the preppies. I started dressing preppy and being very label-conscious. I cut my hair differently and looked really conservative. A lot of people had a hard time with my name change when I came back. They didn't understand why I did it. But they didn't have to live with it, and I did. So I switched social groups, and that really helped me finish school.

CERRIDWEN FALLINGSTAR: Gail and I continued to be in contact. She felt like I was the voice of sanity from her childhood. At fifteen she went to go live with the Zells for a year or so and go to high school. She called me up one night, all angry and freaked out, and said, "I went out on a date last night. And my mother handed me a condom at the door! I said, 'Mom, I'm not that kind of girl! You want to know what gets me orgasmic? Shopping malls!'" She was totally rebelling and going to the other side: materialism. She would call up periodically to complain.

MG: My idea as a parent was that being a mother of a daughter meant giving my daughter the kind of possible tools to develop herself, including sexually, in ways that would be safe and whole and together. So that she wouldn't have to end up pregnant or with a disease or all screwed up with guilt and a whole lot of stuff that was inflicted upon my generation. It's always like that—we always try to give our kids what we would have liked to have had when we were growing up, but they have a whole separate constellation of needs. So, it's like we give them what we would have wanted to have as opposed to what they need.

So I was trying to give my daughter the benefit of the sexual freedom and birth control information that was not available to me as a teenager, which women had fought so hard to gain access to. But instead, she felt that she was being rushed into sexuality, which was never my intention.

She didn't yet have a handle on how to really express her differing needs and often pretended to be a lot more knowledgeable than she really was at the time. I was also pretty hard-headed and strident about my viewpoints. We did enjoy sharing heavy metal music together though, and went to a Dio concert together.

I certainly felt it was her right to change her name when she came into her selfhood; after all, I did. Frankly, I think she chose well: a gale is a kind of storm, and, being a Scorpio, it really fit her personality a lot better. It's kind of funny because Gary and I had actually considered naming her Stormy at one point, but then we figured we should cut us all some slack and go for something a little more cheerful.

DIANE DARLING: Morning Glory and I were very happy, because we were both bisexual, and we each had a wife, which was so cool for us. We would gang up on Otter when he would start to get too out there. Otter and Morning had a very contentious relationship. I was never a part of that because I am so not the drama queen that she was at that time.

MG: Living next door to Diane was great because I had a best girlfriend and eventually co-wife to share everything with. We were both into animals (especially horses), magickal and ritual stuff, medical stuff, and women's issues, as well as polyamory. It was during this time as part of an attempt to explain the rules of the road that OZ and I had painstakingly hammered out together, that I came to coin the term *polyamory*. At the time there were a half-dozen different words being used to describe what we were doing, but a lot of them seemed to define themselves by what they weren't doing—*non-monogamy*, for example—and I always think it's better to have a single, clear, positive word to use when attempting self-definition.

Otter and I still fought a lot, because we were two really strong egos that continually came into collision. We wanted to forge a magickal partnership—the vows that we swore at our wedding had to do with coming together as a single unitary being. We were working on melding our souls, and we were really going for it. And in doing so—it's not exactly what you would call a natural process. But we were convinced that we could make it happen, and we weren't going to quit.

I suppose it can all be boiled down to the words *great expectations*. The problem with expectations is that you project what you want to create onto something, as opposed to appreciating what it is now. In order to forge a lasting bond, we had to get over our assumptions about what that bond had to be before we could actually manifest it. So we fought for ten years over what it was and how we could still maintain our discrete personalities, while melding ourselves into a cosmic union. We would have these amazing, magickal sexual bonding events in our lives, and then not long after that we would be having a really horrible argument that would go on for hours and hours, and days and days, and be really painful.

This went on all the way through Greenfield and till we moved to the Old Same Place. Then it really came to a peak. One night we'd had one of these huge arguments that had started out with us planning to go out to have this wonderful evening together, and then instead, we had a big argument. This went on till like three in the morning, and we were both finally exhausted sitting in the bedroom, and I had my head in my hands and I said, "Why do we always do this? Why do we always fight like this?"

And OZ looked up and he had this clear look on his face, like he does when he has a visionary breakthrough, and he said, "I think I actually know, but you probably won't let me get the words out or you probably won't listen if I tell you."

I was completely drained emotionally. I got very quiet and then I said, "I'll listen to what you say without interruption. I really do want to understand." Because what we were arguing about—even though some of it was actually productive like learning how to lay down rules, and how to conduct a triad relationship fairly, how to go about making a genuine apology when necessary, and how to be in an honest relationship 24/7 with each other—a lot of it was just tailspinning and arguing about trivia.

And so he said, "Well, I was on the debate team when I was in high school. And you were on the debate team when you were in high school. And we both really love a good debate. And we click into that debate mode, and everything else goes out the window. And we lock horns, and we're carried away by the process of affirmative versus negative."

He said that, and it was like a giant light bulb went off above my head. I said, "You're right. That's absolutely it! We get locked into a pattern that we were trained for. And when we turn that ability against each other, it just spins itself into this huge, devouring, catastrophic black hole." So at that point I said, "Well, you know, what we need to do is find some way that we can play for ten points and then quit."

And he said, "Yeah, because we're never going to not argue; we are never going to agree on everything. But it doesn't have to mean the end of the world. It doesn't have to mean that we don't love each other, that we don't want to be together, and that there is something wrong with us. It's just that we're having a debate. And we need to create some distance from it, instead of having every single disagreement be a cosmic event."

From this breakthrough, we were able to heal our wounds and work towards better ways to deal with our arguments. We did a lot of study, took classes, went to workshops, read a lot of books on new ways that we could interact together that would maximize the amount of productiveness in our conflict, and turn the conflict around so that it would be productive (as opposed to destructive). So we weren't tearing each other apart. What we were working on was taking a hypothesis, and tearing that apart, and testing it, and recombining, until it was something that we could both look at and say, "That's good! Now we're both in agreement."

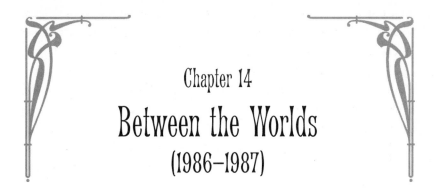

Chapter 14
Between the Worlds
(1986–1987)

We shared our lovers, shared our Hope;
We shared our household with a zoo.
We learned from others how they cope
But no one could be like us two!

With kids and cats and snakes and rats,
Mistakes we made and lives to mend.
I'd do it with you once again;
I'd do it with you once again.

—FROM "LOVE OF MY LIFE," BY MORNING GLORY ZELL

NARRATOR: After Gerald Gardner died in 1964, the contents of his Museum of Magic and Witchcraft were sold to the "Ripley's Believe It or Not!" organization. They put some of the stuff they'd bought on display in their museum in the Fisherman's Wharf area of San Francisco, which was not too far from the Ranch where the Zells were raising their Unicorns in the late 1970s. In the 1980s, when Ronald Reagan was president and religious conservatism was sweeping the country, the Gardner collection was moved around and then was eventually sold to private collectors.

Though tourists were no longer able to gawk at Gardner's ritual tools, his influence in the Pagan community continued to increase. In 1986 Raymond Buckland, an initiated Gardnerian who had started his own tradition, published his *Complete Book of Witchcraft*. This was a step-by-step course of instruction that became a major resource for aspiring Wiccans. It was authentic, packed with information, and it was widely available. By then, multiple bookstore chains were in operation around the United States, including Waldenbooks and Barnes & Noble, so just about anyone had a place nearby where they could walk in and buy Buckland's book.

OZ was, of course, an old friend of Buckland's, and he didn't need a book to tell him how to cast a circle. His magickal circle already covered the whole planet, and his Pagan education would continue to take him all around it in some unexpected ways. He took one such trip in 1987.

OZ: During the summer of 1982, when MG and I were estranged from each other and spent four months apart traveling around the country with the Unicorns, both of us had some interesting romantic encounters. At the Texas Ren Faire I met a woman named Belladonna. She had a booth at the faire also called "Belladonna." She made beautiful metal-framed mirrors of all shapes and sizes, with postcard pictures on the backs.

In camping at the Faire, you spend all day while the Faire is open with the tourists. But in the evening, after the Faire closes, people start campfires and drift around and get to know each other. I ran into Belladonna at such a fire, where we were talking and telling stories. She invited me back to her place for coffee and a nightcap. One thing led to another, and I ended up spending the night—and many more to follow. One of the things that she was attracted by were my stories of ancient times and legends of far-off places. She said that if she could ever possibly afford it, she would love to take a trip to places like that with me as a tour guide. There she was, a Hippie living in a little trailer. And the idea of her having enough money to take a trip to Europe was sort of amusing.

Well, a number of years later she contacted me, and she said her father had just died and left her an inheritance. And he said, "You should take this money and travel. Go see the world." She offered to buy airline tickets for both of us, so in March of 1987 we went off to Europe together.

Belladonna and I flew into Madrid, took a train up through France, spent a glorious time in Paris, and then went down to Italy, where we visited Florence, Rome, Etruria, Parga, and Pompeii. We concentrated on ancient ruins and temples—as well as museums. Then we took an overnight ferry over to Greece, where we made pilgrimage to sites in western Greece such as the Necromanteion, Dodona, Delphi, Mycenae, and more. After visiting the Parthenon in Athens, we took another ferry to Crete, where we explored Knossos, then back to Athens, from whence we flew home.

A large focus of our trip became journeys through the Underworld. We visited tombs, catacombs, and other Underworld places. There were thousands and thousands of years of it, going back to the painted caves at Les Eyzies, in the Dordogne Valley of southwestern France. I saw stuff that I'd never imagined, because you just can't get it from words or books or photographs. I had seen pictures of the deer and buffalo painted on the cave walls. But the photographs don't convey the three-dimensional qualities.

I read that the Cro-Magnons took advantage of rounded projections to paint the images. What they don't tell is that natural hollows were also used, and a lot of images were painted in those hollows in a way that reversed them. When something is painted like that, and you move past it, it appears to be moving and to follow you, simply because of the way the shadows move and the way our brain interprets it. A lot of them were done that way, so it was really eerie. The images of the animals were all moving from the depths of the cave facing towards the entrance.

So we imagined people would be blindfolded and taken in for an initiation. We saw lots of little shelves that had been used for clamshell lamps, with bear fat and a wick or something in them, and that had been the lighting. If you were an initiate you would have carried one of these lamps to find the way back out. And while doing that, you would see on the walls around you these images of animals moving in the same direction that you were, moving out of the womb to be born. Some of them are simply flat pictures, but if you go through holding a single point of light like you would get from a lamp, the hollow ones would appear to be coming alive and leaping off of the wall.

We discovered the Catacombs of Paris with their hundreds of thousands of skeletons and skulls—some of them not entirely human, with divided frontal bones. Just going through that was amazing. And climbing down into the Tarquinian tombs of Tuscany, and walking the once-buried

streets of Pompeii—it brought history alive. We even traveled to the recently excavated Necromanteion at Ephyra, overlooking the Acheron
river in northern Greece, where Odysseus had been sent by Circe to consult the ghost of Tiresias. We don't have any places like that here, that are
part of our legends and stories. In America you can visit Mesa Verde, and
it's an ancient ruin where somebody used to live once upon a time, but
you don't have any names or stories to associate with it. When you go to
Mycenae, you know that it was the citadel of Agamemnon, and you know
the story of the Trojan War and the heroes who fought in it.

That trip was a life-changing experience. It formed the foundation for
my eventual work with the Eleusinian Mysteries. To go into the Underworld like that means to go through a passage from life to death to rebirth.
It's the rebirth part that is the crucial element. All of these places were not
places of death; they were wombs from which new life would be born.
That was the essence that permeated all of this over thousands of years,
from the caves to the tombs. It was a constant theme. There was no sense
that the Underworld was the final destination. It was a transitional phase,
a place to enter into the Mysteries and then be born again.

In many ways my whole life has been a succession of lives and symbolic deaths and rebirths into new lives. I have reinvented myself on
numerous occasions, which is part of what has made this possible—the
sense that it is a cycle, that there is a continuum; there is a series of
phases, and our lives are like beads on a string. There are so many metaphors. But the point of them all is that you begin again. You come to the
end of a phase; you go through a transition; and then you start over
again with something new.

This was the first time I really got that sense of being able to go
through that transition and come out the other end and create a new
life. I think many people can't do that. They get to the end of a phase of
their life and they think, "Well that's it. It's all over. I'm done." They
don't have that sense that, "Okay, I can come back again and do a new
life. This is an opportunity to create a whole new existence." I think that
is an important thing in life and magick.

I have what I call "the attitude of gratitude." Every day I would go
down to the Rushing River at the Old Same Place, and I would say to
myself, "This is just wonderful. This is beautiful." I wouldn't put things

down by saying, "This isn't quite good enough" or "Gee, I wish this was better." I never look at things that way. I'm not comparing them against something that they're not. Ever. Whether it's people, or a place, or a situation, I say, "This is really great. And someday, I may not be here, I may not be a part of this. For this too will pass. So I want to fully appreciate it while I've got it." So I look at every bit of it as if it's brand-new and I'm falling in love.

NARRATOR: OZ returned to his job at the Green Mac, in Ukiah, California, and began a foray into a new business venture alongside it.

OZ: After a full year of my working at the Green Mac, another storefront next to it went vacant. The owners of the Green Mac asked me if I had any ideas of what they could do with it. I said that Morning Glory and I had an idea for a store that would carry all this really cool stuff that we liked—magickal, environmental, and science-related, and also things like comic books and plastic models. The name that we had for it was "Between the Worlds."

NARRATOR: Stores such as the one the Zells dreamed of had, by the late '80s, become an important strand in the web of Pagan activity. Thanks to Buckland's instructional manual and others like it, there were growing numbers of Witches who were working alone. They were called "solitaries," and Scott Cunningham's *Wicca: A Guide for the Solitary Practitioner*, published a couple of years after *Buckland's Complete Book of Witchcraft*, went on to become a hugely popular resource for them. And once these people got comfortable with their books, they then had to find the tools of Magick for their home practices.

New Age and occult stores had evolved into one-stop shopping destinations for people like them, who were stocking their home altars with candles, statues, incense, wands, athames, and the like. For those interested in doing ritual with other human beings, and lucky enough to find some to do them with, these kinds of stores became a regular stop along their path in between the times when they'd be getting together with their group. Since rituals were often only held eight times a year or on full moons, having somewhere to just drop in anytime was a nice option.

(And stores were indoors, and not dependent on the weather to determine if they'd be open or not.)

OZ had already tried to reach the public with a magazine, a coffeehouse, a storefront temple, and a nest in his living room, and none of those had lasted. Likewise his dream of a permanent rural home for his Church had not come true either. But when he got the opportunity for a retail store, it was another assignment from the Goddess, and he jumped right in.

The Zells' idea of a friendly neighborhood Pagan shop was different from what other stores were doing, because their neighborhood was unique. They did have a "Magick" section with books, Tarot decks, candles, crystals, incense, oils, tools, and dolls. And they had a back room, which they reserved for meetings and gaming—*Dungeons & Dragons* was very popular. But there was a lot of homegrown Paganism in the area, including many people who were involved in the activist group Earth First! (EF! had been co-founded years earlier by OZ's original waterbrother, Lance Christie, as part of his plan to create change from behind the scenes.) So when the store was set up as a cooperative, Gary and Betty Ball were brought in with T-shirts and a lot of environmental things.

BETTY BALL: Ukiah, and all of Mendocino County, was just full of back-to-the-landers who came up there in the '70s. And so there were a lot of Hippies, Pagans, and people doing alternative kinds of work. I think everybody thought that kind of business would really make it there. There is a huge environmental community up there. We were doing a T-shirt booth at fairs and festivals at the time, and we were looking for something more stationary, something where we could be part of a business every day instead of just on weekends.

GARY BALL: We were pretty involved in Earth First! We had a lot of shirts from environmental organizations, literature, petitions, bumper stickers, and handouts. The store was a bigger version of what we could carry on the road with us. The redneck community wasn't that pleased about it, but I think they all thought it would fade away soon enough. But the progressive community welcomed us with open arms.

BETTY BALL: We just loved getting to know Otter and Morning Glory, Diane, Zack, and all of their friends who were in and out of there. It was great to get to meet Polly. She was a wonderful, joyful person. She was all-encompassing and loved everybody and always welcomed everybody. I don't think there was a person on Earth that Polly didn't love.

OZ: For several years in the early '80s, Marion Zimmer Bradley and her Berkeley clan put on annual "Worlds of Fantasy" conventions in the Bay Area. MG and I attended all of these as long as they were happening, and we became good friends with many of the sci-fi and fantasy authors who were guests of honor. So when we had the store, we'd invite them to come up for special book signings, which were a big hit with everyone. And then, of course, we'd take them home for dinner and an evening of conversation.

DIANE DARLING: It was fun for a while. I loved doing the windows and having events. One of the events that we had was for Easter. We wanted to have an Easter-egg-decorating contest. But since we weren't Christians, it wasn't going to be obviously Easter. So the theme was "Life springs from Mother Earth." And we invited kids from all over Ukiah to decorate eggs, and we had prizes: Otter made bookmarks that were threaded with Unicorn hair.

GARY BALL: We all worked at both places. I did typesetting, databases, and computer operations, basically. Betty typeset a book. I did lists for movie rental places, spreadsheets, mailing lists, and that kind of thing.

NARRATOR: OZ was actively rebuilding the CAW during all this, and doing regular rituals with them at the Old Same Place and Annwfn. And as a well-known citizen of Ukiah, he got the chance to create a ritual for the entire community where he was living and working.

OZ: One of our friends was Richard Johnson, who published the *Mendocino Grapevine*. I started working for his newspaper as a journalist, staff artist, and editorial cartoonist, doing art and writing articles. I also did layout and pasteups. One day I was sitting down with Richard and talking about stuff, and he said that the town really needed some kind of special event. I said, "Morning Glory and I have done all these Renaissance Faires, and we have a pretty good idea of how such a thing could be put together. Why don't we start a hometown festival? It can be in the fall, around harvest time." The grape harvest was a big thing up there, and in the counterculture it was time to harvest marijuana. So it meant a lot of people had money, and they had reasons to celebrate.

Using the newspaper and my contacts through the chamber of commerce, we started building it up. And the city of Ukiah became the sponsor of our Home Town Harvest Festival, which we kicked off in September of 1986. It involved a parade, closing off the streets, and having bands and performers, big decorations, and sidewalk vendors. It was all happening downtown. The idea was to bring people down there instead of to the malls and big-box stores that were opening up. They were on the edge of town by the freeway, and the downtown area was drying up.

Morning Glory and I led the parade down Main Street in our full Ren Faire regalia. We were the Wizard and the Enchantress, and we marched with our Unicorn. We continued leading the parade every year we were there. Behind us would be the Shriners and the marching bands and floats. Our Unicorns had become so popular that one local artist even produced a comic book featuring "Ukiahcorn," a superhero Unicorn with a spiffy uniform and cape. So of course eventually I had to make such a uniform for Lance when we marched him in the parade, and everyone loved it.

NARRATOR: Another cultural change that had happened while the Zells were off in the woods, and that he was still catching up on in Ukiah, was the rebirth of the comic book industry. In the 1970s all the major superhero characters were owned and published by corporations. They weren't doing anything very interesting, sales were dropping, and comic books didn't appear to have much future. Then a new batch of writers and artists appeared on the scene and revitalized everything. They created new characters, published independently, and all sorts of fun stuff was happening. The mid-1980s were an exciting time—it was possible to walk into a comic book store and find new issues of titles like

Alan Moore's *Watchmen*, Frank Miller's *The Dark Knight Returns*, and the Hernandez brothers' *Love and Rockets*.

OZ and I are both comic book fans, and we agree that comic books are not only updated versions of ancient myths, but that they also can become modern mythology themselves. OZ tried to make comic books a part of Between the Worlds, where, in theory, they could have fit right in. But, in mythology past and present, there are Gods and Goddesses of both love and war, and they don't always get along.

OZ: Between the Worlds began to pick up business from a wider spectrum. When Morning Glory and I set up the store, what we wanted it to be was this place where we had different kinds of stuff brought together. Like our whole life's work, we were trying to weave together disparate elements into something new and neat. One of the things that we had in there was comic books. We had the only comic book store in Ukiah. We had a guy named Ron Grossi, who was really into comics, set it up.

After we got it launched, we brought Diane in as a buyer for the store—we operated on the principal that nepotism begins at home. We always try to bring the people who are closest to us into whatever we do. Most of these projects have been ones that we actually initiated—that is a crucial element in all of this. We initiated many projects, then we brought in our friends. We haven't had a lot of experience with other people initiating projects and then bringing us in, but every now and then something like that does happen. And our attitude has always been that whoever initiated it is pretty much in charge. That is something that we have always taken for granted, but that has not necessarily been shared by everyone who has been involved.

Diane's job was to look at all the catalogues that we got, and bring her recommendations for new products that we should carry to our meetings. She wasn't involved in the comic book stuff—that wasn't her department. She didn't read them or care for the medium. But that didn't keep her from thinking that she had to have a say in that department. That was our first real conflict in all the years that we had been together. We tried to make it work, but we just couldn't.

One of the things that Morning Glory and I were not prepared to deal with in other people—and it took us years before we were finally able to get a handle on this—is that we operate from a position of *inclusiveness*. We look at what can we *include* in whatever we are doing. Whereas we find ourselves occasionally with people whose whole attitude revolves around *exclusiveness*. They're coming from a place of: "What can we keep *out* of this?" What they want is to have something that is pure and uncontaminated by extraneous or incompatible factors. Morning Glory and I do not consider purity to be a value. Our idea is: "What can we bring into the mix that will make it more interesting?"

Anodea eventually wrote an insightful article about this phenomenon of inclusivity versus exclusivity for *The Scarlet Flame*, our Church newsletter, called "Innies versus Outies." It became a thing that haunted us for years and eventually was at the root of the total destruction of the Church and *Green Egg*. But the "comic book war" at Between the Worlds was the first time it really got specific.

Diane didn't particularly like any comics. She accepted some of them, like *ElfQuest*, and a few others we tried to turn her on to. But she simply wanted to keep out of the mix certain things that she did not approve of, particularly comics that had violent or warlike themes. The comic book that she most objected to was *G.I. Joe*, which at that time was the single most popular title. She just absolutely hated it. She thought it glorified war and military stuff. I of course was not even remotely interested in war comics, so I didn't read them. But if that was what the customers wanted, it was our job to sell it to them. I didn't see it as a moral issue.

Ron was in charge of the comics, and he wanted to stock the ones that were the most popular, so as to make the most sales. We never had a conflict with him. Our feeling was that it was his department. The point was to get customers into the store, and if we could get people who were in there to buy comic books, maybe they'd look around and buy other stuff too. Maybe they'd even buy other comics that were more obscure and that they might not have known about. But if we only carried the more obscure comics, those people wouldn't even come in.

This became a serious clash, and Diane simply would not give it up. We went round and round with it, and Ron just got more and more fed up. He couldn't get along with Diane, and eventually we couldn't either. He was the one who understood the comics business, and he couldn't understand why someone was trying to interfere with him trying to make it work.

From Diane's point of view, she had some kind of principle that she felt was really important. We felt like we were dealing with Republicans who didn't want people to have sex that they didn't approve of. Our feelings were: "If you don't like it, don't do it! But don't try and tell somebody else what to do or not to do." I never have understood people who wanted to be puritanical about things.

DIANE DARLING: My bottom line was that I didn't want any comic books in the store that were just going to be off-the-wall violence. I just wanted to have comic books that portrayed the world that we wanted to live in. Well, that was fine for a while. But then the guy who was running the comic book end of things felt that we were losing business. So basically they would have these meetings, and I wasn't there because I worked. I had a job. And then they called a meeting at a time when I was going to be there, and they told me that they were going to have a full line of comic books, and that I could either take it or leave it. And I left it.

OZ: Eventually the conflict escalated to the point where Ron quit. He took the comics and started his own store. It was a very successful store. And when we lost that section, we lost the youth market. Word got out to a lot of our customers who thought we were being stupid and petty—and MG and I had to agree with them.

The problem was, of course, that we kept trying to operate on some kind of consensus basis, where we could sit down and work things out and reach an agreement. Consensus doesn't really work with people who have a different agenda on a fundamental level. Eventually the whole store collapsed.

NARRATOR: There is a happy epilogue to all the brouhaha in this chapter: Betty and Gary Ball moved on to start the Mendocino Environmental Center, where they worked for the next ten years.

BETTY BALL: It was just wonderful. The Green Mac and Between the Worlds were pretty much steppingstones for us to what we really wanted to be doing. And it provided us with the opportunity to get acquainted with the community, connect with the environmental community, and start doing environmental work and getting the word out about environmental issues. When we opened the Mendocino Environmental Center, a lot of people came to us and said, "We know you're starting with nothing, whatever you need, just tell us and we'll get it." And that's just an amazing response from a community.

GARY BALL: The Mendocino Environmental Center still exists. It's a nonprofit. We had a tremendous number of people from the community helping us make the MEC go. That certainly didn't happen with the commercial ventures. We wanted to do environmental work all along. We were doing it at Between the Worlds, and it just expanded into the Environmental Center, which sort of was our dream all along anyway.

NARRATOR: The Zells remained active in local culture and politics, and a few years later Earth Firster Darryl Cherney became an official Bard of the Church of All Worlds. And the revival of *Green Egg*, which will be covered later in the book, came about directly as a result of OZ working at the Green Mac.

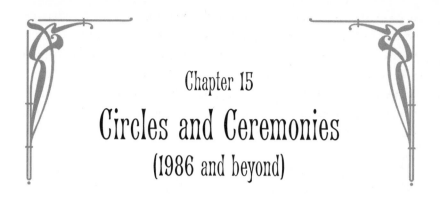

Chapter 15
Circles and Ceremonies
(1986 and beyond)

Though you thought you had destroyed
The memory of the Ancient Way,
Still the people light the bale fires
Every year on Solstice day
And on Beltane Eve and Samhain
You can find us on the hill
Invoking once again
The Triple Will!

—FROM "WE WON'T WAIT ANY LONGER"
BY GWYDION PENDDERWEN, 1980

NARRATOR: The revived Church of All Worlds was a tax-exempt corporation, just like the original had been in St. Louis. The primary functions of their board of directors were the secular, legal, and business aspects of running the Church, which were minor in comparison to the Priesthood Council, which handled the primary religious and liturgical aspects. The rituals, beginning in 1986, were written and organized by the Clergy: Priests and Priestesses. The board of directors had nothing to do with the rituals other than a few other legal matters like making sure the liability insurance was current.

The primary ritualists were the Zells, Anodea Judith, and Marylyn Motherbear. Tom Williams and Avilynn Pwyll did a few, and others occasionally. It was, as always, an eclectic mix of people, and the rituals reflected that. Though OZ had studied Witchcraft and learned from it, and MG was, of course, a Witch, the CAW was (and is) not a Wiccan tradition. It is always evolving and being shaped by the lives and experiences of its members as they explore their relationship to each other and to Mother Earth. Motherbear had decades of experience doing the back-to-the-land trip. Anodea was involved with chakra work, yoga, and psychology. (She has since written several books, including *Wheels of Life: A User's Guide to the Chakra System* and *Waking the Global Heart: Humanity's Rite of Passage from the Love of Power to the Power of Love*.) With this structure, and these people, the CAW regularly held eight celebrations each time the Earth went around the sun.

OZ: Morning Glory, Diane, and I designed and held our first May Games to select our first official May Royalty in 1987. We invented a series of games—some based on traditions and others that we made up—that were erotic competitions to be engaged in by couples. The first one was "Strip Your Partner." The first couple who managed to get each other completely undressed would run over to a bell and ring it. Whichever couple would get the highest total score after all the games were finished would then become the new May King and Queen.

So Friday night we would have the Walpurgisnacht ritual; Saturday we would have the games; and then on Sunday we would set up the Maypole. The men would carry the pole in a ritual procession through the forest into the meadow, where the women had dug a hole for it. And the women would decorate it with flowers and ribbons.

The May Queen would reign until the following Beltane. But the King would only reign until Samhain, at which time the crown would be laid to Earth—whether it had his head in it or not. We would then have, as part of our Samhain rite, a ritual to sacrifice the kingship without actually sacrificing the individual person.

Throughout the summer the King and Queen would hold court. For the winter season the Queen would hold court herself. During the time that they held court at each of the rituals, they would dispense favors; give awards, knighthoods, and honors to people; and stuff like that.

Their lives during that period of time would be wrapped around those roles. They would visit people and be welcomed as houseguests, just like a royal tour.

The next year, the couple who had been crowned previously would conduct the May Games to select the next winner. They would pass on the crowns. That was the first time that we created a cycle that involved people taking a role and holding it throughout the entire year.

The winners of the 1987 May Games had entered as a triple, so when they won, we were obliged to have all three of them crowned as May Queen and Kings. As it turned out, that didn't work out very well. They all broke apart just a few months into their reign, leaving us without seasonal royalty for the rest of the year.

From these early experiments, we came to a deeper understanding of the proper role of the May Royalty as the *avatars* of the land and the community—the Sacred King representing all the men, and the Queen representing all the women. So after that we agreed that we would not have any more same-sex couples—or triples—entering the Games (or at least, not eligible to win). This was (and remains) a controversial decision, as the Church of All Worlds has always embraced people of all sexual persuasions and proclivities. But for this seasonal cycle of avatars to work, we realized it was essential that *both* the men and the women of our Tribe be represented in the May couple. And so it has been for more than twenty years.

ZACK DARLING: I started emerging as sort of a kid leader with the whole group of kids. I was the oldest one. So what I did was, I went out with a friend to another part of the meadow where we were holding the May Games, and we built a kids' Circle. We facilitated our own rituals and had kids' May Games. We would elect the May Prince and Princess. It was the first time that we really integrated the kids into the CAW, into festivals and gatherings as an active part of it that we were doing on our own. It was kind of cool, because we kids did our own thing while the grown-ups did their thing.

OZ: The following year, 1988, Morning Glory and I entered the May Games. We were getting a bit long in the tooth by then, but we thought it'd be fun. We were quite surprised when we won the Games and were crowned King and Queen of the May! Just three weeks later (May 27), MG turned forty, so she referred to herself as "the forty-year-old May Queen" (an homage to an underground comic by Ted Richards called *The Forty Year Old Hippie*).

Then, right after becoming the Queen of the May, she hurt her neck badly in a way that paralyzed her for weeks and pretty much crippled her for much of her reign. She was really in bad shape; there were months when she couldn't even get out of bed, and it wasn't until January of '89 that she was fully recovered. Meanwhile, I had to support the whole family from my job at the Green Mac. I did more and more freelance work to pay for the expenses—including illustrating a book on apocalyptic theology by a fundamentalist Christian preacher! I drew many pictures of Moses, Jesus, the Crucifixion, angels, and Heaven. There were still some circus royalties, but they had begun to peter out at that point.

MG: The year I turned forty was a very "auspicious" year for me. Understand that the word *auspicious* doesn't necessarily mean the same thing as *lucky*; the real meaning is more like "transformational." The first auspicious thing that happened was that OZ and I were chosen in the May Games to be the King and Queen for that year. We had really only played as sort of a lark and to make sure that there were enough players to make it fun for everyone. They say that the best rulers are those who really don't want the job, but it's not as if we actively didn't want it; we could have refused it, but we felt completely surprised and yet honored. Still, there were a lot of jokes about having a forty-year-old May Queen, and I was going to learn a hard lesson about trying to run that Spring Maiden energy through a forty-year-old, out-of-shape body!

Late that summer I saw one of my favorite musicians from the '60s in concert: Country Joe McDonald. Did I mention that I love to dance? I do love to dance, and I am pretty good at it even if I do say so myself. I become completely entranced when I dance, and my body moves of its own volition with no conscious thought on my part about how or where or when; I feel like I'm flying. I used to work as a go-go dancer in the late '60s, and I was an exotic dancer for a while in the '70s. I studied belly dancing and a little Tai Chi, and so all these elements sort of take over when I am dancing. Sexuality, spirituality, and dancing have always come from the same center for me.

Anyway, here I was at this concert dancing my heart out to Country Joe's music, and I started doing some of my old go-go routines that involved a complex movement where I dip my head down, let my hair hang low, touch the floor with one hand, and then push off and leap back upward reaching for the stars with the opposite hand and snapping my head back in ecstasy, which makes my long hair travel in a flashing arc. This movement looks really great and it feels wonderful, like you are freeing your spirit to soar upward. So I repeated it a number of times during that set. I was so high on endorphins that I could not feel any pain as my May Queen spirit expressed itself through a body that had not been living on the Ranch for three years at that point and had slumped into a comparatively sedentary lifestyle.

About two weeks later, OZ, Diane, and I were doing a workshop at Isis Oasis on "Going into the Underworld to Meet the Dark Lady." It was sort of an outgrowth of the work we were visioning about the Eleusinian Mysteries. We had been planning this for months and had worked like mad on this fantastic script. Everything was going great, and then I started having this sharp pain in my neck, which kept getting worse and worse until it reached the proportion of a migraine. Diane gave me some medicine for migraine headaches, and I pushed myself to finish the ritual in spite of the dizziness, nausea, and difficulty in seeing. But I had to leave as soon as I could get away. I could barely drive myself home, I was such a wreck. I'm lucky that I made it safely because I stupidly didn't ask for anyone to drive me; I just wasn't used to asking for help like that. OZ and Diane had decided to stay longer at Isis Oasis to enjoy the rest of the event, which seemed reasonable. I always hate to rain on anyone's parade; and why make a fuss about a pain in the neck?

NARRATOR: Morning Glory was alone for the rest of the weekend till a friend learned of her situation and came over to help her. The next morning she woke up and found herself paralyzed and in agony. Her neck was locked into a frozen position and she could not move her head. When OZ came home, he tried to help her but there was little he could do to fix the situation. After a phone conference with a doctor, she got some prescription drugs but nothing helped. It was twelve days before she was even able to find a position where she wasn't in pain so that she could sleep.

MG: The hardest thing of all for me to understand was Diane's reaction. As a lover, sister, and fellow medical person I would have thought that she would be sympathetic and certainly curious as to what the hell was going wrong with my body. But that was not the case. Oh, she got me an appointment and helped me get to the doctor when I could finally move at all. But when the x-ray did not show what the problem was, she decided that there was nothing really wrong with me and that I was just faking it to get attention; and what's more she began to tell this story to my friends, who would of course believe her because she was a nurse.

Now, the karma for being a drama queen really came down on me like a ton of rocks! I couldn't believe this was happening when I was in such desperate straits; I guess it was partly the fallout from my years of lying to people. Even though I had changed my ways, some people still did not trust me and there was no way that I could prove what I was going through.

As it was, since pain medicines did not really work, we ended up trying some pretty far-out therapy, and one that finally worked was laughter . . . yeah, that is pretty nutty. But it turns out that direct nerve pain responds to the brain's own endorphin rush better than any other synthetic pain remedy. One of the best ways to pump out endorphins is through laughter . . . so it really is the best medicine. That and a $25 over-the-door traction unit put me on the road to recovery, along with a visit to my chiropractor when he finally returned.

All this trouble was actually caused by a ruptured disc between my C4 and C5 vertebrae. This happened when I was dancing my head off at the concert. A ruptured disc can act like a slow leak and take weeks to finally go flat. When mine finally did, it settled down and locked hard onto a pair of spinal nerves, pinching and grinding them into the flayed agony that I experienced. Eventually, I had another x-ray done, and by that time it showed up so I finally had proof I could point to; but the damage was done, trust was breached, and many people never got around to finding out the truth of the situation. For my own self I discovered that a lie can run around the world before the truth can get its boots on. Eventually the injury stabilized naturally. I did not want to get surgery at that time even if I could have afforded it, because the state of neurosurgical medicine was still pretty primitive and the outcome of such surgeries had a high failure rate. It took two years to stabilize naturally, and in the long run it was probably for the best.

I learned some of the hardest and most important lessons of my life during this journey into my own heart of darkness. I eventually learned to befriend the pain and the darkness, to use the sleeplessness and hallucinations as visionary journeys. I found out that I was a lot tougher than I ever thought. I learned that I had true friends who came through for me. And most important of all, I learned that OZ would not abandon me in my need nor would he believe a calumny against me even when it came from someone he also loved and trusted. Knowing that my lovemate would continue to love me even at my worst was evidence that he would come through for me as a lifemate for the rest of my life no matter what tricks the future decided to play on either of us.

OZ: At Samhain (Hallowe'en) of '88, it was time for me to lay down the crown of the May King. While we had been holding our Samhain rites every year at Annwfn, on this particular year Richard Ely—a professional "Gaeologist" and Anodea's husband—arranged to hold our rites at Pinnacles National Monument (now Pinnacles National Park), not too far from Salinas, California.

Pinnacles is a remarkable geological site. It's where the first crack of the San Andreas fault first tore apart the California landscape with a huge outpouring of molten lava called a shield volcano. It was in the largest and uppermost cave that we held our Samhain rites that year. As the outgoing May King, I was the first to be sent down the long, winding stairs cut into the walls of the caves into the Underworld. Being that my consciousness was already enhanced by sacrament, it was a very spooky descent—down into the deepest, darkest depths of the San Andreas fault. Glow sticks were placed here and there to provide enough illumination to avoid deadly missteps.

Finally arriving at the bottom of the descent—which had seemed to go on forever—I came to a barred gate, before which stood a masked figure, who read to me from a scroll, informing me that I was to pass through the gate to meet the Queen of the Underworld Herself. Proceeding further along the cavernous corridor, I came to the throne room of the Goddess, who welcomed me and set me to meditation on my life, my journey, and my Mission. As I did so, I had a profound revelation based on my travels with Belladonna throughout the caves, tombs, catacombs, and Underworld sites of old Europe—especially those in Greece. I envisioned a restoration of the ancient Eleusinian Mysteries to be held in these caves.

As I came to the gate on the way out, I was told that I must now replace the Gatekeeper. The mask and scroll were turned over to me, and the former Gatekeeper returned up the stairs to the cave above where everyone was gathered—sending another to descend into the Underworld. After the next pilgrim had completed his encounter with the Goddess, and had in turn taken my place as Gatekeeper, I returned up the long stairway to present my revelation to the assembly. And everyone agreed that re-creating the Mysteries of Eleusis at this site would be a wonderful thing to do.

NARRATOR: At Mabon (Autumn Equinox) of 1990, the Church of All Worlds returned to Pinnacles National Monument to do their first Eleusinian Mysteries cycle.

OZ: Morning Glory and I had been doing all this historical research since Samhain of 1989, and together with Anodea we worked up an elaborate ritual, replete with her lovely poetry and songs.

ANODEA JUDITH: And so I talked to Otter about it, and he said, "Well, let's do the Eleusinian Mysteries there." So he and Morning Glory did research and crafted a bunch of the tools, masks, and headpieces. I wrote a lot of the music, poetry, and script. We got permission from the park service to do a re-creation of the Mysteries.

The cave is like a half-mile long. A lot of it is steps carved into rock walls that go down around a waterfall. It's a remarkable place, and we had a very powerful ritual there.

OZ: The Mysteries of Eleusis were founded around 1600 BCE and continued uninterrupted for two thousand years, until the Roman emperor Theodosius I closed the sanctuaries in 392 CE. The last remnants of the Mysteries were obliterated four years later, when Alaric, King of the

Goths, invaded, accompanied by Christian monks "in their dark gar-ments," bringing in Arian Christianity and deliberately desecrating and destroying the old sacred sites.

Traditionally the Mysteries were held at the Harvest Moon in Greece, during the week leading up to and culminating in the full moon nearest to the Autumn Equinox. We followed the same schedule ourselves—only on a single weekend—so that on the night of the Mysteries, there would be a full moon to illuminate them.

The park gave us special permission to stay there overnight, but only for a certain number of people. We had to arrange it every year. And the other factor was simply how many people we could process in the course of a night. We came up with a total number of twenty, and almost half of those were needed to conduct the rites. All the participants had to wear authentic Greek costumes. When it was almost dusk, and the park was closed to everyone else, we would come in and everyone would then pro-cess up along a winding path to a particular area. Nobody had been al-lowed to go up there before that. People would come for the whole weekend, and this would be done on Saturday night in the particular area where the caves were. And the landscape is so bizarre and alien that you would have no idea they were there until you turn the corner. It's like step-ping into another world.

So as people went along the path, they would encounter little tableaus. It was basically a walking version of the kind of rituals that we had created before—especially for Walpurgisnacht. But instead of having the tableaus in the center of the circle, they would be at various stages in the journey, like a "stations of the cross" kind of thing. At each place, the characters would enact the next little part of the story.

MG: I had been at several rituals with other groups dedicated to the Ele-usinia, but I wanted to be part of the creation of something different—something more intense and shamanic that would reach down across the centuries and try to recapture a sense of the power, pageantry, and most important of all, the transformational quality of the original cultic Mys-tery that was so influential in shaping a part of Western spirituality for two thousand years. During its time, thousands of the most influential people in classical antiquity—like Pythagoras—had been initiates of the

Mysteries. Though there are a few personal testimonials surviving that tell of how people's lives were changed for the better by their experiences, actual specific information about the Mysteries themselves is almost non-existent. All those people over all that time never broke their sacred oaths of silence and managed to take their knowledge with them to the grave. Certainly that was an amazing tribute to the enduring power of Eleusis, but it sure made it a bitch to try and dredge up enough facts to re-create a real ritual!

Oddly enough, some of the only extant information on details of the Mysteries exists in the form of the Christian diatribes against the practices dating from the spread of Christianity into Greece. How ironic that those ancient poets' and priestesses' only chroniclers would turn out to be the very people who railed against them and eventually succeeded in extinguishing their sacred flame. So we were able to gather bits and pieces of material from an assortment of authors, but we needed to take lots of it with spoonfuls of salt since some of the information came from such biased sources.

Fortunately, there is a kindred spirit in Pagan peoples from all over the world, and certain themes that are rooted in the worship of divine Nature replay themselves constantly, becoming universal themes. We were able to stitch together those fragments and find the common threads that allowed us to glimpse the underlying truth of the original Mysteries and then re-create and reframe those truths so that they would be accessible to a modern English-speaking Pagan. The original script that we wrote for the Mysteries has been fiddled with and changed around by each and every Priestess and poet who has taken them on since we first started performing them; what has occurred is a kind of evolution, where the ancient Gods and Goddesses have been provided with vessels to speak through and are allowed to continue the process of working out these ancient family dynamics in ways that teach us and are applicable to our modern lives. Given enough time, even the Gods themselves evolve.

OZ: The *Homeric Hymn to Demeter* pretty much lays out the narrative of the whole story of the *exoteric* ("outer") Mysteries. It tells how Demeter's daughter, the flower maiden Kore, is out picking flowers and she sees a mysterious black narcissus. When she pulls it, the ground opens

CIRCLES AND CEREMONIES   255

and up comes Hades, Lord of the Underworld, in his black chariot pulled by black horses. He sweeps Kore up and carries her off into the Underworld to become his Queen (henceforth called Persephone). Demeter goes searching for her. And in her grief and anger she doesn't attend to the nurturance of the land—the land grows cold and barren, and winter comes upon the Earth. The harvest fails and people are hungry. The Gods aren't getting their sacrifices, and everything is falling apart.

So the Gods say that this has to be settled. Demeter tells them that she will not relent until she has her daughter back. So then they try to reason with Hades to release her, without success. That's where, eventually, the mortals come into play. A pact is made between the Gods and the humans. To fulfill their pact, the humans have to go into the Underworld and try to persuade Hades to release Persephone. And that's tough—how do you persuade the Lord of the Underworld to relinquish his Queen?

In the *esoteric* ("secret") Mysteries, each of the pilgrims one at a time has to be prepared to go into the Underworld to encounter Hades (and Persephone) on their own. And there they discover things about themselves and the nature of Life and Death and the Mysteries. They have to confront their darkest fears. But before they go down, they are brought before the throne of Demeter to give their last words. Demeter asks, "If you don't return, how would you like to be remembered?" And people have to sort of give their own eulogy.

We have conducted these Mysteries over many years now. And as people were initiated, they also began to contribute songs and stories. People would return in the following year, and the stories would evolve. It finally all concludes as the dawn sun arises and the world returns to normal.

ANODEA JUDITH: I participated every year. I played several different parts. I priestessed the ceremony. I played Hecate. One time I played Demeter and my daughter played Persephone.

We did it for about ten years, and then an endangered species of bat moved into the cave, and the park service closed the cave so we couldn't go in there anymore. But we have continued holding the Mysteries at Pinnacles to this very day—just no longer inside the main caves.

NARRATOR: OZ also continued doing rituals elsewhere, with people who weren't involved with the Church of All Worlds, and with people who weren't even Pagans. His biggest public ritual since the 1979 eclipse came about as a result of his involvement with his local community. He and Morning Glory were representing the Church of All Worlds at planning meetings for an interfaith ceremony to mark the twentieth anniversary of Earth Day in 1990, and found themselves facilitating all the planning due to their prior experience with interfaith ritual. They brought a wide swath of people of different beliefs—Catholics, Jews, Chinese Buddhists, Pomo Indians, Sufis, Krishna followers, Tibetan Buddhists, several congregations of Protestants—together in creating a unique and touching ritual by asking each group what they'd most like to contribute to the ceremony and hanging it on a ritual framework.

OZ: And so we went, singling out each faith group to do what they most wanted, and plugging their part into the basic liturgical structure we'd used for years in Pagan ceremonies.

On the day of the ceremony, after the four directions were called, each faith group did an invocation or prayer to their respective deities. I think no one will ever forget the voluptuous Morning Glory, naked under her diaphanous blue Priestess gown, standing proudly in the center of the Circle intoning Doreen Valiente's "Charge of the Star Goddess" in her stage-trained voice!

Ayisha passed a large inflatable Earth ball with a pledge to the Earth; the Methodist minister led "A Confession of our Carelessness" responsive reading; and various songs and chants were sung.

The Working was the planting of a Tree for the Future by the Methodist youth group, while Tibetan Lamas intoned a trance-inducing "Auoommm . . ." The Krishnas served *prasadam* (holy food) for Communion; everyone thanked their respective deities; the Pomos concluded their pipe ceremony; and the Catholic priest delivered the final benediction.*

(* This story originally appeared in a longer version in Oberon and Morning Glory's 2006 book *Creating Circles and Ceremonies*.)

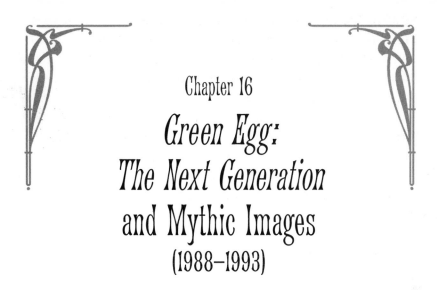

Chapter 16
Green Egg:
The Next Generation
and Mythic Images
(1988–1993)

Say!
I like green eggs and ham!
I do! I like them, Sam-I-am!
And I would eat them in a boat.
And I would eat them with a goat.

—FROM *GREEN EGGS AND HAM*, BY DR. SEUSS, BEGINNER BOOKS, 1960

NARRATOR: *Joseph Campbell and the Power of Myth*, a PBS documentary mini-series, was broadcast for the first time in 1988. The Public Broadcasting Service was, at that time, an important source of news, culture, and entertainment for liberal-minded folks across the United States, and the response was very enthusiastic. *Myth* was shown over and over again, and a companion book, featuring transcriptions of interviews with Campbell by Bill Moyers, became a bestseller.

Campbell and Moyers talked at length about Gáea, the Earth, storytelling, ritual, shamans, Goddess worship, the circle of life, and other subjects that were familiar terrain to contemporary Pagans. (Paganism was, it seemed, reaching the "Public"!) Campbell tied it all together by explaining how these things could all be found in the mythologies of different cultures around the world. He was even able to examine *Star Wars* in mythology terms, and George Lucas himself said that an earlier book by Campbell (*The Hero with a Thousand Faces*) had been a big influence on him.

Campbell talked at length about "following your bliss," which OZ had been doing already for quite a while—though he usually referred to it as "getting an assignment from the Goddess." He continued to do so that same year when he once again began to publish *Green Egg*.

OZ: For years and years we kept hearing about our old magazine, *Green Egg*, and reading about it in books. Every new Pagan zine would be compared with the long-defunct *Green Egg*—and usually unfavorably! Periodically we'd get letters from people asking us to put it out again. At that point I had been working at the Green Mac for several years and learning page layout and desktop publishing, so the idea of reviving *Green Egg* started becoming a viable possibility. It crystallized at the point that I got my own computer. They upgraded at the office, so I was able to take a Mac 512 home with me. I set up a little office in one of our bedrooms. We started talking about how we would do it.

We got a $300 check as seed money from a generous investor. So I sat down and composed a letter saying that *Green Egg* was coming back. I put in a bunch of quotes from people saying how much they had missed it. On the back of the page I put information about advertising rates. The $300 paid for printing and postage to send out the letter. And people sent in their ads and money. It was just about the time that we were ending things with the store (Between the Worlds) that we were starting up things with *Green Egg*, so our main attentions were shifted from the store to the magazine. We let it go and moved on.

By this time we had brought the Church of All Worlds back from its long languishing when we were living up in the woods. There was now a board of directors. We went to them and said, "This is what we are going to do." And they said that we were on our own—they weren't going to bankroll it, but we could use the Church's nonprofit status to get a mailing permit. (At that time there was a big savings for anyone using a nonprofit permit to mail. That has diminished in subsequent times, but it was a huge factor back then.)

At that time Morning Glory was adamantly opposed to the affiliation with the Church. She said, "Look, you guys are starting this on your own; you're going to be doing all the work and putting in all the money. If you put the Church's name on it, somebody might try to take it away from you." I said that nobody would ever want to do that. The board had made it really clear they didn't want anything to do with it. How naïve I was!

Morning Glory and I had worked together on the old *Green Egg* in St. Louis. Diane was a really good editor. And we pulled together a really cool first issue. It came out at Beltane, 1988, with issue #81. The previous fall a new TV series called *Star Trek: The Next Generation* had premiered, so we put a banner across the front cover proudly proclaiming, "Green Egg: The Next Generation," with my artwork of a colorful rising Phoenix. I resurrected a two-plate printing technique from the '60s called split fountain. And I found a guy named Verge Belanger, who used to run a printing press for the underground papers in San Francisco. He knew how to do it, and nobody else did. We found a friendly printing shop in Ukiah that was willing to let him come in and operate their press and do the split fountain colors.

What "split fountain" means is that you create little inserts in the fountain where the ink goes, and you put a different color ink in each one. So when the paper runs through, the colors blend together. If you do that just right, you can get some amazing rainbow effects. So we would do two press runs. We would do a background in rainbow colors, and then print a black ink over it in the foreground. And it was just spectacular. We used that technique for years, just to get it going, until we could go to actual four-color printing.

It got us off the ground. At that time we were the only Pagan publication that had a color cover. People loved it—we had to do a second printing of the premier issue.

Sadly, Robert Heinlein died on May 8, 1988, so he never got to see the new incarnation of the magazine he used to enjoy in the '70s. In the second issue—#82, Lughnasadh—I wrote a tribute to him, and published some of our personal correspondence, especially his lengthy discussion of *Stranger in a Strange Land*, in which he'd written:

"Well, what was I trying to *say* in it?

"I was asking questions.

"I was *not* giving answers. I was trying to shake the reader loose from some preconceptions and induce him to think for himself, along new and fresh lines. In consequence each reader gets something different out of that book because *he himself supplies the answers.*" (R. A. Heinlein to Tim Zell, January 20, 1972)

When we first started, MG, Diane, and I all worked together and did everything. But it soon worked out that I was the publisher—I ran the circulation and promotion of it, and was responsible for the overall mix and design and getting it out there. I also did the database and maintained the subscriptions and advertising. Diane was the editor—she contacted the contributors and did the typesetting.

A lot of people sent in art and articles. In the middle of each issue I put a section for Church of All Worlds stuff, but it was like pulling teeth to get anybody to contribute. Eventually I put in Church membership applications—I basically gave the CAW lots of free advertising and promotion. But it wasn't just a CAW publication. I noted periodically that a very small number of CAW members actually subscribed to the magazine. But that was all right. It wasn't intended as a propaganda device to promote the specific vision of the Church—I had my sights set on a bigger picture. I intended to use the magazine to forge and foster a global Pagan community.

Anodea wrote articles, but they weren't about the CAW—they were about chakras and things like that. Primarily, *Green Egg* was about discussing issues, and presenting concepts and ideas to people. It was directed at shaping a global Pagan community and feeding into it the kind of information that I thought people ought to know about, or think about, or talk about.

To get it launched, we exchanged subscriptions with other Pagan publications. There weren't many that were very professional at that time—most of them were just little newsletters. But a few of them became larger. In exchange for the subscription, we would run ads for their magazine, and they would run ads for *Green Egg*. This kind of brought us to people's attention, and the subscriptions picked up. As we did that

I looked through other publications looking for ads for metaphysical stores and got them to carry *Green Egg*. Eventually that became a substantial part of our circulation. We encouraged our readers to go into their local stores and get them to carry it.

And eventually we found some distributors for it. We had a lot of problems with that, but it was necessary to reach into new markets. Chain stores would not buy directly from us—they would only buy from distributors. If we wanted to get into Borders and Barnes & Noble, we had to deal with distributors. We were hoping that we would be introduced to new audiences, who would then eventually subscribe.

DIANE DARLING: I was working for a doctor, and I had that job for fifteen years. Originally I was recruited just to do some proofreading and to write a few articles. I'd never used a computer at all. But within a few months I found myself pretty much doing all the work.

That was back before we had email, so everything came in on paper and had to be typeset. Otter is a fast typist, and really accurate. He did a lot of the typesetting, and I did a lot of the editing. Over time we got to be quite a team in selecting what should go into *Green Egg*. He traveled a lot, going to festivals and stuff like that, and I stayed home and kept my fingers in the dike. So, eventually, as it became less of a thing that we were just kind of doing for fun and started to turn into a business, a lot of the nuts and bolts of it fell to me. I ended up working way too hard, doing both all the business and the editing.

Our review section gave a lot of exposure to Pagan musical artists and writers. Through our columnists, especially Denny Sargent and Diana Paxson, we were able to present a lot of still-practicing Pagan groups from around the world, such as Shinto (which was one of my favorites), to show that we are not alone in our Pagan practices. We were able to confront the ritual abuse community, who was constantly calling us Satanists. We provided places for very thoughtful articles on people like Robert Heinlein, Aleister Crowley, and Jack Parsons.

We did a lot of important stuff while I was there. We created a showcase of Paganism as it was being practiced on the planet during those years. I thought *Green Egg* worked really well to invigorate and promote growth in the Pagan population.

OZ: Humor has always been an important element of our lives and work. Because we had a magazine called *Green Egg*, people kept asking us if we were gonna do another one called "Ham." Though we hadn't made the connection ourselves, many people immediately associated "Green Eggs and Ham" from the popular children's book of that title by Dr. Seuss. So we decided that it would be a great idea to put out a companion zine for kids, and call it *HAM*, which we made an acronym for *How About Magick?* I talked Zack into editing it, and I did the layout. The first issue came out as an insert in *Green Egg* #86 (Litha, 1989). After that, it became an independent publication for many years, changing editors as each one outgrew the appropriate age (13–16).

ZACK DARLING: *Green Egg* was going really well, and Otter asked me if I wanted to do a kids' magazine. And I was into it. So he taught me about layout and basic design. I was already a pretty decent writer at that point—I was fourteen. Starhawk later took one of the articles I wrote about youth and lovemaking, which basically was about sex education from one kid to another, and she reprinted it in her book *Circle Round*.

I learned page design on the computer, the old-school Macs. Otter got me into it and taught me how to do it. I started my own comic strip called "I Was a Teenage Son of a Witch," about an apathetic teenager with a crazy Witch mom who kept making him do wild stuff. OZ encouraged me artistically.

Later on I went to Mendocino College, and after the first week I got put in the most advanced creative writing class that they offered there— I kind of jetted through the English department because they placed me based on my writing. After that I took over the job of the editor-in-chief of the Mendocino College newspaper, because of my experience having done publications and work with layout and stuff. And the guy who ran the journalism department was someone Otter had worked with at the Green Mac years before. He knew I was a good writer and had some experience in publishing, and the editor of the newspaper at the time was graduating. I had my own office with three computers and my own keys to the school, and I could come and go anytime I wanted. It was awesome, and it was all based on the skills that I had learned from Otter.

I ended up leaving and moving down to Santa Rosa, where I currently live, and going into the graphics department at Santa Rosa Junior College. I decided that was what I really liked—the art, layout, and design. Now I do graphics for a living—I'm an art director for a marketing company, and I have my own graphics company. I have had up to seven people working under me.

NARRATOR: Otter had worked at the Green Mac and taken care of the family finances the whole time that he was also working at Between the Worlds and then when he was beginning to revive *Green Egg*. Then the money that he was able to bring in began to decrease, and the family had to start looking for other sources of revenue.

OZ: Over time more and more people got computers and learned how to use PageMaker, so they didn't need to come to me anymore to do their flyers and catalogues. Fortunately, my work was able to sustain us through MG's ill health. Once she had recovered from that, she took a job at the hospital doing labwork. She worked there for a year or two during the early phases of *Green Egg*. So I was able to devote more of my time to the magazine. And Morning Glory kind of pulled out of the magazine and first put her energies into working in a lab to contribute financial support.

MG: We were up against the wall for money. *Green Egg* couldn't afford to pay much and the Unicorn money was gone, so I started working at the Ukiah Valley Medical Center as a histology tech in the laboratory. It was a job I had trained for and was originally certified for, but I had not even looked at a rotary microtome for twenty years or more. Since Otter was spending all his time working on *Green Egg*, I figured I would take on the role of breadwinner so the magazine would continue to grow and prosper. He kept telling me how one of these days the magazine would be able to pay him a living salary, and then I could go back to working on my own life's work.

It was difficult to go back into the mundane world after living in the Faery world at Greenfield and do a steady nine-to-five-type job. Actually, the hours tend to be a bit more extreme; since histology is basically about preparing slides of human cellular tissue removed in surgery so that it can be examined by a pathologist to determine whether there is disease present, especially malignant disease, it was mostly necessary to be at the lab around 6:30 or 7:00 a.m. This was not kind to the nocturnal creature I had become since I had last practiced this discipline. I immediately found out that many of my skills were not only rusty, but that my ASCP credentials had lapsed and they had recently upgraded the job definition, now requiring an A.S. degree that I lacked. So instead of taking a job as an actual histologist, work I genuinely enjoyed, I ended up being demoted to a pathology technician.

My job was basically to assist the pathologist in taking samples of formaldehyde-preserved organs and whatnot, for gross analysis (aptly named), then labeling and preparing those samples to be mounted on slides and stained so you could see the cellular structures and determine the presence of disease. This is not very pretty work (that's putting it mildly!); the pretty part came at the microscope end. My job involved standing on concrete floors for eight hours with my hands up to the wrists in various toxic substances and diseased tissue. My immediate boss was an older woman who had been doing her job for twenty-five years, and was a very strict disciplinarian who didn't like to explain how to do a task but wanted it done exactly right the first time. I was probably her worst nightmare, and she was certainly close to being mine, but I tried to look hard at her and see the Goddess within. That Goddess was definitely the Crone, and She did not suffer fools gladly.

One day I was standing on a stool and reaching up for a five-gallon jar full of cancerous breast tissue preserved in formaldehyde when my hand slipped and the jar fell on top of me. It opened up and I found myself covered in foul, greasy tissue, blinded and reeking with formalin fumes. I headed for the sink to wash myself off, and as I pulled off the sodden lab coat and flushed my face and body with soap and water, I kept thinking over and over: "This will be the death of me; I will end up in one of these jars if I don't get out of this job."

But, of course, *Green Egg* still wasn't making enough money to pay a salary, and the bills had to be paid, so I kept at it. But I also had made up my mind that I needed to find a way out of this trap. I called on the Goddess for help, and she replied in the form of a new applicant for the job I had originally wanted as histologist. This new woman was completely qualified with years of experience so they sadly informed me that they were going to hire her instead of me. They explained that they would lay me off, which would entitle me to collect unemployment while I found new work. I managed to squeeze out a tear . . . and fervently thanked the Goddess.

I was determined that while I was on unemployment, I would devote myself entirely to creating a business that would support us financially, which neither *Green Egg* nor the Church of All Worlds was doing. I was also desperate to return to my own life work and make it somehow into a real career.

That summer I attended a very germinal series of workshops put on by CIIS (California Institute of Integral Studies), featuring Marija Gimbutas, and it was a tremendous breakthrough for me as a researcher. I was able to dialogue with many other Goddess historians like Merlin Stone, Elinor Gadon, and Patricia Monaghan.

My life work as a Priestess has been teaching Goddess history and Goddess lore. I traveled around and told people wonderful tales of the mythology, lore, and practices of the ancient Goddess religion, and about ancient Goddesses and Gods and the cultures that worshipped them. I would teach at schools, bookstores, metaphysical shops, and Pagan gatherings. By then I had a fairly large collection of Goddess figurines from all over the world and throughout history. I would take some of these images with me and use them as tactile illustrations of various aspects of the Goddess.

One of the most fulfilling things about this work for me is watching women's reactions to the wide range of body types portrayed in these statues. Far too many women have a pretty lousy self-image about their bodies from all the years of negative comparisons we are subjected to, so realizing that whatever type of body a woman possesses, at one time and place in the world, it was considered not only to be beautiful but to be divine—that can be a tremendously liberating and uplifting experience.

Otter had begun making me new Goddesses that were museum reproduction-quality images. He made Goddesses from the Stone Age and from the Bronze Age, one from Crete and one from Czechoslovakia. I also got involved and made a couple of pieces.

OZ: When the California Academy of Sciences opened an exhibit of "Ice Age Art," I went down to San Francisco and spent two days sitting on a little folding camp stool in front of the case of Paleolithic Goddess figurines. I had my box of Sculpey and my clay modeling tools, and I shaped precise replicas, by hand and by eye, of each of the little Matrikas on display. I managed to buffalo the guards who tried to throw me out ("No photos allowed" says nothing about sculpture . . .), and I enjoyed the reactions of the people coming to view the exhibit. Many stopped to ask me what I was doing, and I got to speak to them of the Goddess and my devotion to Her service.

On the second day I met several women who indignantly challenged me: "What right did I, *a man*, have to be involved with the Goddess?" These women seemed to regard Her as their exclusive property, and me as an interloper. I patiently explained that men can love women, and that sons as well as daughters can love their Mother. I diplomatically refrained from calling to their attention the fact that women make up the vast majority of worshippers in the Christian church, with its all-male pantheon.

NARRATOR: With the help of some friends, the Zells were able to make some molds and start producing and selling copies of their statues. They would eventually name their business Mythic Images, after a quote from Joseph Campbell. In the beginning, for a trial period, they did this in connection with the CAW. Then MG decided she wanted to control the rights to the business.

MG: I filed the necessary legal paperwork to get a business license and tax ID, and Mythic Images was born. Of course I had a huge argument with Otter about this because he was determined to keep the statuary business as part of CAW. He wanted to set up another income stream for the Church and avoid paying taxes for what was essentially religious work. But I was adamant that I was not going to have another "Little Red Hen" scenario like the house in St. Louis play out with me as the loser. I would rather build a profit-making venture and pay my taxes than to see my business be crippled by people with lots of differing opinions, no experience, and no interest in seeing the thing succeed. I'd had my fill of people with their own agenda who didn't want to support me or my work when push came to shove. So I finally told him, "If you don't like it, you can't have any" and set up MI as a sole proprietorship with me in charge. I figured OZ could run *Green Egg* any way he wanted and I would run Mythic Images the way I saw fit; then we would see which one survived the longest and actually supported us. In hindsight, I can never think of a more important argument that I actually won with him.

OZ: Once we were able to do it ourselves, we could do most of the work in our kitchen. So gradually our laundry room became a factory for hand-making statues. Soon we developed a product line, and advertised on the back cover of *Green Egg*. Our first ad (in the Samhain 1990 issue) included T-shirts with my artwork and the first nine of our statues. We were mostly doing everything ourselves. We weren't farming anything out, but Morning Glory, starting with Rainbow and her friends, would occasionally hire the local teenagers as production workers. Many of them saved up the money for their first car by doing piecework for Mythic Images. We kept expanding and growing.

When we started *Green Egg* up again, we picked up the numbering where we had left off. So the Phoenix issue was number 81. When we got to issue #100 (Spring 1993), we were totally jazzed. We made it a double-length issue and had a full-color center spread. We did a retrospective on the history and an envisioning of the future of the Pagan community. It was an amazing issue. And the back cover was a full-page ad for our family business of Goddess figurines.

With every new issue, when it came back from the printer, we would look at it and go, "Wow, this is the best one ever!" There was such a sense of excitement, pride, and joy that we all had about it. The forum became great—every time we had an article, people would comment on it and go back and forth on it. It was everything I dreamed it would be. All the best artists were sending us their stuff—as an artist myself, I made sure that the reproduction of the art was top of the line. Eventually we got other people to come in and do other things around the office. But I had, for many issues, done all of it myself—from typesetting to art to photography to putting mailing labels on the magazines and hauling them off to the post office. Eventually that became all completely automated. But in those days it was all done by hand.

NARRATOR: Otter, Morning Glory, and Diane decided to get married as a triad in 1989. I asked OZ why they did this, because it seemed to me that by this point in their group relationship, they were having a lot of problems. And this is what he told me:

OZ: We had developed a deep triadic relationship with Diane for six years before we decided to have a triadic handfasting. We had been together all through the Great Unicorn Adventure, living on Greenfield Ranch, the Mermaid Expedition, Between the Worlds, the resurrection of CAW and *Green Egg*, college ceramics, and the beginning of what became Mythic Images, the Home Town Harvest Festivals, amazing rituals, several moves, and raising three kids together. We were a set—and a powerful team. Sure, Diane always had a streak of sanctimonious Puritanism in her personality—just as I have a strong tendency to OCD perfectionism and MG has severe ADD and is chronically late for everything.

But MG and I regard people as unique individuals, perfect with all their idiosyncrasies. We pretty much live unconditional love and acceptance, and we have a strong tendency for inclusive rather than exclusive relationships. So we indulge others the way we would like to be indulged, and put up with their difficult aspects as we hope they will put up with ours. Only when someone actively turns against us do we finally come to the realization that we can no longer include them in our lives.

So despite those difficulties with Diane that were appearing around that time (1989), we felt that we already had been with her six years (since the fall of 1983), and shared so much of our lives, Vision, and Mission that we wanted to make it a real commitment through handfasting. Mostly our ten years with Diane were really wonderful. Do I regret our time together? Certainly not! It was one of the best periods of our lives!

We created a beautiful ceremony and had a triad wedding on March 19, 1989. It was probably the first triad wedding that anybody had ever done or created, as far as I am aware. We came up with a symbol to represent our relationship: a *triskelion*, which is basically a yin-yang symbol with three parts instead of two. We decided that we were going to formally declare ourselves to be a family, and we took the name "Triskelion" for ourselves.

DIANE DARLING: We decided to get handfasted at Ostara (Spring Equinox). It was really juicy. We had a miniature Unicorn who was a baby then (born March 9), and he was just so cute. His name was Oberon. We had matching triskelions made by a friend of ours. We had a beautiful handfasting, a life-braiding of the three of us. It was really quite wonderful. There was a moment just before the wedding when we were standing with baby Oberon, kind of getting ready, and put the triskelions on a pillow like you would do with wedding rings. We took our eyes off of the Unicorn for like one minute, and turned around and he had pulled one of the triskelions off and was chewing on it. We pulled it out of his mouth, but one of the pins was missing. So we had to wrestle with the baby Unicorn and put our hands in his mouth to get the pin out. That got our adrenaline up for the ceremony. I was a physician's assistant, so I drew blood from each of us and mixed our blood together in a chalice and put drops of it on each other's foreheads.

NARRATOR: Whatever family unit Morning Glory and Otter were in was always open to change and experimentation. That was just a part of how they lived their lives, and always had been. So they decided to try and bring MG's first husband, Gary, back into the family.

OZ: Gary lived in Eugene and rarely went anywhere else. Morning Glory visited him and Rainbow off and on, and sometimes we would both go up there and see him for the Oregon Country Fair. For many years that was an annual pilgrimage. Somewhere along in there it occurred to us that Gary and Diane might have a lot of potential together, and that we should introduce them to each other. And, if we could do it and make it work, it might bring the families together permanently, so it seemed like a good arrangement.

So in 1988 Diane and Morning Glory both drove up to Oregon for the Country Fair. They made a girls' road trip out of it. And so Diane and Gary finally got to meet, and they fell in love. Before long he decided to move away from Eugene and in with Diane. Morning Glory and I did a spectacular handfasting ceremony for them on June 25, 1989. But Gary never really quite assimilated into the Triskelion family thing. When you add a fourth person, it's no longer a triad! Four people have

a tendency to break into two couples. Diane, Morning Glory, and I continued to have our relationship, and Diane and Gary developed their
own relationship that was separate from that. It was complicated to try
to describe it or make sense of it, but it all seemed to work. Gary and
Morning Glory continued to be good friends and co-parents.

MG: Gary and I took a stab at trying to renew our old flame, but too much
time and too much pain had passed between us, and so we decided that
the deep and caring love we had managed to hang on to was enough as it
was, so there was no need to try and turn back the clock.

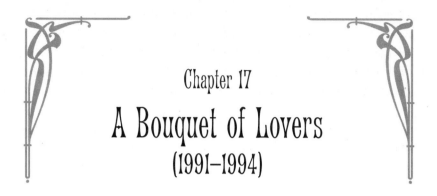

Chapter 17
A Bouquet of Lovers
(1991–1994)

Of all my Lovers that I love;
Of all my Friends I've ever known,
We go together hand in glove;
We fit together flesh and bone.

For twenty years of joy and tears;
For best and worst, through thick and thin.
I'd love you better now and then;
But I'd choose you all the same again!

—FROM "LOVE OF MY LIFE" BY MORNING GLORY ZELL, 1993

NARRATOR: Another sea change that the Zells had missed while they were living in "Faerie" was the beginning of the Pagan festival movement across the nation. These festivals were, and still are, rural gatherings where Pagans of diverse traditions manage to find common ground together for several days of celebration. Since festivals are held on private land, attendees can just be themselves and not have to worry about the outside world—there is usually even the option of not wearing clothing during the entire event. (This is called being "skyclad," a practice that seems to have been picked up from Gerald Gardner's lifestyle, though OZ had already been doing ritual, and living, without clothes on whenever possible since college.) There are a variety of daily activities to choose from, including rituals, classes, music, and shopping. (No Pagan festival would be complete without a big selection of dealers selling jewelry, art, and even clothing—which can presumably then be worn somewhere else.)

As soon as OZ and MG had a home phone again, they started getting invitations to attend various festivals around the country. They were both well known on the Pagan scene, though not as well known as some—they had, after all, disappeared for almost ten years, and they weren't allowed to talk about the Unicorns. The stars at Pagan festivals, at least in the beginning, were generally those who represented a specific system of Magick, often some kind of Witchcraft, and were there to teach something about it. And that wasn't what the Zells were doing.

Morning Glory would go to festivals as a Goddess historian, and Otter would go as a living piece of Neo-Pagan history, in the flesh. He was nearing fifty, and though for some fifty is the new forty, OZ was ready to be the wise, mature sage with gray starting to appear in his beard. And while some of the other featured festival guests would do their thing and then go spend the rest of their time away from the crowd hanging out with just the other presenters and VIPs, OZ would spend the whole weekend mingling with the multitudes. After his moment in the spotlight, which would usually be Gaea-oriented, he'd spend the rest of the festival making himself available to anyone who cared to talk. In the daytime he'd set up a table in the dealers' area where he'd have his statues and copies of *Green Egg*. At night he'd roam from campfire to campfire, joining the random festivities till it was time to go back to his tent—or maybe someone else's.

The Zells weren't, at first, getting paid to make these appearances, but they'd get their transportation and other expenses covered, and it was a chance to promote the magazine and statue business. It was also a chance to meet new lovers. In the Beltane 1990 issue of *Green Egg* (#89), Morning Glory's epochal article "A Bouquet of Lovers" was published. In seeking for a good term to describe people who were into having multiple simultaneous lovers, MG combined Greek and Latin roots to coin the terms *polyamorous* and *polyamory*, meaning "having many lovers" (in contrast to the term *polygamy*, which means "marrying many"). With this terminology to describe it, another entire movement was catalyzed, and doors were opened to even more interesting adventures.

OZ: Over Labor Day weekend of 1991, Deborah Anapol and Ryam Nearing of PEP (Polyfidelitous Educational Productions) and IntiNet co-sponsored a PEP-Con in Berkeley. The Church of All Worlds was invited to be a major participant—not only presenting workshops but also conducting the opening and closing rituals. This was the historic first contact between the poly-sexual community and Pagans. Many of us in CAW—inspired by *Stranger in a Strange Land*—had been polyamorous all along, but we'd never made an especially big deal about it. But when Morning Glory coined the terms, we suddenly found ourselves the center of considerable attention!

We set up a table directly across the hall from the oldest and most famous poly organization around—Kerista, a utopian visionary cult that had been started in New York City back in 1956 by John Peltz "Bro Jud" Presmont. Kerista was premised on the ideals of sexual *polyfidelity* ("faithful to many") and creation of intentional communities centered around a very rigid concept of group marriages of twelve partners. Never more than a couple dozen people, they had moved to San Francisco in 1971, forming the Kerista Commune, in which the terms *polyfidelity* and *compersion* (i.e., "taking pleasure that your partner is experiencing pleasure, even if the source of their pleasure is other than yourself") were coined.

Throughout the conference (which Jud did not attend), people kept coming over to the CAW table after gathering literature from Kerista. They'd ask, "What are *your* rules?"

Somewhat nonplussed, we'd reply, "Rules? Um, 'Be excellent to each other'?"

And they'd say, "Well, the Keristans have eighty-seven rules, and 111 standards."

And all we could say to that was, "Wow. That's a lotta rules! How do they keep track of 'em all?"

NARRATOR: Kerista had an active public profile in the late eighties when they, like OZ, got involved early on with Mac computers, which they also sold and repaired. They published a free newspaper that helped spread the word about open relationships to the general public. It was distributed in San Francisco in sidewalk newspaper boxes throughout the city, where anyone who was curious could pick up a copy.

The Kerista commune broke up in 1991 as the discussion of poly-amory was beginning, and MG and OZ took the ball and ran with it. Their Pagan spirituality and their poly lifestyles were a good match, and here's why: in theory, at least, a person of any faith could fall in love with more than one person at once. It's happened a lot in the past and there have been difficulties—in a monotheistic religion you only get to have one God, and you only get to have one partner. But if you have a polytheistic religion, then you can have as many Gods and Goddesses, and as many partners, as your heart desires. (The same monotheistic argument is currently being used in the battle for the legalization of same-sex marriage—fundamental Christians argue that not only can you have just one God and one partner, but also you can only choose your partner from one sex.)

OZ: As Morning Glory and I started getting out into the world more, we found our "Bouquet of Lovers" rapidly expanding. We saw it as a kind of invisible network permeating the growing Pagan community, and connecting all these divergent groups through bonds and relationships among their members with those in other groups. Much like "The Force" in *Star Wars,* which ". . . surrounds us, penetrates us, and binds the galaxy together." MG and I in particular made it a joyous practice to cast our nets as widely as possible—and we were able to do so more than perhaps anyone because we were getting all these invitations to travel all over the country (and even to Australia) to give workshops and presentations.

In June of 1991, I went to the Midsummer Gathering of Tribes, which was held at a Renaissance Faire site in Georgia. I presented a plan for a new ecumenical alliance to be called the Universal Federation of Pagans—my model for this was the United Federation of Planets on *Star Trek.* And I did a knock-out presentation of my slide show of the whole history of Gaea. It required a musical soundtrack and two slide projectors that alternate back and forth.

One of the people who was there was a sweet and precocious little girl who was about three years old. She kind of danced around and then we talked. Her name was Tam Songdog. Her dad, Talyn Songdog, was also there.

For the closing ritual of that festival, everybody formed a big circle and the guests were asked to call the Quarters and invoke the Gods and

Goddesses. I did an invocation to Fire. There was a woman standing right next to me—a little tiny woman—and there was some kind of connection between us. It gathered during the ritual. We didn't talk much or anything, but there was electricity. When we hugged at the end, there were sparks jumping between us! It felt totally cosmic.

It would have been nice if the Circle had opened and then we could have had some time to talk and find out about each other and exchange addresses. But the car to take me to the airport showed up just as the Circle was ending, and the driver said, "We gotta go right now or you're gonna miss your flight!"

As we were driving away, all I was able to call out was, "What's your name?"

And she hollered back, "Kadira!" That was it. There was something awesome there, but I had no way to pursue it. I didn't have any other information. I didn't know where she lived, whether that was a magickal or mundane name, or anything!

Some of the most significant and life-changing relationships we developed during that period began the next year, at the 1992 Gathering of the Tribes, where Morning Glory and I were both brought in as guests. It was held at Lady Hecate's wolf farm in Georgia over the Autumn Equinox.

MG: It was the year I turned forty-four. I was still recovering from that major injury four years previously where I'd ruptured a disc in my neck, and I was still in a lot of pain much of the time. I was trying to get myself back together but I still wasn't very happy with where my life was going.

Oberon had been working with various people from around that area; he had gone there the year before. They wanted both of us to come this time, and for me to do a Goddess presentation. So I agreed to do it. The deal that Oberon had cut was that we didn't get paid, but we got free booth space and at least they were going to put us up in a motel. Because I said, "Look, I have this neck injury and I really can't sleep on the ground on an inflatable mattress that always goes flat in the middle of the night."

The night before we left, OZ had a conversation with the guy putting on the event and he reported that they were not putting us up in a motel room after all, but that they were going to get us a really good tent! At that point I just lost my basket. All I could see was hours and days of misery lying ahead of me. Out of my state of pain and fear I was also being an insufferable jackass about it. At one point Oberon said, "Don't forget to pack plenty of condoms."

And I said, "Go ahead and pack them in *your* suitcase, because I am never going to meet anybody in the Deep South that I would ever have sex with in a million years!" (Remember I grew up there . . .)

Never name the well you will not drink from, because at that point Aphrodite went, "Oh yeah? Let's just see about that!"

OZ: The Gathering was focused around the Universal Federation of Pagans, which had grown from the seed that I had planted the previous year. We had created a structure, incorporated it, and gotten a 501(c)(3) nonprofit status. Part of my longtime dream has been to have some kind of a Pagan interfaith alliance, like the World Council of Churches, that all Pagan groups could be a part of. And something like a hundred groups were already interested in signing up for the UFP. I worked hard that weekend helping to hammer out articles and bylaws and map out the concept.

MG: Oberon had said, "Watch out in your workshops because you may see a special little girl here, and she is really quite extraordinary."

So I show up for my workshop and start my discussion, whereupon this little girl around four years old comes in and plops herself in the center of the Circle. I said to her, "Honey, would you like to come and sit with the rest of us around the circle instead of right in the center?"

And she said, "I'm not Honey. I'm Tam. And I'm happy where I am."

And I said, "Oh, okay!" So she continued to sit there; she kept pretty quiet except when she asked very cogent questions.

OZ: After a day of UFP meetings I came back into the festival campground and saw Kadira. I hugged her, and she said, "I'll set up my tent and see you later." Well, later never happened because it started to rain. By the evening it was a downpour and everybody was huddled under their tents, which were all set up along the creek bank.

MG: Oberon and I were supposed to perform a handfasting. Right about the time when it was due to start, all of a sudden the sky opened up and started coming down like it can only come down in the South, or maybe someplace like New Guinea. You practically had to have gills. We were hiding underneath the marquee where all the booths were. And the young couple that we were supposed to do the handfasting for said, "We put a lot into getting this together. Even our parents are here." And there was no tent big enough for them to hold the handfasting in. Everything was out-of-doors.

It kept getting more and more tense. The little girl was there riding on a man's shoulders and steering him by the ears. And the man came up to me and said, "I hate to bust your bubble, but this rain isn't going to stop. This doesn't look good to me. There is a creek right down here. We are in a valley. If this floods, it could be really bad. And I don't want my family here." There were a couple of women with them, and one of them was holding a young baby around four months old.

TALYN: I offered Oberon and Morning Glory a dry place to sleep. My oldest daughter really liked Oberon, and we go by our intuition in these things.

MG: We all loaded up into assorted cars, because these people—the man with the little girl and the two women with the baby—were the best friends of the couple that we were going to do the handfasting for. So Oberon went with the handfasting couple, and I went with the other people.

OZ: Well, down in that area the ground is red clay. And driveways that go downhill tend to have gullies and ruts and erosion like miniatures of the Grand Canyon. So we're driving out of there and the car was slipping and sliding and getting stuck in these ruts, and we kept having to get out of the car and push to keep it going.

MG: We forded a stream that was rapidly rising. We tried to drive up a hill, and the rain was coming down in sheets and the mud was just like liquid peanut butter. We were in a big, old American eight-cylinder car, and the guy who was driving was flooring the gas pedal and it was spinning its wheels and was not going up the hill. The car was skidding sideways and we were about to go over a cliff.

I was sitting there thinking, "Oh, shit, I don't believe this. Here I am in a car with people I don't even know. And Oberon is in another car and I don't even know where he is. And he and I had a squabble and now I'm gonna die! And I'm not even gonna be able to tell him how much I love him!" It was just one of those moments where you go, "Please, if I ever get out of this I'll do better, I promise!"

At that point the guy who was driving said, "Okay, women and children out of the car!" So we get out and he guns the engine and starts fish-tailing the car up the hill in the sheeting mud.

I was standing there in the driving rain and watching this big old car going up the hill, sometimes sideways, but still going up, and thinking, "Who is this guy?" Because I'm a pretty good driver; my dad who was a mechanic taught me, and hell, I lived on Greenfield Ranch! I have driven on some incredible roads in incredible conditions, and the idea of trying to drive up that slope through those sheets of liquid mud was just astounding to me. But he did it!

So I and the other two women carried our stuff and the kids, trudging up the hill like refugee Russian peasants, slipping around and wading in the Georgia red clay mud, but we made it to the top of the hill and got back in the car. We were soaking wet all the way through to the skin. We drove along for quite a ways over a lot of back roads and then we stopped off at a little convenience store, and they told me, "Be cool and don't say anything, because this is major Ku Klux Klan territory."

And I'm like, "Okay, great! Welcome back to the South."

TALYN: We brought them to our home and gave them food and a place to stay. That's part of who my lady, Maggie, and I are. We create a haven for people to come and be safe. It's part of our personal juju to try to always have a place to share.

MG: We got showered and cleaned up, and they loaned us spare clothes 'cause ours were covered in mud, so we went on ahead and did the hand-fasting inside the house. After that we were all sitting on couches, and I was next to the man who was the driver, and he put his arm around me. I was thinking, "Okay . . . so far."

We talked some more and he was playing with me a little bit, kind of petting me. I was looking towards the two other women and wondering which one of them was his wife. I didn't want to get in trouble because it definitely seemed like the guy was coming on to me and the women were just talking. I was trying to catch one of their eyes to find out, "Is this okay?" And they were just totally acting oblivious.

Finally they took pity on me, and the guy said, "Well, I'm really glad to be able to get you guys here so that we can have a private talk because your life has been very inspiring to us. We have a polyamorous relationship."

And then it all went *click*, and I thought, "Oh, got it! A man, two women, a baby, and a little girl—it's a poly family!" So I relaxed. We went out and rounded up what luggage we had with us—there wasn't a whole lot—and we were taking it up to where we were put for the night. And the man in question was helping me carry stuff upstairs. Just as we got the stuff up and put it into the bedroom, he turned around and I turned around and we looked at each other and he stepped up and gave me this little friendly kiss, like "I'm glad you're here and I'm glad everything is okay—here's a hug and here's a little kiss."

And at that moment it was like both of us stuck our fingers in a light socket. We looked back at each other in surprise because neither of us expected anything like that at all. I was literally shocked: "Ohmigod!" We had both got bitten badly from that very moment; it was two irresistible forces on a cosmic collision course.

OZ: The next morning we returned to the festival, and the place was total devastation. All the tents, all the booths, all the merchandise, even the wolf pens—everything that had been below the level of four feet was washed away. We came back to a sea of mud. The wolves were wandering around and putting their noses into people's stuff. Things were totally lost forever. People's cars that had been parked down at the bottom were simply gone. But nobody was injured or killed, and that was a miracle.

KADIRA: Most of us, including me, were naked when it hit because we were in the skyclad area. We were only allowed to be skyclad down by the creek. We were sitting in this tent when we noticed that it started raining. The next thing we knew, the water was around our ankles. A young man who was one of the security people carried me, naked, on his shoulders across this raging flood to get my purse and car keys out of my tent. Some woman who had managed to be camped up on higher ground had some dry clothes that she passed around to people. I spent the night holding these older men who were freezing.

MG: The tents were all swept away. All the booths were completely strewn around. There were condoms and paper money and Pagan literature plastered all over the trees for miles downstream. Meanwhile, the guy who had booked us into this festival, and then changed his mind about letting us stay in a motel, was still up in his motel and didn't even know what was going on.

It was a disaster, but at the same time what did happen is that people really came together for each other. But I'm glad I did not have to go through that because I might have been seriously injured or caused someone else to be injured trying to help me—I was still in a physically vulnerable place at that point in my recovery. Oberon had a certain amount of guilt for not staying there and helping with the rescue, but it was what it was.

NARRATOR: Unlike the Federation Starfleet in *Star Trek*, the Universal Federation of Pagans never got off the ground. Due to some unfortunate problems in the Pagan community, the project was abandoned soon after the Gathering of the Tribes.

MG: For me the whole experience had imprinted itself indelibly on my soul. I could barely contain myself after I got back to California. I wrote reams of poetry, I wrote songs; I drove all my friends nuts talking about it. Talyn and I wrote to each other and had long, soulful phone conversations. I returned in January and that really cemented it. Talyn and I had this powerful chemistry. The magick between us, the current, was so strong, there was almost nothing that we couldn't do. You could see sparks flying off of us. And we would have all kinds of incredible visionary experiences when we were doing magick together. It was like every touch was a miracle.

I kept thinking how lucky I was: "This has happened to me twice in my life, first with Oberon, and now here comes yet another intense and completely overpowering love affair!" I felt so blessed by the Goddess— Aphrodite had rocked me in her arms and given me gifts the likes of which I should be grateful for the next ten lifetimes, even while she made a fool of me over my rash proclamation about Southern boys.

TALYN: Physically, if you saw pictures of her when we first were together, and then a few years later, she actually looked about ten years younger. She regained a whole burst of youthfulness. She lost weight. Her skin started glowing. Her hair even stopped graying. She became more beautiful physically. And it was an amazing aspect of the relationship.

Oberon was really happy with it, too. Because I think some of the stuff that had been kind of fallow in their relationship blossomed again. They love each other hugely, and they always have. But I think their relationship had quieted down a bit, and this rekindled some of what they had going.

MG: And I pursued this, and Talyn pursued it. He introduced me into some juicy, kinky stuff that I had never gotten into before. He very lightly introduced this as part of the romantic connection, and I jumped in. I'm never one of these people who just sticks her toe in the water. I plunge right in.

TALYN: I expected it to be playful. I did not expect it to go to the dark, intense, magickal levels that it went to. There is sex, there is sex-play, and then there is sacred sexuality that can be expressed that way too.

MG: And that was a gift to me, to introduce me to a whole side of my personality that I had not been in touch with. I learned that the warrior woman had a vulnerable, submissive side. And I was able to teach him to release and channel the Magick that was bubbling so close to the surface in him. Maggie, who is his wife and primary partner, was always a terrific magickal woman. But she never could manage to break through his stubbornness and share this with him. With all that they shared, they just weren't on the same wavelength to make that breakthrough together. Sometimes it just happens like that; there were things that OZ and I couldn't teach each other also.

TALYN: When I met my wife I was pretty much an atheist. She started studying Wicca. Her group had no male energy, so occasionally they would drag me into the Circles to play the God part. So I looked at the basic rules of the setup. One of them was recognizing that you are part of an ecosystem. And I consider that to be very important. I liked the ethics of personal responsibility. And I liked the fact that they were divorced from a lot of sexual hangups. So, frankly, I was able to get sex and not feel guilty about it.

At that point I did not believe in either Magick or God/Goddess energy. I rationalized most of those things as the placebo effect. But I got along with it, and I got along with the community. So I was able to play along quite comfortably. When I met Morning Glory, a number of things happened that my scientific mind had to look at and go, "Hmmm, that wasn't very likely." We did some rituals that were unbelievably powerful and not explainable through normal, rational means. So I had to set aside some of my logical brain and accept that magick stuff was happening. I realized that she had some real stuff to teach me.

MG: I said, "Yes. It's going to be a daunting thing to give you magickal training when we're at opposite ends of the country, but we'll find a way." And as it turned out, that was really good. I had to create focused lessons and unique ways of communicating.

Eventually, after some long-distance lessons, Talyn came out here and I gave him a magickal initiation. He died symbolically and was reborn as a different person. He was reborn as a Priest. And he is now one of the most powerful and wonderful Priests in the magickal community. So that relationship really flowered and was one of the major moving and shaking things in both of our lives for many years.

All of the erotic loveplay aside, the other important parts of this whole thing are my relationships with Talyn's daughter, Tam, and his wife, Maggie; and as time went on, the baby grew up into another magickal child. I connected to Tam's sister Tir as well. I wrote Maggie a poly love song—a song from one woman to the other woman in the relationship, honoring her and praising her relationship with the man.

And Tam—I made so many mistakes with my daughter, Gail. I never got to really be there for her as much as I wanted to when she was little. There are lots of happy memories that I have of when she was growing up. But there were big pieces of her childhood that I missed. You can't ever go back again, but with Tam I tried to do some of the things that I never really got to with my daughter.

TALYN: After Morning Glory left, we had to debrief the kids a little bit. We taught our kids fairly early what things they could share with the kids in school and what to hold back. We had to teach them both how to hide being Pagan, and how not to talk about our sexuality. The sexuality is actually the bigger issue. Our religion is quite legal. But polyamory, in a lot of areas, would be cause for taking your children away.

We're very open with our kids about our sexuality. But at the same time, everything that we do that is sexual is always behind closed doors. Still it's sort of obvious when two people go behind closed doors—kids are smart, they figure things out. They know when either I or my wife take a lover. So we had to explain that that is not normal, in terms of regular society, and that it is very private. Then we had to explain why—that some people don't like it when you don't play the game the same way they do, and they can be pretty mean.

Both Morning Glory and Oberon didn't understand about being in the closet. They're in a pretty nice place in California. How nice is it to be able to create a whole chunk of world and community where you can live exactly the way that you want to? Where you can have sex with multiple partners and not even think about it as unusual, and you can do ritual right in public and no one bats an eye. If we did ritual in public parks here, it could be trouble. You could end up with a cross burning on your lawn. So we had to coach the kids on how not to spill the beans.

MG: I would try three or four times a year to go and spend two to three weeks with them. I could always manage to get a gig out there doing a presentation or a Goddess talk. Their whole family came out here to visit us in California.

OZ: Our families became very close. Tam became Morning Glory's and my Goddess-daughter—it was agreed that should anything ever happen to her parents, we would be the next in line to raise her and her sister. Every time when we would be back East for festivals, we would stay with them and renew our connections. So that relationship has continued over all these years. We've had the privilege of watching both the girls grow up into beautiful and brilliant young women.

NARRATOR: While at a Samhain festival in Tennessee in 1992, OZ was taken on a side trip to see the full-size replica of the Parthenon in Nashville, which includes a forty-two-foot-tall statue of Athena. He got the idea to hold a pageant and ritual and a Panathenaic games there, just like they had been held in ancient Greece. At the first Panathenaea, held in 1993, OZ and Kadira finally hooked up. MG continued her long-distance relationship with Talyn, and in October 1993, at the Highlands of Tennessee Samhain Gathering, he was there with a man named Wolf.

Talyn and Wolf were old friends from Texas. At one point they had been in a triad relationship with Maggie, the woman who eventually married Talyn. After Talyn went to Germany for grad school, Wolf got involved with another woman who wanted a monogamous relationship. When she got pregnant, they got married. They had a daughter together, but their marriage did not last very long. When Talyn and Maggie returned to the United States and settled in Georgia, they eventually reconnected with Wolf.

MG: I'd been hearing nothing but all these stories about this legendary Wolf person from both Talyn and Maggie, and he had been hearing stories about me and seeing the pictures I had sent plastered all over the house. So sure enough, he shows up at our booth. I swear I could practically hear a drumroll as I watched Wolf and Talyn walk across the field towards me and I thought to myself, "Uh-oh, I am in trouble now!" They were both wearing their black leather jackets and had black hair and beards. Wolf has green eyes and Talyn has brown eyes. Neither of them smiled 'cause they were looking *bad*; as they got closer and closer, I was just standing there and shivering.

When they got to the table, Talyn finally grinned. He didn't say a word. And Wolf looked at me and said, "Hi. I'm Wolf. And we're going to be lovers."

And yes, I was easy; some of my lovers have told me it's one of my sterling qualities. "Okay!" was all I managed to get out. It isn't often that I get tongue-tied, but there are occasions, and this was certainly one of them.

NARRATOR: Later that evening they ended up in a borrowed tent together.

MG: We went into the tent. Wolf pulled out these silk cords and he bound my hands and we had this delicious, rapturous connection. There's nothing like the first time! Our union became even more special when he took a gorgeous cherry opal earring out of his ear, put it in my ear, and said, "Now you're mine. I claim you."

That little claiming was a lot more powerful than he knew. It was one of those things that you do on impulse, that you think is very sweet love-play—he meant it from the heart, don't get me wrong—but sometimes you do things and you have no idea what the consequences of that action are gonna be down the line.

NARRATOR: After that, MG and Wolf went to the cabin where OZ and Kadira were.

MG: Wolf and I got all snuggled up cozy together and tried to sleep. But it didn't last very long—suddenly, sleeping was the last thing on our minds. So we were playing around, and then Oberon joined in, so we had a three-way thing going. And then Oberon and Kadira got back involved with each other again. Finally we all collapsed. And at that point Oberon and I looked at each other and went, "Ohmigod—we forget to even introduce these two guys!"

And so Oberon took Kadira's hand from her side of the bed, and I took Wolf's hand from his side of the bed, and stretched them both all the way across to the middle and shook them together and we said "Wolf, meet Kadira. Kadira, meet Wolf!"

KADIRA: Oberon and I were lying there cuddling, and Morning Glory came in with Wolf. I wasn't too freaked out about it because I so trusted Morning Glory. I knew she wasn't going to bring anybody into the bed who would do anything inappropriate with me. And I could tell that she and he were really focused on each other. I'm really shy at first, and I'm really respectful of other people's relationships and their space. But once somebody lets me know that something is okay with them, and I really sense that they're sincere about it, that their actions back up their words, I'm not an inhibited person at all.

OZ: We then proceeded to have a night of lots of sex and keeping everybody else in the cabin awake. We were trying to be quiet, but we were giggling and having a lot of fun. The other people who were in the cabin with us certainly weren't having nearly as much fun as we were. They stayed in their bunks and tossed and turned and muttered a bit. But they were mostly pretty indulgent about the whole thing. It wasn't a surprise to them—it must have been our reputation! We just take it for granted that this is how it is with us. But I understand that not everybody operates the way that we do . . . even in the Pagan community.

MG: We did the festival one weekend, then we all went back and spent the next week at Talyn's in Georgia; OZ had to go back to California, but I stayed on. And one of those nights, Wolf, Talyn, and I spent the night together. I used to have this fantasy of being able to be with two very special but different men, and I've been privileged to have that experience several times in my life—it's been very powerful, wonderful, and moving, but this left it all in the dust. Talyn has a phrase he uses: "I'm over-meeting your needs." That's when your wildest fantasy is about a 5, and the actual experience is like about a 20.

Since Talyn had been an SCA, Society for Creative Anachronism, fighter, we also made swashbuckling-style fencing sessions part of our regular foreplay whenever we would visit each other. Wolf and I tried out a couple of bouts, but he staunchly remained more of a lover than a fighter. A number of folks from our fencing clan also had connections to the BD/SM communities, and sometimes it was hard to tell just where you managed to get that particular bruise. Still, it was all in good fun, and we were working hard on learning ways to explore the experiences of conflict, passion, power, and partnership along with the dynamics of dominance and submission that are hardwired into all animal species. Taking turns winning or losing, being on top or on the bottom, practicing good sportsmanship, and practicing safe and consensual sexuality were all part of our lives at that time.

The experience that Wolf, Talyn, and I shared together is an example of how people can use sexuality—especially when there is a magickal component and the people are magickal people—in a way that isn't just about sex, it's about initiation. You can push past the boundaries of erotic fantasy and into the realm of sacred sexuality. I'm always such an active and outgoing, take-charge type of dominant woman, and so it has been a revelation and a wonder to me to experience the power of surrendering that dominance, of letting go and just being able to receive pleasure until you can no longer hold on to consciousness. I think I fainted three times that night, the pleasure was so exquisite!

When Oberon went to Italy in 1987 and he was touring Tuscany, where they have the tombs of the Etruscan kings in Tarquinia, he took pictures of paintings that were on the tomb walls. One of the tomb paintings depicted a woman having sex with two men. The men were wearing ritual masks, and it was clearly an amazing initiatory experience. I've often wondered: was that the tomb of the woman, or one of the men? I'll bet it was her tomb, and she was an initiate of that Mystery. It had to have been one of the high points in her life as it was in mine, and if I ever have anything painted on my tomb, it will be that—like the Tarquinian priestess.

Chapter 18
The Ravenhearts
(the 1990s)

We are more than one, we are more than two,
We are more than the sum of our parts.
So we cherish the old and rejoice in the new;
And we meet in the haven of our hearts!
—FROM "THE HAVEN OF OUR HEARTS" [RAVENHEART FAMILY THEME SONG]
BY LIZA GABRIEL, WYNTER, AND MORNING GLORY, 1996

NARRATOR: This events that are in this book aren't all in chronological order—what happens in one chapter may be taking place at the same time as something that is happening in a previous or following chapter. I have tried to group together related events rather than sticking to a timeline (but if you ever get lost, you can refer to a very abbreviated timeline at the end of this book). The Zells always have a number of balls up in the air at once, and though, of course, everything is connected, some things are also easier to explain when looked at on their own.

This chapter, and the next few that follow, all mostly take place in the 1990s, and those were exciting times for Pagans. 1992 was the year the Church of All Worlds became the first non-Christian church to be legally recognized in Australia. William Jefferson Clinton, a Democrat, was elected the forty-second president of the United States in 1992. He seemed like a politician who could do a good job, and there were a lot of things about him that were likeable: he played saxophone; he named his only daughter after a Judy Collins song ("Chelsea Morning"); and he was the first Baby-Boomer president (four years younger, in fact, than OZ). His vice president, Al Gore, had written a bestselling book (*Earth in the Balance: Ecology and the Human Spirit*) that any Pagan reader could find things in to agree with.

It was the decade that PBS brought Canadian director Donna Read's trilogy of Goddess documentaries to American viewers (a lot!). The first, *Goddess Remembered*, prominently featured the Goddess history theories of Marija Gimbutas and interviews with Merlin Stone, Luisah Teish, Starhawk, and other prominent Pagans. This was followed up with *The Burning Times* and *Full Circle*. So, with the help of the Public Broadcasting System, more information about Earth-based spirituality reached the masses.

The decade was a momentous one for Oberon and Morning Glory as well. Two major developments played out in their lives simultaneously: the vicissitudes of *Green Egg* magazine and the building of a loving, polyamorous family.

DIANE DARLING: As *Green Egg* got bigger and bigger, there was more and more nuts-and-bolts stuff that had to be kept together. And Otter is like totally not a nuts-and-bolts guy. He is all right-brain. I felt like I was doing a huge amount of work on it: keeping all the books, editing all the articles, soliciting new articles, and dealing with bookstores and distributors. Otter managed the art, layout, and subscription lists. It got to be harder and harder. When you're just fooling around with a couple of Macs, that's one thing, but when you're running $150,000 to $200,000 a year through an account, you have to keep some records, and that was me. I didn't like doing it but I am capable of doing it, so I did, and maybe I did too much of it.

NARRATOR: OZ and Diane Darling had a major disagreement about whether or not to publish the work of a particular artist. OZ and Diane both agreed, and they told me so in separate interviews years after this happened, that the artist was talented but that he was not a very likable human being. For Diane this was reason enough to not put his art into *Green Egg*, but OZ felt differently.

DIANE DARLING: He was a very good artist, and a real shithead in person. Otter is not really a good judge of character. I had the distinct feeling that he was trying to insinuate himself between me and Otter with a mind to getting some control over the magazine as a vehicle to promote his art. He was presenting himself as being part of a team of a man and a woman, but actually it was just him. So he was being disingenuous from the start, and as I got to know him better I decided that I didn't want him to be part of anything that I was part of, and I had good reasons at the time.

OZ: I felt that I was the one who determined that—after all, it was my magazine. I conceived it and designed it. So her attempts to censor out stuff that she disapproved of were ones that I just utterly resisted. I told her that she was the editor, and I was the publisher, and I was the one who ultimately made the final decisions about what went into the magazine. That's what a publisher does. I took her feelings and opinions into consideration, as I did with everybody, but I reserved to myself the right to make the final decisions.

DIANE DARLING: In retrospect I can see why he felt he was being excluded increasingly, and he was. He was calling himself the publisher, and he wasn't doing any of the publisher things. He wanted to do what he was not good at, instead of sticking to what he *was* good at. And I've seen so many people make that mistake over and over again.

In the spring of 1994, I decided I was going to turn the editing responsibilities over to our friend Maerian, a CAW Priestess and two-time Queen of the May, and then I was going to turn the bookkeeping and business end over to her partner, Orion.

The stress of trying to do *Green Egg* together broke us up. It got to be harder and harder. Morning Glory and I kind of drifted away from each other, and then Otter and I had this blowup at one point that put an end to it forever. But when it was good, it was very good.

NARRATOR: Morning Glory and Oberon ended their ten-year relationship with Diane in April of 1994. They had a formal handparting, cutting the cord of their handfasting and burying it on Annwfn on Beltane. But these kinds of losses often lead to new beginnings; and in OZ's case, he was about to get a new name, a new family, and then *another* new name.

OZ: In the fall of '94 we held the Eleusinian Mysteries again, and that year, for the first and only time, I was selected to take the role of Hades. That was a major change in my life, because, ever since the blowup I'd had back in '73 with Jodie, I had totally turned away from the dark, shadow side of my existence. Morning Glory and I created this whole series of mystery play–type rituals, and in the cast of characters we would often have something like the "Dark Lord," and I would always assign that role to someone else. And I would always take the role of the kindly, wise old Wizard, who advises the heroes on what they need to know to go off on the quest, and that kind of thing.

But the way we had it worked out in the Mysteries was that one of the pilgrims who made the journey, and received initiation, would come back from it with the sense that she had been tapped to take the role of Persephone in the following year. This always happened, year after year—we just accepted it as part of the Magick. So we would then build up the rest of the cast of characters around her. So the first thing we would ask when planning the next year's cycle would be, "So, if you are going to be playing Persephone, who would you chose to be Hades?" They had to in some way manifest being the King and Queen in the Underworld.

What happened in 1993 was a woman named Serendipity, who came back having been tapped to become next year's Kore, was asked who she would choose to be Hades. And she chose me; that was quite a shock. I couldn't refuse this, but it was definitely not something that I was comfortable with or ever would have sought. When I immersed myself in the ritual and the Magick, I had to deal with all these things inside of myself that I had suppressed—all these aspects of myself and my life that I had denied and buried and pushed away.

Morning Glory did not attend the 1994 Eleusinian Mysteries, as she wasn't taking any active role that year. Instead she went to a sex symposium in San Francisco that was on the same weekend. She met some folks there; they hit it off; and she invited them to come up to the Old Same Place. I came back from the Mysteries quite overwhelmed from the experience. Within days, for example, I had to deal with the death of a man in our community. Serendipity was living in an apartment above his house and helping with his care, and he died of AIDS. So she called me and I drove down there. It was the first time I had ever even seen a dead person, yet in a way it was all part of taking on this role as Lord of the Underworld.

The following weekend these folks that MG had met came up. Their names were Devaka and Kai—they were New Age Tantrikas, and these folks were really into the sexuality scene. So that's where they intersected with us. At that time we were very active in the polyamory community, from the CAW/Pagan perspective. We attended a lot of workshops and conferences around sacred sexuality, and there would be these other folks coming from the opposite side of the world from us, from this Hindu-based mythology.

So, they showed up and I met them. We went down to the river and were hanging out. Devaka is one of these people who names other people. It was a big thing in their own community to give new names to people. Nobody could keep the name they came in with. A new name would be given to them as a part of some kind of initiation ritual. So, when she was introduced to me, she said something remarkable: "Well, I don't really see you as an Otter. When I look at you, I see . . . *Oberon*." She laid it all out with a magickal intensity.

And I felt it. I felt this mantle of an identity settle over me like a cloak on my shoulders. In Shakespeare's *A Midsummer Night's Dream*, Oberon was the King of the Faeries, and the whole mystique of that fit in with the Hades aspect that I'd been given—and I had to hold that energy for the next year.

I'd given the name Oberon to a cat and a Unicorn, so I liked the name, though I'd never thought about claiming it for myself. But the way Devaka laid it on me was something that I found irresistible. So I asked Kai, who had experience with this sort of thing, to baptize me with the new name. And so there in the Rushing River, Morning Glory, Devaka, and Kai submerged me under the water, then raised me up and bequeathed on me the new name of Oberon.

MG: It was just the weirdest time for both of us. I was spending a lot of my time traveling around the country and promoting Mythic Images as well as being involved in my relationships with Talyn and Wolf. Our relationship with Diane had imploded, and it seemed like OZ and I hardly had any time together anymore. I had brought up a couple of interesting people to visit us from the International Sex Symposium where I had been on a panel about polyamory. Oberon and I still made the effort whenever possible to bring new people into each other's lives. But I must admit that I was somewhat taken aback when he just totally went along with the renaming thing that Devaka had put out to him. I was sort of hornswoggled into the role of helper in this baptism rite, but I just figured it would be sort of a special magickal name that he would use in special ceremonies or whatever. When he announced that he was permanently changing his name to Oberon, I was utterly flummoxed.

For one thing, he had no real background in Faerylore, and to take on a name of power like that without doing your homework seemed like rank folly to me. I had been doing quite a lot of research on the Fey since I had gotten into this Fairy partnership with Talyn and his family. One thing I learned right away is that the "Gentry" can really resent hubris, so someone with no previous experience in their universe turning up and taking the name of a famous King seemed the height of hubris. The last thing you want to do is to piss off the Faeries. I felt like there was so much chaos in our life at that point, it was like waving a red flag in front of a bull.

Then of course everyone seemed to expect me to change my name to Titania! That was ridiculous; no woman in her right mind with a forty-eight-inch bust names herself Titania unless she is a porn star or a stripper. Not that I have anything against either of those professions, mind you, but I had spent most of my life as Morning Glory; I had put a lot of energy into building my reputation as Morning Glory. Why in the world would I ever want to risk angering the Gentry by taking the name of a Queen?

I guess I was so amazed that OZ would just up and do something this important and irreversible without even talking it over with me. We always step aside and consult with each other before we make some life-changing decision. But he was completely adamant. I came to believe that he felt so beleaguered with Diane and the *Green Egg* and CAW problems that he had just decided he was not going to listen to any more criticism from anyone about anything, myself included. The way he went about taking this name for himself seemed like he was drawing his line in the sand; he came to equate it as "taking back his power." Now as a woman and a student of Goddess lore, I know how important that process can be, and so in the end I just shrugged my shoulders and said it was his life and his choice.

OZ: But the new name did affect my life in a very significant way, as things like that do. It set my feet on a different path. From that point things really changed in nearly every aspect of my life—both positive and negative. And where I am now is a place where Oberon is, but Otter could not have been.

NARRATOR: Morning Glory continued her cross-country relationship with Wolf, and began to look for ways to continue to see him without having to travel so much.

MG: My relationship with Wolf was absolutely wonderful. We had a ball together. He and Talyn just drove me nuts. Between the two of them I was living in a state of peak experiences all the time. I wrote more poetry and was more creative and really present and just happy and wildly productive during that period of my life than I have been probably at any other time period—except for the time when I first met Oberon and fell in love with him. New relationship energy is powerful stuff; the oxytocin pheromones are pretty psychedelic.

OZ: Morning Glory made several trips to Texas to be with Wolf. Up to that point I hadn't had a chance to get to know him. He had been hanging out with her entirely, and they had just been in their own little world. They were having this big, mad fling. I just stepped back and watched the fur fly. They were corresponding and calling each other all the time and having these long, passionate phone conversations. But I wasn't in on any of that, though quite often MG would drag me off to the bedroom for wild sex after one of these sessions. She was pretty hot most of the time, and I certainly enjoyed the benefits of that state of mind. Our erotic relationship went into some wild and wooly territory during that period.

MG: When I met Wolf, he was living in Houston. I started courting him, and he and I formed this powerful, passionate relationship. I said to Oberon, "Look, we've done it your way. We've had the two-women-and-one-man situation. Let's see if I can't find you a co-husband here. I want it to go my way for a while. Let's try two husbands."

And he went, "Well, I'm game. Good luck!" Because he's always been more of a woman's man. He's always gotten along better with women than with men. But Wolf and I had this powerful sex-magick thing going on—a dark, kinky energy, and a lot of juice.

OZ: The crucial thing is that all of us were open in not resisting in any way whatever connections might be made. And so we simply found them by allowing them to emerge. We don't have any kind of built-in limit on how far we're willing to go. We're willing to go however far somebody else is up for going. So if somebody is really ready to ride it all the way, well, we'll ride it all the way too.

NARRATOR: Wolf was able to get a transfer within the company that he was working for from Texas to San Francisco, and so he made the big move to the West Coast. When he first arrived, he lived in the city itself and, for a while, shared an apartment with Morning Glory's daughter, Gail. (Wolf's own daughter remained behind with his ex-wife. After that he continued to pay child support, but would only see her when she would come out from Texas in the summer to visit.) On his days off, he would ride his motorcycle up north to see MG.

OZ, now *Oberon Z*, was not left alone while his marriage to Diana was breaking up and MG was with Wolf—he always had someone else to be with. But then someone new entered his life that completely surprised him, and her name was Liza. She lived on the East Coast at the time.

LIZA GABRIEL: Oberon was in love with one of the other members of my community. And she set us up. The particular situation was they were supposed to do a presentation together at an East Coast Pagan festival. And my friend called up Oberon and said, "I can't make it to this thing. I'm really sorry. But I know someone who'll do a great job—you're gonna love her."

OZ: We started corresponding. In our correspondence we planned workshops we could do together so that we would have a presence at the con. It was like a blind date, but a little bit more involved.

LIZA: Before Oberon ever got there, we were already aligning magically, and our values were coming to the fore. We were planning to meet at Craftwise in Waterbury, Connecticut, and do some workshops together. So we concocted the Pool Water-Sharing Ritual by phone. And then we met at the house of the people who ran Craftwise, the night before the festival began. I was coming from Massachusetts, where I lived then.

OZ: I flew out to Hartford, and was picked up and taken to a farmhouse out in the country. It had a huge kitchen, but the rest of the rooms were small. There was already quite an interesting crowd of people there, including Janet and Stewart Farrar. They lived in Ireland, and it was their first visit to America. I sat on the living room floor—there were only so many sofas and chairs and there were a lot of people—and began telling stories with Stewart and having a fine old time. My back was to the front door. And the door behind me opened, and suddenly I just felt a presence. It was like a psychic thing. I rose up in a spiral from where I was sitting and turned around, and there was Liza right behind me. We locked eyes and embraced.

That night all the guests were stacked like cordwood around the farmhouse. Wall-to-wall bedrolls like sausages. Liza and I managed to squeeze in. We didn't have sex—it was just a nice cuddle-pile.

LIZA: The next night we stayed in a hotel; we consummated our relationship (we didn't even know we were going to be lovers), and then we did the ritual. It was a powerful magical working for us personally, because we really became a Priest and Priestess as we were becoming lovers.

OZ: Liza and I did other workshops—some together and some individually. But we put on a full slate of stuff. After the weekend was over, we went back to her place and we tripped on acid and got connected on deep levels.

LIZA: The center of my attraction to Oberon, and probably the center of his attraction to me, was that we were both intoxicated by serving community, and by being Visionaries. It wasn't simply personal, although there was definitely a lot of personal erotic passion there. It was fueled by this greater Vision. That was why I went to such extraordinary extremes to enhance and preserve our relationship. It wasn't just a relationship. It was a Vision and a Calling.

My roots were always in yoga, energy, Kundalini, and all of those kinds of things. Oberon and I were so intoxicated by the vision of planetary consciousness that we barely noticed that we had very little in common personally. These kinds of relationships are so unusual. They don't fit into a pattern that allows people to understand them easily. I was already deeply immersed in magical and sexual work, and I was already leading erotic ritual very successfully. It wasn't that I became that way when I met him. I saw him as a partner in that. I saw him as my Priest. When a true Priest shows up in her life, a Priestess doesn't squabble. She says "yes" in whatever way she can. During our first Ecstasy trip, at the most intimate, intense moment when the first rush of the drug was coming over us, he asked in a magical voice of command, "Are you ready for me in your life?" I said yes. And that was before I visited his home and met Morning Glory.

Entering the Zells' home for the first time, already madly in love with Oberon and knowing he returned that passion, I inwardly wept. Later when I helped Oberon and Morning Glory move out of the Old Same Place, I witnessed that the corner where their long-deceased great horned owl, Archimedes, had perched had never been cleaned and there were years of owl poop soaked into the bookcase and magazines beneath. Also their possum, who slept in the bottom of the linen closet, had never been entirely housebroken.

Presented with this scene and the chaos it implied, I did what any red-blooded American girl would do. I went on a ritualized LSD trip with the two of them, had sex with Morning Glory on short acquaintance, and acted as if all that was happening was normal. In short, I swept an enormous pile of excrement under the rug from the very start, just as my hosts were doing.

Morning Glory was warm, welcoming, and met me at the airport with roses, yet the atmosphere that unfolded was one of vivid magick, erotic play, intimate psychedelic ritual, and the beauty of the river and surrounding wooded hills, coupled with grinding poverty and entrenched conflict.

The morning after I arrived at the Old Same Place, the caretakers at Annwfn called. A bear and her cub had been breaking into people's homes. The caretaker had to shoot them both. Oberon and Morning Glory were the only ones in the tribe who knew how to skin and butcher a bear and harvest its magical parts. They never succeeded in passing this messy art down to any of the young people.

So off we went in their little old Toyota to the sacred land to butcher the bear. On the way, Morning Glory began to scream at Oberon. I do not remember the content, but even with her vast experience, and the fact that she was so in love with Talyn, it can't have been easy for her to see Oberon so besotted with a person who didn't seem to her like quite the right match.

When she left the car for a moment, I said to Oberon, "Don't say anything, just let her go on." And with those words I entered into codependent entanglement. There was no way I could have understood at that moment how deep and karmic their bond went. They had vowed at their handfasting to be bound in this and all future incarnations. To be tangled up with the two of them was a level of challenging complexity that I am still working out.

Oberon told me he loved me completely and yet, at the same time, the kind of relationship he could have with me was entirely dependent on how well I got on with Morning Glory. Yet I think it was evident to Morning Glory that the train had already left the station and the wreck was already well under way. Both Morning Glory and I were in impossible positions, and we proceeded to make the best of it with discomfort and yet mutual deep respect for a decade.

At the time, I was alarmed by some of the rancor of Oberon and Morning Glory's conflicts, and over time I came to witness a number of women in Oberon's life come completely unhinged. I guess I might have seemed a bit unhinged myself occasionally, although I did not exhibit the dramatic breakdowns I saw in others. What would it be like to bind yourself eternally to Oberon as Morning Glory had done? I might scream myself under those circumstances. I am not sure what it is about him that inspires women to madness, but if I had to guess, I would say the talent for holding an irrational position unswervingly under any and all circumstances.

I dove headfirst into certain disaster. That was something Morning Glory and I shared. You can say whatever you want about psychological health and self-esteem, but no one and nothing trumps love—not even death, as the *Song of Solomon* reminds us. This seems like a romantic cliché from the outside, and it is. At the same time, from the inside, it's a doorway into Mystery.

Then I came back again for like six weeks. It was not just me who was in this obsessive state. Oberon was there too. Every time he could get a ticket back East paid for by someone else, he would come and spend a week at my house with me, and then we would lead workshops and rituals together at East Coast festivals like Rites of Spring and Starwood. I remember Oberon saying to me at the time, "I never thought that at fifty I would have this kind of experience." In other words, being so completely immersed in another human being. We were totally enamored of each other. When he met me, he said, "When I dive into you, there is no bottom."

We both fell all over ourselves and made many sacrifices in order to spend time together. Oberon continually found excuses to go to the East Coast, which I think contributed to his problems at *Green Egg* and CAW, because he was somewhat distracted from his responsibilities. He met them, but if he had been more on his watch he would have seen some of those problems coming in a way that perhaps he didn't.

NARRATOR: And there were more surprises in store for everyone when a young woman named Wynter joined the ever-expanding circle of lovers that centered around MG and OZ. (And it did indeed center around them—they were the primary couple, and no matter how many other people each of them would be involved with, the Zells always knew that they would remain together.)

OZ: In February of '96—right after her seventeenth birthday—Wynter showed up at our house. She had been one of the kids who had sort of hung around the edges of the Tribe. Her family was not part of the Church of all Worlds, but many of her teen girlfriends were. She wasn't known as Wynter at that time. But then she went away for a while—she just disappeared.

When she showed up again, she had undergone such a complete transformation that many people didn't even realize that it was the same person: she was totally different from the awkward little girl who had been around before. She showed up on our doorstep and told Morning Glory, "I've been hanging around this group for years, and I've been watching all the grown-ups. And you're the one that I most wanna grow up to be like. So I wanna be your apprentice and your protégé. And I wanna learn to be like you. And I won't go away!"

WYNTER: When I was nine, my parents got divorced. After that I went back and forth between my parents. When I was thirteen, I lived with my mom and went to school in Laytonville, California. In school I met another oddball, and she introduced me to her parents, who were Pagan and members of the Church of All Worlds. I started getting into trouble with this young woman—just basic teenage girl stuff like going out, getting drunk, and staying out all night with boys. She and I went to a Brigid festival and had a lot of fun with other Pagan kids. At this particular gathering, by choice, I lost my virginity. In my opinion it was the best place in the world to have done that—it wasn't like I was on the couch in the basement watching *Jeopardy!* And my first experience was really awesome.

I was fourteen, going on fifteen. I ended up moving in with that young woman and her family. So I went away and didn't have any contact with the Church of All Worlds for about two years.

After my seventeenth birthday I returned—at that point I had changed my physical appearance so much that nobody recognized me. I was a new person and had assumed a new name to go along with that. I had dyed my blondish/reddish curls black and returned as a Goth girl. I wore all black all the time.

MG: Wynter was a young woman who had grown up near us and had wanted to be part of the Church of All Worlds, but her mom got crossways with some of the folks and kept her apart from us. But Wynter had still admired us and longed to be part of the community the whole time. Finally, it turned out that she and I had a lover in common. She asked him to bring her over to my house, and so he dropped her off. She showed up on my front doorstep and told me that she wanted to be my apprentice. I was busy trying to pack to go back to Georgia for a Goddess presentation and for a visit with Talyn and family, and I really couldn't afford to spend time visiting with anyone just then, but she asked me to tell her all I needed to do. Then she said if I let her come in and visit with me that evening, that she would help me pack my Goddess collection and iron some of my silk shirts. What could I say! Here was this adorable Gothy gamine begging to be part of my life! We visited and worked at packing and whatnot and found that she and I totally clicked, even though it turned out that she really didn't know how to iron silk at that point. When I found out how old she was, I kept the visit as platonic as possible, but we still ended up talking until late into the night and beginning the process of a long, slow fall into love.

This new relationship with Wynter was just the most unlikely Autumn/Spring–type thing, and Talyn was extremely wary about it when I told him, mostly because of her age, I think. But various folks' reservations notwithstanding, I hired her to work for me making statues for Mythic Images, and later that same month we got her mom's permission to let her move in with us in the spare room.

Talyn may have had his doubts about the situation, but Wolf was another matter. When I told him about Wynter, he just lit up like he had a premonition, so I told him that I would be happy to introduce them at Beltane. Wolf and I had a wonderful partnership. We were lovers and just all kinds of co-conspirators. But that very special kind of soul relationship that I have with Oberon was not something Wolf and I had together. I knew that he was going to be looking for a woman that he could have that with. I hoped it could be with a woman who got along with me, too.

OZ: But at that time Wynter was seventeen. And we were very concerned about the whole underage thing. So before they began a serious relationship, Wolf went to her mother on Mother's Day and basically asked for permission to begin a relationship with her daughter. It was all beautiful, romantic, and totally cool.

WYNTER: I met Wolf at Beltane, which was the week before Mother's Day. Then Wolf and I went to my mom with a bouquet of roses and took her out to lunch, where he formally asked my mother's permission to be with me romantically. She really grilled him. And he was as charming as he could be, and Wolf can be very charming. So he won her over.

OZ: So we talked about different possibilities for extending our family. And the one that was the most exciting and promising involved the V-M Ranch, where we'd held the CAW Grand Convocation in 1992. The V-M Ranch was ninety-four acres; it had woods and a ten-acre pond; and there was a huge house that had been built by Chester Van Atta. He had been an aerospace engineer and an inventor, and worked on the Van de Graaff high-voltage generator. Originally V-M stood for Van Atta and another owner. But since the lead character in the book that had inspired the whole CAW, *Stranger in a Strange Land*, was named Valentine Michael Smith, these initials seemed auspicious to us; and so, in our typical fashion of renaming things to suit our own mythos, we called the place the "Valentine Michael Ranch"—which allowed us to retain the original initials.

LIZA: Oberon and I had this period of long-distance romance which was about a year and a half in length. And then there was this period when I had decided to move to the West Coast. I almost pleaded with Oberon, "Can't I just move to Marin County and live in my own apartment?" But he wouldn't have it. He was fixated on us all living up on the Ranch. I became a willing accomplice to that determination.

In 1996 I drove cross-country and showed up on his birthday. I had already given the Van Attas the deposit. I already knew where I was going to live. And so we all moved to the Ranch together and into that house. And they presented me with Wynter. I had no choice. I was never asked about Wynter. They simply presented me with the fact that Wynter was also moving in. So I tried to get to know her. I remember saying to Wynter at the time, "These people can't take care of themselves; how can they take care of you?"

OZ: So we moved into the V-M Ranch. There was an enormous garage that we set up our statuary business in. Originally designed to accommodate two entire families, the house had essentially two wings. There was a central area that had a living, dining room, and kitchen, all of which were very spacious, and there was a huge fireplace. Then at opposite ends of it there were these two bedroom wings, which each had two huge bedrooms, bathrooms, closets, and stuff like that. So Liza and I took one end of it, and Morning Glory and Wynter took the other end. And so there we were, all cozy! The offices of CAW Central and *Green Egg*, along with about five other CAW members, also moved onto the V-M Ranch.

LIZA: Mythic Images was a cottage industry before any of us came on the scene. And Morning Glory had founded it. At the Old Same Place they molded statues in the kitchen, so the kitchen was sometimes full of noxious chemicals. (It wasn't always like that—they didn't pour molds every day.) Friends would come over and they would pay them by the piece to sand down the statues and detail them.

That business continued when we went to the V-M Ranch. Imiri was the head production person and worked on the statues. At one point the power went out in our all-electric house for four days in the middle of winter. And it was a very bad winter, and it rained practically the whole four days. We ran out of firewood, and there was none to be obtained in the county. So we were walking around in the rain, picking up pieces of dead trees that were soaking wet, bringing them into the house to set by the fire until they were dry enough to go into the fire. Because it was the only place that was warm enough to dry out the statues, the whole

Mythic Images assembly line was happening in the living room of the V-M Ranch House. It was quite a scene. We had to make statues because it was right before one of the big festivals we sold at, and we had to have merchandise.

It was the formation of TheaGenesis LLC, the actual legal corporation, that Wolf and I had a part in. This was the Clinton era, and we were optimistic.

Wolf was living in San Francisco. He was Gail's roommate at the time. He didn't live with us. But both Morning Glory and Wynter were commuting down to see him. So I made an offer to Wolf. I said, "How much child support are you paying? What are the monthly expenses that you absolutely cannot do without?" I said I would loan TheaGenesis the money so that he could move to the Ranch and make it into a legitimate business, which he did.

Actually that was not in my best interest. Wolf and I never got along. But at that time I was a creature of the group energy. I saw the group's well-being as more important than my own.

WOLF: When I met Morning Glory and Oberon, they were kind of doing the stuff with the statues, but they weren't doing it real well. They weren't making very much money on it. After their move to the V-M Ranch, the business was in limbo; it was out of money, out of stock, and with no orders. So I helped generate orders, modernize the bookkeeping, and put it together as a legal, straightforward business structure.

OZ: Since we had created this intentional family and were all living together, the obvious thing to do was to come up with a new last name that we could all adopt simultaneously rather than people just taking mine or something. So we started trying to come up with something that would be suitable. We tossed around a lot of ideas, but nothing really came to the fore.

MG: Then, all of a sudden, we were visited by ravens. There was this huge colony of ravens that you saw everywhere flying around. They were quite prominent. But at first we didn't really take them too seriously in that regard. They were just part of the landscape.

OZ: We were driving to Las Vegas and stopped to have a lunch at a picnic ground in Death Valley. While we were sitting at the picnic table, this raven flew down and landed on the table right in front of us and started "talking" to us, and asking for handouts. That was pretty trippy. We had a box of Cheez-Its, which is one of the little snacky things that we like. (It's a snackrament in the CAW!) So I took a Cheez-It and held it out to the raven. And she took it out of my fingers very delicately. She put it down on the table in front of her. And then she looked up at me and cocked her head as if to say, "How about another one?" So I handed her another one. And she carefully stacked it on top of the first one.

I thought, "Well, that's interesting." So I handed her another one. When she had a stack of about four Cheez-Its, she carefully put her beak around them and flew off. We figured that she must have a nest and babies that she was taking them back to. A few minutes later she flew back again. We kept giving them to her and she didn't fly away. She kept stacking them until she had quite a big stack, all neatly piled on top of each other. She could barely open up her beak wide enough to contain them. But she did. And finally she took the whole stack of Cheez-Its and flew away.

MG: Back home again at the V-M Ranch, we started looking up the mythology of what "Raven" was about. Who is Raven? I knew him as the North American trickster bird and as the Norse God Odin and the Celtic Goddess Morrigan's companion. But then I found out that in many traditions he is a conveyer of Magick! He is the shadow that steals the sun, and is the messenger that carries the Magick from the place where it's conceived to the place where it needs to be delivered and dropped off. He is a very important character in many cultures. And if tricks and humor are part of it, that's because he's a communicator. Humor is a great lubrication for communication. Sometimes you have to play tricks and amuse people to get your point across.

OZ: We looked more into ravens and came to realize how cool they are, and how incredibly intelligent. They are regarded in many cultures in different parts of the world as birds of wisdom and intellect. So we thought, "Ravens would be a pretty cool totem animal for us."

MG: And Liza was doing a lot of heart chakra work. So she was talking about, "Well, whatever the name is, it's got to be about the heart because that's what we are: a bunch of hopeless romantics who have ended up together. We're as different as can possibly be. And yet we're coming from a place of Love. Because Love is the only universal solvent that will dissolve the boundaries and allow us to manifest our dreams and our hearts' desires."

Finally I had an epiphany. I said, "I understand what it is. We are Ravenhearts. Raven is about communication, and about Darkness and Magick. And we are beings of the Heart and of Love. And this Family is about Love and the Heart. We're about communicating what Victor Anderson always called 'the Dark Heart of Innocence.' We're about communicating the Secrets of Love, and being able to transmit and translate the Mysteries of the Heart into the world."

OZ: At that point we all agreed to adopt *Ravenheart* for the Family name. And so it was.

PART FOUR

The Demise of the CAW

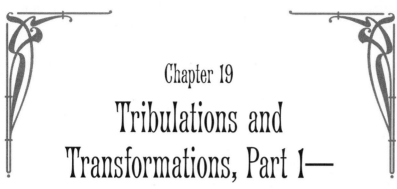

Chapter 19
Tribulations and Transformations, Part 1—
The Shadow Side of a Sex-Positive Religion

It's the sovereign state of confusion
When She shows Her darkest Face.
Where's the One who loves us?
Who's this bitch that's in Her place?
The shit flies thick and heavy,
We cry and clutch our breast.
It's only Mamma Kali come
To shake us out of our nest.

—FROM "A GREETING TO OLD FRIENDS—THE KALI YUGA SONG,"
BY DIANE DARLING, 1987

NARRATOR: With great freedom comes great responsibility. Oberon and Morning Glory had consciously unmoored their sexuality from the constraining mores of the mainstream, and while it was joyous for their family, it caused far more problems within CAW than any of them could have foreseen. They were about to come into close conflict with the shadow side of a sex-positive lifestyle and spirituality.

So far this book has had many twists and turns, but none quite like these. The events that you will be reading about in this chapter were spread out over many years and happened concurrently with what was going on in previous and following chapters. Perceived improprieties among Hippies who just decades before had all lustily embraced free love became a wedge that began to drive people apart, eventually destroying *Green Egg* and even the Church of All Worlds itself.

Let's back up a bit. The first time the compost hit the fan was in 1992 on the V-M Ranch. This was where the Ravenhearts would end up living years later, but at the time Orion was calling it home, and OZ and Morning Glory had not yet even met Talyn, Wolf, Liza, or Wynter. The CAW decided to hold their thirtieth anniversary Grand Convocation and annual meeting there.

OZ: The V-M Ranch at that time was not well known to many of us, but it seemed like a good place to hold a larger gathering because Annwfn is too small, with a more fragile ecosystem; consequently, it has a ceiling of around a hundred people. But the V-M Ranch was ninety-four acres of gentle, rolling grasslands dappled with lovely mixed deciduous and pine forest; it even had a huge pond. It was around the first of August. We had rituals, workshops, entertainment, and music. We swam in the ten-acre pond. We had a campground. We built a big stage.

For the main ritual, Lance and I came into the center of the Circle and shared water, in commemoration of our first water-sharing ritual thirty years earlier. Then we invited the next people who had shared water with us, and the next, and we kept on doing that, inviting people from subsequent years to come forward, until everybody was in the center. And we did a working that this beautiful land would come into our hands and become a new home for us. We had all fallen in love with it. We had such powerful energy that there was a great magickal working for that.

We also scheduled a "tea dance." The idea was that everybody would come in lingerie and have a big dance party. That was something that Diane's long-lost cousin, Andy Conn, came up with. He had a lot of interesting ideas. He had been involved in the edgy, men's group kind of stuff, so he was bringing a certain other kind of energy into the thing that hadn't previously been much a part of our traditions. But as far as I was concerned, everything was welcome. And evidently, tea dances had already been held successfully at both Pagan Spirit Gathering and the

Ancient Ways festivals, nudist camps, and elsewhere, so there was precedent.

A lingerie party seemed like a cool idea. Most of the time we would just be naked. We had a skinny-dipping pond and mudbaths. But dressing up seemed like fun, and everybody brought stuff. There were whole boxes full of lingerie that people brought so that everyone would have something. The kids especially really got into it—they thought it was fun to dress up. And everyone had a real blast, strutting their stuff on the little stage to a great mix of music.

ANDY CONN: I was in a polyamorous relationship with Anodea Judith and Richard Ely, and I was pretty active in the Church of All Worlds. I was asked to do an event for the convocation. I had been involved for a long time in the all-night dance movement, including the early rave movement, going all the way back to 1975 when it was primarily gay and bisexual men and women. So what I decided to do was put on what was sort of like a rave, but the ultimate object was to get everyone into a trance state through dance and movement. There was another member of the Church who went by the name of Mongo, who was an aerobics instructor and a beautiful gay man. He and I decided to put on this trance dance together.

The mix of music was created by Rick Hamouris, along with Mongo and me. Rick had a recording studio and was also in the CAW. Rick had written the all-time classic Pagan song "We Are a Circle," so he had a divine place in the Pagan community. We choreographed a number of different songs where there would be costume changes. We also enlisted Zack, Diane's son, and this was his first actual encounter with the rave movement. I had sort of taken Zack under my wing at about that time. My son Nick was also involved. They were both about fifteen or sixteen. They were sort of enlisted to do art projects during this—do paintings and create sculptures along with a lot of the other Pagan kids.

Now, the whole theme of it was "Come as Your Favorite Fantasy." And, in the typical way that the Church of All Worlds puts on events, Tom Williams put in the flyer, "Come in Lingerie." Well, the flyer wasn't changed.

NARRATOR: There was also some confusion as to the timing of the dance; Morning Glory and Andy Conn both remember the tea dance as having been scheduled after the main ritual, but they were swapped, with the dance occurring under the blazing sun of a hot August day, and the main ritual occurring closer to dusk, which was not optimal for either event.

ANDY CONN: So I put on the tea dance with music that was primarily from the early rave culture. And I began to put people into a trance through music, through sound, through dancing, and through the outrageous costumes that we were using. People started coming up on the stage and dancing; people started losing their inhibitions, and I brought everyone into a sort of Dionysian state.

But it was broad daylight. Now it should have been done at night. People did things that I believe they probably wouldn't have done if they weren't in a trance state. There was an incredible energy that went through this. So the rave went on for I would guess about an hour and a half. Once it ended, and people started coming out of the trance, they said, "Oh my god, there were children around." But there was no blatant sexuality, with the exception of my son and his sixteen-year-old girlfriend making out onstage.

For god's sake, sixteen-year-olds make out in public! There were little kids all dressed in ribbons and things like that. They all seemed to be having a good time. There was certainly no inappropriate behavior between anyone that was a minor and anyone over eighteen.

OZ: Some people apparently felt that if word got out about it, their children could be taken away from them. Morning Glory and I found this utterly baffling. It seemed to be a problem only for the adults and not for the kids. We talked to the kids about it, which nobody else was doing. They said they had loved it. Everybody had a good time. There was nothing that we considered to be sexual. But a few people did, including Orion and Tom Williams—Tom didn't even have any kids, but Orion had a daughter.

At the CAW annual meeting on Sunday, which was very large, the question of whether or not this was moral became the central issue and bone of contention. At that time Tom Williams was president of the board. He started shouting at me, and accusing me of not having appropriate boundaries. I shouted back at him that my boundaries were around not doing harm, and there was no harm done of any sort. Who was harmed? It degenerated into a shouting match, and it became really horrible.

ANDY CONN: Cerridwen Fallingstar got quite upset that there were children present at this. And the next day they decided to have this huge town meeting, where they sort of tried to pillory Mongo and me. It was right out of *The Crucible*. It was a wonderful sham sort of mock court, and they made Mongo cry. The two people who came to support us, in their old truck pulling up the hill to get to this meeting, were Jack and Ace, who were both in the early Pirate movement. And so those guys stood with me and said, "Get over it. It was a successful ritual."

I stand by that, by the way. Quite frankly, I was absolutely thrilled with the outcome of the ritual. It achieved everything I possibly wanted to achieve. It put everyone in an altered state, and everyone had a blast while they were in that altered state. No one was harmed. And probably the only mistake was Tom Williams putting "Everyone Come in Lingerie" rather "Come as Your Favorite Fantasy" in the program book. The tea dance was a grand success. Twenty years later, people are still coming up to me and telling me they were there.

OZ: The odd thing was that nobody had objected to it beforehand. It was in the program. And people had been walking around naked all weekend. During the event nobody had come forward and said, "Stop! This can't go on!"

NARRATOR: Perhaps the backlash had something to do with their fears of how Pagans would appear to the outside world. A photographer on assignment from *National Geographic* magazine was attending and photographing the convocation that weekend as part of a larger project; he was asked to surrender the roll of film he'd taken of the tea dance because certain CAW members realized it could appear fairly scandalous, and he complied. His piece ultimately never ran in the magazine.

DIANE DARLING: People were pretty upset that lingerie-based dancing was publicly exposed, because we all knew the photographer was there. It was a little bit more risqué, I think, than what a lot people expected. Accusations were hurled, and so on and so forth. I'd say it was at that point that the integrity of the convocation started to fall apart. It was stupid to have an outdoor event in Laytonville in August. People were getting way too hot. I don't think anybody actually went to the hospital, but we had people who were fainting from the heat and from not having enough water. Things were kind of tense after that.

OZ: Another thing that happened that set a tone at that time was that Joi Wolfwomyn came to the convocation. I don't remember what prompted this, but she came forward at this meeting and made an appeal for the acceptance in our community of BD/SM. But at this time, BD/SM was really a bone of contention. Morning Glory in particular just came down on Joi like a ton of bricks. She was an outraged feminist, and questioned how BD/SM could possibly be justified in our community. She equated it with abuse. It was quite intense, and became an awful shouting match between them. There were a lot of tears and a lot of anguish.

MG: The reason I reacted so badly to Joi Wolfwomyn's statements was that seeing her bruised body being proudly flaunted brought up all my unresolved anger at my father for abusing my mother and at my mother for letting herself be abused. It was a visceral, automatic reaction from someone who had experienced that sort of pain involuntarily. Later I came to understand that BD/SM is the arena that a lot of people use to work through their trauma and desensitize themselves to their own memories of suffering. Eventually I began to experiment with it myself, and I came to see what a valuable tool it could be. But changing my tune in this department led to the loss of a number of friends and lovers who had the same reaction to me that I had to Joi. Later, at an Ancient Ways gathering, I literally got down on my knees and begged Joi to forgive me for my nonconsensual verbal abuse of her in public. Happily, she forgave me and reminded me that when you venture into dark waters, you become a mirror for people's fears. So I ended up becoming as much of a projection screen for many of the CAW folks as Joi had been for me. Ain't karma a bitch?

OZ: It was one of the very few times I have ever seen Morning Glory on the other side of that particular line. Ultimately this led into some incredibly transformative stuff for her. She ended up coming around full circle on this subject, eventually making a public apology to Joi, guest-editing a whole issue of *Green Egg* devoted to the theme, and becoming a major advocate of it.

That transformation also widened the gap. The same people who had been opposed to the tea dance remained on the opposite side from us on this issue. The fact that Morning Glory and I eventually came to accept something this outrageous became another reason why we were considered so immoral and reprehensible, and that we had no business being in charge of the CAW. This was the key event that had started the rift. It was the beginning of our disaffection.

It never occurred to me that the decision on whether or not somebody was being victimized would not be up to the alleged victim, but rather up to some third party to decide on their behalf—and over their objections. My feeling is, if somebody is not complaining about something that's happening to them, then there is not a problem. And if you don't like it, you can't have any! But the parents of underage children feel that they have to be the overriding opinion about what is right and wrong for their kids, regardless of their kids' opinions. Of course parents have to teach their kids these things from the time they are born, and where are you going to draw the line? Different people draw the line in different places.

ANDY CONN: Everyone always liked to shake their fingers at Oberon. I know that Oberon was the one who was always set up to take some sort of fall, or to be blamed for something, because Oberon always thought everything was a really good idea. "Hey, that sounds like a good idea. Let's do that." If anything, Oberon probably got scolded because he put his seal of approval on the tea dance.

OZ: I think it had to with the fact that we had a second generation of kids growing up in the Church. Suddenly, behavior that had been acceptable to the first generation of people, many of whom had come in themselves when they were young—now suddenly when they were parents and had teenage kids, they took a whole different attitude about it. And this is not an uncommon phenomenon in the world.

MG: I believe that the Feminist Revolution brought a spotlight on an aspect of human behavior that had destroyed many people's lives and souls—and that is childhood sexual abuse. I believe that was the "elephant in the living room" in the brouhaha about the tea dance. We were in a phase in the social revolution where many people were examining their childhoods, and finding that they remembered being sexually abused as children, and were working on coming to terms with it.

I guess we were going through a period that was kind of a backlash against the whole sex-positive, free-love era of the '60s. I found out that I was totally unique among most of my women friends in that I had never been molested as a child or raped as an adult. I was one of the few lucky ones. So my attitude that sex is a wonderful thing was really an off-key song to be singing at that particular time and place. I understand now that I lacked empathy with people who had experienced these traumas; I had certainly been physically abused, so I figured that I understood where they were coming from. But it is another whole territory that sexual abuse takes a person into—a territory of guilt and shame and obsessive needs for secrecy. Many of the people at the tea dance who had issues around sexuality and children had the same sort of visceral reaction to that experience as I'd had to Joi Wolfwomyn and the BD/SM issue.

This whole viewing of sex as a negative thing was the direct antithesis of what I have stood for all my life. I have always been loudly pro-sex and extremely critical of the American sexual double standard: "Do what I say, not what I do." I have always felt that sex was a natural part of life, and that it was a healthy thing, and that parents should allow their kids to see the positive side of sexuality as well as educating them about the negative things. By this I don't mean having sex with the kids, for heaven's sake— just being open with them and allowing them to hang around where that kind of energy is happening and talking in positive ways about it.

I've always believed passionately that what is wrong in our society is that it is okay to expose your kids to gory violence, but if you expose them to even positive examples of sexuality, you can go to jail. I think it says a lot about how twisted and deformed the average American's sense of right and wrong is. But then, on the other hand, I guess I was pretty much of a failure myself at that sort of thing with my daughter, since she was decidedly put off by my ideas and I definitely was out of the majority opinion in this circumstance.

NARRATOR: The 1992 "Tempest in a Tea Dance," as it came to be called, seems to have set the stage for what happened later on in the decade: discord and uncomfortable feelings regarding the younger generation and their interactions with sexuality. But at least for Diane's son, Zack, the tea-dance ritual turned out to be a very meaningful and influential experience. He is he now a popular Bay Area DJ, and he is also involved in theater and stage production and management.

ZACK DARLING: I'm one of the board members of the Health and Harmony Festival in Santa Rosa. That's a 30,000-person music festival, and I'm in charge of the nighttime event called the Mystic Beat Lounge. The whole experience of growing up with Pagan gatherings warmed me up for what's happening now, and it pretty directly tied into Otter.

The Earthdance Festival is an international festival for world peace. It happens in 350 cities in sixty different countries. The main one happens up in Laytonville. They're huge, and the central event happens here in Northern California, and I do all the artwork and design for it. For me, I love the fact that this is ritual, this is ceremony, and it's accessible to anyone. You don't have to subscribe to any particular theology to be able to have a profound, enlightening experience.

NARRATOR: Sadly, the Tempest in a Tea Dance was not the only sexual scandal to rock the close-knit community; two more developed in this decade, one involving a man known as Red Daniel, and another involving a man known as Adam Walks-Between-Worlds.

It all started out innocently enough, as these things often do. Morning Glory began taking fencing classes in the early 1990s as a way of getting back in shape when she was recovering from her neck injury. She got involved with a group of people who got together regularly to practice the sport.

MG: One of the major players, in every sense of the word, in my life came into it through the fencing club. His name was Daniel Bloomfield, but we all called him Daniel the Red, or Red Daniel. He was a tall, tawny fox of a man with a lighthearted laugh and a cynical smile. He was kind of a guttersnipe, but he had his own funny sense of pride and strict code of honor. He was a superb artist and he was surprisingly literate, being self-educated about the same kind of science and history stuff that fascinated OZ and me.

He was brought to our Ostara Sabbat in 1992 by a mutual friend who owned our favorite pizza parlor in Ukiah. But he really started registering on-board when he showed up at the Old Same Place for fencing bouts. He connected easily with most of our gang. One day he and I had fenced several bouts together and worked up a lot of juicy energy, and then a bunch of us ended up over at Diane's house watching old *Conan* movies. We had built up quite a charge, and so I invited him over to my house to play. I explained that Oberon and I had an open marriage and that we both had other lovers and that we liked to know the person the other one was with, but that it was okay.

He looked pretty dubious, but allowed himself to be drawn into the house. And then I introduced him to OZ and asked if it was convenient for us to use the bedroom for a while. OZ just grinned at us and said, "Sure." So we disappeared into the back room and had a wonderful romp, and I discovered he was a very talented fencer in more ways than one. Later, OZ came in and joined us, and we all ended up having a great time and talking late into the night.

Over the years, Daniel and Oberon became quite good friends, though Daniel and Wolf never trusted each other. OZ and I got up to all manner of mischief with Daniel, and I came to love him dearly for his high-hearted romanticism that clashed with his world-weary cynicism—but, above all, for his roguish charm. Daniel, however, had some fatal flaws. It's not that I was unaware of them; rather, it's that with some I sympathized and others I thought he could learn to outgrow. Many a woman has wrecked her ship on a similar set of rocks. He was exactly the dashing and dangerous sort of scoundrel that appeals to a certain sort of woman regardless of her age. I was one of them, and there were several others. However, one of Daniel's problems lay in that he was not concerned about age when it came to the women in his life. He liked them whether they were young or old—and nobody cared much when he liked them old, but when he liked them young, it created no end of problems.

The "age of consent" is a thorny problem that has no set answer. The age even varies from state to state, with some being as young as fourteen and others being as old as twenty-one. Of course, the problem with all this is that chastity is a kind of Pandora's box, and no matter how many rules society makes, when it comes to the power of the force of sexuality, most of these rules are pretty unenforceable. If they were not, there would be no teenage pregnancy. But the laws that have been written on this subject can be extremely draconian if you happen to step over the wrong line in the wrong state. Many a young man languishes in jail not because he forced a young lady, but because her parents caught them having a good time together. The fact that she may have even been the instigator has no force whatsoever in a court of law when it comes to the crime of statutory rape.

I grew up asserting my sexuality at a pretty young age—fifteen, I believe it was, when I happily flung my virginity to the winds. I suppose it might have been quite a scandal if I had ever been caught, but I wasn't, so it wasn't, if you take my meaning. I have always enjoyed the company of older men and women; I found them wiser and more caring than most kids my own age. I learned about life and about love from these people in my teens and I was never molested, coerced, or harmed in any way. I never got pregnant or was given a disease, and I learned a lot about compassion as well as passion. So I was very much in the minority of most women's experience in that arena. I felt strongly that young women past the age of reason should have the right to choose their lovers and it was nobody's business but theirs with whom they chose to share their bodies and their hearts. This was the strong and somewhat rebellious stance of an Aphrodite Priestess, and the Goddess Hecate herself couldn't have said it in a more straightforward manner.

Of course, the world is littered with the broken hearts and ruined lives of women who did not have my good fortune and who were terribly abused and taken advantage of by men who were old enough to know better but who didn't really care. Of course, just as many girls have been taken advantage of by guys their own age too; so this is why there is such a tremendous negative charge around teenage sexuality, especially where girls are concerned.

The word *sex* is a neutral word; it is biological in nature. It does not have any positive or negative moral or emotional attachments by itself. But no other word in the English language is so fraught with both positive and negative associations for people. Americans in particular are obsessed with sex—perhaps because of our Puritan background. We are either engaged in decrying rampant sexuality or else furiously indulging in it. Sometimes people do both at the same time, in the sense that they like to indulge their own sexuality while decrying other people's. This is usually done in a very hypocritical fashion, but it can also be done from a place of care and concern. Sometimes these things overlap and it is hard to tell where one ends and the other begins.

When sexual abuse became such a huge national cause within the women's movement and the psychological communities, the laissez-faire standards that I had grown up with in the '60s changed radically. The '60s radicals had become the parents of teenagers, and they did not want to see their daughters abused the way so many women had been. Our community had grown quite a crop of lovely young teenage girls, and since they had been raised Pagan in a sex-positive community, they were raring to go. In fact, it was a disaster waiting to be unleashed upon the community, and Red Daniel was going to be the spark that would blow everything to hell.

A number of the young women sought Daniel out and let him know that they were available, and he was only too happy to oblige them. He had a devil-may-care attitude and a naturally rebellious streak, so he felt that if these Pagans believed in the glories of sexuality and in women's freedom of choice, then where was the problem?

Well, the problem was that the parents of the teenage girls had loved them since they were babies and did not want to see their daughters hurt or taken advantage of by a guy who didn't really love them but only wanted to have sex with them. They felt that they were in charge of their daughters' well-being until they were eighteen, and they were going to do everything they could to protect them from would-be scoundrels. They felt, in fact, pretty much like their parents had felt about them . . . if they were girls. There were boys in the community who had had liaisons with older women, and it generated little or no comment because, unfortunately, the double standard is just as present in the Pagan community as it is in the world at large.

At any rate, several of these young women looked up to me as a role model since I had such an "out there" and positive relationship with my sexuality. So when the girls started getting involved with Daniel or with other guys, they would often come to me as a Priestess to confide in me about the relationships. It was a somewhat awkward situation for me, because on one hand I was friends with some of their mothers and fathers, and at that point in their lives the girls frequently found themselves in an adversarial relationship with one or more of their parents around issues of sexuality.

But young people desperately need a reliable confidant at this time in their life—someone who will not judge them for their thoughts, feelings, or actions and who can validate their positive experiences, while at the same time giving them some necessary advice about how not to get in over their heads. In order to be a successful confidant, you have to have the credibility that comes with walking your talk.

So I became the Sister Confessor for a number of girls who were starting to experiment with their burgeoning sexuality. I listened and I advised, but mostly I listened. Often I counseled them to open up a dialogue with their parents, but under the Clergy Code of Confidentiality I could not convey any of these confidences directly to the parents. This is a difficult position to be put in, but it is strictly necessary to allow a confessor the right to be heard by a Priest or Priestess who absolutely will not violate their trust. This right to privacy has been upheld time and again by the courts of the United States and other countries all over the world. It is a sacred trust that holds even when someone confesses that they are engaged in a crime. All rules about mandatory reporting of crimes do not apply to Clergy Confidentiality, period.

Now, as I have said before, everyone has strong opinions on underage sexuality and almost everyone is convinced that their opinion is the one, true, right, and only way to view the subject, and anyone who disagrees with them is somehow morally defective. So I found myself sitting on a powder keg. Perhaps I should have refused to counsel the girls as a Priestess because I was involved with a man with whom some of them were also involved. But at the time, it seemed to me and Oberon and also to them that this gave me a unique insight into their situation—both the good parts and the problems. So I went ahead and took this on. Word soon spread about it, and at first some of the parents welcomed the situation because they agreed that I seemed to handle my sex life in a happy and responsible way. At one point, I even set up a sex-education evening where the young women who were coming or had come of age could learn more about the positive as well as the negative aspects of sexuality.

At first everything seemed to go well, but girls will be girls, and, as we know from the song, they just wanna have fun. So stuff was said and done after I had gone to bed alone in my room that created a huge brouhaha, and a number of the parents decided that I was no longer a trustworthy confidante for the girls. The firestorm started to pick up steam, and before long I found myself up before a meeting of the Clergy Council to explain my behavior or to be impeached. During that meeting, I was denounced by several people for my strict stance on Clergy Confidentiality, but attorneys were consulted about the laws and to everyone's great surprise but mine, I had in fact acted impeccably and well within the letter of the law as well as its spirit. You might think that would end it, but it did not by a long shot.

Both Oberon and I sincerely advised the parents who were so violently upset to talk to the police if they felt they had a case. There was a Clergy vote, from which we abstained due to conflict of interest. The outcome was that Red Daniel was banished from attending Church functions, especially ones that took place on Annwfn.

OZ and I were pilloried for our friendship with him, and we were put in a very conflicted position. Though at that time we were both ready to cheerfully strangle both him and a couple of the girls, we both felt very strongly that there were principles of loyalty, friendship, and individual freedom of choice at stake. Also, the majority of the young women vigorously defended both us and Daniel at some of these CAW meetings, insisting that no harm had been done to them, and since we all gave credence to the Wiccan Rede—"An it harm none, do as thou wilt"—we found ourselves having to ask exactly what harm had been done.

As it turned out, the harm that had been done most dramatically was done by our compassionate support of the girls, which drove a wedge between them and some of their parents and the Church. This whole affair lasted for just a few years, until the girls turned eighteen, but it served to tear the Church apart and to bring a lot of discredit on us through a concerted campaign of rumors throughout the Pagan community. OZ and I were accused of everything from collusion in improprieties to out-and-out child molesting. We were appalled! Once a thing like that starts going, it's like an avalanche, almost impossible to stop because people love to gossip and they especially love to hear terrible things about well-known people and eagerly pass them on without bothering to check whether or not they are true.

I did a lot of soul-searching before I made the decision to rake over these old coals in this book; and though I have made my peace with many of the people who disowned me at the time, I felt that there were lessons I learned from those experiences that needed to be shared lest others make the same mistakes. Ultimately, although your right to swing your fist ends at the place someone else's nose begins, challenging the dragons of accepted traditions can be a painful and sometimes fatal game to play.

Red Daniel was a consummate player at that kind of dragon tag. He danced on the edge all the time. He flaunted his sexuality and his kinkiness, and he was a magnet for rebellious teenage girls. He also had some seriously damaged parts of his personality. He was so much into arguing with everybody about everything that he could never hold down a job for more than a couple of weeks at a time. He was so lacking in personal discipline that he could never succeed as an artist, in spite of considerable talent. And he sometimes liked to play around with more dangerous drugs than pot or acid. He romanticized the sleazier side of society much like a lot of modern rap artists and old blues singers. He was never happier than when he was running hell-bent-for-leather five feet away from the lynch mob. In short, he was what we call a "Weenie Wagger."

Now, Oberon and I also have a certain amount of weenie-wagging tendencies—more so when we were much younger. It is a very typical adolescent attitude that took us a long time to grow out of, and some people like Daniel never grow out of it. Maybe the reason why he got along so well with teenagers was that fundamentally he still was one. He was an adolescent Peter Pan—the darker, scruffy one in the books, not the cleaned-up Disney version. This is a quality that can be somewhat endearing when one is young and dashing, but much less so the older one becomes. Eventually it can settle into middle-aged stubbornness and intractability, and much later into a grumpy old-manhood.

NARRATOR: The other controversial character was a talented Bard in their community.

OZ: Other significant conflicts arose in the fall of 1996, the most serious concerning one of our Bards, Adam Walks-Between-Worlds Rostoker, who stood accused of numerous improprieties around sexual manipulation ("Sleep with me, baby, and I'll make ya a High Priestess!"). Unfortunately, those few of his victims who dared to break his imposed vow of silence to complain to members of the Clergy did so individually and in strict "Clergy confidence." It was only when a few of us (MG, me, and Anodea) began to hear more than one complaint that we broke confidence and consulted with each other, leading to a big hearing and extensive, heated debate concerning the issues raised on all sides. At the hearing, nearly twenty victims showed up, and letters were read by that many more who could not attend in person. Due to the severity of the concerns, Adam resigned his position of Bard and was banished from the Church.

LIZA: Oberon and Morning Glory made a point of befriending people who were controversial. It was never their own behavior; it was the behavior of these controversial friends and Oberon and Morning Glory's defense of them that really got them into trouble. Part of what so enraged the Clergy was that they virtually sacrificed themselves, and their reputations, in order to defend a few dubious characters, while neglecting people who perceived themselves as having been faithful and true to them for many, many years. I used to say to Oberon, "Why don't you take Orion out and buy him a hamburger?" I doubt it would have made a difference, but he never did.

MAERIAN MORRIS: When people behave in this way, and they are the face of a minority, whether they are polyamorous people or members of a religious minority like Paganism, it really does not serve the community well. When you put in as much time as I did, breaking your bum to try to be of some service to something that you heartily treasure—the ideas of water-brotherhood, the ideas of the sacredness of the Earth and our responsibility to the Earth as a living creature, of which we're all part—to have this happen is just demolishing to one's sense of hope. I became conflicted over the use of the word *Pagan*; for one thing, it carried a lot of connotations that people didn't even understand. And for another thing, if this was the way Pagans behaved, was I Pagan? What was I?

OZ: On February 20, 1997, Adam Walks-Between-Worlds was found shot to death in the home he was visiting in Orange County, California. Investigating detectives regarded the case as a homicide—a crime of passion. To this date, his murder remains unsolved.

NARRATOR: All of these personal incidents relating to their core values alienated OZ and Morning Glory from many of their closest friends and fellow CAW members. As you'll see in the next chapter, the members of CAW and *Green Egg* were no longer simply small groups of friends and lovers doing ritual and a magazine together. Both had grown into something much larger, and increasingly they nudged Oberon and Morning Glory to the side.

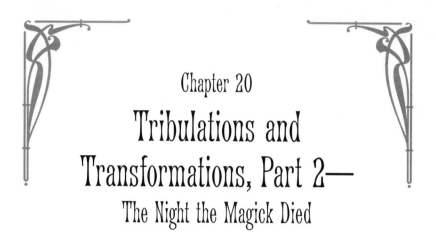

Chapter 20
Tribulations and
Transformations, Part 2—
The Night the Magick Died

Now all the truth is out, be secret and take defeat
From any brazen throat, for how can you compete,
Being honor bred, with one who, were it proved he lies,
Were neither shamed in his own nor in his neighbors' eyes?

—FROM WILLIAM BUTLER YEATS,
"TO A FRIEND WHOSE WORK HAS COME TO NOTHING"

NARRATOR: The events that you will be reading about in this chapter were spread out over many years and happened concurrently with what was going on in the previous chapter. The roots of them go way back, to at least the early days of the CAW in St. Louis. At that time, in order to receive recognition as a tax-exempt religion, the Church became incorporated and established a board of directors. This meant that what was essentially a bunch of Hippies and college students had to become part of the "establishment"; but they wanted to be able to exercise their right to freedom of religion, and so they took that chance.

With the rebirth of the CAW in California in the mid-1980s, there were many more dues-paying members than just the select few you are reading about in this book, and there was Annwfn, which by the 1990s had become valuable real estate. (It was primo rural acreage in the heart of Mendocino County, where growing and selling marijuana had become a major local industry.) And there was *Green Egg*, which had become a professionally published, slick magazine that was sold on newsstand racks in chain bookstores alongside the likes of *Playboy*, *Sports Illustrated*, and *Rolling Stone*. And all of this belonged to the Church, which was still legally incorporated.

No one on the staff in the early years in California had much experience running a business, and as it grew as a business the problems grew. Neither the Church itself nor the magazine had a professional bookkeeper, and the financial records were still being kept, and not very well, by hand. And the legal and financial matters of the Church were controlled not by OZ and not even by the Clergy, but by the board of directors.

When Tim Zell set up his Church for legal recognition in the '60s, he not only had to incorporate it, but he also had to give the whole setup some kind of structure other than simply sitting around in a circle telling stories. The only social group he'd ever belonged to, other than the Boy Scouts, was his fraternity. So that's what he used as a model.

That meant that the religious organization that Tim had wanted to be libertarian and leaderless had to follow rules that had been established by the U.S. government and, to a certain extent, the college Greek system—and that included how the board, and its meetings, were run. And so when things began to fall apart, that's what was used to try and keep them together. And in the mid-'90s, they started to fall apart pretty badly.

Much of this was done in meetings that were closed to the public. And since this was the beginning of the Internet age, there was lots of back and forth, done quicker than anyone could have previously imagined possible, with Internet lists and groups that were also closed. (This also meant that rumors and gossip were spreading at a crazy new pace, which didn't seem to help matters.)

I don't want to take sides in this, or create any kind of appearance that there is some simple, obvious explanation of what went on. But suffice it to say that by the mid-'90s, Oberon felt beleaguered by both the *Green Egg* staff and the CAW board of directors, who were mostly made up of *Green Egg* staff at that time.

(And as the researcher, interviewer, organizer, and de facto editor of this book, I have decided that it is in everybody's best interests, including those of the reader, to not try and analyze what happened at every CAW board meeting during these years. This is an oral history! My inspirations for this book are journalists like Studs Terkel and Legs McNeil, not Bob Woodward and Carl Bernstein.

And with that in mind, we will now continue with this chapter.)

OZ: In October of '93, we finally moved the *Green Egg* offices out of the spare rooms in our homes and rented a real office building, which became the administrative office of the Church as well. Two years later, we moved everything into a large storefront in downtown Ukiah, where we provided walk-in copy services to the public. And of course in 1996 the *Green Egg* and CAW offices moved to the V-M Ranch.

Over the years the staff of *Green Egg* expanded to include a number of talented and dedicated people. It grew to a circulation that reached about 30,000 readers. But with all this success, and so many people involved, there soon arose conflict, contention, and power struggles. In July of 1994 after our triad broke up, Diane, a brilliant editor, left *Green Egg*, and went on to edit *Green Man*, and later *PanGaia*. She was succeeded as editrix by Maerian Morris, newly wedded to Orion Stormcrow (with MG and me officiating), who ended up responsible for bookkeeping.

NARRATOR: Orion's perspective on things is conspicuous in its absence from this book, and that was his choice. He declined my interview request. Unfortunately we're going to go ahead and consider some of it without Orion's perspective, but we will include that of Maerian, his partner at the time.

The relationship between Orion and OZ seems to be one of those mysterious things that nobody, including the two of them, really understands. One person I interviewed described the CAW Clergy as "a twenty-five-person dysfunctional family with thirty years of history," and certainly what went on between those guys was among the most dysfunctional of all. They have loved and cared for each other for decades, but also have had many great conflicts.

After Diane left *Green Egg*, Orion became increasingly involved in its day-to-day operations, and found that he had the same differences with Oberon as Diane had had—namely, that of who had final say over what ran in the magazine, from art and essays to advertisements. Oberon summed up the staff's position as "Oberon insisted, as publisher, he had absolute authority to publish anything he saw fit to. Orion insisted he didn't."

OZ: And that was exactly true. I'd created the magazine (twice!), and each incarnation had become a legendary success. And like any other founding publisher of any other journal, I fully maintained my right to include in it anything I felt belonged there; indeed, that was the entire purpose of my creating the magazine in the first place, and the essential prerogative of being publisher—as well as the key to its success.

Orion, however (like Diane before him), was adamant in his desire to exclude submissions by people he didn't approve of personally. As far as I was concerned, personal approval of the behavior or lifestyles of contributors was never a criterion in my decision to include their material— but rather whether their contributions would enhance the content and vision of the magazine and be of interest to the readers. We had many heated exchanges around this issue, and I always maintained that the final decision was mine to make, not Orion's.

Like many of my Hippie/Pagan peers, I had not been part of the high school "in-crowd" cliques, whose very *raison d'être* was about exclusion. I encountered the same thing in college fraternities, churches, and social clubs. And I resented the hell out of it. I was determined to create something different—a "club" in which everyone who wanted to join could belong, and be welcomed.

But it seems to be a basic aspect of human nature to want to form associations defined more on who (or what) is excluded than on who (or what) is included. My conflicts within CAW were invariably around my welcoming in people others didn't want to associate with. I've actually had people threaten to blackball events I've held if I allowed so-and-so to attend!

MAERIAN MORRIS: During that period of time, just before Orion began to deal with some of the publisher's jobs, *Green Egg* switched to a model where the board of directors of CAW, who actually owned the magazine, would hire *Green Egg* staff as employees of the Church. I was thus hired by the board with Otter's strong recommendation. The CAW board included all members of the Clergy and several scions, and these people were legally responsible for business decisions. Of course they listened to the publisher and the founder, but they had final decision-making power over the magazine.

It's important to understand that this was a nonprofit religious magazine, with a tiny staff, most of whom were CAW scions and Priests or Priestesses—most of us wore a lot of hats at the same time. The goals and ideals of the Church recognized divinity within each of us, and were about helping people discover it in within themselves. Unfortunately, these goals did not always transfer into action in the CAW. There was a big difference between Pagan ideals and the laissez-faire culture of the Pagan community. This culture often conflicted with the business requirements of running an organization.

Otter is a visionary. He's interested in Magick; he's interested in being a Wizard. He was less interested in the managerial stuff. Otter liked to do the fun parts of it. He's gregarious and charismatic and funny and lovable when he's out there being Otter. And there's another side. And that, I think, has to be said. And it has to be said by somebody who is trying to say it in a loving way. He is not good at the management side of things. His life history proves that. You don't give your house to the Church and then say, "Send me my money." A publisher needs to be a good manager. I know what good business practices are. And believe me, these were never successfully implemented at *Green Egg*.

OZ: So when Orion was elected president of the board of directors in August of 1996, the very first meeting held thereafter, on September 13, stripped me of all control and decision-making—in absentia. The "conflict of interest" was absolute, as all of the board of directors officers who voted on it were also staff members of *Green Egg*. But since the minutes of that fateful meeting were never published, the rest of the membership had no way of knowing what had actually come down. I was handed the honorary title of "publisher emeritus," with no more say in the content, vision, or direction of the award-winning magazine I had created, and the position of publisher was given over to Orion.

NARRATOR: It would be easy, and ultimately unfair, to frame all of this as just another episode in their ongoing drama—indeed, even after this incident, the next year the Ravenhearts still invited Orion and his family to move into one of the homes on the V-M Ranch.

OZ: Although devastated by what I felt to be profound betrayals, I continued to write for the magazine, as I believed it to be an essential service to the greater Pagan community, and I didn't want to see it disappear again.

NARRATOR: Still, this infighting between water-brothers, in addition to the sex scandals explored in the previous chapter, took its psychic toll on Oberon.

OZ: When I brought up my own pain and sense of betrayal over that action at the following Samhain rite, I was loudly condemned by Orion and accused of "breaking the chalice" of CAW trust and water-brotherhood. This interpretation, supported by the entire board and most (but, significantly, not all) of the Clergy Council, left deep wounds and alienation for many years thereafter, planting a poison of mistrust and a sense of betrayal deep within the heart of our core group. These were the darkest years of my life.

NARRATOR: Tom Williams has known OZ, and had been active in the CAW, since the original St. Louis Nest. Here he shares some of his memories of, and insight into, the experiences that caused him and many others to quit the Church.

TOM WILLIAMS: The night was Samhain 1996, and the Tribe had gathered at Annwfn, the sacred landhold of the Church of All Worlds in Northern California. It was part of an established magickal cycle that had been building momentum for some ten years and infusing that magickal energy back into the land from the love and dedication of hundreds of devotees of the Goddess and those who loved this place. We had poured our feasting, revelry, lovemaking, song, passion, tears, and ritual intent into this place to produce a truly enchanted sanctuary.

That was the bright side. There was another side. CAW has long been beset by controversy, rivalry, upset, and political intrigues that had caused many a long and agonizing encounter among Clergy and members in general. Up until this night we had mostly been able to keep these darker issues separate from our sacred workings or even, at times, to turn the energy generated at those workings towards healing or trying to heal the sorrier aspects of our entity as a Church. Seldom, if ever before, had those controversies intruded directly into a circle dedicated to magickal working focused on the health of the Tribe and the well-being of the land of Annwfn.

This night would be different. This night would signal a sea change in the energy flow that constituted the gestalt of the Church of All Worlds. This night the chalice would be shattered in the midst of the Magick Circle. This was the Night the Magick Died.

That night did not happen out of nowhere. There were seething conflicts afoot concerning the then Primate [Oberon] and his dealings with the Clergy and the membership. This night, however, broke the veil that separated the mundane world of organizational and business dealings from the world of the true magickal mission of the Northern California CAW. This was the Night the Magick Died.

In order to understand what was lost that night and how it has led to this situation, which signals the actual demise of the Church of All Worlds as an effective Neo-Pagan organization, it is necessary to understand what the magickal energy surrounding Annwfn actually was. I will probably not be believed in this by those who have only experienced CAW and its Magick at festivals, through Nests in remote places like the East Coast or the Midwest. What they have known of the magickal energy and vitality of the CAW in those parts of the country as opposed to its full power in its Northern California incarnation at Annwfn and at its celebration of the Eleusinian Mysteries at the Pinnacles caves is but a pale shadow. Indeed, they know not, though they think they do.

Of all the things CAW has done, the cycles of the Eleusinian Mysteries and the Beltane/Samhain fertility cycle enacted at Annwfn are the most meaningful and significant contributions to Magick and the understanding of the meanings of life's enigma we could have imparted to those members fortunate enough to experience them in the time in which they prevailed. This is not something that those who experienced CAW only from printed literature or online discussions can remotely comprehend. An understanding of Magick can only be achieved by an experience of Magick. That is why I considered the entire online presence of CAW to have been utterly worthless and degrading to the vision we once held.

They were two interwoven magickal/mythical cycles, the Mysteries and the Corn Cycle. Of the Mysteries, I can speak but little, for I have twice carried the energy of Lord Hades and refuse to profane those sacred rites by revealing their secrets to the uninitiated. Suffice to say that a sincere participation in those rituals could bestow on the initiate a deep appreciation for and understanding of the endless round of birth, life, death, and renewal and bring to that person a reverence for his or her place in the tapestry of existence. But perhaps I have already spoken too much.

Of the Corn Cycle I may speak more openly, although it, too, concerns the cycle of birth, death, and rebirth, albeit on a more "Earthy" level. In truly and faithfully enacting this cycle on the landhold of Annwfn, we not only involved ourselves and our co-worshippers in the magickal energy of birth, death, and renewal. We also infused our magickal energy into the land itself, making it a sacred and sanctified place that welcomed our Tribe and opened itself to our Workings.

Four great Sabbats were dedicated to these two cycles: Mabon and Ostara to the Eleusinian Mysteries, and Beltane and Samhain to the rites of the Corn Cycle. Thus did the cycle turn through the year for our Tribe. This, then, is the magickal wonder that was shattered on the Night the Magick Died.

On the Night the Magick Died we were in a sacred Circle that was a Samhain Circle dedicated to continuing the cycle. It was here that these mundane controversies of Clergy and member strife boiled over into that sacred Circle and broke the Circle. Since that night, the steady decline of magickal energy at Annwfn and in both cycles—Eleusinia and Corn—has continued to this day. I wish I had not witnessed the hurt and anger and pain that were brought into that Circle that night. Nothing has ever been the same since.

After that night, the National Park Service denied access to the Pinnacles caves where the Mysteries were performed (breeding time for bats). Since that night, the May couples have experienced misfortunes to the point that this past Beltane the May energies were buried and returned to the Earth as if we were no longer worthy to carry them. I have little hope that they will ever be resurrected by a CAW ritual again. Since then the Magick has died. It died that night—the Night the Magick Died.

This night was neither the cause nor the end result of the problems plaguing CAW. There was an almost pathological denial of obvious dysfunction that allowed totally unqualified persons to be ordained as Clergy. There was also a long-standing feud over the allegations of teenagers having sex with adults. Over a number of years we allowed a charming sexual predator into our midst in the person of Adam Walks-Between-Worlds. This creature had a habit of insinuating his sexual attentions on women (often young and impressionable) with promises of magickal initiation. Another ploy was to break up relationships and then move in on the female. This latter tactic may be what ultimately got him murdered in L.A.—a case that has yet to be solved. His "seductions" left a number of women emotionally wounded and traumatized, and several of them complained directly to individual Clergy members. Still, CAW remained blind to his depredations for years, although to its credit, the Clergy finally did take action.

Given this background, the Night the Magick Died was what is called a "signal event." It was a sign—had we been able to heed it—that there had been a change. That change began before that night and continued long after it.

NARRATOR: There were major ramifications from all of this. I would just like to point out that I don't think anybody was pleased with the end results. The hurt feelings, anger, mistrust, and sense of betrayal went on for years, and just when it seemed like the conflict might be over and that it couldn't possibly get any worse, it did. In 1998, Oberon was "impeached," and although some would disagree with his word choice, no one can dispute that it happened. A few years later the CAW board of directors dissolved *Green Egg* altogether, and, once again, Pagandom's most legendary publication seemed destined to become but a footnote in history.

Right around the beginning of the millennium, a new board of directors was established, and the board operations were moved to Ohio. By this point there were about 1,300 CAW members across the United States (and elsewhere) who were connected by members-only CAW email lists, and who had full voting privileges. In 2002, Oberon was not even invited to the fortieth-anniversary annual meeting of the church. Under the leadership of Jim Looman, an Ohio resident who got elected president, the board of directors was able to change the ways the Church was run to their own personal financial advantage. They proceeded to gut the Church's treasury and other resources like corporate raiders. The extent of what they did, and why they did it, will probably never be understood, because all the records have been "lost."

OZ: The officers of the board of directors in Ohio voted themselves an unprecedented income, to pay for which it was rumored that they intended to sell off the Church's sacred land of Annwfn (bequeathed to CAW by our late Bard, Gwydion Pendderwen, upon his tragic death in a car accident in 1982) and take the money. I was appalled.

Most of the finest people who had been inspired by CAW over all those years, and had gathered together into its worldwide Tribe, left in dismay and disgust. I could no longer recommend that anyone become involved in the new "CAW Inc.," which embraced ripping off and fucking over as a matter of company policy. And—following my principle of "If you don't like it, you can't have any"—I denied my permission for them to use any of my own writings and artwork in their new organization. Let them write and illustrate their own sermons, theological treatises, histories, handbooks, FAQ sheets, liturgy, tracts, etc.!

To counter this painful estrangement somewhat, Liza Gabriel-Ravenheart composed a brilliantly succinct synopsis of "The Church of All Worlds Tradition"—as distinct from "CAW Inc.," the corporation. This document summarized beautifully the essence of the religion that I had worked so hard to create, and in which I still deeply believed. I hoped eventually to develop a website dedicated to the "Church of All

Worlds Tradition," which would make available to everyone the forty years' worth of good stuff we conceived and created when CAW was a Pagan religion and a "congregational" Church, rather than a secular business, as "CAW Inc." was set up.

LIZA: I wrote the seminal document "The Church of All Worlds Tradition," later published in *Creating Circles and Ceremonies*. The idea to write it was Morning Glory's, but the actual document was written by me and at my initiative. This document became the focus of a high-volume list-serve among CAW members. It helped catalyze the rebirth of the Church of All Worlds after its demise. This was a magical working that resonated with the "Open Source" movement in software today. By setting the CAW tradition free from its institutional moorings, we empowered anyone and everyone to participate—and they continued to do so!

To his credit, Oberon saw the wisdom in this. I still consider myself a proud practitioner of the CAW tradition—beholden to no one and connected, through water, to everyone. I later discovered that translating the vision of a group or individuals in this way is a gift I can give to anyone who is open to it, and it is a major part of my work now, something I continue to be excited about.

OZ: At the CAW annual general meeting, held on August 1, 2004, Jim Looman was re-elected president, and the board of directors (BoD) issued "A Resolution for Implementing the Dormancy of Church of All Worlds, Inc." It stated:

> *Be It Resolved that the Board of Directors, Church of All Worlds, Inc., authorizes the Officers and the Director of Operations to take whatever actions necessary to wind up its affairs and cease doing business by September 1, 2004 or as soon thereafter as possible, and Be It Further Resolved that the Board of Directors, Church of All Worlds, Inc., authorizes the following specific actions: To cease to accept new memberships and the renewal of existing memberships by authority of {3.8} of the Constitution; To cancel all lifetime memberships by authority of {3.8} of the Constitution; To terminate or all publications, websites, email lists and any other form of public contact. To notify all*

individual members and Local Congregations of this decision so that they may go their own way or organize and affiliate as they wish; To terminate all business relationships; To terminate or escrow all Licenses; To satisfy all creditors possible, either fully or partially, in any legal way possible until there is nothing of value left; To close all bank accounts; To inform the proper sections of the IRS that we are ceasing operations so that they may retire our EIN, our 501(c)(3) status, and our group exemption letter; To complete all of the above by June 1, 2005 VOTE: 6 aye, 2 stand aside, 1 nay.

But immediately afterwards, the entire BoD resigned en masse, and none of those items were actually implemented. And in October, Jim Looman died. Thus ended in ignominy the second incarnation of the Church of All Worlds: 1985–2004. *Requiescat in Pace.*

NARRATOR: The year 2004 also saw the end of the story of Red Daniel, started in the previous chapter. He had eventually settled down into a long-term relationship with one of the young women he'd been involved with. It lasted for over ten years, until she was well into her twenties.

MG: When his relationship with his lady finally failed and she left him in a fit of despair and frustration with his perpetual self-destructive adolescence, he completely went to pieces and started drinking and doing speed—hanging out with genuine low-life types.

We let him sleep on our sofa and spent time counseling him and helping him get his life back together. And then finally, his only daughter, who had gotten married, had a baby and invited him to come up and spend some time with his grandchild. He was making plans to get a truck and camper setup so he could do that. He had been working at a sort of farm where the owner rented to speed freaks, and Daniel had been promised a truck in exchange for his work. When he went to pick up the vehicle on August 18, 2004, he was met by one of the tweakers, who shot him down and left him for dead.

NARRATOR: In 2006 a jury convicted James Zook of first-degree murder for killing Daniel; he was sentenced to fifty years to life in a state prison.

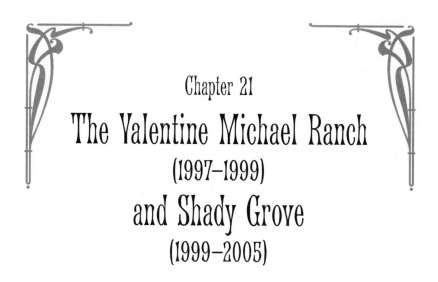

Chapter 21
The Valentine Michael Ranch
(1997–1999)
and Shady Grove
(1999–2005)

We've jumped gaping chasms, done impossible things;
Where there were walls we've somehow made open doors.
And I know that whatever the future may bring,
We will Love ever deeper than before!

—FROM "THE HAVEN OF OUR HEARTS" [RAVENHEART FAMILY THEME SONG]
BY LIZA GABRIEL, WYNTER, AND MORNING GLORY, 1996

NARRATOR: From 1996 through 1999, during some of the most difficult times described in the previous chapter, the Ravenhearts lived on the V-M Ranch. As OZ became less active in the Church, and, eventually, not active at all, he put more and more of his energy into the Family business.

It was also during those years, in September 1997, that Morning Glory led an expedition sponsored by CAW's Ecosophical Research Association (ERA) to ancient sacred sites in Greece and the Aegean Islands. She stayed in Greece for six weeks.

MG: My journey to Greece felt like a homecoming. I paid my first visit at Eleusis to the Plutonion where Hades made his entrance into the Underworld, and all the hairs on my body just stood straight up. There were several little cave openings, but you couldn't really get inside any of them. However, in one entrance it was clear that the Dark Lord still had his worshippers, because there were offerings of bread and pomegranates and other things lying inside the opening where the cavern got bigger. We made our offerings of bread to Demeter in the Telesterion, and the guide pointed out that a little church that had been built on the hill above the ruins still received the gift of the first loaves of bread baked after the harvest and had done so for the last two thousand years. So the customs were still being observed though the altars had changed places.

NARRATOR: After the group tour ended, she stayed in Greece and went back to Eleusis with a local Pagan named Sirius.

MG: I felt that I had unfinished business with Hades. So we went back to Eleusis. I went to the opening of the cave and sat on the stone, putting my head and shoulders inside the opening. I made an offering of a pomegranate that I had brought all the way from Crete. As I sat on the cold stone gazing into the cavern, I felt an electric thrill travel through the stone and up through my body. And before my very eyes one of the stone formations in the cave shifted shape into the face of the God, and He spoke inside my mind. His face looked like a composite of all the lovers I have ever had who carried dark energy, and His voice had the quality of a knife slicing through black silk. He told me many things that were private, but in the end I cried and asked Him not to leave me.

He laughed: "I am always here, I never leave; it is you who always comes and goes." I felt a lightness and comfort in my heart and was grateful for that and all the other insights I received. Then He told me before I left that Hecate wanted to speak to me and gave me precise directions how to get to Her precinct. I didn't want to leave; it was orgasmically wonderful just gazing on His face like that. His image never wavered before my eyes until I forced myself to tear them away. I heard His voice say in farewell, "Don't worry, you will see Me again, everyone always does sooner or later . . ." So I arose and stretched the kinks out of my back and followed His directions to find Hecate's shrine.

I entered Her precinct and found an altar of broken stone near a twisted fig tree. I placed an offering of a ripe prickly pear smeared with my own blood on the stone and listened inward; almost at once I heard Her voice in my ear: "We used to be such good friends." And then I remembered how I used to love to go out in the dark when there was no moon and listen to the night.

Hecate continued, "But once you took up with Aphrodite you never came to Me anymore." I felt consumed by guilt and shame.

"That's all right, I hold no malice; such are the ways that mortals dance to Nature's tune. Besides, soon you will be Mine." I felt an icy needle prick at my heart—what exactly did She mean by that? Considering who She was, that statement could have a variety of meanings.

"Lady, what do You mean?" I asked, trembling inside.

She laughed. "Don't be in such a hurry; you'll find out soon enough." It was the same answer that I had gotten over thirty years before from the woman who had died on my shift in the ER. I asked Hecate if She had any other messages for me, but Her voice was silent and the sense of Her presence was gone.

NARRATOR: When she returned to the States, Morning Glory, Wolf, and Oberon were joined in a triad handfasting. Liza and Wynter participated as "ladies-in-waiting."

OZ: We felt that since Wolf had been the first to come into our relationship, he should be the first to be handfasted to us. Next would be Liza and then, finally, Wynter. But despite our impeccable intentions in handfasting each partner sequentially by seniority, this apparently didn't go down well with Liza and Wynter, who evidently thought we should do it all together. The whole issue of seniority in relationships, which is fundamental to the way MG and I operate, was always difficult for them to accept.

MG: OZ and I had proposed to Wolf long before we all moved in together, and so it felt like this would just be part of the unfolding of the natural sequence of events. The three of us seemed to take it for granted that we were sort of the founding triad, but that did not set well with Wynter and Liza. On the other hand, they did not really talk to me about it much, but there was a certain amount of moping about. I did everything I could to include them in the ceremony.

LIZA : Oberon and I were quite deeply involved at the time of that handfasting, and he was handfasting with someone who was hardly speaking to me. That did not seem like honoring our connection. I'm not complaining about this. I had to deal with what I had, because I was in that kind of a state of passion where you don't turn back because it's hard—no matter how hard it is, you just do it. Part of that was because of the impersonal nature of my relationship with Oberon, because of the vision. The vision trumps everything—it trumps any kind of irrational weirdness that goes on. No one ever dragged me kicking and screaming; I always had the option to leave. But one becomes more and more invested.

Wynter and I were both maids of honor dressed in black. It was a charade from our point of view.

WYNTER: Partly we wore black to the wedding because that's what Morning Glory wanted. She was wearing red, and she wanted something to complement that. But partly we wore black because we were both really distraught over the wedding. We were both coping the best we could. It was hard on both of us for different reasons. For me, it was like I was falling in love with Wolfie, and his response to falling in love with me was to marry another woman. As open-minded and out there as I am, that threw me. I had two of my best friends and lovers marrying each other and not me. I was young and pissed off.

MG: I never understood what the problem was, because for me when you love someone, you want them to be happy; and when the people you love are in love with each other, it should make everyone even happier. It is from such assumptions when they are not equally shared that idyllic faerie castles fall into ruins.

WYNTER: Wolf was my principal primary partner, and he came first in all things—second only to me! We shared a lot of triad experiences. On specific nights I slept with Morning Glory or Wolf—we tried to keep it fair as much as is emotionally possible.

But sometimes I would sleep with Wolf just so he wouldn't sleep with Morning Glory, and this kind of behavior affected my relationship with both of them. Another thing: Morning Glory had to go from being his primary partner—the only woman in his life—to being the secondary. And I was none too gentle about claiming my position and my emotional turf as primary partner with Wolf.

NARRATOR: As the Ravenhearts' interpersonal relationships grew difficult, they continued to perform handfastings among the various members, almost to try to patch things up when the going got rough. The next couple to handfast were Morning Glory and Wynter because, in Morning Glory's words, their relationship "was the one that needed a boost." At this handfasting in 1998, it was Oberon and Liza who were left feeling excluded from the decision.

Meanwhile, their family business continued to blossom. After working on her for two years, OZ finally finished his sculpture called the Millennial Gaia in 1998, which became one of their bestsellers.

WOLF: I introduced the color catalogues, and we started going to trade shows and doing a lot of promotion. Oberon did a lot of sculpting. Our inventory was growing. We had the new Millennial Gaia, which was a really big deal. That was possibly the single most important piece that they ever did. It provided the majority of sales.

NARRATOR: The plans to buy the V-M Ranch did not work out, which was partly another consequence of the conflicts described in the previous chapters. So the Ravenhearts had to find another place to live and to continue the Family business in 1999. As usual, their new household included other friends and lovers in addition to the Ravenhearts.

MG: We packed up and moved to Sonoma County, to a house we called Shady Grove that we found in Penngrove. Liza's mother took out the mortgage; Liza made the down payment; and we divided up the $2,000-per-month mortgage payments in the form of rent to be paid on the various dwellings and offices on the parcel.

LIZA: It was a very happy, perky family in some ways when we first moved there. Wolf and Wynter were all romantic, and they were happily ensconced in their apartment. Oberon and Morning Glory were living in the main house, and so was I. [Oberon's lover] Ariel was living in a downstairs apartment in another building; [MG's lover] Alejandro was living upstairs; and Jon was living in the back cottage. [Jon was Liza's lover at the time.] It took a while for this all to take place. We had no idea, but as soon as we moved there our friends wanted to live with us. It quickly became a wonderful, warm kind of environment where we really liked all of the people we were living with. Then things began to decay a little bit, as things will. We had business meeting after business meeting after business meeting. No matter what we talked about, no matter what we decided, it didn't seem to make any difference to the outcome. I shouldn't say nothing was accomplished, but very little. Wolf just never, ever got along with me.

NARRATOR: The final handfasting of this group was between Wolf and Wynter in 2000.

WYNTER: I think that both of us always assumed that we'd get married, because of the depth of our relationship. Not only did we assume that we'd get married, but our community and our families also assumed that we'd get married. And we didn't take the time to step back and say, "Is that where we really are now in our life together?" We were both caught up in "this is what we must do." Not that there wasn't love and desire there, and strength in our relationship. But if we had taken the time to step back and look at the situation, I think we might not have gotten married. And that's not to say that I didn't want to marry him. But we were two very different people by the time we reached the altar. I felt like it was more of a celebration of the relationship that we'd had than the relationship that we were going to have.

And during that time, right around the time we moved to Shady Grove, I was developing a deep relationship with a couple. I was spending a lot of time with them. There was a lot of stuff going on there that I won't go into.

OZ: August 11, 1999, was the long-awaited final total solar eclipse of the millennium, with the path of totality crossing the entire Eurasian continent from Cornwall, England, to the Bay of Bengal. Ariel and I flew to London right after Starwood, carrying magickal talismans from many people. Of all the dozens of Witches, Druids, Magicians, Priests, and Priestesses who had worked together twenty years before, creating the first phase of this Millennial Eclipse ritual, only I was able to complete the final component at the ancient stone circle of Boscawen-ûn in Cornwall.

I got home just in time for the Eleusinian Mysteries, which our whole Family was putting on this year. Morning Glory was Priestess; Wynter was Persephone; Wolf was Hades; Liza was Hecate; and I was the Poet. The entire all-night ritual went fabulously, with perfect timing, culminating at sunrise. It was exactly the ritual that MG and I had been envisioning from the beginning, so many years ago.

MG: I had wanted to Priestess the Eleusinian Mysteries for many years. My research and my poetry were germinal in creating the original script; I had undergone initiation and then participated actively, taking many different roles over the years. Then several times I had put my name in the hat to be the Priestess of the Rites. It was largely a role that Anodea had made her own, and as long as she wanted to keep doing it, no one else wanted to stand in her way because she was doing a great job. But the Mysteries were evolving and moving into directions that I felt took it away from the intent of its original creators and its ancient focus, so I really was itching for an opportunity to do a cycle that refocused them back into an earlier direction. Finally it came down that Anodea no longer wanted to handle the Mysteries, so at that point I just swept in and said, "Look, I'm doing it this year. I have the cast, I have the script, I have the props, and that's that." At that point I had gotten pretty fed up with asking permission and being told I wasn't worthy to be Priestess, especially when I had been a major part of the creation of the thing in the first place.

I had already gotten the ball rolling by the time I went to Greece, so I was able to really use my time at Eleusis to bring in some very powerful magickal connections to the ancient rites. For a number of years Wynter and Wolf had been working with the Persephone and Hades archetypes in their relationship, and it just seemed like the Fates had stirred all these things together into a Ravenhearts' Eleusinia. The last piece in the puzzle was when Liza said that she wanted to take on the role of Hecate.

LIZA: The year that the Ravenhearts did it, I was in charge of providing breakfast. I wasn't careful enough, and the whole thing was eaten by feral pigs in the night. They were huge. Not quite the size of Volkswagens, but they looked like black Volkswagens. You did not want to argue with these guys.

We held these archetypes the entire year and invited all the initiates of the Mysteries to our home. Hecate is the Goddess of Death, of the crossroads and of divination. I performed a divination with the Tarot that day for every initiate who wanted one.

MG: We had a great group of pilgrims that year, and Talyn decided he wanted to be initiated so that he could bring the Mysteries back to his part of the country. The all-night ritual is always somewhat of an ordeal and it is intended that way, but this year we had an additional crisis in that one of the pilgrims injured his ankle. But he decided to tough it out and continue through until the dawn. When the dawn came and the rite reached its climax, it was almost as though it was the moment of greatest triumph and cohesion for our Ravenheart Family as well. It was a moment that in spite of pigs and sprained ankles and exhaustion transmuted all the lead of our exertions into pure gold. For one single, shining moment we were all united in something ancient, powerful, and greater than all of us combined—and we had worked together to co-create this miracle of transformation. I think we all felt the Gods move through us and within us, and regardless of whatever else was to come, for that one moment we came together as One entity.

LIZA: The most extraordinary thing [because the Eleusinian Mysteries were cancelled in 2000 due to a crisis, and no Mysteries were held in 2001] was that during our reign as the Archetypes of the Underworld, 9/11 happened. The evening of September 11th we spontaneously performed what was in my memory the most powerful magical working we performed as a family. We gathered, dressed in our ritual costumes, and with very little preparation we said, "Okay, we're taking on our archetypes." We called a few people who circled with us often and were local there, and we said, "Do you want to come?" A few people joined us, but it was basically us and our lovers and friends who happened to be onsite at the time, and Wynter's two large boas.

We each spoke spontaneously, from our archetypes, our blessing, and our reassurance and guidance for the souls who had died and were dying. The towers had fallen less than twelve hours before. In that ritual we were able to use the sense of being in these archetypes to help these souls cross over to another place. It wasn't a sense that the souls were going to be Pagans and opt into the Underworld as we saw it. It was more a sense that people had died in terror, and that we could help ease their journey. Now, whether we eased anyone's journey or not I have no idea. But I do know that it was a meaningful ritual. And that it can be helpful, when you're dealing with horrors, to feel like you have some contact with death and the Underworld to help mediate an experience like that.

NARRATOR: In spite of their magickal compatibility, in the real world people drift apart and relationships change. In the early years of the new millennium, the Ravenheart Family structure continued to morph. Oberon, Morning Glory, and Wolf left on a business trip that was also meant to rekindle the spark and reconnect with each other as a triad. Unfortunately, they all got the flu and it was a disaster. While they were gone, their home was broken into.

WYNTER: I was home one weekend by myself. I had gone out briefly and I came back, and my house had been broken into. The door was broken and the house was open—I was just violated. All of my grandmother's jewelry had been stolen. At the time Wolf was in Florida with

Oberon and Morning Glory on a trip that he didn't want to be on, because he was really sick. It was supposed to be some kind of getaway, and the whole time was very miserable for all of them for different reasons. Liza was away for the weekend at a sacred sex workshop. So I put the house back together as best I could, and I hightailed out to the home of the couple that I was in a relationship with.

There was something about my relationship with Wolf that kind of broke during that time. He was so caught up in whatever was happening in his relationship or whatever was going on with him and Morning Glory and Oberon that he couldn't pull away and come take care of me in my time of need. It was a situation that created depth in one relationship and distance in another.

There was me finding out what I needed, and what was happening in my life and where I wanted to go. I looked at the future and thought, "If I'm doing this for the next ten or fifteen years, where will I be?" And I didn't want to be in the same place. I didn't want to be in my thirties and making statues and living hand-to-mouth and overdrawing the checking account because we're not bringing in enough. There were a lot of wonderful things about living with Oberon and Morning Glory, but they have a difficult time with reality, with the world at large as it is now.

WOLF: Anytime you're dealing with any kind of relationship, whether you're dealing with multiple or single relationships, whether it's poly or monogamous, there are always issues of people simply going in different directions. The major thing that went on is that Morning Glory and Oberon were really pretty much headed down one particular path, and all of us kind of shared that path for a while, but it really wasn't ours. Wynter left first, going off and doing her own thing, having more of a young person's life; the thing about life is it changes.

NARRATOR: During the years that followed, Wynter spent more time away focusing on new relationships and less time at the house with the Ravenhearts, until finally she was gone. Morning Glory's life became further complicated when she realized that she was going into menopause.

MG: Then I had a flash of insight about my visit with Hecate in Greece. When She said, "You've been spending all your time with Aphrodite, but that's all right because soon you will be Mine"—suddenly I understood what She meant. She is the Goddess of Transformation, and I was on the threshold of one of the major transformations in a woman's life. So I decided that if Hecate had spoken to me about this, it meant that She intended to be my guide through this transition. And if that was so, then I needed to do a Hecate vision quest and find out what She intended for me.

NARRATOR: On her vision quest, MG got her assignment: to create a Hecate statue, and to spend more time with her mother to learn what it means to grow old.

MG: In honor of all the wisdom that the Goddess shared with me during that time, I created a statue of Her that was to be my masterwork the way that the Millennial Gaia is Oberon's masterwork. I asked Her what She wanted from me and She said, "Many people need me in their lives as much as you do. You are an artist; put me on their altars." So Hecate is now on many altars all over the world because of that Vision and my efforts. There are times in your life when you can be satisfied with your work and proud that you have done the right thing, and this was one of those times for me.

And I started visiting my mother, Polly, more often. It had been hard for her when I left to move from Ukiah to Laytonville and then again down to Sonoma County. But she was deeply involved with her church and its community of friends, and so everything seemed to be going along on cruise control for a while. But one of the things I found out when I spent more time with Polly was that her precarious health was going downhill, and it was becoming increasingly hard for her to maintain her separate life alone. First I got her a housekeeper and cook, but then just getting around the house was too hard, so her doctor recommended that she be put in a rest home. I was appalled because I knew that a person without an effective advocate in a rest home usually does not last very long, and I lived too far from her for that.

What Polly needed was assisted living, but we certainly couldn't afford that. After calling every single elderly assistance program in the county and visiting every possible facility, I reached a point of complete despair. I was sitting in the living room with my head in my hands when Liza walked through and asked what the problem was. I explained it to her, and she thought about it for a few minutes and then she said, "Well, why don't we move her in here with us? She could move into Jon's apartment since he moved out."

I was flabbergasted at her suggestion. It would never have occurred to me to ask Liza to even consider moving Polly into our community because I knew how she valued her privacy and how involved she was with the Sacred Sexuality community. I couldn't imagine how we could make something as disparate as an old Christian lady and weekend sex seminars somehow coexist in the same backyard. But Liza said that Polly was a very special person with a very special point of view about love; so if anybody could manage to pull it off, we would be the ones. I just broke down crying, and I hugged her and thanked her and then went around to everybody else and asked them all if they were open to the possibility of having Polly live at Shady Grove. And to my deep relief, Polly had found her way into everyone's heart. I called Polly and told her that everyone had invited her to come and live with us and to have her own space and that I would be her caregiver. Polly tearfully agreed, but it was hard for her to leave behind all her friends and her Christian church and move to a new place where the only people she knew were her Pagan family. But she quoted from the Bible what Naomi had said to her daughter-in-law Ruth: "Whither thou goest I shall go, and thy people shall be my people." And so it was.

In the midst of all this grief around CAW and the ups and downs of Ravenheart Family dynamics, there were lots of truly wonderful times. We had many Family feasts together and spent long hours lounging in the hot tub. We created some fantastic art, Wynter's Elemental plaques of the Bird Goddess and the Sea Goddess, Oberon's Odin sculpture, my Hecate statue. We spent time laughing and having pillow fights, going to movies and concerts together. We grew a terrific garden every year, which was mostly Oberon and Liza's bailiwick. We raised chickens and rabbits and had our own fresh eggs. Our houses were invaded by possums, raccoons, skunks, and rats, but we found it to be more amusing than distressing. We made lots of new friends and traveled to many gatherings and festivals together, having great adventures along the way.

OZ: About that time, a British author named J. K. Rowling started writing a series of books about a young wizard who was going to school to study magick and sorcery. She opened up this place in the universe where suddenly it was reasonable to talk about Wizards and Wizardry. Before that, you couldn't say it. People would look at you and go, "Huh?" Then suddenly it's all over the place.

Every now and then something creates a breakthrough, an opening in the world for something to appear. We humans are storytellers—that is our greatest magick, and one of our first. We sat around the campfire and we created ourselves; we created humanity by telling stories. The stories, in turn, create us—they shape us: the myths, the legends, the common references and metaphors. All these things are deeply rooted in our collective psyche. When a story attains a level of popularity like the *Harry Potter* books, millions of people have read this common story and therefore share this common mythos.

When J. K. Rowling created the *Harry Potter* stories, she incorporated an aspect that many people seem not to have noticed. In other stories of magick, from *The Wizard of Oz* to *The Lord of the Rings*, *Narnia*, and *Star Wars*, it's all someplace else—somewhere over the rainbow, or in a long-lost ancient world, through a magick wardrobe, or even in another galaxy, a long time ago and far, far away. But the *Harry Potter* saga is set in our world, and in our time. Its central premise is that just beyond the mundane, everyday reality that you see is a sort of hidden and invisible society. But they're real people, and they could be walking down the streets passing by you and you might never even know it. They have their places that they go to, and it's all right here in the present-day world. And this is true.

In the *Harry Potter* mythos there is a magical world, with magical people, just around the corner. If you could find the right alley, or knew the right password, maybe you, too, could get in there. Maybe you belong there.

MG: It seems to be just the universe next door, and most of us as kids were desperate to find the key that would unlock that door and become part of that universe. Many things have changed in the world but not the desire of certain special kids to find their way into the realm of magick.

OZ: For a number of years I'd been lamenting at presentations in the Pagan community, and especially in the Wiccan community, that we didn't really have a way to assimilate our kids. The whole thing was set up for adults only. You had to be eighteen before you could even apply to start studying or to join a coven or something. All of the online services there were available you had to be eighteen. There really wasn't anything major for kids to get involved with except some programming at Pagan Festivals.

NARRATOR: Following the popularity of Rowling's growing trend, Oberon was offered a book contract by New Page Books to write what he described as "a book of apprentice Wizardry, sort of a *Boy Scout Handbook* for young Wizards; what you need to know when you start off; what I wish I could have gotten hold of when I was eleven." He was eager to dive in.

OZ: What I wanted to do was bigger than just what I know. I know a lot of stuff, because I've been around awhile. But one of the most important things I know is how many people know more than I do. Our community is full of Wizards, sages, and mages. These people are the world-class experts on magickal stuff. And really, this was something that should not just be a one-person job. This should be something in which the collective wisdom of our community could be compiled into one place, and offered to the next generation.

So I started talking to these folks, and we decided to form the legendary Wizards Council.

Part of the mythos and legend of Magick and Wizardry throughout all the ages of both history and of myth, is the idea of the Council of Wizards, such as the White Council in *Lord of the Rings*. There have been many schools and councils and associations of mages and Wizards and such. Unlike the village Witch, who is usually just all by herself on the edge of the village somewhere, Wizards tend to create schools, starting with Plato's Academy in ancient Athens, founded in 387 BCE. So we started talking about this, and it wasn't very long before we had gathered a rather amazing group of people and formed the Grey Council.

Utilizing the same skills and contacts I'd developed over a forty-year career as a writer, editor, and publisher of *Green Egg*, I coordinated and integrated contributions from many of the leading teachers in the magickal community, wrote everything else I felt needed to be said, drew many illustrations, formatted, and laid it all out in PageMaker.

NARRATOR: It was around this time that an old flame returned to OZ's life. Her name was Julie, and he had first crossed paths with her back in the late '80s and early '90s.

JULIE EPONA: My then-husband Dr. Aidan Kelly and I ended up living in Los Angeles in the early '90s. We became involved with a CAW Nest that was started in Hollywood and then went to the San Fernando Valley. As a part of that Nest, we attended the 1992 Grand Convocation of the CAW. It was very hot and very dry. I was camping with a two-year-old boy, which was quite an endeavor. What Aidan had worked out was that he'd get one night and I'd get one night, because you can't go off and leave a two-year-old in the tent. The fog came in and I happened to wander down towards the drumming. It was getting chilly, and there was the Wizard with his huge, gray wool cloak lined with green flannel, and he offered to wrap me inside of it with him. Well, no girl in her right mind would refuse such an offer. So I snuggled in next to him. There was drumming, storytelling, and various frivolities going on.

I sat there and enjoyed my time with the Wizard. I wandered off in the fog with him. We couldn't see much beyond the edges of the trail we were on. He had a beautiful staff named Pathfinder. At that point it was very much like walking through the forest with Gandalf. We were getting to know each other, and lo and behold we ended up at his tent instead of mine and spent an absolutely wonderful night together. We really established a magical connection that held us in very good stead. We saw each other a couple of times over the next year. I participated in the Eleusinian Mysteries and a Beltane ritual. But his life took him off on some very different adventures, and mine became very focused on trying to raise my son and provide for him. So we lost track of each other for a while.

NARRATOR: Unbeknownst to Oberon, she'd split from Aidan Kelly (a famous Witch in his own right, he'd co-founded the New Reformed Orthodox Order of the Golden Dawn), remarried, and moved to Santa Rosa, settling down in order to provide a stable home for her son Aidan O'Ryan Kelly.

JULIE EPONA: We reconnected in 2003 while he was working on his *Grimoire for the Apprentice Wizard*. When we picked up the conversation again after nearly ten years, it was like there had never been a break in it.

NARRATOR: By the next year, she would break up with her then-husband; her son would go to Washington state to live with his father; and she would move in with the Ravenhearts at Shady Grove.

OZ: She settled right into life with the Ravenhearts, and joined MG and me in our Mythic Images booth and presentations at PantheaCon, a huge Pagan conference held every February in a San Jose hotel, where the three of us bonded wonderfully as a great team. She landed Wolf a great job with the company she worked for, and he has worked there ever since.

JULIE EPONA: My relationship with Oberon has always been that of a girlfriend, and I have always been a girlfriend to both him and Morning Glory. My relationship wouldn't be possible for me without my practice of polyamory, and really honoring their relationship as primary, and all that entails in terms of communication, honesty, and working together to make sure that all the juice is going to support everyone in the group. There is no one true right and only way to being polyamorous, anymore than there is any one true right and only way to be Pagan. But it's the constant communication and negotiation that allows it to work.

NARRATOR: Even before she moved in with the Ravenhearts, she helped Oberon with his *Grimoire*.

JULIE EPONA: I contributed to some of the material in the *Grimoire* regarding young men, because I am primarily a single mom, and I had been a Cub Scout leader and was participating in the Boy Scouts at the time. So, in bringing some of that understanding of what young men are facing today in terms of ethics—it hadn't occurred to Oberon to look at the gang violence and extreme peer pressure and bullying as a form of black magick.

OZ: I spent all of 2003 working on the book. If you read the *Grimoire*, and note carefully, you'll see that the reading level goes up a year chapter by chapter. I worked with an editor who had worked with children's books and could set the vocabulary and the style and reading level to progress over a seven-year period. So, by the time you're reading the last chapter, you're reading it at seven years advanced from the very first one. Sort of like what J. K. Rowling did with the *Harry Potter* series. I sent the disc off to New Page on December 16, and my author's copy of the *Grimoire* arrived on Brigit's Day, February 1, 2004. The *Grimoire* was a big hit—soon ranking as the number-one bestseller for New Page. But before it was even out, we knew we needed something more.

NARRATOR: In retrospect, it seems almost incredible that Oberon had not written a book before that point, given all the writing and editing he'd done over the course of his life. The *Grimoire* basically started a new career as author for him. In the years that followed, he would go on to publish *Companion for the Apprentice Wizard* and *Creating Circles and Ceremonies*. Both were very successful, making it onto New Page's list of "Bestsellers" in the #2 and #4 spots, respectively—right behind the *Grimoire*. He also later co-authored another book, *A Wizard's Bestiary*, with Ash "LeopardDancer" DeKirk; it was the book he'd conceived back in the mid-'70s while doing research with Morning Glory, and it included more than 1,500 illustrations. But when the *Grimoire* first came out, he had only one thing on his mind: a magickal school.

MG: The thing that makes *Harry Potter*, the whole cycle of those books, catch fire for kids and for adults, especially in the mundane world, is that they think, "I know there has got to be something more out there than going home and watching TV, or going to work, or going to school at this dull place where people bore me." Because they can feel the Magick streaming behind everything in the universe.

When the first *Harry Potter* book came along, I read it, and I went, "Oh, that is so cool! I want to teach at that school!" I had all these great stories that I made up about it. I tried to go on some of the websites to play around with some of the other folks, but the problem was that I already had access to a much richer world. And what they were trying to do with those websites was to be just about the *Harry Potter* books, and it only went that deep. And I thought, "Boy, there really needs to be something that goes all the way down, that's all about the real stuff."

So OZ and I, Liza, and the other Ravenhearts started dialoguing about it, and what we could do to create such a school. And of course the Internet was the perfect place to do it.

OZ: For one thing, it should not be religious—not even overtly Pagan, because we're not trying to recruit people's kids into some funny religion, even if it's our own. But Wizardry is not a religion. It's like philosophy or science. You can have philosophers, scientists, or Wizards in any tradition or religion. Every culture has produced great Wizards, and we needed to preserve that. I didn't want this to be identified as just a Pagan thing. It had to be universal.

Wizardry is the most authenticated profession that has ever been. That's because the Wizards of old have left us their teachings and writings. They wrote stuff down. In many cases they were the only literate people in the community. Thus we have an entire history of Wizardry— it's worldwide, and it's in every culture. It connects with shamanism at one end and science at the other.

When I began writing it, I figured that I'd design the *Grimoire* itself as a course of basic studies, and then simply refer readers to various websites and online schools of Wizardry where they could go for further teachings. Since I'd taken particular pains to design a book that would be accessible to teenagers, I also wanted to make sure that sites I would be referring my readers to would be teen-friendly as well.

I had heard there were a lot of online schools of magick, so I went looking for a website that was teaching magick in a non-religious context. I wanted this to be for readers as young as eleven, like the book.

But I simply couldn't find any online sources or schools dedicated to serious Wizardry or Magick that were suitable for teens, and that weren't specifically Pagan or Wiccan-oriented. Paganism and Wicca are *religious* orientations, whereas Magick and Wizardry are *studies* and *practices* that are independent of any particular religion.

Moreover, just like covens, all of the serious websites and online schools that offered magickal studies at all were for adults only—operating at a college level, and not admitting anyone under eighteen.

A third factor was the unconscionably high rates of tuition in nearly all the online schools I looked into. I felt that these costs were way out of the price range of many of my readers—especially teens! And, finally, I wanted to direct my readers into a full curriculum in all aspects of Wizardry, with many highly qualified teachers in specialized areas.

When I get an idea for something I really think should exist, but doesn't yet, I often take it as a "Mission Impossible" assignment to make it so. This was such an assignment. By the time I figured out what I wanted to refer my readers to, I realized that I would have to create it myself. Well, the obvious model was sitting right out there in front of me. It was created by J. K. Rowling. The idea of a "Hogwarts" kind of school seemed so natural.

I got all excited about this idea of the online school. At Samhain of 2003, I was attending a Pagan Pride event out in Salem, Massachusetts, and I found myself sitting down for lunch with a guy named Steve who had created a website for the local group. I said, "We'd really like to do something like that and have an online school."

And he said, "Wow, that sounds really great! Count me in—I'll be your website designer."

For six months after that, it was a matter of me and other people who came on board feeding Steve ideas of things that we wanted to see—which were utterly impossible, yet he did them. Basically, the Grey School is a virtual online equivalent to J. K. Rowling's fictional Hogwarts. Only we don't teach just fantasy magic—we teach the real thing: true Wizardry, the Wisdom of the Ages, real Magick (with a *k*), alchemy, divination, psychic arts, sorcery, healing, wortcunning, beast mastery, spellwork, ritual, and so much more!

The earliest age of admission was set at eleven, and the classes were designed for junior high and high school level. I took on the responsibility of being headmaster, and the *Grimoire* became the basic foundational textbook. The *Grimoire* had already created an organization of classes and lessons. So I took a lot of them and retooled them and created study guides, exams, assignments, and all kinds of stuff. These were our first classes, but other teachers soon began creating their own, and today there are well over four hundred classes available!

With an initial faculty of thirty qualified and dedicated teachers, the Grey School of Wizardry opened its virtual doors at www.GreySchool .com on Lughnasadh (August 1) 2004, to quite a rush of new students. What we didn't expect was that three-quarters of the students enrolling turned out to be adults—some into their seventies! So we had to develop adult programs and systems as well as those for teens. The neat thing is many of them are parents who are enrolling with their kids.

MG: There are a lot of kids who would like to be in it, and their parents are Mundanes and won't let them. We can't push the envelope with that, because there are legal issues; kids under fourteen have to have signed parental permission.

NARRATOR: One more bit of Magick awaited them in 2004. After successfully working at a salon for a few years, Gail and her supportive boyfriend bought a Victorian house in Oakland and decided to get married.

MG: I asked her if she was planning a church wedding since Joe, her fiancé, was raised Catholic, but she said, "No way! They make you promise to raise your kids in the Church, and there is no way I'm going with that program." She had picked out a beautiful mansion in Marin County that rented to wedding parties and was just looking for someone to perform the ceremony, but they had to be legally registered with the state. So I suggested that she contact her dear friend and childhood confidante, Cerridwen Fallingstar. She did, and Cerridwen agreed to be their Priestess. I must admit that I was pretty delighted that when push came to shove the most logical solution to the dilemma of what to do for a wedding ceremony was to make it a modern Pagan-style wedding.

I knew that Cerridwen would do a wonderful job, because despite our differences we have always respected each other as fellow Priestesses.

OZ: Gail and Joe were married on October 1, 2004. Polly was there, and so was my son, Bryan, who flew in from Florida. Developing and administering the Grey School occupied much of my time over the following months, along with the usual round of parties, festivals, holly-daze, and travels for speaking engagements around the country.

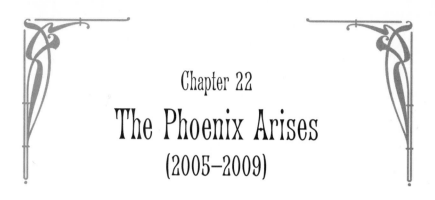

Chapter 22
The Phoenix Arises
(2005–2009)

NARRATOR: The Ravenheart Family business was hurt really badly by the economic downturn that followed 9/11. After that, Wolf and Wynter both had to stop working for Mythic Images full time. Wynter got a job in San Francisco and eventually moved in with Morgan, her lover there. Morning Glory learned to use the software that Wolf had designed and took over as business manager.

MG: Of course the other full-time occupation that was consuming my attention at this same time was taking care of my mother, whose deteriorating health made constant demands on my time and attention well beyond the simple basic things like cooking, cleaning, and doing her laundry.

This was one of the hardest times of my life. I was losing two of the people whose daily presence had made my life sweet and juicy, and though we still cared about each other, it was not the same and it never would be again. I was carrying a lot of grief about that as well as grappling with the increasingly debilitating effects of menopause. But I found the most wonderful thing when I started reading to Polly in the evenings.

It started out as a bit of an experiment to calm her down and help her to sleep better without all the drugs that messed up her memory and blood pressure. She never really read much herself except for the Bible or maybe some fundamentalist religious tracts, but she did love to hear stories, so I got the notion that she might enjoy hearing stories read to her from some of the fantasy books that had been so meaningful in my life. It was a way of sharing a part of my spirit with her without it being about religion. So I decided to read her *The Hobbit* by J. R. R. Tolkien.

She absolutely loved *The Hobbit* and we actually went through the book fairly quickly, even just reading a chapter or so every few days. So when it was over, she was so eager for more that I decided to take a leap into a pretty ambitious possibility and read her the entire *Lord of the Rings* trilogy and show her the movies too.

Oberon also really got into the spirit of the thing. He would bring all his little *Lord of the Rings* model toys and action figures that he collected over to her house and set up little dioramas and scenes for the characters and events that would be in that night's chapter. Lots of people were amazed that she had made such a turnaround in her health after leaving Ukiah and moving to Shady Grove. They would say things like "Polly, we are surprised you are looking so well; we thought you were about ready to die."

Polly would just tell them proudly, in her thick Southern accent, "Well, I cain't die till I find out what happens to Frodo!"

OZ: In March of 2005, one of the caretakers at Annwfn showed up and asked me, "How would you like to have your Church back?" In updating the insurance for our upcoming Beltane, he had discovered that despite the perfidious Ohio board of directors supposedly discorporating the Church of All Worlds the previous year, they had failed to notify the IRS, and had overlooked the fact that our California incorporation was still extant. All we needed to do was file a change of address for our primary office from Toledo to Cotati, and we were back in business!

At our first Church of All Worlds board meeting on Annwfn at Beltane, May 1, I was reinstalled as Primate and President of the BoD, with High Priestess Morning Glory as Vice President.

The Ohio BoD had pretty much burned the whole Church down to the ground. When we contacted the surviving members of that board, they wouldn't even send us the records of their tenure, memberships, bookkeeping, or anything else. They claimed that all the files had been destroyed in a flood. Over the next few years we would begin re-conceptualizing and rebuilding our beloved Church from the ground up—a wonderful opportunity, actually, as it allowed us to learn from our successes and failures, and to incorporate those lessons into what we came to call "The Third Phoenix Resurrection of the Church of All Worlds" (the two previous ones being in Ukiah in the mid-'80s, and St. Louis in the late '60s). As we started rebuilding the CAW, many old and new Waterkin started showing up to become involved.

NARRATOR: In 2005 the community at Shady Grove was broken up. What basically happened was a "poly" divorce—Liza met someone new and fell in love, and the two of them decided they did not want to live there. They eventually evicted the other residents of Shady Grove and sold the property. As with most divorces, it was difficult for *all* involved.

One of Oberon's favorite sayings is from *Spider-Man* comics (as written by Stan Lee), and it goes like this: "With great power comes great responsibility." I think that could apply to this situation and what led up to it. Polyamory gives people great power. Anyone who decides to live a polyamorous lifestyle has opportunities that were unimaginable just a generation ago. They have the power to *love more*. And much discussion, communication, and hard work has gone into creating a system that is ethical and, yes, responsible for all concerned. But most of this is still relatively new. Just how much responsibility, and what kind of responsibility, is required in a situation where multiple partners decide to live together, and then break up, is something that the polyamorous community will have to consider as it continues to grow and evolve.

OZ: Right after returning from a trip in July, I was slated to appear on a major TV show in Australia called *The Sunday Program*. A camera and sound crew were being dispatched to our home to tape me responding to the host, who would be phoning in his side of the interview. We walked in the door at 1:30 and were met by Wolf, who said, "I have bad news. We've all been evicted."

No sooner had he spoken these words than the TV crew arrived—two hours earlier than they'd said they'd be here. There was simply no time at all for me to process the news of the eviction, and I was in a state of shock as I attempted to give a coherent interview.

It was 5:30 before they finally cleared out, and we all collapsed together in the kitchen. Liza had gone away incommunicado for the next two months with her new fiancé, and then had someone come in and tape sixty-day eviction notices to all our doorknobs.

LIZA: Sending out those notices was a hard decision. The kind you go over and over in your mind to see if there could have been a better way. I don't think there could have been, unless it was not getting involved with Oberon and Morning Glory in the first place.

Sitting in meetings with Oberon and Morning Glory for a decade, I had learned that action was the only language they fully honored, so I spoke as clearly as I could in a language they could not ignore.

Each notice included a general letter to the community and a personal letter to the individual offering to pay moving expenses (which I did) and generally trying to explain myself. Each letter said I was open to suggestions about how to proceed, that I was available by email for any kind of dialogue but not in person.

None of the negotiations I was open to ever took place because within a few days of receiving my notices, rather than respond to me, Oberon wrote a letter to everyone I knew and everyone he knew dramatically discrediting me by giving an alarming version of my actions out of their full context.

So I, Oberon's magickal partner and devoted friend, became his enemy. It was amazing. I had seen them both forgive people for much more damaging things. But not me. I love these people. They don't have the power to erase that. It brought to mind a chant I had written for a workshop on the shadow Oberon and I had led together:

> *I salute you, beloved enemy*
> *Full of darkness death and mystery*
> *Spread your dark wings inside of me*
> *Touch me with your wisdom and beauty*

MG: Polly had loved and trusted Liza like a daughter and had been promised that she would be able to spend the last years of her life in peace. Still and all, if Liza hadn't let her move into Shady Grove in the first place she would never have had these last few wonderful years to share with us. So perhaps the karma balances out in some painful way. Unfortunately, OZ was too busy writing the next book he was under contract for to be much help with finding a place, and so I tackled that by going online and checking the papers and finally joining a rental search program.

OZ: I had a really tight deadline schedule for the next book I was writing, *Companion for the Apprentice Wizard*. I couldn't possibly handle a housing search, financing, moving, and so on in the next two months and still finish the book on time. And we had a business to run, which involved working every day filling orders, shipping, invoicing, etc.

While Wolf and his girlfriend Kat were out house-hunting, Morning Glory, Julie, and I held a New Moon Circle to envision our future. We laid out a huge sheet of blank paper and drew on it everything we wanted in a new home, which would include Polly, our business, a place to swim, facilities for animals, and possibly more. As we had done so many times before, we would all move forward, shifting probabilities to create a new reality and a new life out of the ashes.

After a month of intense house-hunting and even more intense Magick, MG finally found what would be the absolutely perfect new home with plenty of room for Morning Glory and me, our business, and Polly. The major drawback was that there would be no room for Wolf, Kat, Linda, or Julie, but they were all pretty much in the process of finding other places on their own. It was really sad to have to break up the

Family, as we had enjoyed living together so much. It felt like the end of an era for certain.

We packed up everything and finally made the move on the first of October, 2005.

MG: Wolf and Kat moved into their own place nearby, and we continued to get together and enjoy each other's company; we all considered each other to be part of our extended Family as we do Morgan and Wynter and Julie and Aidan. The people may change roles in our relationships, but whenever possible we try not to burn our bridges so that the Love can still remain.

Our new house is on a dead-end street, and I would take Polly out and push her down the street in her wheelchair to see the horses and sheep that were there. I kept trying to keep her interest in the world alive but it felt like something had broken inside her. She was in constant chronic pain, and that was taking its toll.

OZ: Thanksgiving that year was graciously picked up by Morning Glory's daughter Gail, and her husband Joe. At dinner, Gail and Joe made a wonderful announcement: Gail was pregnant! Polly was happy over the prospect of finally becoming a great-grandmother, but at the same time she quietly bemoaned the thought of having to stay alive another eight months to see the newest member of her beloved family. By this time she had pretty much concluded that she was done with this life, and all she wanted now was for Jesus to come and take her home to Heaven.

NARRATOR: Polly's condition worsened, and she had to be moved into a hospital.

MG: On February 11, 2006, Gail and I were both going to sit with her together when I got the call from the nurse that Polly had stopped breathing. So we raced over, and Gail and I went into her room to find that her spirit was still there. We could sense it like an enormous sparkling feeling of release fluttering around above her old shell of a body and laughing and laughing: "I'm free, I'm free! I can fly, I can fly!" It was so amazing to share this overwhelming sense of joy at her release that we couldn't really be sad; we could only laugh with her. We were laughing and crying at the same time. Then we covered her body with all the flowers that had filled her room and kissed her goodbye. Gail gathered up her stuff and went back to the house while I waited for the mortician.

After he left with Polly's body, I walked slowly to my car and turned for a moment, looking back towards the room where she had been—and I saw a large cloud hanging in the air directly over the rest home in the shape of an angel. Polly loved angels and she loved clouds. She had an angel collection and a comforter with clouds on it; I had even written her a poem called "My Mother's Wings." I just stared at this huge angelic apparition and my jaw dropped. I sucked in my breath, and all of a sudden the sun, which was setting, came out of a cloud bank and lit up the angel cloud with brilliant red and gold colors like a stained-glass window. At that very instant I heard my mother's voice say, "Anytime you need to talk to me or show me anything, you just call out my name and tell it to me; I will hear you just fine because I'm everywhere now."

I was so much in awe that I couldn't even cry. I just said, "Wow, Polly! What a way to go!"

OZ: A living vessel of unconditional Love who lived her faith with every breath she took, she graced the life of everyone she met. Polly loved everybody, and everybody loved her. As many of Polly's Hippie and Pagan friends showed up for her funeral as did the Christians.

One by one, Christians and Pagans got up and took turns telling anecdotes of their experiences with Polly. Polly's favorite hymns were sung, concluding with Artemisia, our Bard, singing an exquisite rendition of Annie Lennox's "Into the West," from the final credits of *Return of the King*, which Polly had specifically requested after seeing the movie. It was a beautiful and moving service for Christians and Pagans alike

NARRATOR: Oberon and Morning Glory started having health issues of their own. When her back didn't recover for months after a fall the day before her mother's funeral, Morning Glory saw a neurosurgeon who immediately checked her into the hospital for the biopsy. The next day, she got the bad news: it was cancer.

MG: The next morning right after the biopsy, my doctor woke me up to tell me that the biopsy had come back positive for multiple myeloma, that it was incurable but it was treatable. He told me that it looked like this cancer had been growing in me for about four or five years, which was why my bones kept breaking—in other words, while I was under all the stress with the business, menopause, taking care of Polly, the breakup of our Family, and our eviction. I have never experienced such a heart-breaking moment as when I had to tell OZ and Gail that I had an incurable cancer. But the nurses in the hospital and even a representative from the insurance company were the kindest people I have met in many a day.

My doctor did some more surgery on me. This time he fixed my broken vertebra with a kyphoplasty, which is a fancy way of putting you back together with a surgical version of Bondo. After that, they released me and I was ecstatically happy to be back home in my wonderful new place with the people I love. The next day I woke up to the sound of beautiful female voices singing May Carols, and it was Artemisia's women's chorus rehearsing on the porch outside my bedroom. The sunshine streamed in and the smell of all the hanging wisteria blossoms filled my heart with sheer gratitude for being alive. From now on, I have become aware that every day I live is a gift to be cherished for as long as possible.

OZ: Fortunately, a center for treatment of multiple myeloma—and one of the foremost doctors, Dr. Marek Bozdech—is right here in Santa Rosa, only five miles from our home. The oncologist in San Francisco told MG that if she'd come in with this condition ten years ago, they'd have given her only a couple years to live. But while multiple myeloma is still presently incurable, he said that current treatments can now keep her going for another fifteen years—by which time, hopefully, better treatments or even a cure will be available.

I am so glad that now we had medical insurance; it was one of the things that Liza had insisted on for which we owe her thanks, and so Morning Glory was able to begin treatment immediately.

The most amazing thing was the overwhelming community response to the news of MG's cancer. Our friends at WitchSchool.com put up a special website for her healing. Cards, letters, and emails started pouring in from dozens, then hundreds, of supporters—sending love, prayers, magick, and all kinds of healing energy. Monthly "Rolling Thunder" rituals were created on the full moons, with people joining in around the world. It was deeply moving, and really helped Morning Glory get back on her feet. Her doctors were very impressed by the degree of her steady progress towards remission, which currently has stabilized at 98 percent.

MG: Gail's daughter was born by caesarian at 8:55 p.m. on Friday evening, July 28, 2006; Joe was able to be with her the entire time, even in the operating room. Times have sure changed since Gary and I opted for a home birth because they wouldn't let fathers into the delivery room. She named the baby Alessandra Salvador. Alessa was absolutely the most perfect, adorable baby that ever there was, except for her mother. She was born with a full head of lush black hair, just like both her parents. Joe finally brought Alessa in for us to coo and gush over, and as we all sat there together, I saw Polly with my peripheral vision sitting in the corner with a big smile on her face reaching out her arms to hold her great-granddaughter—four generations of women now.

NARRATOR: After moving out of Shady Grove, confronted with Polly's death and Morning Glory's medical problems, it wasn't until 2007 that Oberon was finally able to construct display cases and unpack Morning Glory's Goddess collection.

MG: All through the darkest time in my life—the death of my mother and my bout with cancer—I had been without my Goddess collection. I was overjoyed to be able to have all their familiar images to consult with and share my inner thoughts. It may sound odd because of course the statues of Goddesses are just statues; but at the same time since I know all their stories the figurines become object links connecting me to the energetic forces that are the true forms of the deities. Before too long the Goddesses began whispering to me about reaching out again and teaching other people about them—finding new Priestesses to hear their tales and touch their power.

NARRATOR: Oberon had been rebuilding his relationship with his father over the past several years, due in part to Liza's encouragement. As they came to relate on better terms to one another, Charlie had even helped Oberon make a connection to a factory in Taiwan in the mid-'90s where they could produce some of Mythic Image's statuary, which they used until 1998. He was particularly proud of his son's Millennial Gaia.

LIZA: I pointed out to Oberon that his relationship with his father was an important thing on many levels. I also set an example with my own family. I helped him to understand that it was worthy of his time and attention to cultivate a relationship with his father, and that it didn't have to be about his father agreeing with him, or thinking that he was a good guy. And he developed a better relationship with his father. He went to visit his father regularly, and his father eventually came to visit us. I couldn't help but feel somewhat that his father was a difficult man, it's fair to say. But we did our best to be welcoming and hospitable to him.

OZ: I think we'd both gotten mellower over the years, and it was nice to feel a deepening of our filial connection, which was for so long rendered well-nigh impossible by the extreme antithesis of our respective lifestyles, religions, politics, and philosophies. It had been a real challenge, for me at least, to find some common ground we could both stand on! But I held to the conviction that we both really did love each other, despite our considerable differences and disagreements.

During a visit in 2008, my father informed me that he had put me back in his will. That was nice—I hadn't known that I'd been disinherited for all those years! He also told me that one of the reasons why I'd never been included in any family events and adventures—such as reunions, weddings, funerals, holidays, vacations, etc.—was because I was "too interesting." He told me that whenever I show up, I'm always the center of attention, and everyone else is just eclipsed. I guess there is something to think about always having to be the center of attention; I didn't really realize that was how it might seem to others.

MG: I found out that I had also inadvertently caused a large part of the estrangement. I had first met Charles at our wedding, but I didn't meet his second wife, Helen Marie, until almost seven years later, and I'm afraid that I was still in a somewhat confrontational adolescent headspace. Unthinkingly, I made a really nasty remark about the newly elected president, Ronald Reagan. I said, "Maybe we'll be lucky, and he'll die in office." I was quoting my father, who used to say stuff like that all the time. And though they were too polite to show it, they were both completely horrified, because Reagan was actually a personal friend of theirs. In fact, Charlie had worked on Reagan's campaign in one of the early, and very important, state primaries for the election.

For years we had no idea that this was an issue, and I had completely forgotten the event; it had come from such a non-conscious part of me anyway. But as years went by I stopped attending any family gatherings where Charlie and Helen Marie would be, because I sensed they didn't like me and I didn't want to inflict my presence on them. I still urged OZ to attend, however, because I have always felt it was crucially important to stay connected to your biological family if at all possible, regardless of your differences.

OZ came back from one of these visits with his dad after Helen Marie had passed on, and Charlie had confided this story to Oberon. OZ was really taken aback! That they had taken this insult in such a deeply personal way that I had delivered flippantly and then carried it around like a festering wound all these years was an intolerable burden. When he told me about this, I spent a lot of time in grief about the damage that an unthinking attitude can do to people's lives and about how you can't fix something until you know about it. But I was determined to do the right thing. I put myself in their place and imagined how I would have felt if a stranger that I had just met had made a heartlessly cruel comment about one of my close friends. I certainly would not have wanted to spend time hanging around with them.

So I sat down and spent a couple of days writing a lengthy and heart-felt apology to Charlie for the stupid thing I said so many years ago. I have certainly grown as a human being since then, but even at the time, if I had known the hurt I had caused I would gladly have apologized. The ability to be honest about who you are and to understand and acknowledge your flaws is the only way you can ever get beyond them.

Charlie read my apology and graciously accepted it, and we both ended up in tears over the tragic misunderstanding that had blighted our lives for so long. I was only sorry that Helen Marie was no longer around to be part of the experience.

OZ: Actually my dad was sort of amazed that Morning Glory could just come right out with an apology like that, as it is apparently not the sort of thing that happens very often in his circle of friends. But as far as I was concerned, he was always the one who taught me that it takes a big person to admit when they are wrong. So I guess he understands Morning Glory a lot better now and why I continue to love her and support her even when she is wrong—because she does the same thing for me, and we both have learned to make a practice of admitting to each other whenever it becomes apparent that we were wrong about something. It has certainly been a feature in transforming our relationship and reducing the number of bitter fights that used to be one of its worst characteristics and the one that lost us so many good friends.

NARRATOR: After that visit to his dad, Oberon went in for a routine physical and was urged to have his first colonoscopy. Unfortunately, they discovered he had a large tumor in his descending colon and immediately scheduled him for surgery.

OZ: On August 29, 2008, I underwent the surgery. I stayed in the hospital for a week, suffering the worst pain I'd ever experienced. The only thing that kept me going was the knowledge that actual pain cannot be remembered later. And so it was. Morning Glory came in every evening to massage my back and read me Charles de Lint stories.

And now I, too—just like Morning Glory the previous year—began to receive a vast outpouring of love, prayers, and healing magick from all over the world. I felt buoyed up and supported like never before.

NARRATOR: The doctors discovered that one of the lymph glands was also cancerous, so Oberon had to go through six months of chemotherapy.

MG: We have a lot of friends who've had cancer and gone through chemo, so it was helpful to be able to consult with them about what to expect. My birthday sister Jessica went through the whole breast cancer routine and lost her hair to chemo, so she was able to give OZ some good suggestions about things. And our dear friend Gary Ball, who was our partner in the Between the Worlds venture back in Ukiah, had the same kind of cancer as OZ, so he was able to be a great support person. It really does help when someone else has walked before you on the road you have to travel. And now that we ourselves have walked that road, we can be guides to others.

OZ: I am hardly alone. It seems that every month I hear of someone I know having cancer. One of these was Lance Christie. When I learned this, I told him, "Don't you think this is carrying this water-brother thing a bit too far?"

LANCE CHRISTIE: In September of 2008 I was diagnosed as having pancreatic cancer and quickly arranged to have a Whipple procedure done.

After undertaking a course of chemotherapy, tests in April showed me to be free of cancer. If cancer does recur, I have several agents identified that can stop tumor progression, turning cancer into a manageable chronic condition with which one can live with no particular inconvenience until one dies at a ripe old age from something else.

NARRATOR: In spite of all their personal setbacks and heartbreaks, OZ, CAW, and even *Green Egg* continued on.

OZ: At Ostara 2007, *Green Egg*, which had ceased publication in 2000, rose again from the ashes as a downloadable e-zine with a spectacular Phoenix on the cover, painted by Ian Daniels, who had done the cover and chapter illustrations for my *Wizard's Bestiary*. This third incarnation began with volume 39, issue #137. Our old friends Tom Donohue and Ariel Monserrat were now at the helm, and doing a beautiful job! I am listed on the masthead as "Founder," and I am very proud to see it back again. With a new motto of "Legends never die," it can be found online at www.GreenEggzine.com.

After our respective cancer treatments, in 2009 we were back at PantheaCon, pulling out all the stops. We had just received the first prototype of a thirty-inch-tall Garden Goddess of my Millennial Gaia statue, and we set Her up in front of our Mythic Images booth. Everyone loved Her, and it was a real delight to see small children come up and hug Her—even give Her a kiss. Our biggest offering that year was a spectacular "Phoenix Rising" ritual. It would dramatize the resurrection of the Church of All Worlds, the healing of MG and me personally, and the new sense of hope engendered by Obama's election, in these darkest of times. We spent months writing and rehearsing the script, casting all the parts, and making props, masks, and costumes.

At PantheaCon, on Valentine's Day, the room was packed, and the ritual was a tremendous success. It began in near-darkness, with fog machines filling the center of the circle with mist. Participants became passengers on a "ship of fools," guided by a navigator and arriving at a forgotten island, where the last Priestess tended the hearth in the temple of Gaia. But the sacred fires had gone out, and all that remained was a large mound of ashes. Helios, the Sun God, crossed from east to west, bringing a bit of illumination, as Gaia entered, reciting Algernon Swinburne's evocative poem "Hertha." The Priestess told her sad tale, of how all her hopes, dreams, and work had turned to ashes, and invited the "passengers" to identify with their own lives, tossing their ashes onto the heap, and fanning the coals. As they caught fire, a Phoenix emerged from under the gray, ashen blanket and rose to full height, wings outstretched. I was that Phoenix; and this is what the Phoenix said:

> I arise. I arise from the ashes, reborn yet again. I am the Phoenix, ever-dying, ever-resurrecting. I am the hope in every heart, never dying, however wounded. I am the dream in every head, never forgotten, however diminished its grandeur in coming true. I am the light in every eye, still burning, however dimmed by remaining open through the darkest times. I am you.
>
> I am born of the dance of the Earth and the Sun—as are all of you. You are my people, and I am your avatar. We are one.

We are Pagans and magickal folk—bound to the endless cycles of the Spiral Dance, from the vast wheeling galaxies to the double helix within your every cell. We know that there are cycles of destruction and creation, times of despair and times of hope, darkness and returning light, death and rebirth—all reflected in the Mystery of the Phoenix. We know that what goes around comes around, and Darkness must always yield to Light.

Black holes turn inside out to become brilliant quasars, filling the universe with energy. The bitterest winter rolls around to balmy spring, when Life springs forth anew. Out of every Dark Age is born a glorious Renaissance, in which all good things flower and flourish. Death eternally comes 'round to rebirth. And the deepest, darkest, longest night inexorably yields to the blazing sun of a New Dawn.

We have lived through rising tides of prosperity and the still waters of peace. And we have lived amidst gathering clouds and raging storms. Our spirit remains strong, and cannot be broken. We will not turn back; nor will we falter.

There may come a day, billions of years hence, when Light fails, Entropy triumphs, and Darkness falls forever over all the worlds. But this is not that day! For this day, dedicated for millennia to Love, heralds a New Dawn, and a new Rebirth. On this day, we choose hope over fear, unity of purpose over conflict and discord. We choose rebirth!

In the glory of the rising Phoenix, Hope shall be rekindled in every heart; forgotten Dreams shall be reawakened in every mind; and the light of Love shall burn in every eye. This is the way of things, and it shall not be denied! Thus shall it be in our personal lives, in our Religion, in our Nation, and on our Planet. And thus the long tragedy of human history brings us inevitably towards the Awakening of Gaea!

They thought us dead, along with our hopes and dreams for a better world. But they were wrong. We live! We Are Alive!

MG: I made up my mind that the summer of 2009 was going to be the turnaround point for me with my life's Work in the field of Goddess history. I sat down and wrote up a series of outlines for Goddess Retreat weekends and chose dates and then got OZ to create flyers for me to advertise them. I started with a little lecture for Sonoma County Pagan Network to show what I know and generate some local interest.

OZ: In June, I flew out to St. Louis for the Illinois Grey School Conclave, held about sixty-five miles from St. Louis in Illinois, and it was every bit as wonderful as the previous two I'd attended. When it ended we broke camp and drove back to St. Louis in time to set up our Grey School/ Mythic Images booth for the two-day Pagan Picnic. When Morning Glory and I left St. Louis for the West Coast in June of 1976, there were maybe a couple dozen Pagans in the area—nearly all of them members of our own Church of All Worlds. So I was completely blown away to discover that this event—then in its seventeenth year—was attended by around five thousand people! Paganism has certainly come a long way in the past thirty-plus years, and this was a dramatic example.

MG: While OZ was gone we had a wonderful time at my first Goddess Retreat. This one was dedicated to Our Lady of Love and Pleasure; and even though it was a small, first-time affair, it was terrific. We were able to spend lots of time getting to know the Goddesses I passed around. That evening we swam in the pool and had a ritual bath in the hot tub, learning ritual songs and chants. Then I led a meditation to take people to meet the Goddess who had chosen them.

The next day we made Goddess talismans in the form of beautiful beaded necklaces, sitting out in the sunlight on the Fairy Porch next to my bedroom. We wove a wreath of jasmine for the large concrete Aphrodite statue in our garden, then had a little procession to crown Her wearing our talismans. I did an invocation from Sappho, and we sang Her some of the chants we learned that day. We processed on into the temple room, where the altar was filled with all the images of Goddesses of Love and Beauty from my collection: a plethora of pulchritude! Then we did some trance work and held a Council of Goddesses where each Goddess got to speak Her truth through the woman She chose.

It was simple but profoundly moving; we all learned a great deal in the process. I especially felt like I had taken the first step on the road to reclaiming my life's Work; and by learning from this event what worked and didn't work, I will be able to continue to build this experience, fine-tuning it until it is the ideal teaching technique for me to share my knowledge with the community in a setting that is accessible for me to use and enjoyable for anyone to experience.

I feel like I am really beginning to come out of the cocoon that I have been withdrawn into for the last few years. I recognize that I needed that time and space for healing, and that from time to time I will still have to go gently and listen to my body. I pushed it too hard for too many years, and it finally broke down and forced me to pay attention. I will not make that mistake again. I am working on trying to reinvent myself once more. I've been a child, a maiden, a mother, and a sex-crazed lover; now I am ready to embrace the Crone. I'm no longer sad about it; instead I feel a real sense of renewal. Whether it is the change in the political climate or the change in my inner self, either way it feels like the sun just came out after a long, cold winter.

OZ: The Pagan Picnic closed on Sunday afternoon, and as soon as we got everything broken down and packed up, we drove down to my old teacher Deborah Bourbon's store, Pathways, where I was scheduled to talk and sign books. Debbie (then Deborah Letter) had opened her first store, The Cauldron, way back in 1968, and when she offered classes in 1970, I was among her first students. When we arrived, there was a big cake with "Welcome Back, Oberon!" written on it.

After a lovely time at Pathways, we decided to go to the famous St. Louis Gateway Arch. None of us had been up in it, though I'd watched it being completed when I first moved to St. Louis in 1965. I was still in full Wizardly regalia, so we anticipated a bit of "freaking the Mundanes." But everyone was delighted with us, and many tourists had to have their photos taken with the real Wizards! Even the security guards and the clerks in the gift store were friendly—they all seemed to know about the Pagan Picnic, and were tickled that we'd come all dressed up. There was not even the slightest hint of negativity—what a difference from thirty-three years ago!

I feel that this return visit to St. Louis brought me full circle, and it is an appropriate place to conclude this narrative of The Story So Far.

We shall not cease from exploration
And the end of all our exploring
Will be to arrive where we started
And know the place for the first time.

—FROM "LITTLE GIDDING" BY T. S. ELIOT, 1942

Afterword:
The Making of This Epic Story
by Elysia Gallo

I'm a senior acquisitions editor at Llewellyn Worldwide, and when I first took on this project, I didn't really know what I was getting into! I had met Oberon at PantheaCon, and he was eager to share his life story—and what a life story it has been. John Sulak offered to do the painstaking work of stitching together all these threads, interviewing folks who knew Oberon and Morning Glory over the years, and sitting down for long, long tales told by Oberon and Morning Glory themselves.

In one of Oberon's first emails to me, sent in 2006, he told me, "You might find it of interest to know that 'Elysia' was the name I'd chosen for my first child, had it been a daughter. Instead, a son was born to my first wife and me, on September 15, 1963. We named him Bryan. But I've always loved the name Elysia, and if I'd ever had a girl . . ." So I guess in some way I was meant to become part of this story, and here it is.

In 2009 John Sulak sent me the first draft of this manuscript. It was 370,000 words long. For those of you who don't deal with word counts every day, that's more than twice the length of the book you hold in your hands. That's 1,155 typed pages. Not counting the six appendices that were sent separately!

Publishing is a funny industry. For reasons that could take up a book of their own, here at Llewellyn it was agreed that we needed to have John and Oberon trim the book to 150,000 words or less; otherwise it would have become a prohibitively expensive, gargantuan doorstop that readers could neither afford nor lift. I advised Oberon to save that manuscript for his children and his grandchildren because it truly was a treasure trove, but that we needed to seriously narrow our focus.

There was an entire chapter on Gwydion Pendderwen, for example, which perhaps one day Oberon can publish as an article. There was an entire chapter on Leonard Lake, a bit player in the story you've just read. There were complete genealogies of Oberon's and Morning Glory's families and a recounting of every summer job either of them had had. There was a reincarnated cat, a cat who liked to ride on the roof of the car, and at least three sad cat burials. There were cars broken down at the side of the road (and the names of complete strangers who towed them), dead skunks, storage lockers, dirt bikes, a World's Fair, and snakes in the snow. There were three stories that had to do with people being naked and getting poison ivy. There were pages and pages of drug trips.

But more than anything—there were names. Names of every friend and lover, every dearly loved CAW member, every helping hand in the course of their lives, every enemy. As a publisher with a healthy dose of caution, Llewellyn needs to be very careful about what it prints because of privacy concerns. We aimed to secure the permission of every named or identifiable person in this book if they weren't a contributor or a "public figure." And that led to a lot of people having their names changed or left out of this book. This was not Oberon's wish, and he fought me every step of the way—after all, his desire to be inclusive in the telling of his life, not excluding anyone who meant anything to him, is basically the theme of his life.

So, if you saw yourself anywhere in this book and we changed your name or masked your identity in some way, but you'd like to stand on the record, as it were, please write to Llewellyn's reprint committee (our address can be found at the back of this book or on the Internet) and let us know, and perhaps we will be able to change it in the next printing with your permission. Likewise, if you're wondering why you aren't in this story at all, disguised or otherwise, and are now wondering whether you were important to Oberon and Morning Glory after all, I'm here to reassure you that you are. You *were* in the book, I can guarantee that, but your contribution to this great story was somehow left on the cutting-room floor. We take full responsibility for that; we just couldn't get it all in there and still get this important story published.

This book has been a fun challenge, through four years of rewrites, meetings, and long conversations. I hope you enjoyed the ride.

Appendix I
Brief Timeline

1961   OZ begins freshman year at Westminster College, in Fulton, Missouri, where he meets Lance Christie and Martha McCance.

1962   Lance and OZ read *Stranger in a Strange Land* and share water (April 7), vowing to begin living according to concepts set forth therein. They form a Nest, and OZ begins publishing *The Atlan Torch*.

1963   OZ marries Martha (April), and they have a son, Bryan (September).

1965   OZ graduates from Westminster, begins graduate school at Washington University in St. Louis; begins new Nest of CAW there.

1966   OZ quits graduate school, begins working for Human Development Corporation as a Head Start counselor.

1967   On Labor Day, OZ first goes public with Church of All Worlds, applies for incorporation. He immediately begins using the term *Pagan* as self-identification for this new religion. He completes Life Science College for a Doctor of Divinity degree, becomes ordained as first Priest of CAW (December 21).

1968   CAW receives corporate status on March 4; opens a coffeehouse / temple on Gaslight Square in St. Louis. OZ begins publishing *Green Egg* (all in March). The temple closes in September.

1969   With Fred Adams of Feraferia and others, OZ co-founds the Council of Themis—the first Pagan ecumenical council. OZ attends his first World Science Fiction conventions (St. Louiscon) and meets many people (including John C. Sulak).

1970   April: CAW opens a new storefront temple. OZ does his first acid trip (at the solar eclipse, March 7); he meets Jodie Parker (April 1); CAW major participant at first Earth Day (April 22). CAW gets its IRS 501(c)(3) (June 18). OZ begins Witchcraft training under Deborah Letter at her occult shop, The Cauldron. On September 6, OZ has major Vision of the Living Earth, which he writes up as "TheaGenesis." This is the first publication of what later becomes known as "The Gaea Thesis."

1971   Martha and OZ separate, later to divorce. Jodie, Bryan, and OZ travel to the East Coast for sci-fi Noreascon (Labor Day). They meet Susan Roberts, Ray Buckland, Leo Martello, Robert Rimmer, and many famous Witches.

1972   Council of Themis dissolves due to internal dissension; Jodie and OZ attend WorldCon in Los Angeles; they meet many California Pagans, see Greenfield Ranch for the first time.

1973   Jodie and OZ break up in the spring. OZ attends the Gnostica Aquarian Festival (Gnosticon) in Minneapolis at Mabon, as a keynote speaker on TheaGenesis. There he meets and falls in love with Morning Glory. She moves in with him.

1974   MG and OZ are married in a huge public Pagan handfasting in Minneapolis (April 14). Isaac Bonewits and Carolyn Clark officiate; Margot Adler sings Gwydion's songs.

1975   On his thirty-third birthday, OZ quits his job. OZ and MG buy and fix up an old school bus, "The Scarlet Succubus."

1976   MG and OZ leave St. Louis for the West Coast. They end up in Eugene, Oregon. Their research uncovers the lost secret of the unicorn. Back in St. Louis, *Green Egg* folds. Soon, so does CAW.

1977   MG and OZ move onto Greenfield Ranch as caretakers on a 220-acre parcel named *Coeden Brith*, owned by Alison Harlow. Their next-door neighbor is Gwydion Pendderwen. They form Holy Order of Mother Earth (HOME) with Alison. They begin real land-based Pagan life, transfer CAW HQ to California.

1979   Total eclipse of the sun (February 26) over full-scale Stonehenge replica in Washington state. OZ and MG officiate at rites, along with many other Pagan luminaries. Three thousand to four thousand people attend. OZ receives new name of "Otter."

1980   March—first baby Unicorns born. OZ and MG's lives change radically as they find themselves traveling to make appearances, doing Ren Faires and other appearances over next few years.

1981   July—OZ, MG, and Bryan go on Chautauqua with performers from the Oregon Country Fair.

1982   Doing Ren Faires all summer, MG and OZ don't see each other for four months. At Samhain, Gwydion is killed in a car wreck—it's the first death in the Tribe.

1983   In the fall, taking pottery classes at the local college, OZ meets and falls in love with Diane Darling.

1984   OZ and MG sign a four-year exhibition lease for several of their Unicorns with Ringling Brothers/Barnum & Bailey Circus. Diane and her son, Zack, move in with them.

1985   OZ, MG, and Diane mount a diving expedition to New Guinea to solve the mystery of the "Mermaids" sighted there. On the way, they visit Australia, connect with local Pagans. In the fall, they leave Greenfield Ranch and move to "the Old Same Place."

1986   MG and OZ create their dream store, Between the Worlds, bringing in Diane and several others.

1987   In March, OZ goes on a month-long pilgrimage with Belladonna to Spain, France, Italy, Greece, and Crete.

1988   OZ, MG, and Diane resurrect *Green Egg* twenty years after the first issue.

1989   March 19—MG, Diane, and OZ handfast as a triad.

1990   CAW participates in an interfaith ritual for the twentieth anniversary of Earth Day. In the Beltane issue of *Green Egg*, MG coins the term *polyamory*. CAW begins conducting elaborate annual recreations of Eleusinian Mysteries.

1991   Labor Day—CAW does a major presentation, opening and closing rituals, at big Poly-Con in Berkeley.

1992   CAW becomes first legally incorporated Pagan church in Australia. In September MG and OZ meet Talyn, Maggie, and the kids of the Songdog Family, who become a major part of their lives for many years.

1993   OZ and MG meet Wolf at Samhain Gathering in Tennessee.

1994   Diane quits *Green Egg*, and Maerian comes on board as the new editor. At Beltane, MG and OZ formally terminate their handfasting with Diane. In September, after serving as Hades in Eleusinia, OZ receives the new name of "Oberon."

1995   In April, OZ meets Liza Gabriel at the Craftwise Festival in New England; they begin a serious relationship. In November Wolf moves from Houston to San Francisco.

1996   Wynter Rose moves in with OZ and MG in February, meets Wolf at Beltane. CAW board of directors (BoD) remove OZ from any control over the magazine he'd founded. In December, Liza moves to California, and Liza, Wynter, MG, and OZ all pull up stakes and move to V-M Ranch, committing to a two-year lease with an option to buy.

1997   Wolf moves in with the others, and they all take the Family name of "Ravenheart." MG leads Goddess tour to Greece and Crete. MG, OZ, and Wolf are handfasted as a triad, with Liza and Wynter as ladies-in-waiting.

1998   OZ finishes creation of "Millennial Gaia" statue. In early August, OZ is "impeached" as Primate by the CAW BoD, and takes a one-year sabbatical from Primacy. MG and Wynter handfast.

1999   Ravenhearts decide not to buy V-M Ranch. They find a new home for all Ravenhearts in Penngrove, name it Shady Grove, and support themselves with their statuary business, Mythic Images: www.MythicImages.com. In August, OZ travels with Ariel Monserrat to England and France for the final eclipse of twentieth century. The entire Ravenheart Family conducts spectacular Eleusinian Mysteries in September, with Wolf and Wynter as Hades and Persephone.

2000   OZ convenes committee of Pagan leaders and initiates the "Papal Apology Project" to ask the Pope to include Pagans in his apology for the horrors of the Inquisition, etc. Over six thousand signatures are gathered. The Pope does apologize for "crimes against indigenous peoples." Wolf and Wynter are handfasted in August; MG and OZ officiate.

2001   OZ's final year of involvement with CAW, whose BoD is increasingly hostile to OZ personally.

2002   Board of directors tries to consolidate power, and OZ formally disaffiliates from CAW. He is commissioned by New Page Books to write book of Wizardry for the "Harry Potter generation." OZ assembles "Grey Council" as advisory council for this project.

2003   OZ spends entire year writing *Grimoire for the Apprentice Wizard*.

2004   *Grimoire* published. OZ creates online Grey School of Wizardry (incorporated March 14). CAW BoD in Ohio dissolves CAW Inc. The entire CAW BoD in Ohio resigns en masse, and CAW's corporate status reverts to California: www.CAW.org.

2005   Liza evicts Ravenhearts from Shady Grove, and they all go separate ways. MG and OZ find a wonderful place in the Sonoma County countryside, outside of Cotati.

2006   *Companion for the Apprentice Wizard* and *Creating Circles and Ceremonies* are both published. MG's mother, Polly, dies on February 11. In March, MG is diagnosed with cancer. With CAW now back in California, OZ is now President of BoD, and begins total overhaul of entire structure. Granddaughter, Alessandra, born July 28.

2007   Ariel Monserrat and Tom Donohue revive *Green Egg* as an e-zine at www.GreenEggzine.com.

2008   Julie Epona becomes OZ's personal assistant. OZ is diagnosed with colon cancer and has surgery on August 29. In October, he begins six months of chemotherapy.

2009   *Green Egg Omelette* comes out in January. OZ Travels to St. Louis for Grey School Conclave and St. Louis Pagan Picnic—attended by five thousand people. MG starts offering Goddess Retreats.

2010   OZ travels extensively as a presenter.

2012   OZ writes an e-book in conjunction with Harvey Wasserman: *Prophecy & the End of the World (as We Know It)*. OZ also creates definitive poster map of *Barsoom* (the Mars of Edgar Rice Burroughs's "John Carter" novels).

2013   OZ and John Sulak complete work on this autobiography and submit it to the publisher for publication in 2014.

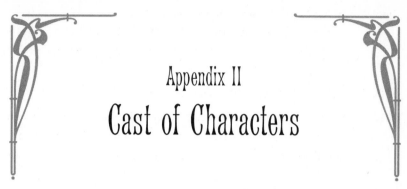

Appendix II
Cast of Characters

Note to the reader: Italicized words reflect the role the person played in this book, while up-to-date descriptions follow in roman type.

Margot Adler

A researcher who met the Zells on several occasions. Margot, author of *Drawing Down the Moon*, lives in New York City and is a New York correspondent for National Public Radio.

Betty and Gary Ball

Betty and Gary worked with the Zells at the Green Mac and Between the Worlds. After that, they opened the Mendocino Environmental Center and later moved to Boulder, Colorado. Gary died in May 2011. Betty continues her activism, working at the Rocky Mountain Peace and Justice Center.

Wynter Rose Anduin-Weiss

A partner of Morning Glory and Wolf, and member of the Ravenheart Family. Born in 1979, Wynter grew up mostly Pagan in a poly-friendly family on the Mendocino coast, and later became part of the Church of All Worlds. She moved in with Morning Glory and Oberon in April of 1996, and met Wolf at the following CAW Beltane. Wynter and Wolf were married in 2000 but divorced a few years later. In April of 2010 she married her best friend, Morgan Anduin-Weiss; they continue to live, work, play, and create magick in San Francisco.

Kadira Belynne

A lover of Oberon's. Kadira lives in Middle Tennessee and is single. Currently, she works for a communications company producing education support materials.

Richard Lance Christie

Oberon's first water-brother and life-long friend. Lance entered Westminster College in 1961, where he met Tim Zell. Lance received an M.A. in experimental social psychology from UCLA. He designed and operated management information and computer systems, helped launch several environmental organizations (including Earth First!), designed and built renewable energy systems, and managed behavioral health care systems. Lance succumbed to pancreatic cancer on October 28, 2010. His book, *The Renewable Deal*, is at www.earthrestoration.net.

Carolyn Clark

The first ordained Priestess of the CAW. During the early 1970s, Carolyn and Oberon were the public face of CAW, lecturing and giving interviews to radio, television, newspapers, and magazines. She now lives quietly with her second ex-husband and two cats, happily retired from a career in nursing.

Catherine Crowell (C9)

A friend of MG's in Eugene, Oregon. In 2005 Catherine retired and moved to Portland, Oregon, and then to Las Vegas, where she died of lung cancer on October 30, 2009.

Diane Darling

A triad partner of OZ and MG who lived with them on the Ranch and the Old Same Place. Diane edited *Green Egg* magazine and assumed many organizational and priestessly duties for the burgeoning American Neo-Pagan movement. Later she edited *The Green Man* and *PanGaia* magazines. Today she is semi-retired and living rurally with her parrot, tiny dog, horse, and donkey.

Zack Darling

Son of Diane Darling and like a son to MG and OZ. Zack has a career in graphic design, marketing, high-end websites, and stunning digital artwork (Zack Darling Creative Associates, www.zackdarling.com). He lives in Santa Rosa, California, with his beloved wife, Monicka.

Deborah Dietz

A runaway who lived with Tim and Martha in their St. Louis days. Deborah has lived in Taos, New Mexico; Ajijic, Jalisco, Mexico; and has settled in Tucson, while considering becoming an expat in Latin America or even farther away. She remains single and childfree, without living relatives, but has a large wealth of friends. Her memories are great company, too.

Cerridwen Fallingstar

A fellow CAW member who also lived on the Ranch. Cerridwen has published hundreds of columns, articles, and short stories, and has been interviewed extensively by print, radio, and television media. She has published two books: *The Heart of the Fire* (1990), a historical novel about Witchcraft in sixteenth-century Scotland; and *White as Bone Red as Blood* (2009), set in twelfth-century Japan.

Gary Ferns

MG's first husband and father of her only child. Gary is a devoted grandparent whose current interests range from history and politics to music, spirituality, and healthful living.

Farida Fox

A fellow CAW member who also lived on the Ranch. Farida has been a Witch for at least forty years and proudly maintains the honorable title of Low Priestess. Her extended family includes four grandchildren and two step-grandkids. She spends almost every waking moment in her garden.

Liza Gabriel

Partner of Oberon and member of Ravenheart Family. Liza has been a nationally recognized workshop leader, writer, and Bard whose work is focused on building spiritual and erotic community. She was a founder and three-year coordinator of The Body Sacred and a founding member of Sacred Connections. She currently lives in Los Angeles with her husband, Reed.

Alison Harlow

Owner of parcel on Ranch that OZ and MG lived on for years; CAW member. In 1982 Alison moved onto a thirty-two-acre plot of land in the Santa Cruz Mountains, creating a residential cooperative community called Eclectia. During the last eight years of her life she served on the Women's Commission of Santa Cruz County. After a brief battle with cancer, she died on June 13, 2004.

Anne Hill

Released Gwydion Pendderwen's music on CD. Anne Hill is co-author with Starhawk of *Circle Round: Raising Children in Goddess Traditions.* Anne writes for the *Huffington Post, SageWoman Magazine,* and the Blog o' Gnosis; hosts Dream Talk Radio; and is on the faculty of Cherry Hill Seminary. See http://annehill.org.

Ayisha Homolka

A fellow CAW member who also lived on the Ranch. Ayisha completed a bachelor of science in nursing in 1994. Primary areas of her nursing practice have been as a sexual-assault nurse examiner and an ER nurse.

Anodea Judith

A fellow CAW member who also lived on the Ranch. Anodea received her M.A. in psychology and Ph.D. in mind-body health. Twice married, she has a grown son, Alexander. She teaches workshops worldwide on the chakras, healing, and cultural transformation. See www.sacredcenters.com.

Anna Korn

Friend in Eugene, Oregon, who lent her driveway to the Scarlet Succubus. Anna has devoted her professional life to the life-sciences ecology and laboratory medicine.

Eldri Littlewolf

A fellow CAW member who also lived on the Ranch. Eldri is currently living in Berkeley with two dogs and a snake, keeping a garden.

Polly Love Moore

Morning Glory's mother. Born Pauline Browning in 1917, in Tutwiler, Mississippi, she was the youngest of thirteen children. She dropped out of college to marry James Moore in 1937, and they moved to California during World War II, where James worked in the oil fields. When James died in 1982, Morning Glory brought Polly to live in Ukiah, where she attended the Gospel Tabernacle and later the Ukiah Valley Bible Church. She died on February 11, 2006, just two months short of her eighty-ninth birthday.

Maerian Morris

Editor of Green Egg *magazine and a High Priestess of the Church of All Worlds.* Maerian is the founding Priestess of Westernesste, a Nest of CAW that evolved into a separate nonprofit religious organization, and she is the creative director of the Sidhevairs, Westernesste's virtual world and community (www.sidhevair.org).

Julie Epona O'Ryan

OZ and MG's girlfriend, who lived with them at Shady Grove. Julie has served on the board of directors for CAW and the Grey School of Wizardry, sharing her extensive business knowledge and experience. She now lives in Guerneville, California, with her son, Aidan O'Ryan-Kelly.

Gail Salvador

Morning Glory's daughter, who changed her name from Rainbow to Gail at age fifteen. Gail worked for more than ten years as a veterinary technician, where she met her husband, Joe Salvador. They married in 2004, and their daughter, Alessandra, was born in 2006. She is now working as a high-end hairstylist and education director at Festoon Salon in the Bay Area. Gail lives with her family in Oakland, California.

Jeffrey Siegel

Promoter that brokered Unicorn deal with Ringling Bros. Jeff produces two of the larger Renaissance Festivals in the United States, held in Arizona and North Carolina annually (www.royalfaires.com), and operates his production company, Supply Studio, out of a historic warehouse in Minneapolis, Minnesota.

Talyn Songdog

Lover of Morning Glory. Born in 1963, Talyn's wife and soulmate is Maggie, and Morning Glory and Oberon are godparents to their two amazing daughters, Tam and Tyr. He lives with his family in Georgia and works as an engineer.

Wolf Dean Stiles

Partner of MG and Wynter, and member of Ravenheart Family. Wolf is now with the incomparable Miss Kat, and the two of them work together at *The Green Sheet,* where Wolf is a website designer.

Orion Stormcrow

A fellow CAW member and onetime publisher of Green Egg.

John C. Sulak (NARRATOR)

Narrator of this story. John is co-author of *Modern Pagans* (RE/Search Publications, 2001). When he was sixteen years old he went to the World Science Fiction Convention in St. Louis, and it was there that he first learned about

Paganism and began the journey that would result in this book. In addition to interviewing people for *The Wizard and the Witch*, John also edited all the material together into the story arc that it now has. He is currently investigating polyamory and sacred sex in San Francisco for his next gonzo journalism endeavor. John writes a theatre blog (voxtheatricum.wordpress .com), and his email address is voxtheatricum@gmail.com.

Martha Turley

Oberon's first wife and mother of his only child. After college, she worked as a Montessori teacher, and later for the Salvation Army. She and Oberon divorced in 1972, and she remarried twice. She currently lives in Florida.

Donald Wildgrube

Water-brother and CAW member. Now retired, Don lives in a suburb of St. Louis and is still teaching and active in the Pagan community, establishing a CAW retro-Nest, based on the original teachings of the 1960s.

Tom Williams

Water-brother and CAW member. After almost thirty years of activity as a CAW Priest, Tom retired from Clergy work to devote himself to his rural homestead in Santa Cruz County, where he raises alpacas and spends his time with his shrunken-head collection and his memories.

Barry Zell

Oberon's brother, born in 1946 in Pennsylvania. In 1989, Barry found his soul-mate, Nancy, and they married in 2002. Some of his current interests are traveling, collecting antiques, and proofreading. Barry is a Christian and a political conservative.

Bryan Zell

Oberon's son. Born in 1963 in Elgin, Illinois, Bryan is the only child of Martha and Tim (Oberon) Zell. He earned a college degree in geriatric nursing, serving in that field for several years. In 2002, he moved to Florida to help care for his mother, working as a nurse's aide.

Charles Zell

Oberon's father. Charles was born in Harrisburg, Pennsylvania, in 1914. A devout Christian and a conservative Republican, Charlie was deeply involved in Ronald Reagan's first presidential campaign. He lived in a suburb of Minneapolis until his death from a stroke on March 8, 2011. He was ninety-six.

Morning Glory Zell (MG)

Oberon's soulmate. Born Diane Moore in Long Beach, California, she met her soulmate, Oberon, in September 1973 at the Gnostic Aquarian Festival in Minneapolis. They were married April 14, 1974. In 1977, the Zells moved into a Hippie homesteading community in Northern California, where they lived for eight years, raising Living Unicorns. They handfasted with Diane Darling in a ten-year triad, followed by another decade with Wolf, Wynter, and Liza as the Ravenheart Family. In 2006, Morning Glory was diagnosed with multiple myeloma (bone and blood cancer), for which she is in continuing treatment. Her greatest joy is her granddaughter, Alessandra.

Oberon Zell (OZ)

Morning Glory's soulmate. Tim Zell was born in St. Louis in 1942 to Vera and Charlie Zell. He has a brother, Barry, born in 1946, and a sister, Shirley, born in 1948. He grew up in Crystal Lake, Illinois, and attended Westminster College in Fulton, Missouri, from 1961 to 1965, receiving a B.A. There he met Lance Christie and the two of them founded Atl, the forerunner of the Church of All Worlds (CAW). Tim married Martha McCance in February 1963, and they had a son, Bryan, born the following September. Tim met Morning Glory in Minneapolis at Autumn Equinox of 1973, and they were married there the following Easter. Moving to a Hippie community in Northern California in 1976, Tim changed his first name to "Otter" in 1979. OZ and MG returned to civilization in 1985, handfasting with Diane Darling. Otter took the name "Oberon" in 1994, and they began a new relationship with Wolf, Wynter, and Liza, which became the Ravenheart Family. OZ founded the Grey School of Wizardry in 2004.

Vera Zell

Oberon's mother. She was born Vera Bedell in St. Louis, Missouri, in 1917. She attended William Woods College in Fulton, Missouri. Her father, a dentist, died in 1941. She met and married Charlie Zell in 1940, and their first child, Tim, was born two years later. A second son, Barry, was born in 1946, after Charlie returned from the war, and their daughter, Shirley, was born in 1948. Vera and Charlie divorced in 1966. She moved to Phoenix, Arizona, to be near Shirley and her family. She died on March 25, 2010.

Acknowledgments

We would like to thank the many people who agreed to be interviewed. They are:

Charles Zell (OZ's father)

Vera Zell (OZ's mother)

Barry Zell (OZ's brother)

Shirley Kaye (OZ's sister)

Lance Christie (OZ's first water-brother, 1962)

Gale Fuller (OZ's former college professor and mentor)

Martha Turley (OZ's first wife, Bryan's mother)

John B. (met OZ in 1964 as an impressionable teenager)

Barry Zell (OZ's brother)

Bryan Zell (OZ's son)

Tom Williams (CAW Priest and co-adventurer)

Debbie Dietz (lived in the CAW temple on Gaslight Square as a teenager)

Michael Muddypaws (previously Hurley; CAW St. Louis)

Carolyn Clark (CAW High Priestess, St. Louis)

Don Wildgrube (CAW High Priest, St. Louis)

Polly Love Moore (MG's mother)

Carolyn Whitehorn (MG's oldest friend from the '60s in Long Beach, California)

Carl D. (Carolyn's ex-husband in Long Beach)

Gary Ferns (MG's first husband)

Catherine Crowell (MG's friend since 1971)

Margot Adler (author of *Drawing Down the Moon*)

Steve F. (longtime CAW member from the St. Louis days)

Pendragon (dear friend and lover from St. Louis)

Cerridwen Fallingstar (lover, author, Priestess)

Anna Korn (close friend, met in Eugene, Oregon, 1976)

Alison Harlow (owner of Coeden Brith; invited OZ/MG to become caretakers and raise Unicorns)

Marylyn Motherbear (CAW Priestess, early Greenfield Ranch pioneer)

Kirsten (Kiri) J. (Greenfield neighbor and Oberon's first apprentice)

Anodea Judith (lover, CAW High Priestess in California)

Eldri Littlewolf (lived with OZ/MG on Coeden Brith)

Ayisha Homolka (lived on Greenfield with Gwydion)

Artemisia (met as a teenager—longtime friend and lover)

"Matthew Eberhard" (Alison's lawyer, agent for the Living Unicorn)

Elan P. (met Unicorn as a child in 1980)

Gail Salvador (MG's daughter)

Jeffrey Siegel (booking agent for Unicorn Ren Faire saga)

Daniel Blair Stewart (co-adventurer on Mermaid expedition)

Diane Darling (third partner in triad marriage for ten years, editor *Green Egg*)

Zack Darling (Diane's son, OZ and MG's stepson)

Maerian Morris (CAW High Priestess)

Darryl Cherney (CAW Bard)

Farida Fox (dear friend and lover)

Gary and Betty Ball (friends/partners in Between the Worlds)

Julie O'Ryan (OZ's lover since 1992 and still dearest friend)

Tom Donohue (MG's lover, best friend, helped launch Mythic Images)

Elantari L. (daughter of Aeona, and a dear friend since childhood)

Talyn Songdog (MG's lover)

Tam Songdog (Talyn's daughter, MG and OZ's water-daughter)

Kadira Belynne (OZ's lover)

Wolf Stiles (Ravenheart Family member)

Liza Gabriel (Ravenheart Family member)

Wynter Rose (Ravenheart Family member)

Ariel Monserrat (OZ's lover—lived at Shady Grove for a while, now publishing *Green Egg*)

And finally, we'd also like to thank Orion Stormcrow, who joined CAW in 1969 and was our co-adventurer for many years. His delightful "Unicorn Song Part 2" charmingly summarizes the great Unicorn Saga.

John C. Sulak would like to thank Elysia Gallo for her help in shaping the many drafts of this book. He would also like to express his gratitude to Alisa Highfill, Deborah "Oak" Cooper, Nancy Harris Dalwin, Ken Montgomery, Bert Huckelberry, V. Vale, and Ron Ward for their love, friendship, and support during the many years he was working on *The Wizard and the Witch*. May they all live long and prosper!

Morning Glory and Oberon Bibliography

Oberon Zell-Ravenheart is featured, quoted, interviewed, or otherwise referenced in the following books:

As Tim Zell (1972–1978)

1. *The New Pagans*, by Hans Holzer (Doubleday & Co., 1972)
2. *Black Magic, Satanism & Voodoo*, by Leo Louis Martello (Castle Books, 1973)
3. *Witchcraft, The Old Religion*, by Leo Louis Martello (University Books, 1973)
4. *Religious & Spiritual Groups in Modern America*, by Robert S. Ellwood (Prentiss-Hall, 1974)
5. *Directory of the Occult*, by Hans Holzer (Henry Regnery, 1974)
6. *Occultism, Witchcraft & Cultural Fashions*, by Mircea Eliade (University of Chicago Press, 1976)

As Otter G'Zell (1979–1994)

1. *Drawing Down the Moon: Witches, Druids, Goddess-Worshippers, and Other Pagans in America Today*, by Margot Adler (Beacon Press, 1979; Viking, revised and expanded 2nd edition, 1987)
2. *The Encyclopedia of American Religions*, by J. Gordon Melton (Gale Research Co., 1979; Triumph Books, 2nd edition, 1991)
3. *Do You Believe in Magic?* by Annie Gottlieb (Times Books, 1987)

4. *Encyclopedia of Witches & Witchcraft*, by Rosemary Guiley (Facts on File, 1989)

5. *Larson's New Book of Cults*, by Bob Larson (Tyndale House Publications, 1989)

6. *Le Livre de la Licorne*, by Yvonne Caroutch (Pardes, 1989)

7. *Coincidance: A Head Test*, by Robert Anton Wilson (New Falcon Publications, 1991)

8. *The Truth About Unicorns*, by James Cross Giblin (HarperCollins, 1991)

9. *Heaven on Earth/Dispatches from America's Spiritual Frontier*, by Michael D'Antonio (Crown Publishers, 1992)

10. *The World's Most Incredible Stories: The Best of the Fortean Times*, ed. Adam Sisman (Avon Books, 1992)

11. "Counterpoint: Old Souls in New Vestments," by Robert S. Ellwood, *The '60s Spiritual Awakening: American Religion Moving from Modern to Postmodern*, by Robert S. Ellwood (Rutgers University Press, 1994)

As Oberon Zell (1995–1999)

1. *The Pagan Path: The Wiccan Way of Life*, by Janet and Stewart Farrar and Gavin Bone (Phoenix Publishing, Inc., 1995)

2. *Paganism Today*, by Graham Harvey and Charlotte Hardman (eds.) (Thorsons Press, 1995)

3. *America's Alternative Religions*, by Timothy Miller, ed. (State University of New York Press, 1995)

4. *People of the Earth: The New Pagans Speak Out*, by Ellen Evert Hopman and Lawrence Bond (Inner Traditions/Destiny Books, 1996)

5. *Magical Religion & Modern Witchcraft*, James R. Lewis, ed. (State University of New York, 1996)

6. *To Ride a Silver Broomstick: New Generation Witchcraft*, by Silver RavenWolf (Llewellyn Worldwide, 1997)

7. *Ecoterror: The Violent Agenda to Save Nature*, by Ron Arnold (Free Enterprise Press, 1997)

8. *Contemporary Paganism: Listening People, Speaking Earth*, by Graham Harvey (New York University Press, 1997)

9. *Heretic's Heart*, by Margot Adler (Beacon Press, 1997)

10. *The Encyclopedia of Cults, Sects, and New Religions*, by James R. Lewis (Promethean Press, 1998)

11. *Goddess Worship, Witchcraft and Neo-Paganism*, by Craig Hawkins (Zondervan Publishing, 1998)

12. *Religious & Spiritual Groups in Modern America*, by Roger Ellwood and Harry Baxter Partin (Prentiss-Hall, 2nd edition, 1998)

13. *Encyclopedia of Witches & Witchcraft*, by Rosemary Guiley (Facts on File, 2nd edition, 1999)

14. *Peculiar Prophets: A Biographical Dictionary of New Religions*, by James R. Lewis (Paragon House, 1999)

15. *Religious Leaders of America*, by J. Gordon Melton (The Gale Group, 1999)

16. *Triumph of the Moon: A History of Modern Pagan Witchcraft*, by Ronald Hutton (Oxford University Press, 2000)

As Oberon Zell-Ravenheart (2000–present)

1. *Encyclopedia of Wicca & Witchcraft*, by Raven Grimassi (Llewellyn Worldwide, 2000)

2. *The Writers Complete Fantasy Reference: An Indispensable Compendium of Myth and Magic* (Writer's Digest Books, 2000)

3. *Practicing the Presence of the Goddess: Everyday Rituals to Transform Your World*, by Barbara Ardinger, Ph.D. (New World Library, 2000)

4. *Make Love Not War: The Sexual Revolution: An Unfettered History*, by David Allyn (Little Brown & Co., 2000)

5. *Odd Gods: New Religions & the Cult Controversy*, ed. by James R. Lewis (Prometheus Books, 2001)

6. *The New Believers: A Survey of Sects, Cults and Alternative Religions*, by David V. Barrett (Cassell Academic, 2001)

7. *Being a Pagan: Druids, Wiccans, and Witches Today*, by Ellen Evert Hopman (Inner Traditions/Destiny Books, 2001)

8. *Modern Pagans*, by John Sulak and V. Vale (RE/Search Publications, 2001)

9. *Neo-Pagan Sacred Art & Altars: Making Things Whole*, by Sabina Magliocco (University Press of Michigan, 2001)

10. *My Misspent Youth*, by Meghan Daum (Open City Books, 2001)

11. *The World of Wizards*, by Anton and Mina Adams (Lansdowne Publishing/Barnes & Noble, 2002)

12. *The Practical Pagan: Common Sense Guidelines for Modern Practitioners*, by Dana Eilers (New Page Books, 2002)

13. *Witches: True Encounters with Wicca, Wizards, Covens, Cults & Magick*, by Hans Holzer (Black Dog & Leventhal, 2002)

14. *Contemporary Paganism: Minority Religions in a Majoritarian America*, by Carol Barner-Barry (Palgrave Macmillan, 2003)

15. *Nelson College Prep Biology 11*, by Giuseppe Fraser, LeDrew, and Roberts (Nelson Thompson Learning Publishing, 2003)

16. *Crop Circles: Signs of Contact*, by Colin Andrews (New Page Books, 2003)

17. *Shadows of a Witch*, by Shewolf Silver Shadows (WitchesWay Publishing.com, 2003)

18. *New Age & Neopagan Religions in America*, by Sarah Pike (Columbia University Press, 2004)

19. *Pop! Goes the Witch*, by Fiona Horne, ed. (The Disinformation Co., 2004)

20. *Gaia Eros*, by Jesse Wolf Hardin (New Page Books, 2004)

21. *Rites of Pleasure: Sexuality in Wicca & NeoPaganism*, by Jennifer Hunter (Citadel Press, 2004)

22. *Cyberhenge: Modern Pagans on the Internet*, by Douglas E. Cowan (Routledge, 2004)

23. *Plural Loves: Designs for Bi and Poly Living*, by Serena Anderlini-D'Onofrio, ed. (Harrington Park Press, 2004)

24. *Celebrating the Pagan Soul*, by Laura Wildman, ed. (Citadel Press, 2005)

25. *Encyclopedia of Religion & Nature*, by Bron Taylor (Thoemmes Continuum, 2005)

26. *Religion & Popular Culture: A Hyper-Real Testament (Gods, Humans, & Religions, No. 7)*, by Adam Posasamai (Peter Lang, 2005)

27. *The Pagan Man*, by Isaac Bonewits (Kensington Citadel Press, 2005)

28. *Introduction to Pagan Studies*, by Barbara Jane Davy (Altamira Press, 2005)

29. *Pagan Polyamory*, by Raven Kaldera (Llewellyn Worldwide, 2005)

30. *Not in Kansas Anymore: A Curious Tale of How Magic is Transforming America*, by Christine Wicke (HarperSanFrancisco, 2005)

31. *Cakes & Ale for the Pagan Soul*, by Patricia Telesco (Celestial Arts, 2005)

32. *Earthly Bodies, Magical Selves*, by Sarah N. Pike (2006)

33. *Odyssey: Wisdom's Children*, by Anita L. Wynn (a.k.a. WolfWoman) (PublishAmerica, 2006)

34. *Nature Religion Reader in Paganism & Ecology*, by Barbara Jane Davy, ed. (AltaMira Press, 2006)

35. *Her Hidden Children: The Rise of Wicca & Paganism in America*, by Chas S. Clifton (Altamira Press, 2006)

36. *Drawing Down the Moon: Witches, Druids, Goddess-Worshippers, and Other Pagans in America Today*, by Margot Adler (Viking Press, 1979; Penguin Books, revised and expanded 3rd edition, 2006)

37. *Dragonlore*, by Ash "LeopardDancer" DeKirk (New Page Books, 2006)

38. *Gargoyles*, by Susan "Moonwriter" Pesznecker (New Page Books, 2006)

39. *Encyclopedia of Witches & Witchcraft*, by Rosemary Guiley (Facts on File, 3rd edition, 2008)

Books by Oberon Zell-Ravenheart

Grimoire for the Apprentice Wizard (New Page Books, 2004)

Companion for the Apprentice Wizard (New Page Books, 2006)

Creating Circles & Ceremonies: Rituals for All Seasons & Reasons, with Morning Glory Zell (New Page Books, 2006)

A Wizard's Bestiary, with Ash "LeopardDancer" DeKirk (New Page Books, 2007)

Green Egg Omelette: An Anthology of Art and Articles from the Legendary Pagan Journal (New Page Books, 2008)

The Wizard and the Witch, with Morning Glory and John C. Sulak (Llewellyn Worldwide, 2014)

In addition to the above, Oberon was an acknowledged consultant for Marion Zimmer Bradley's *The Mists of Avalon* (1982), and drew up an extensive Bestiary for her "Darkover" science-fiction series. He illustrated Ann Forfreedom and Julie Ann's *Book of the Goddess* (1980), and Anodea Judith's *Wheels of Life* (1987; 1993). The cover of Patricia Monaghan's *New Book of Goddesses & Heroines* (1997) features seven of Oberon's sculptures, and the cover of Carl McColman's *Complete Idiot's Guide to Paganism* (2002) also features his art. Oberon also designed the covers for Urmas Kaldeveer's *Single Fathers' Cookbook* (1986), Phil Snow's *Blast from the Past* (1986), and Jeanne Mara's *Listen to My Heart* (1986). He wrote the introductions for *Gaia Eros*, by Jesse Wolf Hardin (New Page Books, 2004); *Dragonlore*, by Ash "LeopardDancer" DeKirk (New Page Books, 2006); *Gargoyles*, by Susan "Moonwriter" Pesznecker (New Page Books, 2006); and *Composing Magic* by Elizabeth Barrette (New Page Books, 2007). He was an acknowledged consultant for Anodea Judith's *Waking the Global Heart* (Elite Books, 2006). Oberon's work has been seen on the TV shows *Buffy the Vampire Slayer* and *Mad Mad House*. His sculptures have also appeared in the following movies: *The Witches of Eastwick* (1987), *Pickman's Model* (2003), and *The Feast of Love* (2007).

Morning Glory Zell-Ravenheart is featured, quoted, interviewed, or otherwise referenced in the following books:

1. *Drawing Down the Moon: Witches, Druids, Goddess-Worshippers, and Other Pagans in America Today*, by Margot Adler (Beacon Press, 1979; revised and expanded 2nd edition, 1987)

2. *Do You Believe in Magic?* by Annie Gottlieb (Times Books, 1987)

3. *Encyclopedia of Witches & Witchcraft*, by Rosemary Guiley (Facts on File, 1989)

4. *Le Livre de la Licorne*, by Yvonne Caroutch (Pardes, 1989)

5. *The Pagan Path: The Wiccan Way of Life*, by Janet and Stewart Farrar and Gavin Bone (Phoenix Publishing, 1995)

6. *To Ride a Silver Broomstick: New Generation Witchcraft*, by Silver Raven-Wolf (Llewellyn Worldwide, 1997)

7. *Heretic's Heart*, by Margot Adler (Beacon Press, 1997)

8. *Encyclopedia of Witches & Witchcraft*, by Rosemary Guiley (Facts on File, 2nd edition, 1999)

9. *Religious Leaders of America*, by J. Gordon Melton (The Gale Group, 1999)

10. *Encyclopedia of Wicca & Witchcraft*, by Raven Grimassi (Llewellyn Worldwide, 2000)

11. *Make Love Not War: The Sexual Revolution: An Unfettered History*, by David Allyn (Little Brown & Co., 2000)

12. *Modern Pagans*, by John Sulak and V. Vale (RE/Search Publications, 2001)

13. *Neo-Pagan Sacred Art & Altars: Making Things Whole*, by Sabina Magliocco (University Press of Michigan, 2001)

14. *My Misspent Youth*, by Meghan Daum (Open City Books, 2001)

15. *Witchcraft: A Concise Guide*, by Isaac Bonewits, Earth Religion Press, 2001

16. *Pop! Goes the Witch*, by Fiona Horne, ed. (The Disinformation Co., 2004)

17. *Rites of Pleasure: Sexuality in Wicca and NeoPaganism*, by Jennifer Hunter (Citadel Press, 2004)

18. *Plural Loves: Designs for Bi and Poly Living*, by Serena Anderlini-D'Onofrio, ed. (Harrington Park Press, 2004)

19. *New Age and Neopagan Religions in America*, by Sarah M. Pike (Columbia University Press, 2004)

20. *Drawing Down the Moon: Witches, Druids, Goddess-Worshippers, and Other Pagans in America Today*, by Margot Adler (Viking Press, 1979; Penguin Books, revised and expanded 3rd edition, 2006)

21. *Encyclopedia of Witches & Witchcraft*, by Rosemary Guiley (Facts on File, 3rd edition, 2008)

22. *Daughters of Aquarius: Women of the Sixties Counterculture*, by Gretchen Lemke-Santangelo (University Press of Kansas, 2009)

In addition to the above, Morning Glory was an acknowledged consultant for Marion Zimmer Bradley's *The Mists of Avalon* (1982), and had two short stories published in MZB's *Sword & Sorceress* anthologies. She has contributed significantly to the following books:

1. *Book of the Goddess*, by Ann Forfreedom and Julie Ann, eds., 1980 (Nine Goddess invocations and poems)

2. "The Golden Egg" in *Sword and Sorceress*, vol. V, Marion Zimmer Bradley, ed., 1988

3. "A Lesser of Evils" in *Sword and Sorceress*, vol. VI, Marion Zimmer Bradley, ed., 1990

4. "A Bouquet of Lovers" in *Love Without Limits*, Deborah Anapol, ed., 1992

5. *Creating Circles & Ceremonies: Rituals for All Seasons & Reasons*, with Oberon Zell (New Page Books, 2006)

6. *A Wizard's Bestiary*, by Oberon and Ash "LeopardDancer" DeKirk (New Page Books, 2007)

7. *The Wizard and the Witch*, with Oberon and John C. Sulak (Llewellyn, 2014)

To Write to the Authors

If you wish to contact the authors or would like more information about this book, please write to the authors in care of Llewellyn Worldwide Ltd. and we will forward your request. Both the authors and the publisher appreciate hearing from you and learning of your enjoyment of this book and how it has helped you. Llewellyn Worldwide Ltd. cannot guarantee that every letter written to the authors can be answered, but all will be forwarded. Please write to:

John C. Sulak
℅ Llewellyn Worldwide
2143 Wooddale Drive
Woodbury, MN 55125-2989

Please enclose a self-addressed stamped envelope for reply,
or $1.00 to cover costs. If outside the USA, enclose
an international postal reply coupon.

Many of Llewellyn's authors have websites with additional
information and resources. For more information,
please visit our website at http://www.llewellyn.com

PAGAN
POLYAMORY
BECOMING A TRIBE OF HEARTS

RAVEN
KALDERA

Pagan Polyamory
Becoming a Tribe of Hearts
RAVEN KALDERA

The term *polyamory* describes nonmonogamous relationships based on honesty and affection. Presenting a fascinating peek inside the polyamorous lifestyle from a Pagan perspective, Raven Kaldera offers practical insight and spiritual depth into a vastly misunderstood way of life.

Relating polyamory to astrology and the elements (air, fire, water, earth, and spirit), the author addresses all aspects of the polyamorous life, including family life, sexual ethics, emotional issues, proper etiquette, relationship boundaries, and the pros of cons of this lifestyle. Kaldera also discusses polyamory as a path of spiritual transformation and shares spells, rituals, and ceremonies for affirming one's relationships and spirituality.

978-0-7387-0762-4, 288 pp., 6 x 9   **$21.95**

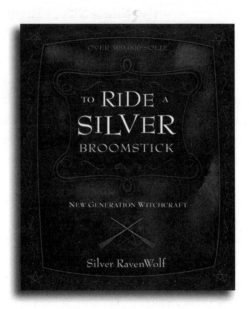

To Ride a Silver Broomstick
New Generation Witchcraft
SILVER RAVENWOLF

Summon. Scry. Spin, spiral, and sweep. Learn how to bend time, draw down the moon's energy, and use mirror magick. Whether novice or adept, a Witch's world is filled with wonder and magick. It's also filled with the hard work and dedication to learning that are part of living the Craft every day.

Silver RavenWolf presents a fascinating introduction to the Craft in *To Ride a Silver Broomstick*, the first volume in the tremendously popular Witchcraft series that also includes *To Stir a Magick Cauldron* and *To Light a Sacred Flame*. This indispensable guide presents tried-and-true Witch wisdom, dished out with Silver's down-to-earth warmth and humor. You'll learn the essentials of Witchcraft, including:

- webweaving
- astral projection, bi-location, and power animals
- stocking your magickal cabinet
- cleansing, consecrating, and charging
- The Summerland: death, reincarnation, and time
- healing techniques
- deities and pantheons
- telepathy, psychometry, and mind power
- The Wheel of the Year
- gems, herbs, and healing
- color, candle, and sympathetic magick

978-0-87542-791-1, 360 pp., 7½ x 9⅛ $16.95

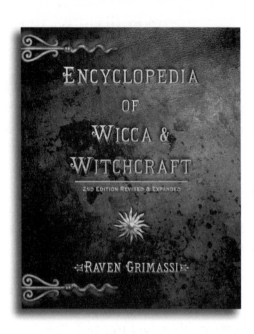

Encyclopedia of Wicca & Witchcraft
Raven Grimassi

Craft Elder and author Raven Grimassi has revised and expanded his indispensable reference work, the award-winning *Encyclopedia of Wicca & Witchcraft*. The first book of its kind to be written by a practicing Witch, this guide presents Wicca/Witchcraft as a spiritual path, connecting religious concepts and spirituality to both a historical background and modern practice.

With a wealth of information on European folklore and Western Occultism, and material relevant to any tradition, you can use this book to research any aspect of the Craft, including:

- theology: pantheons, Wiccan Rede, Three-Fold Law
- history: Craft roots and influence
- places: historical and sacred sites
- verses, rites, and invocations
- ritual objects and tools
- influential Witches, past and present

Encyclopedia of Wicca & Witchcraft also contains a glossary of terminology; book references; listings of Craft websites, organizations, and magazines; magickal alphabets, runes, correspondences, and symbols; and 300 illustrations.

978-1-56718-257-6, 528 pp., 8 x 10   **$27.95**
